The Electric
Kool-Aid Acid Test

TOM

WOLFE

The Electric Kool-Aid Acid Test

BANTAM BOOKS

New York   Toronto   London   Sydney   Auckland

The Electric Kool-Aid Acid Test

A Bantam Book / published by arrangement with Farrar, Straus & Giroux

PUBLISHING HISTORY

Farrar, Straus & Giroux hardcover edition published in August 1968
Literary Guild edition published in August 1968
Bantam mass market edition / October 1969
Bantam trade paperback edition / October 1999

ISBN 0-553-38064-8

Published simultaneously in the United States and Canada

Bantam Books are published by Bantam Books, a division of Random House,
Inc. Its trademark, consisting of the words "Bantam Books" and the portrayal
of a rooster, is Registered in U.S. Patent and Trademark Office and in other
countries. Marca Registrada. Bantam Books, 1540 Broadway, New York, New
York 10036.

PRINTED IN THE UNITED STATES OF AMERICA

20 19 18 17 16 15 14

Contents

Contents

The Electric
Kool-Aid Acid Test

chapter

I

Black Shiny
FBI Shoes

THAT'S GOOD THINKING THERE, COOL BREEZE. COOL BREEZE is a kid with three or four days' beard sitting next to me on the stamped metal bottom of the open back part of a pickup truck. Bouncing along. Dipping and rising and rolling on these rotten springs like a boat. Out the back of the truck the city of San Francisco is bouncing down the hill, all those endless staggers of bay windows, slums with a view, bouncing and streaming down the hill. One after another, electric signs with neon martini glasses lit up on them, the San Francisco symbol of "bar"—thousands of neon-magenta martini glasses bouncing and streaming down the hill, and beneath them hundreds, thousands of people wheeling around to look at this freaking crazed truck we're in, their white faces erupting from their lapels like marshmallows—streaming and bouncing down the hill—and God knows they've got plenty to look at.

That's why it strikes me as funny when Cool Breeze says very seriously over the whole roar of the thing, "I don't know—when

Kesey gets out I don't know if I can come around the Warehouse."

"Why not?"

"Well, like the cops are going to be coming around like all feisty, and I'm on probation, so I don't know."

Well, that's good thinking there, Cool Breeze. Don't rouse the bastids. Lie low—like right now. Right now Cool Breeze is so terrified of the law he is sitting up in plain view of thousands of already startled citizens wearing some kind of Seven Dwarfs Black Forest gnome's hat covered in feathers and fluorescent colors. Kneeling in the truck, facing us, also in plain view, is a half-Ottawa Indian girl named Lois Jennings, with her head thrown back and a radiant look on her face. Also a blazing silver disk in the middle of her forehead alternately exploding with light when the sun hits it or sending off rainbows from the defraction lines in it. And, oh yeah, there's a long-barreled Colt .45 revolver in her hand, only nobody on the street can tell it's a cap pistol as she pegs away, kheeew, kheeew, at the erupting marshmallow faces like Debra Paget in . . . in . . .

—Kesey's coming out of jail!

Two more things they are looking at out there are a sign on the rear bumper reading "Custer Died for Your Sins" and, at the wheel, Lois's enamorado Stewart Brand, a thin blond guy with a blazing disk on his forehead too, and a whole necktie made of Indian beads. No shirt, however, just an Indian bead necktie on bare skin and a white butcher's coat with medals from the King of Sweden on it.

Here comes a beautiful one, attaché case and all, the day-is-done resentful look and the . . . shoes—how they shine!—and what the hell are these beatnik ninnies—and Lois plugs him in the old marshmallow and he goes streaming and bouncing down the hill . . .

And the truck heaves and billows, blazing silver red and Day-Glo, and I doubt seriously, Cool Breeze, that there is a single cop in all of San Francisco today who does not know that this crazed vehicle is a guerrilla patrol from the dread LSD.

The cops now know the whole scene, even the costumes, the jesuschrist strung-out hair, Indian beads, Indian headbands, donkey beads, temple bells, amulets, mandalas, god's-eyes, fluorescent vests, unicorn horns, Errol Flynn dueling shirts—but they still don't know about the shoes. The heads have a thing about shoes. The worst are shiny black shoes with shoelaces in them. The hierarchy ascends from there, although practically all lowcut shoes are unhip, from there on up to the boots the heads like, light, fanciful boots, English boots of the mod variety, if that is all they can get, but better something like hand-tooled Mexican boots with Caliente Dude Triple A toes on them. So see the FBI—black—shiny—laced up—FBI shoes—when the FBI finally grabbed Kesey—

There is another girl in the back of the truck, a dark little girl with thick black hair, called Black Maria. She looks Mexican, but she says to me in straight soft Californian:

"When is your birthday?"

"March 2."

"Pisces," she says. And then: "I would never take you for a Pisces."

"Why?"

"You seem too . . . *solid* for a Pisces."

But I know she means stolid. I am beginning to feel stolid. Back in New York City, Black Maria, I tell you, I am even known as something of a dude. But somehow a blue silk blazer and a big tie with clowns on it and . . . a . . . pair of shiny lowcut black shoes don't set them all to doing the Varsity Rag in the head world in San Francisco. Lois picks off the marshmallows one by one; Cool Breeze ascends into the innards of his gnome's hat; Black Maria, a Scorpio herself, rummages through the Zodiac; Stewart Brand winds it through the streets; paillettes explode—and this is nothing special, just the usual, the usual in the head world of San Francisco, just a little routine messing up the minds of the citizenry en route, nothing more than psyche food for beautiful people, while giving some guy from New York a lift to the Warehouse to wait for the Chief, Ken Kesey, who is getting out of jail.

ABOUT ALL I KNEW ABOUT KESEY AT THAT POINT WAS THAT HE was a highly regarded 31-year-old novelist and in a lot of trouble over drugs. He wrote *One Flew Over the Cuckoo's Nest* (1962), which was made into a play in 1963, and *Sometimes a Great Notion* (1964). He was always included with Philip Roth and Joseph Heller and Bruce Jay Friedman and a couple of others as one of the young novelists who might go all the way. Then he was arrested twice for possession of marijuana, in April of 1965 and January of 1966, and fled to Mexico rather than risk a stiff sentence. It looked like as much as five years, as a second offender. One day I happened to get hold of some letters Kesey wrote from Mexico to his friend Larry McMurtry, who wrote *Horseman, Pass By,* from which the movie *Hud* was made. They were wild and ironic, written like a cross between William Burroughs and George Ade, telling of hideouts, disguises, paranoia, fleeing from cops, smoking joints and seeking satori in the Rat lands of Mexico. There was one passage written George Ade–fashion in the third person as a parody of what the straight world back there in the U.S.A. must think of him now:

"In short, this young, handsome, successful, happily-married-three-lovely-children father was a fear-crazed dope fiend in flight to avoid prosecution on three felonies and god knows how many misdemeanors and seeking at the same time to sculpt a new satori from an old surf—in even shorter, mad as a hatter.

"Once an athlete so valued he had been given the job of calling signals from the line and risen into contention for the nationwide amateur wrestling crown, now he didn't know if he could do a dozen pushups. Once possessor of a phenomenal bank account and money waving from every hand, now it was all his poor wife could do to scrape together eight dollars to send as getaway money to Mexico. But a few years previous he had been listed in *Who's Who* and asked to speak at such auspicious gatherings as the Wellesley Club in Dah-la and now they wouldn't even allow him to speak at a VDC [Vietnam Day Committee] gathering. What was it that had brought a man so high of promise to so low a state in so short a time? Well, the answer can be found in just one short word, my friends, in just one all-well-used syllable:

"Dope!

"And while it may be claimed by some of the addled advocates of these chemicals that our hero is known to have indulged in drugs before his literary success, we must point out that there was evidence of his literary prowess well before the advent of the so-called psychedelic into his life but no evidence at all of any of the lunatic thinking that we find thereafter!"

To which he added:

> "(oh yea, the wind hums
> time ago—time ago—
> the rafter drums and the walls see
> . . . and there's a door to that bird
> in the sa-a-a-apling sky
> time ago by—
> Oh yeah the surf giggles
> time ago time ago
> of under things killed when
> bad was banished and all the
> doors to the birds vanished
> time ago then.)"

I got the idea of going to Mexico and trying to find him and do a story on Young Novelist Real-Life Fugitive. I started asking around about where he might be in Mexico. Everybody on the hip circuit in New York knew for certain. It seemed to be the thing to know this summer. He is in Puerto Vallarta. He is in Ajijic. He is in Oaxaca. He is in San Miguel de Allende. He is in Paraguay. He just took a steamboat from Mexico to Canada. And everyone knew for certain.

I was still asking around when Kesey sneaked back into the U.S. in October and the FBI caught up with him on the Bayshore freeway south of San Francisco. An agent chased him down an embankment and caught him and Kesey was in jail. So I flew to San Francisco. I went straight to the San Mateo County jail in Redwood City and the scene in the waiting room there was more like the stage door at the Music Box Theatre. It was full of cheerful anticipation. There was a young psychologist there, Jim Fadiman—Clifton Fadiman's nephew, it turned out—and Jim and his wife Dorothy were happily stuffing three I Ching coins into the spine of some interminable dense volume of Oriental mysticism and they asked me to get word to Kesey that the coins were in there. There was also a little roundfaced brunette named Marilyn who told me she used to be a teenie grouper hanging out with a rock 'n' roll group called The Wild Flowers but now she was mainly with Bobby Petersen. Bobby Petersen was not a musician. He was a saint, as nearly as I could make out. He was in jail down in Santa Cruz trying to fight a marijuana charge on the grounds that marijuana was a religious sacrament for him. I didn't figure out exactly why she was up here in the San Mateo jail waiting room instead except that it was like a stage door, as I said, with Kesey as the star who was still inside.

There was a slight hassle with the jailers over whether I was to get in to see him or not. The cops had nothing particularly to gain by letting me in. A reporter from New York—that just meant more publicity for this glorified beatnik. That was the line on Kesey. He was a glorified beatnik up on two dope charges, and why make a hero out of him. I must say that California has smooth cops. They all seem to be young, tall, crewcut, blond, with bleached blue eyes, like they just stepped out of a cigarette ad. Their jailhouses don't look like jailhouses, at least not the parts the public sees. They are all blond wood, fluorescent lights and filing-cabinet-tan metal, like the Civil Service exam room in a new Post Office building. The cops all speak soft Californian and are neat and correct as an ice cube. By the book; so they finally let me in to see Kesey during visiting hours. I had ten minutes. I waved goodbye to Marilyn and the Fadimans and the jolly scene downstairs and they took me up to the third floor in an elevator.

The elevator opened right onto a small visiting room. It was weird. Here was a lineup of four or five cubicles, like the isolation booths on the old TV quiz shows, each one with a thick plate-glass window and behind each window a prisoner in a prison blue workshirt. They were lined up like haddocks on ice. Outside each window ran a counter with a telephone on it. That's what you speak over in here. A couple of visitors are already hunched over the things. Then I pick out Kesey.

He is standing up with his arms folded over his chest and his eyes focused in the distance, i.e., the wall. He has thick wrists and big forearms, and the way he has them folded makes them look gigantic. He looks taller than he really is, maybe because of his neck. He has a big neck with a pair of sternocleido-mastoid muscles that rise up out of the prison workshirt like a couple of dock ropes. His jaw and chin are massive. He looks a little like Paul Newman, except that he is more muscular, has thicker skin, and he has tight blond curls boiling up around his head. His hair is almost gone on top, but somehow that goes all right with his big neck and general wrestler's build. Then he smiles slightly. It's curious, he doesn't have a line in his face. After all the chasing and hassling—he looks like the third week at the Sauna Spa; serene, as I say.

Then I pick up my telephone and he picks up his—and this is truly Modern Times. We are all of twenty-four inches apart, but there is a piece of plate glass as thick as a telephone directory between us. We might as well be in different continents, talking over Videophone. The telephones are very crackly and lo-fi, especially considering that they have a world of two feet to span. Naturally it was assumed that the police monitored every conversation. I wanted to ask him all about his fugitive days in Mexico. That was still the name of my story, Young Novelist Fugitive Eight Months in Mexico. But he could hardly go into that on this weird hookup, and besides, I had only ten minutes. I take out a notebook and start asking him—anything. There had been a piece in the paper about his saying it was time for the psychedelic movement to go "beyond acid," so I asked him about that. Then I started scribbling like mad, in shorthand, in the notebook. I could see his lips moving two feet away. His voice crackled over the telephone like it was coming from Brisbane. The whole thing was crazy. It seemed like calisthenics we were going through.

"It's my idea," he said, "that it's time to graduate from what has been going on, to something else. The psychedelic wave was happening six or eight months ago when I went to Mexico. It's been growing since then, but it hasn't been moving. I saw the same stuff when I got back as when I left. It was just bigger, that was all—" He talks in a soft voice with a country accent, almost a pure country accent, only crackling and rasping and cheese-grated over the two-foot hookup, talking about—

"—there's been no creativity," he is saying, "and I think my value has been to help create the next step. I don't think there will be any movement off the drug scene until there is something else to move to—"

—all in a plain country accent about something—well, to be frank, I didn't know what in the hell it was all about. Sometimes he spoke cryptically, in aphorisms. I told him I had heard he didn't intend to do any more writing. Why? I said.

"I'd rather be a lightning rod than a seismograph," he said.

He talked about something called the Acid Test and forms of expression in which there would be no separation between himself and the audience. It would be all one experience, with all the senses opened wide, words, music, lights, sounds, touch—*lightning*.

"You mean on the order of what Andy Warhol is doing?" I said.

. . . pause. "No offense," says Kesey, "but New York is about two years behind."

He said it very patiently, with a kind of country politeness, as if . . . I don't want to be rude to you fellows from the City, but there's been things going on out here that you would never guess in your wildest million years, old buddy . . .

THE TEN MINUTES WERE UP AND I WAS OUT OF THERE. I HAD gotten nothing, except my first brush with a strange phenomenon, that strange up-country charisma, the Kesey presence. I had nothing to do but kill time and hope Kesey would get out on bail somehow and I could talk to him and get the details on Novelist Fugitive in Mexico. This seemed like a very long shot at this time, because Kesey had two marijuana charges against him and had already jumped the country once.

So I rented a car and started making the rounds in San Francisco. Somehow my strongest memories of San Francisco are of me in a terrific rented sedan roaring up hills or down hills, sliding on and off the cable-car tracks. Slipping and sliding down to North Beach, the fabled North Beach, the old fatherland bohemia of the West Coast, always full of Big Daddy So-and-so and Costee Plusee and long-haired little Wasp and Jewish buds balling spade cats—and now North Beach was dying. North Beach was nothing but tit shows. In the famous Beat Generation HQ, the City Lights bookstore, Shig Murao, the Nipponese panjandrum of the place, sat glowering with his beard hanging down like those strands of furze and fern in an architect's drawing, drooping over the volumes of Kahlil Gibran by the cash register while Professional Budget Finance Dentists here for the convention browsed in search of the beatniks between tit shows. Everything was The Topless on North Beach, strippers with their breasts enlarged with injections of silicone emulsion.

The action—meaning the hip cliques that set the original tone—the action was all over in Haight-Ashbury. Pretty soon all the bellwethers of a successful bohemia would be there, too, the cars going through, bumper to bumper, with everybody rubber-necking, the tour buses going through "and here . . . Home of the Hippies . . . there's one there," and the queers and spade hookers and bookstores and boutiques. Everything was Haight-Ashbury and the acid heads.

But it was not just North Beach that was dying. The whole old-style hip life—jazz, coffee houses, civil rights, invite a spade for dinner, Vietnam—it was all suddenly dying, I found out, even among the students at Berkeley, across the bay from San Francisco, which had been the heart of the "student-rebellion" and so forth. It had even gotten to the point that Negroes were no longer in the hip scene, not even as totem figures. It was un-believable. *Spades,* the very soul figures of Hip, of jazz, of the hip vocabulary itself, man and like and dig and baby and scarf and split and later and so fine, of civil rights and graduating from Reed College and living on North Beach, down Mason, and balling spade cats—all that good elaborate petting and patting and pouring soul all over the spades—all over, finished, incredi-bly.

So I was starting to get the trend of all this heaving and con-vulsing in the bohemian world of San Francisco. Meantime, miraculously, Kesey's three young lawyers, Pat Hallinan, Brian Rohan, and Paul Robertson, were about to get Kesey out on bail. They assured the judges, in San Mateo and San Francisco, that Mr. Kesey had a very public-spirited project in mind. He had re-turned from exile for the express purpose of calling a huge meet-ing of heads and hippies at Winterland Arena in San Francisco in order to tell The Youth to stop taking LSD because it was dan-gerous and might french fry their brains, etc. It was going to be an "acid graduation" ceremony. They should go "beyond acid." That was what Kesey had been talking to me about, I guess. At the same time, six of Kesey's close friends in the Palo Alto area had put their homes up as security for a total of $35,000 bail with the San Mateo County court. I suppose the courts figured they had Kesey either way. If he jumped bail now, it would be such a dirty trick on his friends, costing them their homes, that Kesey would be discredited as a drug apostle or anything else. If he didn't, he would be obliged to give his talk to The Youth—and so much the better. In any case, Kesey was coming out.

This script was not very popular in Haight-Ashbury, however. I soon found out that the head life in San Francisco was already such a big thing that Kesey's return and his acid graduation plan were causing the heads' first big political crisis. All eyes were on Kesey and his group, known as the Merry Pranksters. Thousands of kids were moving into San Francisco for a life based on LSD and the psychedelic thing. *Thing* was the major abstract word in Haight-Ashbury. It could mean *any*thing, isms, life styles, habits, leanings, causes, sexual organs; *thing* and *freak; freak* referred to styles and obsessions, as in "Stewart Brand is an Indian freak" or "the zodiac—that's her freak," or just to heads in costume. It wasn't a negative word. Anyway, just a couple of weeks before, the heads had held their first big "be-in" in Golden Gate Park, at the foot of the hill leading up into Haight-Ashbury, in mock observance of the day LSD became illegal in California. This was a gathering of all the tribes, all the communal groups. All the freaks came and did their thing. A head named Michael Bowen started it, and thousands of them piled in, in high costume, ringing bells, chanting, dancing ecstatically, blowing their minds one way and another and making their favorite satiric gestures to the cops, handing them flowers, burying the bastids in tender fruity petals of love. Oh christ, Tom, the thing was fantastic, a freaking mind-blower, thousands of high-loving heads out there messing up the minds of the cops and everybody else in a fiesta of love and euphoria. Even Kesey, who was still on the run then, had brazened on in and mingled with the crowd for a while, and they were all *one,* even Kesey—and now all of a sudden here he is, in the hands of the FBI and other supercops, the biggest name in The Life, Kesey, announcing that it is time to "graduate from acid." And what the hell is this, a copout or what? The *Stop Kesey* movement was beginning even within the hip world.

We pull up to the Warehouse in the crazed truck and—well, for a start, I begin to see that people like Lois and Stewart and Black Maria are the restrained, reflective wing of the Merry Pranksters. The Warehouse is on Harriet Street, between Howard and Folsom. Like most of San Francisco, Harriet Street is a lot of wooden buildings with bay windows all painted white. But Harriet Street is in San Francisco's Skid Row area, and despite all the paint, it looks like about forty winos crawled off in the shadows and died and turned black and bloated and exploded, sending forth a stream of spirochetes that got into every board, every strip, every crack, every splinter, every flecking flake of paint. The Warehouse actually turns out to be the ground-floor garage of an abandoned hotel. Its last commercial use was as a pie factory. We pull up to the garage and there is a panel truck parked just outside, painted in blue, yellow, orange, red Day-Glo, with the word BAM in huge letters on the hood. From out the black hole of the garage comes the sound of a record by Bob Dylan with his raunchy harmonica and Ernest Tubb voice raunching and rheuming in the old jack-legged chants—

Inside is a huge chaotic space with what looks at first in the gloom like ten or fifteen American flags walking around. This turns out to be a bunch of men and women, most of them in their twenties, in white coveralls of the sort airport workers wear, only with sections of American flags sewn all over, mostly the stars against fields of blue but some with red stripes running down the legs. Around the side is a lot of theater scaffolding with blankets strewn across like curtains and whole rows of uprooted theater seats piled up against the walls and big cubes of metal debris and ropes and girders.

One of the blanket curtains edges back and a little figure vaults down from a platform about nine feet up. It glows. It is a guy about five feet tall with some sort of World War I aviator's helmet on . . . glowing with curves and swirls of green and orange. His boots, too; he seems to be bouncing over on a pair of fluorescent globes. He stops. He has a small, fine, ascetic face with a big mustache and huge eyes. The eyes narrow and he breaks into a grin.

"I just had an eight-year-old boy up there," he says.

Then he goes into a sniffling giggle and bounds, glowing, over into a corner, in among the debris.

Everybody laughs. It is some kind of family joke, I guess. At least I am the only one who scans the scaffolding for the remains.

"That's the Hermit." Three days later I see he has built a cave in the corner.

A bigger glow in the center of the garage. I make out a school bus . . . glowing orange, green, magenta, lavender, chlorine blue, every fluorescent pastel imaginable in thousands of designs, both large and small, like a cross between Fernand Léger and Dr. Strange, roaring together and vibrating off each other as if somebody had given Hieronymous Bosch fifty buckets of Day-Glo paint and a 1939 International Harvester school bus and told him to go to it. On the floor by the bus is a 15-foot banner reading ACID TEST GRADUATION, and two or three of the Flag People are working on it. Bob Dylan's voice is raunching and rheuming and people are moving around, and babies are crying. I don't see them but they are somewhere in here, crying. Off to one side is a guy about 40 with a lot of muscles, as you can see because he has no shirt on—just a pair of khakis and some red leather boots on and his hell of a build—and he seems to be in a kinetic trance, flipping a small sledge hammer up in the air over and over, always managing to catch the handle on the way down with his arms and legs kicking out the whole time and his shoulders rolling and his head bobbing, all in a jerky beat as if somewhere Joe Cuba is playing "Bang Bang" although in fact even Bob Dylan is no longer on and out of the speaker, wherever it is, comes some sort of tape with a spectral voice saying:

"... The Nowhere Mine ... we've got bubble-gum wrappers ..." some sort of weird electronic music behind it, with Oriental intervals, like Juan Carrillo's music: "... We're going to jerk it out from under the world ... working in the Nowhere Mine ... this day, every day ..."

One of the Flag People comes up.

"Hey, Mountain Girl! That's wild!"

Mountain Girl is a tall girl, big and beautiful with dark brown hair falling down to her shoulders except that the lower two-thirds of her falling hair looks like a paint brush dipped in cadmium yellow from where she dyed it blond in Mexico. She pivots and shows the circle of stars on the back of her coveralls.

"We got 'em at a uniform store," she says. "Aren't they great! There's this old guy in there, says, 'Now, you ain't gonna cut them flags up for costumes, are you?' And so I told him, 'Naw, we're gonna git some horns and have a parade.' But you see this? This is really why we got 'em."

She points to a button on the coveralls. Everybody leans in to look. A motto is engraved on the bottom in art nouveau curves: "Can't Bust 'Em."

Can't Bust 'Em! ... and about time. After all the times the Pranksters have gotten busted, by the San Mateo County cops, the San Francisco cops, the Mexicale Federale cops, FBI cops, cops cops cops cops ...

And still the babies cry. Mountain Girl turns to Lois Jennings.

"What do Indians do to stop a baby from crying?"

"They hold its nose."

"Yeah?"

"They learn."

"I'll try it ... it sounds logical ..." And Mountain Girl goes over and picks up her baby, a four-month-old girl named Sunshine, out of one of those tube-and-net portable cribs from behind the bus and sits down in one of the theater seats. But instead of the Indian treatment she unbuttons the Can't Bust 'Em coveralls and starts feeding her.

"... The Nowhere Mine ... Nothing felt and screamed and cried ..." brang tweeeeeeng "... and I went back to the Nowhere Mine ..."

The sledge-hammer juggler rockets away—

"Who is that?"

"That's Cassady."

This strikes me as a marvelous fact. I remember Cassady. Cassady, Neal Cassady, was the hero, "Dean Moriarty," of Jack Kerouac's *On the Road,* the Denver Kid, a kid who was always racing back and forth across the U.S. by car, chasing, or outrunning, "life," and here is the same guy, now 40, in the garage, flipping a sledge hammer, rocketing about to his own Joe Cuba and—talking. Cassady never stops talking. But that is a bad way to put it. Cassady is a monologuist, only he doesn't seem to care whether anyone is listening or not. He just goes off on the monologue, by himself if necessary, although anyone is welcome aboard. He will answer all questions, although not exactly in that order, because we can't stop here, next rest area 40 miles, you understand, spinning off memories, metaphors, literary, Oriental, hip allusions, all punctuated by the unlikely expression, "you understand—"

The Bladder Totem

FOR TWO OR THREE DAYS IT WENT LIKE THAT FOR ME IN THE garage with the Merry Pranksters waiting for Kesey. The Pranksters took me pretty much for granted. One of the Flag People, a blonde who looked like Doris Day but was known as Doris Delay, told me I ought to put some more . . . well, *color* . . . into my appearance. That hurt, Doris Delay, but I know you meant it as a kindly suggestion. She really did. So I kept my necktie on to show that I had pride. But nobody gave a damn about that. I just hung around and Cassady flipped his sledge hammer, spectral tapes played, babies cried, mihs got flipped out, bus glowed, Flag People walk, freaks loop in outta sunlight on old Harriet Street, and I only left to sleep for a few hours or go to the bathroom.

The bathroom; yes. There was no plumbing in the Warehouse, not even any cold water. You could go out into a little vacant lot next door, behind a board fence, and take a stance amid the great fluffy fumes of human piss that were already lufting up from the mud, or you could climb a ladder through a trap door that led up to the old hotel where there were dead flophouse halls lined with rooms of a kind of spongy scabid old wood that broke apart under your glance and started crawling, vermin, molting underlife. It was too rank even for the Pranksters. Most of them went up to the Shell station on the corner. So I went up to the Shell station on the corner, at Sixth and Howard. I asked where the bathroom is and the guy gives me The Look—the rotten look of O.K., you're not even buying gas but you want to use the bathroom—and finally he points inside the office to the tin can. The key to the bathroom is chained to a big empty Shell oil can. I pick it up and walk out of the office part, out onto the concrete apron, where the Credit Card elite are tanking up and stretching their legs and tweezing their undershorts out of the aging waxy folds of their scrota, and I am out there carrying a Shell oil can in both hands like a bladder totem, around the corner, to the toilet, and—all right, so what. But suddenly it hits me that for the Pranksters this is *permanent*. This is the way they live. Men, women, boys, girls, most from middle-class upbringings, men and women and boys and girls and children and babies, this is the way they have been living for months, for years, some of them, across America and back, on the bus, down to the Rat lands of Mexico and back, sailing like gypsies along the Servicenter fringes, copping urinations, fencing with rotten looks—it even turns out they have films and tapes of their duels with service-station managers in the American heartland trying to keep their concrete bathrooms and empty Dispensa-Towels safe from the Day-Glo crazies . . .

Back inside the Warehouse. Everything keeps up. Slowly I am getting more and more of a strange feeling about the whole thing. It is not just the costumes, the tapes, the bus and all that, however. I have been through some crewcut college fraternity weekends that have been weirder-looking and -sounding, insane on the beano. The . . . feeling begins when the Flag People start coming up to me and saying things like—well, when Cassady is flipping the sledge hammer, with his head down in the mull of the universe, just mulling the hell out of it, and *blam,* the sledge hammer, he misses it, and it slams onto the concrete floor of the garage and one of the Flag People says, "You know, the Chief says when Cassady misses it, it's never an accident—"

For a start, the term the "Chief." The Pranksters have two terms for referring to Kesey. If it is some mundane matter they're talking about, it's just Kesey, as in "Kesey got a tooth knocked out." But if they are talking about Kesey as the leader or teacher of the whole group, he becomes the Chief. At first this struck me as phony. But then it turned to . . . *mysto,* as the general mysto steam began rising in my head. This steam, I can actually hear it inside my head, a great sssssssss, like what you hear if you take too much quinine. I don't know if this happens to anybody else or not. But if there is something startling enough, fearful, awesome, strange, or just weird enough, something I sense I can't cope with, it is as if I go on Red Alert and the fogging steam starts . . .

"—when Cassady misses, it's never an accident. He's saying something. There's something going on in the room, something's getting up tight, there's bad vibrations and he wants to break it up."

They mean it. Everything in everybody's life is . . . significant. And everybody is alert, watching for the meanings. And the vibrations. There is no end of vibrations. Sometime after that I was up in Haight-Ashbury with some kid, not a Prankster, a kid from another communal group, and the kid was trying to open an old *secrétaire,* the kind that opens out into a desktop you can write on, and he pinches his finger in a hinge. Only instead of saying Aw shit or whatever, the whole thing becomes a parable of life, and he says:

"That's *typ*ical. You see that? Even the poor cat who designed this thing was playing the game they wanted him to play. You see how this thing is designed, to open *out*? It's always *out, in*to, it's got to be *out,* into *your* life, the old bullshit *thrust*—you know?—they don't even *think* about it—you know?—this is just the way they design things and you're here and they're there and they're going to keep coming *at* you. You see that kitchen table?" There is an old enamel-top kitchen table you can see through a doorway in there. "Now that's actually *better design,* it actually is, than all this ornate shit, I mean, I truly dig that kitchen table, because the whole thing is right *there*—you know?—it's there to *receive,* that's what it's all about, it's passive, I mean what the hell is a table anyway? Freud said a table is a symbol of a woman, with her shanks open, balling it, in dreams—you know?—and what is this a symbol of?" He points to the *secrétaire.* "It's a symbol of fuck-you, Fuck *you,* right?" And so on, until I want to put my hand on his shoulder and say why don't you just kick it in the kneecaps and let it go at that.

But anyway this talk just flows. Everyone is picking up on the most minute incidents as if they are metaphors for life itself. Everybody's life becomes more fabulous, every minute, than the most fabulous book. It's phony, goddamn it . . . but *mysto* . . . and after a while it starts to infect you, like an itch, the roseola.

There is also a lot about games. The straight world outside, it seems, is made up of millions of people involved, trapped, in games they aren't even aware of. A guy they call Hassler comes in out of the sunlight screen on Harriet Street and, zoom, he doesn't even wait for the metaphors. I never got into an abstract discussion with a total stranger so fast in my life. We began talking right away about the games. Hassler is a young guy, good-looking with a wide face and long hair with bangs just exactly like Prince Valiant in the comic strip and a turtleneck jersey on with metal stars on it, of the sort generals wear on their shoulders, and he says, "Games so permeate our culture that . . ." rumble rumble ego games judge everything screwed up brainwashing tell ourselves ". . . keep on oppositioning"—here Hassler stiffens his hands and brings his fingertips together like a karate collision—

But my mind is wandering. I am having a hard time listening

because I am fascinated by a little plastic case with a toothbrush
and toothpaste in it that Hassler has tucked under one thumb. It
is shuddering around in front of my eyes as Hassler's hands op-
position . . . What a curious bunch of bohos. This guy with the
generals' stars on his jersey is giving a kind of vesper service lec-
ture on the sins of man and—a toothbrush!—but of course!—he
brushes after every meal!—he really does. He brushes after every
meal despite the fact that they are living here in this garage, like
gypsies, and there is no hot water, no toilet, no beds, except for a
couple of mattresses in which the dirt, the dust, the damps, and
the scuds are all one, melded, with the stuffing, and they stretch
out on the scaffoldings, in the bus, in the back of a pickup truck,
nostrils mildewing—

"—but you know what? People are beginning to see through
the warf of the games. Not just the heads and everybody, but all
sorts of people. You take in California. There's always been this
pyramid—"

Here Hassler outlines a pyramid in the air with his hands and
I watch, fascinated, as the plastic toothbrush case shiny shiny
slides up one incline of the pyramid—

"—they're transcending the bullshit," says Hassler, only his
voice is earnest and clear and sweet like a high-school valedictorian's, as if he just said *may next year's seniors remember our
motto*—"transcending the bullshit—"

—a nice line of light there along the plastic, a straight rigid
gleam from the past, from wherever Hassler came from. Now
I'm doing it again, ah, that amiable itch, I just extracted a
metaphor, a piece of transcendent bullshit, from this freaking
toothbrush case—

"—transcending the bullshit—"

A TALL GUY COMES INTO THE WAREHOUSE WEARING SOME
kind of blue and orange outfit like a mime harlequin's and with
an orange Day-Glo mask painted on his face, so that he looks ex-

traordinarily like The Spirit, if you remember that comic strip. This, I am told, is Ken Babbs, who used to be a helicopter pilot in Vietnam. I get to talking to him and I ask him what it was like in Vietnam and he says to me, very seriously:

"You really want to know what it was like?"

"Yeah."

"Come over here. I'll show you."

So he leads me back into the garage and he points to a cardboard box lying on the floor, just lying there amid all the general debris and madness.

"It's all in there."

"It's all in there?"

"Right, right, right."

I reach in there and lift out a typewritten manuscript, four or five hundred pages. I leaf through. It's a novel, about Vietnam. I look at Babbs. He gives me a smile of good fellowship with his Day-Glo mask glowing and crinkling up.

"It's all in there?" I say. "Then I guess it takes a while to get it."

"Yeah, yeah, right! right! right!" says Babbs, breaking into a laugh, as if I just said the funniest thing in the world. "Yeah! Yeah! Hah hah hah hah hah hah hah Right! Right!" with the mask glowing and bouncing around on his face. I lower the novel back into the box, and for days I would notice Babbs's novel about Vietnam lying out there on the floor, out in the middle of everything, as if waiting for a twister to whip it up and scatter it over San Francisco County, and Babbs would be somewhere around saying to some other bemused soul: "Yeah, yeah, right! right! right!"

The Merry Pranksters were all rapidly assembling, waiting for Kesey. George Walker arrives. Walker has on no costume. He is just like some very clean-cut blond college kid wearing a T-shirt and corduroy pants, smiling and outgoing, just a good West Coast golden boy except for a few random notes like the Lotus racing car he has outside, painted with orange Day-Glo so that it lights up at dusk, skidding around the corners of the California suburbs in four-wheel drifts. And Paul Foster. Foster, I am told, is some kind of mad genius, a genius at computers, with all sorts of firms with names like Techniflex, Digitron, Solartex, Automaton, trying to hunt him down to lay money on him to do this or that for them . . . Whether he is a genius or not, I couldn't say. He certainly looks mad enough. He is hunched over in a corner, in a theater seat, an emaciated figure but with a vast accumulation of clothes. It looks like he has on about eight pairs of clown's pants, one on top of the other, each one filthier than the next one, all black, sooty, torn, mungey and fungous. His head is practically shaven and he is so thin that all the flesh seems to be gone off his head and when he contracts his jaw muscles it is as if some very clever anatomical diagram has been set in motion with little facial muscles, striations, sheathes, ligaments, tissues, nodules, integuments that nobody ever suspected before bunching up, popping out, springing into definition in a complex chain reaction. And he contracts his jaw muscles all the time, concentrating, with his head down and his eyes burning, concentrating on a drawing he is doing on a pad of paper, an extremely small but crucial drawing by the looks of his concentration . . .

Black Maria sits on a folding chair and smiles ineffably but says nothing. One of the Flag People, a thin guy, tells me about Mexicans strung out on huaraches. Doris Delay tells me—

"They're off on their own freak," Hassler continues, "and it may not look like much, but they're starting to transcend the bullshit. There's this old trinity, Power, Position, Authority, and why should they worship these old gods and these old forms of authority—"

"Fuck God . . . ehhhhh . . . Fuck God . . ."

This is a voice behind a blanket curtain to one side. Somebody is back there rapping off what Hassler just said.

"Fuck God. Up with the Devil."

It is a very sleepy, dreamy voice, however. The curtain pulls back and standing there is a wiry little guy who looks like a pirate. Behind him, back in there behind the curtain, all sorts of wires, instruments, panels, speakers are all piled up, a glistening heap of electronic equipment, and the tape is back there going . . . "In the Nowhere Mine . . ." The guy looks like a pirate, as I said, with long black hair combed back Tarzan-style, and a mustache, and a gold ring through his left earlobe. He stares out, sleepily. In fact, he is a Hell's Angel. His name is Freewheeling Frank. He has on the Hell's Angels' "colors," meaning a jacket with insignia, a jacket with the sleeves cut off and the skull with the helmet on it and the wings and a lot of other arcane symbols.

"Fuck God," says Freewheeling Frank. "Fuck all forms of . . . of . . ." and the words trail off in a kind of dreamy way, although his lips are still moving and he kind of puts his head down and trudges off into the gloom, toward the bus, with his hands flicking out, first this side, then the other, like Cassady, and he is off on his trip, like Cassady, and, all right, a Hell's Angel—and the Hassler brushes his teeth after every meal, in the middle of a Shell station tin-can economy—

Just then Kesey arrives.

chapter

III

The Electric Suit

THROUGH THE SHEET OF SUNLIGHT AT THE DOORWAY AND down the incline into the crazy gloom comes a panel truck and in the front seat is Kesey. The Chief; out on bail. I half expect the whole random carnival to well up into a fluorescent yahoo of incalculably insane proportions. In fact, everybody is quiet. It is all cool.

Kesey gets out of the truck with his eyes down. He's wearing a sport shirt, an old pair of pants, and some Western boots. He seems to see me for an instant, but there is no hello, not a glimmer of recognition. This annoys me, but then I see that he doesn't say hello to anybody. Nobody says anything. They don't all rush up or anything. It's as if . . . Kesey is back and what is there to say about it.

Then Mountain Girl booms out: "How was jail, Kesey!"

Kesey just shrugs. "Where's my shirt?" he says.

Mountain Girl fishes around in the debris over beside a bunch of theater seats and gets the shirt, a brown buckskin shirt with an open neck and red leather lacings. Kesey takes off the shirt he has on. He has huge latissimi dorsi muscles making his upper back fan out like manta-ray wings. Then he puts on the buckskin shirt and turns around.

Instead of saying anything, however, he cocks his head to one side and walks across the garage to the mass of wires, speakers, and microphones over there and makes some minute adjustment. ". . . The Nowhere Mine . . ." As if now everything is under control and the fine tuning begins.

From out of the recesses of the garage—I didn't even know they were there—here comes a woman and three children. Kesey's wife Faye, their daughter Shannon, who is six, and two boys, Zane, five, and Jed, three. Faye has long, sorrel-brown hair and is one of the prettiest, most beatific-looking women I ever saw. She looks radiant, saintly. Kesey goes over to her and picks up each of the kids, and then Mountain Girl brings over her baby, Sunshine, and he picks up Sunshine a moment. All right—

Then Kesey loosens up and smiles, as if he just thought of something. It is as if he just heard Mountain Girl's question about how was jail. "The only thing I was worried about was this tooth," he says. He pops a dental plate out of the roof of his mouth and pushes a false front tooth out of his mouth with his tongue. "I had the awfulest feeling," he says. "I was going to be in court or talking to reporters or something, and this thing was going to fall down like this and I was going to start gumming my words." He gums the words "start gumming my words," to illustrate.

Three weeks later he was to replace it with a tooth with an orange star and green stripes on it, an enameled dens incisus lateral bearing a Prankster flag. One day at a gas station the manager, a white guy, gets interested in the tooth and calls over his helper, a colored guy, and says, "Hey, Charlie, come over here and show this fellow your tooth." So Charlie grins and bares his upper teeth, revealing a gold tooth with a heart cut out in the gold so that a white enamel heart shows through. Kesey grins back and then bares *his* tooth—the colored guy stares a moment and doesn't say anything. He doesn't even smile. He just turns away. A little while later, down the road, Kesey says very seriously, very sorrowfully, "That was wrong of me. I shouldn't have done that." "Done what?" "I outniggered him," says Kesey.

Outniggered him! Kesey has kept these countryisms, like "the awfulest feeling," all through college, graduate school, days of literary celebration . . .

"How did it happen?" says Freewheeling Frank, meaning the tooth.

"He got in a fight with a Hell's Angel," says Mountain Girl.

"What!—" Freewheeling Frank is truly startled.

"Yeah!" says Mountain Girl. "The bastard hit him with a chain!"

"What!" says Frank. "Where? What was his name!"

Kesey gives Mountain Girl a look.

"Naw," she says.

"What was his name!" Frank says. "What did he look like!"

"Mountain Girl is shucking you," Kesey says. "I was in a wreck."

Mountain Girl looks repentant. Angels' duels are no joke with Frank. Kesey breaks up . . . the vibrations. He sits down in one of the old theater seats. He is just talking in a soft, conversational tone, with his head down, just like he is having conversation with Mountain Girl or somebody.

"It's funny," he says. "There are guys in jail who have been in jail so much, that's their whole thing. They're jail freaks. They've picked up the whole jail language—"

—everybody starts gathering around, sitting in the old theater seats or on the floor. The mysto steam begins rising—

"—only it isn't their language, it's the guards', the cops', the D.A.'s, the judge's. It's all numbers. One of them says, 'What happened to so-and-so?' And the other one says, 'Oh, he's over in 34,' which is a cellblock. 'They got him on a 211'—they have numbers for different things, just like you hear on a police radio—'they got him on a 211, but he can cop to a 213 and get three to five, one and a half with good behavior.'

"The cops like that. It makes them feel better if you play their game. They'll chase some guy and run him down and pull guns on him and they're ready to blow his head off if he moves a muscle, but then as soon as they have him in jail, one of them will come around and ask him how his wife is and he's supposed to say she's O.K., thanks, and ask him about his kids, like now that we've played the cops-and-robbers part of the game, you can go ahead and like me. And a lot of them in there go along with that, because that's all they know.

"When you're running, you're playing their game, too. I was up in Haight-Ashbury and I heard something hit the sidewalk behind me and it was a kid had fallen out the window. A lot of people rushed up and a woman was there crying and trying to pick him up, and I knew what I should do is go up and tell her not to move him but I didn't. I was afraid I was going to be recognized. And then up the street I saw a cop writing out parking tickets and I was going to go up and tell him to call an ambulance. But I didn't. I just kept going. And that night I was listening to the news on television and they told about a child who fell out of a window and died in the hospital."

And that's what the cops-and-robbers game does to you. Only it is *me* thinking it. Figuring out parables, I look around at the faces and they are all watching Kesey and, I have not the slightest doubt, thinking: *and that's what the cops-and-robbers game does to you.* Despite the skepticism I brought here, *I* am suddenly experiencing *their* feeling. I am sure of it. I feel like I am in on something the outside world, the world I came from, could not possibly comprehend, and it *is* a metaphor, the whole scene, ancient and vast, vaster than . . .

TWO GUYS COME IN OUT OF THE DAYLIGHT ON HARRIET Street, heads by the looks of them, and walk up to Kesey. One of them is young with a sweatshirt on and Indian beads with an amulet hanging from the beads—a routine acid-head look, in other words. The other one, the older one, is curiously neat, however. He has long black hair, but neat, and a slightly twirly mustache, like a cavalier, but neat, and a wildly flowered shirt, but neat and well-tailored and expensive, and a black leather jacket, only not a motorcycle jacket but tailored more like a coat, and a pair of English boots that must have set him back $25 or $30. At first he looks like something out of Late North Beach, the boho with the thousand-dollar wardrobe. But he has a completely sincere look. He has a thin face with sharp features and a couple of eyes burning with truth oil. He says his name is Gary Goldhill and he wants to interview Kesey for the Haight-Ashbury newspaper *The Oracle,* and when could he do that—but right away it is obvious that he has something to get off his chest that can't wait.

"The thing is, Ken"—he has an English accent, but it is a middle-class accent, a pleasant sort of Midlands accent—"the thing is, Ken, a lot of people are very concerned about what you've said, or what the newspapers say you've said, about graduating from acid. A lot of people look up to you, Ken, you're one of the heroes of the psychedelic movement"—he has a kind of Midlands England way of breaking up long words into syllables, psy-che-delic move-ment—"and they want to know what you mean. A very beautiful thing is happening in Haight-Ashbury, Ken. A lot of people are opening the doors in their minds for the first time, but people like you have to help them. There are only two directions we can go, Ken. We can isolate ourselves in a monastery or we can organize a religion, along the lines of the League for Spiritual Discovery"—the League for Spi-ri-tu-al Dis-cov-ery—"and have acid and grass legalized as sacraments, so everyone won't have to spend every day in fear waiting for the knock on the door."

"It can be worse to take it as a sacrament," Kesey says.

"You've been away for almost a year, Ken," Goldhill says.

"You may not know what's been happening in Haight-Ashbury. It's growing, Ken, and thousands of people have found something very beautiful, and they're very open and loving, but the fear and the paranoia, Ken, the waiting for the knock on the door—it's causing some terrible things, Ken. It's re-spon-si-ble for a lot of bad trips. People are having bad trips, Ken, because they take acid and suddenly they feel that any moment there may be a knock on the door. We've got to band together. You've got to help us, Ken, and not work against us."

Kesey looks up, away from Goldhill, out across the gloom of the garage. Then he speaks in a soft, far-off voice, with his eyes in the distance:

"If you don't realize that I've been helping you with every fiber in my body . . . if you don't realize that everything I've done, everything I've gone through . . ."

—it is rising and rising—

"I know, Ken, but the repression—"

"We're in a period now like St. Paul and the early Christians," Kesey says. "St. Paul said, if they shit on you in one city, move on to another city, and if they shit on you in that city, move on to another city—"

"I know, Ken, but you're telling people to stop taking acid, and they're not going to stop. They've opened up doors in their minds they never knew existed, and a very beautiful thing, and then they read in the papers that somebody they've looked up to is suddenly telling them to stop."

"There's a lot of things I can't tell the newspapers," says Kesey. His eyes are still focused long-range, away from Goldhill. "One night in Mexico, in Manzanillo, I took some acid and I threw the I Ching. And the I Ching—the great thing about the I Ching is, it never sends you Valentines, it slaps you in the face when you need it—and it said we had reached the end of something, we weren't going anywhere any longer, it was time for a new direction—and I went outside and there was an electrical storm, and there was lightning everywhere and I pointed to the sky and lightning flashed and all of a sudden I had a second skin, of lightning, electricity, like a suit of electricity, and I knew it was in us to be superheroes and that we could become superheroes or nothing." He lowers his eyes. "I couldn't tell this to the newspapers. How could I? I wouldn't be put back in jail, I'd be put in Pescadero."

—rising—rising—

"But most people aren't ready for that, Ken," Goldhill says. "They're just beginning to open the doors in their minds—"

"But once you've been through that door, you can't just keep going through it over and over again—"

"—and somebody's got to help them through that door—"

"Don't say stop plunging into the forest," Kesey says. "Don't say stop being a pioneer and come back here and help these people through the door. If Leary wants to do that, that's good, it's a good thing and somebody should do it. But somebody has to be the pioneer and leave the marks for others to follow." Kesey looks up again, way out into the gloom. "You've got to have some faith in what you're trying to do. It's easy to have faith as long as it goes along with what you already know. But you've got to have faith in us all the way. Somebody like Gleason—Gleason was with us this far." Kesey spread his thumb and forefinger about two inches apart. "He was with us as long as our fantasy coincided with his. But as soon as we went on further, he didn't understand it, so he was going against us. He had . . . no faith."

No faith!—bay fog turns steam, hissing in the old cranium—

Faith! Further! And it is an exceedingly strange feeling to be sitting here in the Day-Glo, on poor abscessed Harriet Street, and realize suddenly that in this improbably ex-pie factory Warehouse garage I am in the midst of Tsong-Isha-pa and the sangha communion, Mani and the wan persecuted at The Gate, Zoroaster, Maidhyoimaongha and the five faithful before Vishtapu, Mohammed and Abu Bekr and the disciples amid the pharisaical Koreish of Mecca, Gautama and the brethren in the wilderness leaving the blood-and-kin families of their pasts for the one true family of the sangha inner circle—in short, true mystic brotherhood—only in poor old Formica polyethylene 1960s America without a grain of desert sand or a shred of palm leaf or a morsel of manna wilderness breadfruit overhead, picking up vibrations from Ampex tapes and a juggled Williams Lok-Hed sledge hammer, hooking down mathematical lab drugs, LSD-25, IT-290, DMT, instead of soma water, heading out in American flag airport coveralls and an International Harvester bus—yet for real!—amid the marshmallow shiny black shoe masses—

chapter IV

What Do You Think
of My Buddha?

THE CURRENT FANTASY... BY NOW, LATE EVENING, MOST of the Pranksters have cleared out of the Warehouse, off to take a shower at the apartment of Gut, an ex–Hell's Angel who has a psychedelic shop called Joint Ventures, off to here, off to there... Just Kesey and a couple of others left in the Warehouse. Kesey stands in the gloom of the Control Central, over to the side amid the tapes, and cans of movie film marked with adhesive strips, and notebooks and microphones and wires and coils, speakers, amplifiers. The Prankster Archives—and a tape drones on in a weird voice, full of Ouija-whammy:

"... the blissful counterstroke... a considerable new message..."

A considerable new message... The current fantasy... Fantasy is a word Kesey has taken to using more and more, for all sorts of plans, ventures, world views, ambitions. It is a good word. It is ironic and it isn't. It refers to everything from getting hold of a pickup truck—"that's our fantasy for this weekend"—to some scary stuff out on the raggedy raggedy edge . . . like the current fantasy, which is somehow to be told at the Acid Test Graduation. But how to tell it? Kesey rummages through the film cans and assorted . . . Archives . . . It has never been possible, has it, truly, just to come out and *announce* the current fantasy, not even in days gone by, when it seemed so simple. Now, you take Goldhill, who was just in here with the truth in his eyes. He will come closer than most. Kesey could see it. Goldhill was open . . . and into the pudding. He had his own fantasy, the League for Spi-ri-tu-al Dis-cov-ery, and yet he is the rare kind who might even be willing to move with *their* fantasy, his and the Pranksters'. It *takes* a rare kind. Because always comes the moment when it's time to take the Prankster circus further on toward Edge City. And always at that point some good souls are startled: Hey, wait! Like Ralph Gleason with his column in the *Chronicle* and his own clump of *hip*ness. Gleason is one of those people . . . Kesey can remember them all, people who thought he was great so long as his fantasy coincided with theirs. But every time he pushed on further—and he always pushed on further—they became confused and resentful . . . The tape winds on:

". . . the blissful counterstroke . . . through workhorse and intercourse . . . the blood that was available to him in intercourse . . . made us believe he was in the apple sauce for twenty years . . ."

Only lucky dogs and Merry Pranksters can understand this supersonic warble! . . . most likely . . .

". . . the blissful counterstroke . . ."

. . . the current fantasy . . . Even back on Perry Lane, where everyone was young and intellectual and analytical, and the sky, supposedly, was the limit—there was no way he could just come right out and say: Come in a little closer, friends . . . They had their own fantasy for him: he was a "diamond in the rough." Wellllll, that was all right, being a diamond in the rough. He had gone to Stanford University in 1958 on a creative-writing fellowship, and they had taken him in on Perry Lane because he was such a swell diamond in the rough. Perry Lane was Stanford's bohemian quarter. As bohemias go, Perry Lane was Arcadia, Arcadia just off the Stanford golf course. It was a cluster of two-room cottages with weathery wood shingles in an oak forest, only not just amid trees and greenery, but amid vines, honeysuckle tendrils, all buds and shoots and swooping tendrils and twitterings like the best of Arthur Rackham and *Honey Bear.* Not only that, it had true cultural cachet. Thorstein Veblen had lived there. So had two Nobel Prize winners everybody knew about though the names escaped them. The cottages rented for just $60 a month. Getting into Perry Lane was like getting into a club. Everybody who lived there had known somebody else who lived there, or they would never have gotten in, and naturally they got to know each other very closely too, and there was always something of an atmosphere of communal living. Nobody's door was ever shut on Perry Lane, except when they were pissed off.

It was sweet. Perry Lane was a typical 1950s bohemia. Everybody sat around shaking their heads over America's tailfin, housing-development civilization, and Christ, in Europe, so what if the plumbing didn't work, they had mastered the art of living. Occasionally somebody would suggest an orgy or a three-day wine binge, but the model was always that old Zorba the Greek romanticism of sandals and simplicity and back to first principles. Periodically they would take pilgrimages 40 miles north to North Beach to see how it was actually done.

The main figures on Perry Lane were two novelists, Robin White, who had just written the Harper Prize novel, *Elephant Hill,* and Gwen Davis, a kind of West Coast Dawn Powell. In any case, all the established Perry Laners could see Kesey coming a mile away.

He had Jack London Martin Eden Searching Hick, the hick with intellectual yearnings, written all over him. He was from Oregon—who the hell was ever from Oregon?—and he had an Oregon country drawl and too many muscles and callouses on his hands and his brow furrowed when he was thinking hard, and it was perfect.

White took Kesey under his wing and got him and his wife Faye a cottage on Perry Lane. The Perry Lane set liked the idea at once. He could always be counted on to do *perfect* things. Like the time they were all having dinner—there was a lot of communal dining—and some visitor was going on about the ineffable delicacy of James Baldwin's work, and Kesey keeps eating but also trying to edge a word in saying, well, bub, I dunno, I cain't exactly go along with you there, and the fellow puts down his knife and fork very carefully and turns to the others and says,

"I'll be delighted to listen to what*ever* Mr. Kesey has to say—as soon as he learns to eat from a plate without holding down his meat with his thumb."

Perfect! He had been voted "most likely to succeed" at his high school in Springfield, Oregon, and had graduated from the University of Oregon, where he was all involved in sports and fraternities, the All-American Boy bit. He had been a star wrestler in the 174-pound class and a star actor in college plays. He had even gone to Los Angeles after he finished college, and knocked around Hollywood for a while with the idea of becoming a movie star. But the urge to write, to create, had burst up through all this thick lumpy All-American crap somehow, like an unaccountable purslane blossom, and he had started writing, even completing a novel about college athletics, *End of Autumn*. It had never been published, and probably never would be, but he had the longing to do this thing. And his background—it was great, too. Somehow the Perry Lane set got the idea that his family were Okies, coming out of the Dust Bowl during the Depression, and then up to Oregon, wild, sodden Oregon, where they had fought the land and shot bears and the rivers were swift and the salmon leaped silver in the spring big two-hearted rivers.

His wife Faye—she was from the same kind of background, only she came from Idaho, and they had been high-school sweethearts in Springfield, Oregon, and had run off and gotten married when they were both freshmen in college. They once made a bet as to which of them had been born in the most Low Rent, bottomdog shack, his old place in La Junta, or hers in Idaho. He was dead sure there was no beating La Junta for Rundown until they got to Idaho, and she sure as hell did win that one. Faye was even more soft-spoken than Kesey. She hardly spoke at all. She was pretty and extremely sweet, practically a madonna of the hill country. And their cottage on Perry Lane—well, everybody else's cottage was run-down in a careful bohemian way, *simplicity,* Japanese paper lamp globes and monk's cloth and blond straw rugs and Swedish stainless steel knives and forks and cornflowers sticking out of a hand-thrown pot. But theirs was just plain Low Rent. There was always something like a broken washing machine rusting on the back porch and pigweed, bladderpods, scoke and scurf peas growing ragged out back. Somehow it was...*perfect*...to have him and Faye on hand to *learn* as the Perry Lane sophisticates talked about life and the arts.

BEAUTIFUL! . . . THE CURRENT FANTASY . . . BUT HOW TO TELL them?—about such arcane little matters as Captain Marvel and The Flash . . . and *The Life*—and the very *Superkids*—

"...a considerable new message...the blissful counterstroke..."

—when they had such a nice clear picture of him as the horny-nailed son of the Western sod, fresh from Springfield, Oregon. It was true that his father, Fred Kesey, had started him and his younger brother, Joe, known as Chuck, shooting and fishing and swimming as early as they could in any way manage it, also boxing, running, wrestling, plunging down the rapids of the Willamette and the McKenzie Rivers, on inner-tube rafts, with a lot of rocks and water and sartin' death foamin' down below. But it was not so they could tame animals, forests, rivers, wild up-turned convulsed Oregon. It was more to condition them to do more of what his father had already done a pretty good job of—claim whatever he can rightly get by being man enough to take it, and not on the frontier, either . . . Kesey Sr. had been part of the 1940s migration from the Southwest—not of "Okies" but of Protestant entrepreneurs who looked to the West Coast as a land of business opportunity. He started out in the Willamette Valley with next to nothing and founded a marketing cooperative for dairy farmers, the Eugene Farmers Cooperative, and built it into the biggest dairy operation in the area, retailing under the name of Darigold. He was one of the big postwar success stories in the Valley—and ended up not in an old homestead with wood sidings and lightning rods but in a modern home in the suburbs, lowslung and pastel, on a street called Debra Lane. The incredible postwar American electro-pastel surge into the suburbs!—it was sweeping the Valley, with superhighways, dreamboat cars, shopping centers, soaring thirty-foot Federal Sign & Signal Company electric supersculptures—Eight New Plexiglas Display Features!—a surge of freedom and mobility, of cars and the money to pay for them and the time to enjoy them and a home where you can laze in a rich pool of pale wall-to-wall or roar through the technological wonderworld in motor launches and, in the case of men like his father, private planes—

The things he would somehow suddenly remember about the old home town—over here, for example, is the old white clapboard house they used to live in, and behind it, back a ways, is the radio tower of station KORE with a red light blinking on top—and at night he used to get down on his knees to say his prayers and there would be the sky and the light blinking—and he always kind of thought he was praying to that red light. And the old highway used to take a bend right about here, and it seemed like there was always somebody driving through about three or four in the morning, half asleep, and they would see the lights over there in town where it was getting built up and they'd think the road headed straight for the lights and they'd run off the bend and Kesey and his dad would go out to see if they could help the guy draggle himself out of the muck—chasing street lights!—praying to the red beacon light of KORE!—and a little run-in at Gregg's Drive-In, as it used to be called, it is now Speck's, at Franklin Boulevard at the bridge over the river. That was the big high-school drive-in, with the huge streamlined sculpted pastel display sign with streaming streamlined super-slick A-22 italic script, floodlights, clamp-on trays, car-hop girls in floppy blue slacks, hamburgers in some kind of tissuey wax paper steaming with onions pressed down and fried on the grill and mustard and catsup to squirt all over it from out plastic squirt cylinders. Saturday nights when everybody is out cruising—some guy was in his car in the lot at Gregg's going the wrong way, so nobody could move. The more everybody blew the horns, the more determined the guy got. Like *this* was the test. He rolls up the windows and locks the doors so they can't get at him and keeps boring in. This guy vs. Kesey. So Kesey goes inside and gets a potato they make the french fries with and comes out and jams it over the guy's exhaust pipe, which causes the motor to conk out and you ain't going *any* which way now, bub. The guy brings charges against Kesey for ruining his engine and Kesey ends up in juvenile court before a judge and tries to tell him how it is at Gregg's Drive-In on a Saturday night: The Life—that *feeling*—The Life—the late 1940s early 1950s American Teenage Drive-In Life was *precisely* what it was all about—but how could you tell anyone about it?

But of course!—the *feeling*—out here at night, free, with the motor running and the adrenaline flowing, cruising in the neon glories of the new American night—it was very Heaven to be the first wave of the most extraordinary kids in the history of the world—only 15, 16, 17 years old, dressed in the *haute couture* of pink Oxford shirts, sharp pants, snaky half-inch belts, fast shoes—with all this Straight-6 and V-8 power underneath and all this neon glamour overhead, which somehow tied in with the technological superheroics of the jet, TV, atomic subs, ultrasonics—Postwar American suburbs—glorious world! and the hell with the intellectual bad-mouthers of America's tailfin civiliza-

tion . . . They couldn't know what it was like or else they had it
cultivated out of them—the feeling—to be very Superkids! the
world's first generation of the little devils—feeling immune, beyond calamity. One's parents remembered the sloughing common order, War & Depression—but Superkids knew only the
emotional surge of the great payoff, when nothing was common
any longer—The Life! A glorious place, a glorious age, I tell you!
A very Neon Renaissance—And the myths that actually touched
you at that time—not Hercules, Orpheus, Ulysses, and Ae-
neas—but Superman, Captain Marvel, Batman, The Human
Torch, The Sub-Mariner, Captain America, Plastic Man, The
Flash—but of course! On Perry Lane, what did they think it
was—quaint?—when he talked about the comic-book Superheroes as the honest American myths? It was a fantasy world *already,* this electro-pastel world of Mom&Dad&Buddy&Sis in the
suburbs. There they go, in the family car, a white Pontiac
Bonneville sedan—*the family car!*—a huge crazy god-awful-
powerful fantasy creature to begin with, 327 horsepower, shaped
like twenty-seven nights of lubricious luxury brougham seduction—*you're already there, in Fantasyland,* so why not move off
your smug-harbor quilty-bed dead center and cut loose—go
ahead and say it—Shazam!—juice it up to what it's already
aching to be: 327,000 horsepower, a whole superhighway long
and *soaring, screaming* on toward . . . Edge City, and ultimate fantasies, current and future . . . Billy Batson said *Shazam!* and
turned into Captain Marvel. Jay Garrick inhaled an experimental gas in the research lab . . .

. . . AND BEGAN TRAVELING AND THINKING AT THE SPEED OF
light as . . . The Flash . . . the current fantasy. Yes. The Kesey
diamond-in-the-rough fantasy did not last very long. The most
interesting person on Perry Lane as far as he was concerned was
not any of the novelists or other literary intellectuals, but a young
graduate student in psychology named Vic Lovell. Lovell was

like a young Viennese analyst, or at least a California graduate-school version of one. He was slender with wild dark hair and very cool intellectually and wound-up at the same time. He introduced Kesey to Freudian psychology. Kesey had never run into a system of thought like this before. Lovell could point out in the most persuasive way how mundane character traits and minor hassles around Perry Lane fit into the richest, most complex metaphor of life ever devised, namely, Freud's. . . . And a little experimental gas . . . Yes. Lovell told him about some experiments the Veterans Hospital in Menlo Park was running with "psychomimetic" drugs, drugs that brought on temporary states resembling psychoses. They were paying volunteers $75 a day. Kesey volunteered. It was all nicely calcimined and clinical. They would put him on a bed in a white room and give him a series of capsules without saying what they were. One would be nothing, a placebo. One would be Ditran, which always brought on a terrible experience. Kesey could always tell that one coming on, because the hairs on the blanket he was under would suddenly look like a field of hideously diseased thorns and he would put his finger down his throat and retch. But one of them—the first thing he knew about it was a squirrel dropped an acorn from a tree outside, only it was tremendously loud and sounded like it was not outside but right in the room with him and not actually a sound, either, but a great suffusing presence, visual, almost tactile, a great impacting of . . . *blue* . . . all around him and suddenly he was in a realm of consciousness he had never dreamed of before and it was not a dream or a delirium but part of his awareness. He looks at the ceiling. It begins moving. Panic—and yet there is no panic. The ceiling is moving—not in a crazed swirl but along its own planes its own planes of light and shadow and surface not nearly so nice and smooth as plasterer Super Plaster Man intended with infallible carpenter level bubble sliding in dim honey Karo syrup tube not so foolproof as you thought, bub, little lumps and ridges up there, bub, and lines, lines like spines on crests of waves of white desert movie sand each one with MGM shadow longshot of the ominous A-rab coming up over the next crest for only the sinister Saracen can see the road and you didn't know how many subplots you left up there, Plaster Man, trying to smooth it *all* out, *all* of it, with your bubble in a honey tube carpenter's level, to make us all down here look up and see nothing but ceiling, because we all know ceiling, because it has a *name,* ceiling, therefore it is nothing but a ceiling—no room for A-rabs up there in Level Land, eh, Plaster Man. Suddenly he is like a ping-pong ball in a flood of sensory stimuli, heart beating, blood coursing, breath suspiring, teeth grating, hand moving over the percale sheet over those thousands of minute warfy woofings like a brush fire, sun glow and the highlight on a stainless-steel rod, quite a little movie you have going on in that highlight there, Hondo, Technicolors, pick each one out like fishing for neon gumballs with a steam shovel in the Funtime Arcade, a ping-pong ball in a flood of sensory stimuli, all quite ordinary, but... *revealing* themselves for the first time and happening... *Now* ... as if for the first time he has entered a moment in his life and known exactly what is happening to his senses now, at this moment, and with each new discovery it is as if he has entered into all of it himself, is *one* with it, the movie white desert of the ceiling becomes something rich, personal, his, beautiful beyond description, like an orgasm behind the eyeballs, and his A-rabs—A-rabs behind the eyelids, eyelid movies, room for them and a lot more in the five billion thoughts per second stroboscope synapses—his A-rab heroes, fine Daily Double horsehair mustaches wrapped about the Orbicularis Oris of their mouths—

Face! The doctor comes back in and, marvelous, poor tight cone ass, doc, Kesey can now see *into him.* For the first time he notices that the doctor's lower left lip is trembling, but he more than *sees* the tremor, he understands it, he can—almost seen!—see each muscle fiber decussate, pulling the poor jelly of his lip to the left and the fibers one by one leading back into infrared caverns of the body, through transistor-radio innards of nerve tangles, each one on Red Alert, the poor ninny's inner hooks desperately trying to make the little writhing bastards *keep still in there,* I am Doctor, this is a human specimen before me—the poor ninny has his own desert movie going on inside, only each horsehair A-rab is a threat—if only his lip, his face, would stay level, level like the honey bubble of the Official Plaster Man assured him it would—

Miraculous! He could truly *see into people* for the first time—

And yes, that little capsule sliding blissly down the gullet was LSD.

VERY SOON IT WAS ALREADY TIME TO PUSH ON BEYOND AN-other fantasy, the fantasy of the Menlo Park clinicians. The clinicians' fantasy was that the volunteers were laboratory animals that had to be dealt with objectively, quantitatively. It was well known that people who volunteered for drug experiments tended to be unstable anyway. So the doctors would come in in white smocks, with the clipboards, taking blood pressures and heart rates and urine specimens and having them try to solve simple problems in logic and mathematics, such as adding up columns of figures, and having them judge time and distances, although they did have them talk into tape recorders, too. But the doctors were *so out of it.* They never took LSD themselves and they had absolutely no comprehension, and it couldn't be put into words anyway.

Sometimes you wanted to paint it huge—Lovell is under LSD in the clinic and he starts drawing a huge Buddha on the wall. It somehow encompasses the whole—White Smock comes in and doesn't even look at it, he just starts asking the old questions on the clipboard, so Lovell suddenly butts in:

"What do you think of my Buddha?"

White Smock looks at it a moment and says, "It looks very feminine. Now let's see how rapidly you can add up this column of figures here . . ."

Very feminine. Deliver us from the clichés that have locked up even these so-called experimenters' brains like the accordion fences in the fur-store window—and Kesey was having the same problem with his boys. One of them was a young guy with a lie-down crewcut and the straightest face, the straightest, blandest, most lineless awfulest Plaster Man honey bubble levelest face ever made, and he would come in and open his eyes wide once as if to make sure this muscular hulk on the bed were still *rational* and then get this smug tone in his voice which poured out into the room like absorbent cotton choked in chalk dust from beaten erasers Springfield High School.

"Now when I say 'Go,' you tell me when you think a minute is up by saying, 'Now.' Have you got that?"

Yeah, he had that. Kesey was soaring on LSD and his sense of time was *wasted,* and thousands of thoughts per second were rapping around between synapses, fractions of a second, so what the hell is a minute—but then one thought stuck in there, held ... ma-*li*-cious, *de*-li-cious. He remembered that his pulse had been running 75 beats a minute every time they took it, so when Dr. Fog says 'Go,' Kesey slyly slides his slithering finger onto his pulse and counts up to 75 and says:

"Now!"

Dr. Smog looks at his stop watch. "Amazing!" he says, and walks out of the room.

You said it, bub, but like a lot of other people, you don't even know.

LSD; HOW CAN—NOW THAT THOSE BIG FAT LETTERS ARE BAB-bling out on coated stock from every newsstand ... But this was late 1959, early 1960, a full two years before Mom&Dad&Buddy&Sis heard of the dread letters and clucked because Drs. Timothy Leary and Richard Alpert were french-frying the brains of Harvard boys with it. It was even before Dr. Humphry Osmond had invented the term "psychodelic," which was later amended to "psychedelic" to get rid of the nuthouse connotation of "psycho" . . . LSD! It was quite a little secret to have stumbled onto, a hulking supersecret, in fact—the triumph of the guinea pigs! In a short time he and Lovell had tried the whole range of the drugs, LSD, psilocybin, mescaline, peyote, IT-290 the superamphetamine, Ditran the bummer, morning-glory seeds. They were onto a discovery that the Menlo Park clinicians themselves never—mighty fine irony here: the White Smocks were supposedly using *them*. Instead the White Smocks had handed them the very key itself. *And you don't even know, bub . . . with these drugs your perception is altered enough that you find your- self looking out of completely strange eyeholes. All of us have a great deal of our minds locked shut. We're shut off from our own world. Aand these drugs seem to be the key to open these locked doors.* How many?—maybe two dozen people in the world were on to this incredible secret! One was Aldous Huxley, who had taken mescaline and written about it in *The Doors of Perception.* He compared the brain to a "reducing valve." In ordinary percep- tion, the senses send an overwhelming flood of information to the brain, which the brain then filters down to a trickle it can man- age for the purpose of survival in a highly competitive world. Man has become so rational, so utilitarian, that the trickle be- comes most pale and thin. It is efficient, for mere survival, but it screens out the most wondrous part of man's potential experience without his even knowing it. *We're shut off from our own world.* Primitive man once experienced the rich and sparkling flood of the senses fully. Children experience it for a few months—until "normal" training, conditioning, close the doors on this other world, usually for good. Somehow, Huxley had said, the drugs opened these ancient doors. And through them modern man may at last go, and rediscover his divine birthright—

But these are *words,* man! *And you couldn't put it into words.* The White Smocks liked to put it into words, like *hallucination* and *dissociative phenomena.* They could understand the visual skyrockets. Give them a good case of an ashtray turning into a Venus flytrap or eyelid movies of crystal cathedrals, and they could groove on that, *Kluver, op cit., p. 43n.* That was swell. *But don't you see?*—the visual stuff was just the décor with LSD. In fact, you might go through the whole experience without any true hallucination. The whole thing was ... *the experience* ... this certain indescribable *feeling* ... Indescribable, because words can only jog the memory, and if there is no memory of ... The *experience* of the barrier between the subjective and the objective, the personal and the impersonal, the *I* and the *not-I* disappearing ... that *feeling!* ... Or can you remember when you were a child watching someone put a pencil to a sheet of paper for the first time, to draw a picture ... and the line begins to grow—into a nose! and it is not just a pattern of graphite line on a sheet of paper but the very miracle of creation itself and your own dreams flowed into that magical ... growing ... line, and it was not a picture but a *miracle* ... an *experience* ... and now that you're soaring on LSD that *feeling* is coming on again—only now the creation is of the entire universe—

MEANWHILE, OVER ON PERRY LANE, THIS WASN'T PRECISELY the old Searching Hick they all knew and loved. Suddenly Kesey—well, he was soft-spoken, all right, but he came on with a lot of vital energy. Gradually the whole Perry Lane thing was gravitating around Kesey. Volunteer Kesey gave himself over to science over at the Menlo Park Vets hospital—and somehow drugs were getting up and walking out of there and over to Perry Lane, LSD, mescaline, IT-290, mostly. Being hip on Perry Lane now had an element nobody had ever dreamed about before, wild-flying, mind-blowing drugs. Some of the old Perry Lane luminaries' *cool* was tested and they were found wanting. Robin White and Gwen Davis were against the new drug thing. That was all right, because Kesey had had about enough of them, and the power was with Kesey. Perry Lane took on a kind of double personality, which is to say, Kesey's. Half the time it would be just like some kind of college fraternity row, with everybody out on a nice autumn Saturday afternoon on the grass in the dapple shadows of the trees and honeysuckle tendrils playing touch football or basketball. An hour later, however, Kesey and his circle would be hooking down something that in the entire world only they and a few avant-garde neuropharmacological researchers even knew about, drugs of the future, of the neuropharmacologists' centrifuge utopia, the coming age of . . .

Well shee-ut. An' I don't reckon we give much of a damn any more about the art of living in France, either, boys, every frog ought to have a little paunch, like Henry Miller said, and go to bed every night in pajamas with collars and piping on them—just take a letter for me and mail it down to old Morris at Morris Orchids, Laredo, Texas, boys, tell him about enough peyote cactus to mulch all the mouldering widows' graves in poor placid Palo Alto. Yes. They found out they could send off to a place called Morris Orchids in Laredo and get peyote, and one of the new games of Perry Lane—goodbye Robin, goodbye Gwen—got to be seeing who was going down to the Railway Express at the railroad station and pick up the shipment, since possession of peyote, although not of LSD, was already illegal in California. There would be these huge goddamned boxes of the stuff, 1,000 buds and roots $70; buds only—slightly higher. If they caught you, you were *caught,* because there was no excuse possible. There was no other earthly reason to have these goddamned fetid plants except to get high as a coon. And they would all set about cutting them into strips and putting them out to dry, it took days, and then grinding them up into powder and packing them in gelatin capsules or boiling it down to a gum and putting it in the capsules or just making a horrible goddamned broth that was so foul, so unbelievably vile, you had to chill it numb to try to kill the taste and fast for a day so you wouldn't have anything on your stomach, just to keep eight ounces of it down. But then—*soar*. Perry Lane, Perry Lane.

Miles
      Miles
           Miles
                 Miles
                      Miles
                           Miles
                               Miles
                                   under all that good vegetation from Morris Orchids and having visions of

Faces
      Faces
           Faces
               Faces
                     Faces
                          Faces
                               Faces
                                 so many faces rolling up behind the eyelids, faces he has never seen before, complete with spectral cheekbones, pregnant eyes, stringy wattles, and all of a sudden: Chief Broom. For some reason peyote does this . . . Kesey starts getting eyelid movies of faces, whole galleries of weird faces, churning up behind the eyelids, faces from out of nowhere. He knows nothing about Indians and has never met an Indian, but suddenly here is a full-blown Indian—Chief Broom—the solution, the whole mothering key, to the novel . . .

HE HADN'T EVEN MEANT TO WRITE THIS BOOK. HE HAD BEEN working on another one, called *Zoo* about North Beach. Lovell had suggested why didn't he get a job as night attendant on the psychiatric ward at Menlo Park. He could make some money, and since there wasn't much doing on the ward at night, he could work on *Zoo*. But Kesey got absorbed in the life on the psychiatric ward. The whole system—if they set out to invent the perfect Anti-cure for what ailed the men on this ward, they couldn't have done it better. Keep them cowed and docile. Play on the weakness that drove them nuts in the first place. Stupefy the bastards with tranquilizers and if they still get out of line haul them up to the "shock shop" and punish them. Beautiful—

Sometimes he would go to work high on acid. He could *see into their faces*. Sometimes he wrote, and sometimes he drew pictures of the patients, and as the lines of the ball-point greasy creased into the paper the lines of their faces, he could—the *interiors* of these men came into the lines, the ball-point crevasses, it was the most incredible feeling, the anguish and the pain came right out front and flowed in the crevasses in their faces, and in the ball-point crevasses, the same—*one!*—crevasses now, black starling nostrils, black starling eyes, blind black starling geek cry on every face: "Me! Me! Me! Me! I am—Me!"—he could see clear into them. And—how could you tell anybody about this? they'll say you're a nut yourself—but afterwards, not high on anything, he could *still see into people*.

The novel, *One Flew Over the Cuckoo's Nest,* was about a roustabout named Randle McMurphy. He is a big healthy animal, but he decides to fake insanity in order to get out of a short jail stretch he is serving on a work farm and into what he figures will be the soft life of a state mental hospital. He comes onto the ward with his tight reddish-blond curls tumbling out from under his cap, cracking jokes and trying to get some action going among these deadasses in the loony bin. They can't resist the guy. They suddenly want to *do* things. The tyrant who runs the place, Big Nurse, hates him for weakening . . . Control, and the System. By and by, many of the men resent him for forcing them to struggle to act like men again. Finally, Big Nurse is driven to play her trump card and finish off McMurphy by having him lobotomized. But this crucifixion inspires an Indian patient, a schizoid called Chief Broom, to rise up and break out of the hospital and go sane: namely, run like hell for open country.

Chief Broom. The very one. From the point of view of craft, Chief Broom was his great inspiration. If he had told the story through McMurphy's eyes, he would have had to end up with the big bruiser delivering a lot of homilies about his down-home theory of mental therapy. Instead, he told the story through the Indian. This way he could present a schizophrenic state the way the schizophrenic himself, Chief Broom, feels it and at the same time report the McMurphy Method more subtly.

Morris Orchids! He wrote several passages of the book under peyote and LSD. He even had someone give him a shock treatment, clandestinely, so he could write a passage in which Chief Broom comes back from "the shock shop." Eating Laredo buds—he would write like mad under the drugs. After he came out of it, he could see that a lot of it was junk. But certain passages—like Chief Broom in his schizophrenic fogs—it was true *vision,* a little of what you could see if you opened the doors of perception, friends . . .

RIGHT AFTER HE FINISHED *ONE FLEW OVER THE CUCKOO'S NEST,* Kesey sublet his cottage on Perry Lane and he and Faye went back up to Oregon. This was in June, 1961. He spent the summer working in his brother Chuck's creamery in Springfield to accumulate some money. Then he and Faye moved into a little house in Florence, Oregon, about 50 miles west of Springfield, near the ocean, in logging country. Kesey started gathering material for his second novel, *Sometimes a Great Notion,* which was about a logging family. He took to riding early in the morning and at night in the "crummies." These were pickup trucks that served as buses taking the loggers to and from the camps. At night he would hang around the bars where the loggers went. He was Low Rent enough himself to talk to them. After about four

months of that, they headed back to Perry Lane, where he was
going to do the writing.

ONE FLEW OVER THE CUCKOO'S NEST WAS PUBLISHED IN FEBRUARY,
1962, and it made his literary reputation immediately:

"A smashing achievement"—*Mark Schorer*
"A great new American novelist"—*Jack Kerouac*
"Powerful poetic realism"—*Life*
"An amazing first novel"—*Boston Traveler*
"This is a first novel of special worth"—New York *Herald Tribune*
"His storytelling is so effective, his style so impetuous, his
grasp of characters so certain, that the reader is swept along ...
His is a large, robust talent, and he has written a large, robust
book"—*Saturday Review*

AND ON THE LANE—ALL THIS WAS A CONFIRMATION OF
everything they and Kesey had been doing. For one thing there
was the old Drug Paranoia—the fear that this wild uncharted
drug thing they were into would gradually ... *rot your brain*.
Well, here was the answer. Chief Broom!
    And McMurphy ... but of course. The current fantasy ... he
was a McMurphy figure who was trying to get them to move off
their own snug-harbor dead center, out of the plump little game
of being ersatz daring and ersatz alive, the middle-class intellectual's game, and move out to ... Edge City ... where it was
scary, but people were whole people. And if drugs were what un-
locked the doors and enabled you to do this thing and realize all
this that was in you, then so let it be ...
    Not even on Perry Lane did people really seem to catch the
thrust of the new book he was working on, *Sometimes a Great
Notion*. It was about the head of a logging clan, Hank Stamper,

who defies a labor union and thereby the whole community h
lives in by continuing his logging operation through a strike. It
was an unusual book. It was a novel in which the strikers are the
villains and the strikebreaker is the hero. The style was experimental and sometimes difficult. And the main source of "mythic"
reference was not Sophocles or even Sir James Frazer but . . . yes,
Captain Marvel. The union leaders, the strikers, and the towns-
people were the tarantulas, all joyfully taking their vow: "We
shall wreak vengeance and abuse on all whose equals we are
not . . . and 'will to equality' shall henceforth be the name for
virtue; and against all that has power we want to raise our
clamor!" Hank Stamper was, quite intentionally, Captain Marvel. Once known as . . . *Übermensch.* The current fantasy . . .

. . . on Perry Lane. Nighttime, the night he and Faye and the
kids came back to Perry Lane from Oregon, and they pull up to
the old cottage and there is a funny figure in the front yard, smiling and rolling his shoulders this way and that and jerking his
hands out to this side and the other side as if there's a different
drummer somewhere, different drummer, you understand,
corked out of his gourd, in fact . . . and, well, Hi, Ken, yes, uh,
well, you weren't *around,* exactly, you understand, doubledy-
clutch, doubledy-clutch, and they told me you wouldn't mind,
generosity knoweth no—ahem—yes, I had a '47 Pontiac myself
once, held the road like a prehistoric bird, you understand . . .
and, yes, Neal Cassady had turned up in the old cottage, like he
had just run out of the pages of *On the Road,* and . . . what's next,
Chief? Ah . . . many Day-Glo freaking curlicues—

All sorts of people began gathering around Perry Lane. Quite
an . . . *underground* sensation it was, in Hip California. Kesey,
Cassady, Larry McMurtry; two young writers, Ed McClanahan
and Bob Stone; Chloe Scott the dancer, Roy Seburn the artist,
Carl Lehmann-Haupt, Vic Lovell . . . and Richard Alpert himself . . . all sorts of people were in and out of there all the time, because they had heard about it, like the local beats—that term was
still used—a bunch of kids from a pad called the Chateau, a wild-

⌐d Jerry Garcia and the Cadaverous Cowboy,
⌐ng. Everybody was attracted by the strange high
⌐ney had heard about ... the Lane's fabled Venison Chili, a
Kesey dish made of venison stew laced with LSD, which you
could consume and then go sprawl on the mattress in the fork of
the great oak in the middle of the Lane at night and play pinball
with the light show in the sky ... Perry Lane.

And many puzzled souls looking in ... At first they were cap-
tivated. The Lane was too good to be true. It was Walden Pond,
only without any Thoreau misanthropes around. Instead, a community of intelligent, very open, out-front people—out front was
a term everybody was using—out-front people who cared deeply
for one another, and *shared* ... in incredible ways, even, and were
embarked on some kind of ... *well,* adventure in living. Christ,
you could see them trying to put their finger on it and ...
then ... gradually figuring out there was something here they
weren't *in on* ... Like the girl that afternoon in somebody's cottage when Alpert came by. This was a year after he started working with Timothy Leary. She had met Alpert a couple of years
before and he had been 100 percent the serious young clinical
psychologist—legions of rats and cats in cages with their brain-
stems, corpora callosa and optic chiasmas sliced, spliced, diced,
iced in the name of the Scientific Method. Now Alpert was sitting on the floor in Perry Lane in the old boho Lotus hunker-
down and exegeting very seriously about a baby crawling blindly
about the room. Blindly? What do you mean, blindly? That baby
is a very sentient creature ... That baby sees the world with a
completeness that you and I will never know again. His doors of
perception have not yet been closed. He still experiences the moment he lives in. The inevitable bullshit hasn't constipated his
cerebral cortex yet. He still sees the world as it really is, while we
sit here, left with only a dim historical version of it manufactured
for us by words and official bullshit, and so forth and so on, and
Alpert soars in Ouspenskyian loop-the-loops for baby while, as
far as this girl can make out, baby just bobbles, dribbles, lists and

rocks across the floor . . . But she was learning . . . that the world is sheerly divided into those who have had *the experience* and those who have not—those who have been through that door and—

It was a strange feeling for all these good souls to suddenly realize that right here on woody thatchy little Perry Lane, amid the honeysuckle and dragonflies and boughs and leaves and a thousand little places where the sun peeped through, while straight plodding souls from out of the Stanford eucalyptus tunnel plodded by straight down the fairways on the golf course across the way—this amazing experiment in consciousness was going on, out on a frontier neither they nor anybody else ever heard of before.

PALO ALTO, CALIF., JULY 21, 1963— AND THEN ONE DAY THE end of an era, as the papers like to put it. A developer bought most of Perry Lane and was going to tear down the cottages and put up modern houses and the bulldozers were coming.

The papers turned up to write about the last night on Perry Lane, noble old Perry Lane, and had the old cliché at the ready, End of an Era, expecting to find some deep-thinking latter-day Thorstein Veblen intellectuals on hand with sonorous bitter statements about this machine civilization devouring its own past.

Instead, there were some kind of *nuts* out here. They were up in a tree lying on a mattress, all high as coons, and they kept offering everybody, all the reporters and photographers, some kind of venison chili, but there was something about the whole *set*up—

and when it came time for the sentimental bitter statement, well, instead, this big guy Kesey dragged a piano out of his house and they all set about axing the hell out of it and burning it up, calling it "the oldest living thing on Perry Lane," only they were giggling and yahooing about it, high as coons, in some weird way, all of them, hard-grabbing off the stars, and it was hard as hell to make the End of an Era story come out right in the papers, with nothing but this kind of freaking Olsen & Johnson material to work with,

but they managed to go back with the story they came with, End of an Era, the cliché intact, if they could only blot out the cries in their ears of *Ve-ni-son Chi-li*—

—and none of them would have understood it, anyway, even if someone had told them what was happening. Kesey had already bought a new place in La Honda, California. He had already proposed to a dozen people on the Lane that they come with him, move the whole scene, the whole raggedy-manic Era, off to . . .

Versailles, his Low Rent Versailles, over the mountain and through the woods, in La Honda, Calif. Where—where—in the lime ::::: light ::::: and the neon dust—

". . . a considerable new message . . . the blissful counter-stroke . . ."

The Rusky-Dusky
Neon Dust

A very Christmas card,
   Kesey's new place near La Honda.
   A log house, a mountain creek, a little wooden bridge
   Fifteen miles from Palo Alto beyond
   Cahill Ridge where Route 84
   Cuts through a redwood forest gorge—
A redwood forest for a yard!
A very Christmas card.

And—
Strategic privacy.
   Not a neighbor for a mile.
   La Honda lived it Western style.
One work-a-daddy hive,
   A housing tract,
   But it was back behind the redwoods.
   The work-a-daddy faces could

Not be seen from scenic old Route 84,
Just a couple Wilde Weste roadside places, Baw's General
   Store,
The Hilltom Motel, in the Wilde Weste Touriste mode.
With brown wood signs sawed jagged at the ends,
But sawed neat, you know,
As if to suggest:
Wilde Weste Roughing It, motoring friends,
But Sanitized jake seats
Ammonia pucks in every urinal
We aim to keep your Wilde West Sani-pure—
Who won the West?
Antisepsis did, I guess.

La Honda's Wilde Weste lode
Seems to be owed to the gunslinging Younger Brothers.
They holed up in town
And dad-blame but they found a neighborly way
To pay for their stay.
They built a whole wooden store, these notorious mothers.
But them was the Younger Brothers,
Mere gunslingers.
Now this Kesey
And his Merry Humdingers down the road—

—in the :::::: lime :::::: light ::::::

Early in 1964, just a small group on hand as yet. In the after-noon—Faye, the eternal beatific pioneer wife, in the house, at the stove, at the sewing machine, at the washing machine, with the children, Shannon and Zane, gathered around her skirts. Out in a wooden shack near the creek Kesey has his desk and typewriter where he has just finished the revisions on *Sometimes a Great Notion,* now almost 300,000 words long. Kesey's friend from Oregon, George Walker, is here, a blond All-American-looking guy in his twenties, well-built, son of a wealthy housing developer. Walker has what is known as a sunny disposition and is always saying *Too much!* in the most enthusiastic way. And Sandy Lehmann-Haupt. Sandy is the younger brother of Carl Lehmann-Haupt, whom Kesey had known on Perry Lane. Sandy is a handsome kid, 22 years old, tall, lean—high-strung. Sandy had met Kesey three months before, November 14, 1963, through Carl, when Kesey had come to New York for the opening of the stage version of *One Flew Over the Cuckoo's Nest.* Kirk Douglas played McMurphy. Sandy had dropped out of N.Y.U. and was working as a sound engineer. He was a genius with tapes, soundtracks, audio systems and so forth, but he was going through a bad time. It got to the point where one day he tried to enter himself in a psychiatric ward, only to be talked out of it by Carl, who took him off to see the opening of *One Flew Over the Cuckoo's Nest.* And there was Randle McMurphy . . . Kesey . . . and Carl asked Kesey to take Sandy out west with him, to La Honda, to get him out of the whole New York morass. And if there was any place for curing the New York thing, this was it, out back of Kesey's in the lime :::::: light :::::: bower :::::: up the path out back of the house, up the hill into the redwood forest, Sandy suddenly came upon a fabulous bower, like a great domed enclosure, like what people mean when they talk about a "cathedral in the pines," only the redwoods were even more majestic. The way the sun came down through the redwood leaves—trunks and leaves seemed to stretch up for hundreds of feet above your head. It was always sunny and cool at the same time, like a perfect fall day all year around. The sun came down through miles of leaves and got broken up like a pointillist painting, deep green and dapple shadows but brilliant light in a soaring deep green super-bower, a perpetual lime-green light, green-and-gold afternoon, stillness, perpendicular peace, wood-scented, with the cars going by on Route 84 just adding pneumatic sound effects, *sheee-oooooooooo,* like a gentle wind. All peace here; very reassuring!

· · ·

A FEW TIMES SANDY AND KESEY AND WALKER WOULD WALK UP
into the forest with axes and cut some wood for the house—but
that wasn't really the name of it at Kesey's. Sandy could see that
Kesey wasn't primarily an outdoorsman. He wasn't that crazy
about unspoilt Nature. It was more like he had a vision of the forest as a fantastic stage setting . . . in which every day would be a
happening, an art form . . .

He had hi-fi speakers up on the roof of the house, and suddenly out here in God's great green mountain ozone erupts a
manic spade blowing on a plastic saxophone, namely, an Ornette
Coleman record. It's a slightly weird path here that the three loggers take: nutty mobiles hanging from the low branches and a lot
of wild paintings nailed up on the tree trunks. Then a huge tree
with a hollow base, and inside it, glinting in the greeny dark,
here is a tin horse with the tin bent so that the grotesque little animal is keeled over, kneeling, in bad shape.

The terrain Kesey was most interested in, in fact, was inside
the house. The house was made of logs, but it was more like a
lodge than a cabin. The main room had big French doors, for a
picture-window effect, and exposed beams and a big stone fireplace at one end. Kesey had all sorts of recording apparatus
around, tape recorders, motion-picture cameras and projectors,
and Sandy helped add still more, some fairly sophisticated relay
systems and the like. Often the Perry Lane people would drive
over—although no one had moved to La Honda so far. Ed Mc-
Clanahan, Bob Stone, Vic Lovell, Chloe Scott, Jane Burton, Roy
Seburn. Occasionally Kesey's brother Chuck and his cousin Dale
would come down from Oregon. They both resembled Kesey but
were smaller. Chuck was a bright quiet man. Casual and down-
home. Dale was powerfully built and more completely down-
home than either. Kesey was trying to develop various forms of
spontaneous expression. They would do something like . . . all lie
on the floor and start rapping back and forth and Kesey puts a
tape-recorder microphone up each sleeve and passes his hands
through the air and over their heads, like a sorcerer making

signs, and their voices cut in and out as the microphones sail over. Sometimes the results were pretty—

—well, freaking gibberish to normal human ears, most likely. Or, to the receptive standard intellectual who has heard about the 1913 Armory Show and Erik Satie and Edgard Varèse and John Cage it might sound . . . sort of *avant-garde,* you know. But in fact, like everything else here, it grows out of . . . *the experience,* with LSD. The whole *other world* that LSD opened your mind to existed only in the moment itself—*Now*—and any attempt to plan, compose, orchestrate, write a script, only locked you out of the moment, back in the world of conditioning and training where the brain was a reducing valve . . .

So they would try still wilder improvisations . . . like the Human Tapes, huge rolls of butcher paper stretched out on the floor. They would take wax pencils, different colors, and scrawl out symbols for each other to improvise on: Sandy the pink drum strokes there, and he would make a sound like *chee-oonh-chunh, chee-oonh-chunh,* and so forth, and Kesey the guitar arrows there, *broinga broinga brang brang,* and Jane Burton the bursts of scat vocals there, and Bob Stone the Voice Over stories to the background of the Human Jazz—all of it recorded on the tape recorder—and then all soaring on—what?—acid, peyote, morning-glory seeds, which were very hell to choke down, billions of bilious seeds mulching out into sodden dandelions in your belly, bloated—but soaring!—or IT-290, or dexedrine, benzedrine, methedrine—Speed!—or speed and grass—sometimes you could take a combination of speed and grass and prop that . . . LSD door open in the mind without going through the whole uncontrollable tumult of the LSD . . . And Sandy takes LSD and the lime :::::: light :::::: and the magical bower turns into . . . *neon dust* . . . pointillist particles for sure, now. Golden particles, brilliant forest-green particles, each one picking up the light, and all shimmering and flowing like an electronic mosaic, pure California neon dust. There is no way to describe how beautiful this discovery is, to actually *see* the atmosphere you have lived in for years for the first time and to feel that it is *inside* of you, too, flowing up from the heart, the torso, into the brain, an electric fountain ... And ... IT-290!—he and George Walker are up in the big tree in front of the house, straddling a limb, and he experiences ... intersubjectivity—he knows *precisely* what Walker is thinking. It isn't necessary to say what the design is, just the part each will do.

"You paint the cobwebs," Sandy says, "and I'll paint the leaves behind them."

"Too much!" says George, because, of course, he knows—all of us sliding in and out of these combinations of mutual consciousness, intersubjectivity, going out to the backhouse, near the creek, with tape recorders and starting to *rap*—a form of free association conversation, like a jazz conversation, or even a monologue, with everyone, or whoever, catching hold of words, symbols, ideas, sounds, and winging them back and forth and beyond ... the walls of conventional logic ... One of us finds a bunch of wooden chessmen. They are carved figures, some kind of ancient men, every piece an old carved man, only somebody left them outside and they got wet and now they're warped, which sprung them open into their real selves. This one's genitals are hanging out despite he has robes on and carries a spear—

—Have you seen my daughter? Claims I embarrass her. Claims the whole world knows I have cunt on the brain. At *my* age—

—Yes, sir, we have the report. Your daughter's a horny little bitch, but I am the King and I have no choice but to cut your balls off—

—King, I'll throw you for them—

—Your balls?

—Right! With those gold hubcaps you lug about there—

—Right! *In fact, incredible.* Each one of us has a chess figure in his hand and becomes that character and they are rapping off the personalities they see in these figures, and they start thinking the same things at once. *I, too, saw these funny little curves under this figure's hand here,* no larger than the head of a tiny tack, *as . . . golden hubcaps . . . I was about to say it*—

It is the strangest feeling of my life—intersubjectivity, as if our consciousnesses have opened up and flowed together and now one has only to look at a flicker of the other's mouth or eye or at the chessman he holds in his hand, wobbling—

—You wouldn't believe a girl with electric eel tits, would you, King?

—The ones that ionized King Arthur's sword under swamp water?

—The very ones. Dugs with a thousand tiny suction caps, a horny, duggy little girl, I'm afraid, 120 household volts of jail bait if I ever saw one—

—and how, in the wildest operations of chance, could a term like 120 household volts of jail bait arise in all our minds at once—

But the swamps, too—it is no longer all Garden of Eden and glorious discovery for the old Perry Lane crowd. In fact, there's a little grumbling here in the magic dell. Kesey is starting to *organize our trips.* He hands out the drugs personally, one for you, and one for you . . . and just when you're starting to lie back and groove on your thing, he comes in—Hup!—Hup!—Everybody up! and organizes a tramp through the woods . . .

After it's all over, some of them ask Kesey for some acid and IT-290 to take back to Palo Alto. No-o-o-o-o-o, says Kesey, and he cocks his head as if he wants to say this thing just right, because it's a delicate matter.—I think you should come here and take it . . .

Later, on the way back, someone says: We used to be equals. Now it's Kesey's trip. We go to his place. We take his acid. We do what he wants.

But what does he want? Gradually, vaguely, it dawns that Kesey's fantasy has moved on again, beyond even theirs, old Perry Lane. In any case, nobody has the stomach for Kesey's master plan, that they should all move out onto his place, in tents and so forth, transplanting the Perry Lane thing to La Honda. They began to eye Kesey's place as a kind of hill-country Versailles, with Kesey as the Sun King, looking bigger all the time, with that great jaw in profile against the redwoods and the mountaintops. It never develops into an open breach, however, or even disenchantment. They just get uneasy. They get the feeling that Kesey was heading out on further, toward a fantasy they didn't know if they wanted to explore.

OTHER PEOPLE WERE BEGINNING TO SHOW UP AT KESEY'S, AND that was part of the trouble. Some of the Perry Lane crowd didn't know exactly what to make of Cassady. Here he is before us in Kesey's Versailles, coming on, coming on, with his shirt off and his arms jerking and his abdominal obliques jutting out at the sides like a weight lifter's . . . We are hip, we value the holy primitive. Only Kesey is intimating that one should *learn* from Cassady, he is *talking to you.* Which he was. Cassady wanted intellectual communion. But the intellectuals just wanted him to be the holy primitive, the Denver kid, the *natural* in our midst. Sometimes Cassady would sense they weren't accepting him intellectually and go off into the corner, still on his manic monologue, muttering, "All right, I'll take my own trip, I'll go off on my own trip, this is my own trip, you understand . . ."

Or Page Browning. The Cadaverous Cowboy had found his way over the mountain, too. Back on Perry Lane he had been just a Low Rent character popping in from time to time on his route. Only now Kesey is intimating that one can learn from Page Browning. Kesey finds something loyal, brave and creative, *creative,* under that cadaverous face and the Adam's apple and the black motorcycle jacket like a leftover from when he must've ridden with the Hell's Angels—and his thick Shellube pit voice. The primordial Shellube pits . . . could that be it, a little class fear, after all, among the hip . . . genteel . . . intellectuals? A little Ahor, as Arthur Koestler called it, the Ancient Horror, from boyhood—the genteel suburban kid rides his bicycle over to the gas station and there in the grease pit area where they lubricate the cars the hard rocks are hunkered down telling jokes about pussy, with an occasional clinical reference to bowel movements and crepitation. And oh christ don't you remember their forearms with the basilic veins wrapped around them like surgical tubes, gorged with the unattainable lower-class hard-rock power that any moment is going to look up and *spot* us . . . genteel little pudding kids. But Kesey loved this Low Rent stuff. He was ready to swing with it. In time he would even be swinging with the beasts from the veritable Ahor fathoms of the Shellube pits, the Hell's Angels themselves . . .

In fact, only a few of the new retinue that showed up at La Honda were Low Rent in terms of background, but the place became much more down-home than Perry Lane.

One of Kesey's old friends, Kenneth Babbs, showed up, just back from Vietnam, where he had been a captain in the Marines, flying helicopters. Babbs had graduated magna cum laude from Miami University, majoring in English. He had also been a great athlete. He entered the creative-writing program at Stanford, where Kesey met him. Babbs was tall, powerful, a very Rabelaisian creature. Back from the wars, he came on like a great hearty grizzly bear roaring a cosmic laugh. Sometimes he would wear a flight suit for days at a time, no matter where he was, *come fly with me.* And Babbs was capable of some wild flights. He gave the Kesey colony much of its new style . . . Yes. He introduced the idea of the *pranks,* great public put-ons they could perform . . .

And Mike Hagen arrived. Hagen was a fellow Kesey had known in Oregon, good-looking, soft-spoken, well-mannered, from a good family, fairly rich, the kind of kid daddies smile over as he takes their teenage daughter out on her first date, Yup, I've raised her pretty damn well, if I do say so. No riffraff for my girl, just nice Christian boys who say Yes, sir, Yes, ma'am and comb their hair down with water on the comb. About ten minutes after Hagen pulled into Kesey's, he had his Screw Shack built out back of the cabin, a lean-to banged together with old boards and decorated inside with carpet remnants, a mattress with an India-print coverlet, candles, sparkling little bijoux, a hi-fi speaker—for the delight and comfort of Hagen's Girls. Oh christ Hagen's Girls and the trouble they caused—Stark Naked, Anonymous—but they come later. Hagen was a benign but inspired con man in a sweet way. He had a special gift for haggling, bartering, hassling, and Hagen would turn up with his car crammed with gleaming tape-recorder equipment, movie equipment, microphones, speakers, amplifiers, even video-tape equipment, and the audio-visual level started rising around here—

Then one day, for example, one of Kesey's old Perry Lane friends, Gurney Norman, a writer, drove up for the weekend from Fort Ord, the Army camp, and brought along one of his Army friends, a 24-year-old first lieutenant in the infantry named Ron Bevirt. Bevirt put everybody off at first, because he looked totally Army. He was fat and sloppy-looking and had a particularly gross-looking Army crewcut and was totally unsophisticated. Bevirt, however, liked *them* and he kept coming on weekends and bringing a lot of food, which he enjoyed sharing with everybody, and he smiled and laughed a lot and people couldn't help but get to like him. By and by he was out of the Army and he came around all the time. He even started getting leaner and harder and his hair grew out until it was like Prince Valiant's, in the comic strip, and he was a pretty handsome guy and very much into the . . . pudding. By and by he became known as The Hassler and his real name vanished almost . . .

AND BY AND BY, OF COURSE, THE CITIZENS OF LA HONDA AND others would start wondering . . . what are the ninnies *doing*? How to tell it? But there was no way to tell them about *the experience*. You couldn't put it into words. The citizens always had the same fantasy, known as the pathology fantasy. *These ninnies are pathological.* Sometimes it was psychological—what do these kids come from, broken homes or what? Sometimes it was social—are these kids *alienated?* is our society getting rotten at the core? or what? The citizens couldn't know about the LSD experience, because that door had never opened for them. To be on the threshold of—Christ! how to tell them about the life here? The Youth had always had only three options: go to school, get a job or live at home. And—how boring each was!—compared to the experience of . . . the infinite . . . and a life in which the subject is not scholastic or bureaucratic but . . . *Me* and *Us,* the *attune*d ones amid the non-musical shiny-black-shoe multitudes, *I*—with my eyes on that almost invisible *hole* up there in the r-r-r-redwood sky . . .

ONE NIGHT BOB STONE WAS SITTING AT HOME IN MENLO Park—he was still in the creative-writing program at Stanford—and the phone rang and it was Babbs calling from Kesey's in La Honda. Come on over, he said, we're going to get something going. Well, no, Stone said, he didn't feel much up to it, he was kind of tired and it would take an hour to drive over the mountain and an hour to drive back, and maybe some other time—

"Come on, Bob," says Babbs. "It won't take you an hour. You can get here in thirty minutes."

Babbs is in very high spirits and in the background Stone can hear music and voices and they are, indeed, getting something going.

"I know how long it takes," says Stone. "And it takes forty-five minutes or an hour, more like an hour at night."

"Listen!" says Babbs, who is laughing and practically shouting into the phone. "The intrepid traveler can make it in thirty minutes! The intrepid traveler can make it with the speed of light!"

In the background Babbs can hear a couple of voices rapping off that: "The intrepid traveler! The intrepid traveler!"

"The intrepid traveler," Babbs is shouting. "The intrepid traveler just gets up and walks out and he's here!"

And so on, until Stone's resistance wears down and he gets in his car and heads over. He arrives; after an hour, yes.

As soon as he gets out of his car out front of the house he starts hearing the Big Rap, from inside the house, from up in the woods, it's like drums are beating and horns are blowing and Pranksters are ululating and rapping: "The Intrepid Traveler!"

"The Intrepid Traveler!"

"The Intrepid Traveler!"

"The Intrepid Traveler!"

"The Intrepid Traveler!"

He goes through the French doors in the front, mad ochre and lurid lights, gongs, pipes, drums, guitars being banged like percussion bangers—

"The Intrepid Traveler!"

"The Intrepid Traveler—the traveler in a flash!"

"The Intrepid Traveler—"

"—straights out the curves!"

"The Intrepid Traveler—"

"—curves out the straights!"

"The Intrepid Traveler—"

"—a beam of light!"

"The Intrepid Traveler—"

"—a lightning beam!"

"The Intrepid Traveler—"

"—shortens the circuit!"

"The Intrepid Traveler—"

"—short-waves the band!"

"The Intrepid Traveler—"

"—and his band of Merry Pranksters!"

"The Intrepid Traveler!—"

—and his band of Merry Pranksters take a journey to the East.

chapter VI

The Bus

I COULDN'T TELL YOU FOR SURE WHICH OF THE MERRY Pranksters got the idea for the bus, but it had the Babbs touch. It was a superprank, in any case. The original fantasy, here in the spring of 1964, had been that Kesey and four or five others would get a station wagon and drive to New York for the New York World's Fair. On the way they could shoot some film, make some tape, freak out on the Fair and see what happened. They would also be on hand, in New York, for the publication of Kesey's second novel, *Sometimes a Great Notion,* early in July. So went the original fantasy.

Then somebody—Babbs?—saw a classified ad for a 1939 International Harvester school bus. The bus belonged to a man in Menlo Park. He had a big house and a lot of grounds and a nice set of tweeds and flannels and eleven children. He had rigged out the bus for the children. It had bunks and benches and a refrigerator and a sink for washing dishes and cabinets and shelves and a lot of other nice features for living on the road. Kesey bought it for $1,500—in the name of Intrepid Trips, Inc.

Kesey gave the word and the Pranksters set upon it one afternoon. They started painting it and wiring it for sound and cutting a hole in the roof and fixing up the top of the bus so you could sit up there in the open air and play music, even a set of drums and electric guitars and electric bass and so forth, or just ride. Sandy went to work on the wiring and rigged up a system with which they could broadcast from inside the bus, with tapes or over microphones, and it would blast outside over powerful speakers on top of the bus. There were also microphones outside that would pick up sounds along the road and broadcast them inside the bus. There was also a sound system inside the bus so you could broadcast to one another over the roar of the engine and the road. You could also broadcast over a tape mechanism so that you said something, then heard your own voice a second later in variable lag and could rap off of that if you wanted to. Or you could put on earphones and rap simultaneously off sounds from outside, coming in one ear, and sounds from inside, your own sounds, coming in the other ear. There was going to be no goddamn sound on that whole trip, outside the bus, inside the bus, or inside your own freaking larynx, that you couldn't tune in on and rap off of.

The painting job, meanwhile, with everybody pitching in in a frenzy of primary colors, yellows, oranges, blues, reds, was sloppy as hell, except for the parts Roy Seburn did, which were nice manic mandalas. Well, it was sloppy, but one thing you had to say for it; it was freaking lurid. The manifest, the destination sign in the front, read: "Furthur," with two *u*'s.

THEY TOOK A TEST RUN UP INTO NORTHERN CALIFORNIA AND right away this wild-looking thing with the wild-looking people was great for stirring up consternation and vague befuddling resentment among the citizens. The Pranksters were now out among them, and it was exhilarating—look at the mothers staring!—and there was going to be holy terror in the land. But there would also be people who would look up out of their poor work-a-daddy lives in some town, some old guy, somebody's stenographer, and see this bus and register . . . delight, or just pure open-invitation wonder. Either way, the Intrepid Travelers figured, there was hope for these people. They weren't totally turned off. The bus also had great possibilities for altering the usual order of things. For example, there were the cops.

One afternoon the Pranksters were on a test run in the bus going through the woods up north and a forest fire had started. There was smoke beginning to pour out of the woods and everything. Everybody on the bus had taken acid and they were zonked. The acid was in some orange juice in the refrigerator and you drank a paper cup full of it and you were zonked. Cassady was driving and barreling through the burning woods wrenching the steering wheel this way and that way to his inner-wired beat, with a siren wailing and sailing through the rhythm.

A *siren?* It's a highway patrolman, which immediately seems like the funniest thing in the history of the world. Smoke is pouring out of the woods and they are all sailing through leaf explosions in the sky, but the cop is bugged about this freaking bus. The cop yanks the bus over to the side and he starts going through a kind of traffic-safety inspection of the big gross bus, while more and more of the smoke is billowing out of the woods. Man, the license plate is on wrong and there's no light over the license plate and this turn signal looks bad and how about the brakes, let's see that hand brake there. Cassady, the driver, is already into a long monologue for the guy, only he is throwing in all kinds of sirs: "Well, yes sir, this is a Hammond bi-valve serrated brake, you understand, sir, had it put on in a truck ro-de-o in Springfield, Oregon, had to back through a slalom course of baby's bottles and yellow nappies, in the existential culmination of Oregon, lots of outhouse freaks up there, you understand, sir, a punctual sort of a state, sir, yes sir, holds to 28,000 pounds, 28,000 pounds, you just look right here, sir, tested by a pure-blooded Shell Station attendant in Springfield, Oregon, winter of '62, his gumball boots never froze, you understand, sir, 28,000 pounds hold, right here—" Whereupon he yanks back on the hand-brake as if it's attached to something, which it isn't, it is just dangling there, and jams his foot on the regular brake, and the bus shudders as if the hand brake has a hell of a bite, but the cop is thoroughly befuddled now, anyway, because Cassady's monologue has confused him, for one thing, and what the hell are these . . . *people* doing. By this time everybody is off the bus rolling in the brown grass by the shoulder, laughing, giggling, ya-hooing, zonked to the skies on acid, because, mon, the woods are burning, the whole world is on fire, and a Cassady monologue on automotive safety is rising up from out of his throat like weenie smoke, as if the great god Speed were frying in his innards, and the cop, representative of the people of California in this total freaking situation, is all hung up on a hand brake that doesn't exist in the first place. And the cop, all he can see is a bunch of crazies in screaming orange and green costumes, masks, boys and girls, men and women, twelve or fourteen of them, lying in the grass and making hideously crazy sounds—christ almighty, why the hell does he have to contend with . . . So he wheels around and says, "What are you, uh—show people?"

"That's right, officer," Kesey says. "We're show people. It's been a long row to hoe, I can tell you, and it's *gonna* be a long row to hoe, but that's the business."

"Well," says the cop, "you fix up those things and . . ." He starts backing off toward his car, cutting one last look at the crazies. " . . . And watch it next time . . ." And he guns on off.

That was it! How can you give a traffic ticket to a bunch of people rolling in the brown grass wearing Day-Glo masks, practically Greek masques, only with Rat phosphorescent *élan,* giggling, keening in their costumes and private world while the god Speed sizzles like a short-order French fry in the gut of some guy who doesn't even stop talking to breathe. A traffic ticket? The Pranksters felt more immune than ever. There was no more reason for them to remain in isolation while the ovoid eyes of La Honda supurated. They could go through the face of America muddling people's minds, but it's a momentary high, and the bus would be gone, and all the Fab foam in their heads would settle back down into their brain pans.

SO THE HIERONYMUS BOSCH BUS HEADED OUT OF KESEY'S place with the destination sign in front reading "Furthur" and a sign in the back saying "Caution: Weird Load." It was weird, all right, but it was euphoria on board, barreling through all that warm California sun in July, on the road, and everything they had been working on at Kesey's was on board and heading on Furthur. Besides, the joints were going around, and it was nice and high out here on the road in America. As they headed out, Cassady was at the wheel, and there was Kesey, Babbs, Page Browning, George Walker, Sandy, Jane Burton, Mike Hagen, Hassler, Kesey's brother Chuck and his cousin Dale, a guy known as Brother John, and three newcomers who were just along for the ride or just wanted to go to New York.

One of them was a young, quite handsome kid—looked sort of like the early, thin Michael Caine in *Zulu*—named Steve Lambrecht. He was the brother-in-law of Kesey's lawyer, Paul Robertson, and he was just riding to New York to see a girl he knew named Kathy. Another was a girl named Paula Sundsten. She was young, plump, ebullient, and very sexy. Kesey knew her from Oregon. Another one was some girl Hagen of the Screw Shack had picked up in San Francisco, on North Beach. She was the opposite of Paula Sundsten. She was thin, had long dark hair, and would be moody and silent one minute and nervous and carrying on the next. She was good-looking like a TV witch.

By the time they hit San Jose, barely 30 miles down the road, a lot of the atmosphere of the trip was already established. It was nighttime and many souls were high and the bus had broken down. They pulled into a service station and pretty soon one of the help has his nose down in under the hood looking at the engine while Cassady races the motor and the fluorescent stanchion lights around the station hit the bus in weird phosphorescent splashes, the car lights stream by on the highway, Cassady guns the engine some more, and from out of the bus comes a lot of weird wailing, over the speakers or just out the windows. Paula Sundsten has gotten hold of a microphone with the variable-lag setup and has found out she can make weird radio-spook laughing ghoul sounds with it, wailing like a banshee and screaming "How was your stay-ay-ay-ay . . . in San Ho-zay-ay-ay-ay-ay," with the variable lag picking up the ay-ay-ay-ays and doubling them, quadrupling them, octupling them. An endless ricocheting echo—and all the while this weird, slightly hysterical laugh and a desperate little plunking mandolin sail through it all, coming from Hagen's girl friend, who is lying back on a bench inside, plunking a mandolin and laughing—in what way . . .

Outside, some character, some local, has come over to the bus, but the trouble is, he is not at all impressed with the bus, he just has to do the American Man thing of when somebody's car is broken down you got to come over and make your diagnosis.

And he is saying to Kesey and Cassady, "You know what I'd say you need? I'd say you need a good mechanic. Now, I'm not a good mechanic, but I—" And naturally he proceeds to give his diagnosis, while Paula wails, making spook-house effects, and the Beauty Witch keens and goons—and—

"—like I say, what you need is a good mechanic, and I'm not a good mechanic, but—"

And—of course!—the Non-people. The whole freaking world was full of people who were bound to tell you they weren't qualified to do this or that but they were determined to go ahead and do just that thing anyway. Kesey decided he was the Non-navigator. Babbs was the Non-doctor. The bus trip was already becoming an allegory of life.

·   ·   ·

BEFORE HEADING EAST, OUT ACROSS THE COUNTRY, THEY stopped at Babbs's place in San Juan Capistrano, down below Los Angeles. Babbs and his wife Anita had a place down there. They pulled the bus into Babbs's garage and sat around for one final big briefing before taking off to the east.

Kesey starts talking in the old soft Oregon drawl and everybody is quiet.

"Here's what I hope will happen on this trip," he says. "What I hope will continue to happen, because it's already starting to happen. All of us are beginning to do our thing, and we're going to keep doing it, right out front, and none of us are going to deny what other people are doing."

"Bullshit," says Jane Burton.

This brings Kesey up short for a moment, but he just rolls with it.

"That's Jane," he says. "And she's doing her thing. Bullshit. That's her thing and she's doing it."

"None of us are going to deny what other people are doing. If saying bullshit is somebody's thing, then he says bullshit. If somebody is an ass-kicker, then that's what he's going to do on this trip, kick asses. He's going to do it right out front and nobody is going to have anything to get pissed off about. He can just say, 'I'm sorry I kicked you in the ass, but I'm not sorry I'm an ass-kicker. That's what I do, I kick people in the ass.' Everybody is going to be what they are, and whatever they are, there's not going to be anything to apologize about. What we are, we're going to wail with on this whole trip."

HAUL ASS, AND WHAT WE ARE, OUT ACROSS THE SOUTHWEST, and all of it on film and on tape. Refrigerator, stove, a sink, bunk racks, blankets, acid, speed, grass—with Hagen handling the movie camera and everybody on microphones and the music blaring out over the roar of the bus, rock 'n' roll, Jimmy Smith. Cassady is revved up like they've never seen him before, with his shirt off, a straw version of a cowboy hat on his head, bouncing up and down on the driver's seat, shifting gears—doubledy-clutch, doubledy-clutch, blamming on the steering wheel and the gearshift box, rapping over the microphone rigged up by his seat like a manic tour guide, describing every car going by,

"—there's a barber going down the highway cutting his hair at 500 miles an hour, you understand—"

"So remember those expressions, sacrifice, glorious and in vain!" Babbs says.

"Food! Food! Food!" Hagen says.

"Get out the de-glom ointment, sergeant!" says Babbs, rapping at Steve Lambrecht. "The only cure for joint glom, gets the joint off the lip in instant De-Glom—"

—and so on, because Steve always has a joint glommed onto his lip and, in fact, gets higher than any man alive, on any and all things one throws his way, and picks up the name Zonker on this trip—

"—De-Glom for the Zonker!—"

—and then Babbs parodies Cassady—

"—and there's a Cadillac with Marie Antoinette—"

—and the speakers wail, and the mandolin wails and the weird laugh wails, and the variable lag wails-ails-ails-ails-ails-ails, and somebody—who?—hell, *every*body wails,

"—we're finally beginning to move, after three fucking days!"

ON THE SECOND DAY THEY REACHED WIKIEUP, AN OLD WILD West oasis out in the Arizona desert along Route 60. It was all gray-brown desert and sun and this lake, which was like a huge slimy kelp pond, but the air was fantastic. Sandy felt great. Then Kesey held the second briefing. They were going to take their first acid of the trip here and have their first major movie production. He and Babbs and the gorgeous sexy Paula Sundsten were going to take acid—*Wikieup!*—and the others were going to record what happened. Hagen and Walker were going to film it, Sandy was going to handle the sound, and Ron Bevirt was going to take photographs.

Sandy feels his first twinge of—what? Like . . . there is going to be Authorized Acid only. And like . . . they are going to be separated into performers and workers, stars and backstage. Like . . . there is an inner circle and an outer circle. This was illogical, because Hagen and Walker, certainly, were closer to Kesey than any other Pranksters besides Babbs, and they were "workers," too, but that was the way he feels. But he doesn't say anything. Not . . . out front.

Kesey and Babbs and Paula hook down some acid orange juice from the refrigerator and wait for the vibrations. Paula is in a hell of a great mood. She has never taken LSD before, but she looks fearless and immune and ready for all, and she hooks down a good slug of it. They wait for the vibrations . . . and here they come.

Babbs has a big cane, a walking stick, and he is waving it around in the air, and the three of them, Babbs, Kesey and Paula, go running and kicking and screaming toward the lake and she dives in—and comes up with her head covered in muck and great kelpy strands of green pond slime—and beaming in a way that practically radiates out over the face of the lake and the desert. She has surfaced euphoric—

"Oooooh! It sparkles!"

—pulling her long strands of slime-slithering hair outward with her hands and grokking and freaking over it—

"Ooooooooh! It sparkles!"

—the beads of water on her slime strands are like diamonds to her, and everybody feels her feeling at once, even Sandy—

"Oooooooooh! It sparkles!"

—surfaced euphoric! euphorically garlanded in long greasy garlands of pond slime, the happiest slime freak in the West—

—and Babbs is euphoric for her—

"Gretchen Fetchin the Slime Queen!" he yells and waves his cane at the sky.

"Ooooooooh! It sparkles!"

"Gretchen Fetchin the Slime Queen!"

"It sparkles!"

"Gretchen Fetchin!"

And it is beautiful. Everybody goes manic and euphoric like a vast contact high, like they have all suddenly taken acid themselves. Kesey is in an athletic romp, tackling the ferns and other slimy greenery in the lake. Babbs and Paula—Gretchen Fetchin!—are yahooing at the sky. Hagen is feverishly filming it all, Sandy has a set of huge cables stretched out to the very edge of the lake, picking up the sound, Ron Bevirt is banging away with his camera. Babbs and Paula—Gretchen Fetchin!—and Kesey keep plunging out into the mucky innards of the lake.

"Come back!" Hagen the cameraman starts yelling. "You're out of range!"

But Babbs and Paula and Kesey can't hear him. They are cartwheeling further and further out into the paradise muck—

"It sparkles!"

"Gretchen Fetchin—Queen of the Slime!"

But meanwhile Hagen's Beauty Witch, in the contagion of the moment, has slipped to the refrigerator and taken some acid, and now she is outside of the bus on the desert sand wearing a black snakeskin blouse and a black mantle, with her long black hair coming down over it like in a pre-Raphaelite painting and a cosmic grin on her witch-white face, lying down on the desert, striking poses and declaiming in couplets. She's zonked out of her nut, but it's all in wild manic Elizabethan couplets:

"Methinks you need a gulp of grass
And so it quickly came to pass
You fell to earth with eely shrieking,
Wooing my heart, freely freaking!"

—and so forth. Well, she wins Hagen's manic heart right away, and soon he has wandered off from the Lake of the Slime

Euphoria and is in a wide-legged stance over her with the camera as she lies declaiming on the desert floor, camera zeroed in on her like she is Maria Montez in a love scene—and now the Beauty Witch is off on her trip for good ...

BACK ON THE BUS AND OFF FOR PHOENIX IN THE SLIME-Euphoric certitude that they and the movie—The Movie!—many allegories of life—that they could not miss now. Hagen pressed on with the film, hour after hour in the bouncing innards of the bus. There were moments in the History of Film that broke everybody up. One was when they reached Phoenix. This was during the 1964 election excitement and they were in Barry Goldwater's home town, so they put a streamer on the bus reading: "A Vote for Barry is a Vote for Fun." And they put American flags up on the bus and Cassady drove the bus backward down the main drag of Phoenix while Hagen recorded it on film and the flags flew backward in the wind-stream. The citizens were suitably startled, outraged, delighted, nonplused, and would wheel around and start or else try to keep their cool by sidling glances like they weren't going to be impressed by any *weird shit*—and a few smiled in a frank way as if to say, I am with you—if only I could be with you!

The fact that they were all high on speed or grass, or so many combinations thereof that they couldn't keep track, made it seem like a great secret life. It was a great secret life. The befuddled citizens could only see the outward manifestations of the incredible stuff going on inside their skulls. They were all now characters in their own movies or the Big Movie. They took on new names and used them.

Steve Lambrecht was Zonker. Cassady was Speed Limit. Kesey was Swashbuckler. Babbs was Intrepid Traveler. Hagen, bouncing along with the big camera, soaring even while the bus roared, was Mal Function. Ron Bevirt had charge of all the equipment, the tools, wires, jacks, and stuff, and became known as Equipment Hassler, and then just Hassler. George Walker was Hardly Visible. And Paula Sundsten became...Gretchen Fetchin the Slime Queen, of course...

A notebook!—for each of the new characters in The Movie, a plain child's notebook, and each character in this here movie can write in his notebook himself or other people can pick up the notebook and write in it—who knows who wrote what?—and in Gretchen Fetchin it says:

> Bury them in slime!
> She cried, flailing about the garden—
> With a sprig of parsley clutched in
> her hands—which had always been
> clamped in her hands.
>   This is strange business,
> Gets weirder all the time,
> She said, wrapping some around
> her finger, for we are always
> moist in her hand ... "Naturally," she
> said, "The roots are deep."
>   That was no surprise, but she
> was mildly curious to
> know what the hell is
>
>   THAT
>   Whereupon he got very
> clumsy, giggled confidentially,
> and tripped over her shadow,
> carrying them both into
> an unaccountable adventure.

Barely a week out and already beautiful ebullient sexy Gretchen Fetchin the Slime Queen, Gretch, is *synched* in. Kesey, the very Swashbuckler himself, makes a play for her, and that should be that, but she looks at—Babbs—who tripped over her

shadow?—Hmmmmmmmm? So many shadows and shafts of
Southwest sun bouncing in through the windows and all over the
floor, over the benches over the bunk uprights bouncing out of
the freaking roar of the engine bouncing two sets of Gretch eyes
two sets of Babbs eyes, four sets of Gretch eyes four sets of Babbs
eyes eight sets of Gretch eyes eight sets of Babbs eyes all grinning
vibrating bouncing in among one another carrying them both
into an unaccountable adventure, you understand. Kesey sulks
a bit—Kesey himself—but the sulk bounces and breaks up
into Southwestern sunballs. *Drivin' on dirt in Utah, a '46 Plymouth with an overhead cam,* says Cassady. The refrigerator door
squeaks open, gurgle gurgle, this acid O.J. makes a body plumb
smack his lips, Hagen and his Black Witch girl friend hook
down a cup of acid orange juice apiece and Hagen's sweet face
spirals, turning sweet Christian boy clockwise and sweet sly
Screw Shack counterclockwise, back and forth, and they disappear, bouncing, up the ladder, up through the turret hole and
onto the roof where, under the mightily hulking sun of the
Southwest and 70 miles an hour—Pretty soon Hagen is climbing
back down the ladder and heading for the refrigerator and hooking down another cup of orange juice and smiling for all, Christian boy and Screw Shack sly, spiraling this way and that
way—and climbing back up top the bus in order to—

MAL FUNCTION!

If only I had $10, then we
could split ½ a Ritalin order
with Margo—I eat
Ritalin like aspirin
Now, let's charm Brooks Brothers—
impressed?

At night the goddamn bus still bouncing and the Southwest
silvery blue coming in not exactly bouncing but slipping and slid-

ing in shafts, sickly shit, and car beams and long crazy shadows from car beams sliding in weird bends over the inside, over the love bunk. The love bunk'll get you if you don't wash out. One shelf on the bunk has a sleeping bag on it and into this sleeping bag crawl whoever wants to make it, do your thing, bub, and right out front, and wail with it, and Sandy looks over and he can see a human . . . bobbing up and down in the sleeping bag with the car beams sliding over it and the motor roaring, the fabulous love bunk, and everyone—*synch*—can see that sleeping bag veritably filling up with sperm, the little devils swimming like mad in there in the muck, oozing into the cheap hairy shit they quilt the bag with, millions billions trillions of them, darting around, crafty little flagellants, looking to *score,* which is natural, and if any certified virgin on the face of the earth crawled into that sleeping bag for a nap after lunch she would be a hulking knocked-up miracle inside of three minutes—but won't this goddamn *bouncing* ever stop—

THIS BEING A SCHOOL BUS, AND NOT A GREYHOUND, THE springs and the shock absorbers are terrible and the freaking grinding straining motor shakes it to pieces and hulking vibrations synched in to no creature on earth keep batting everybody around on the benches and the bunks. It is almost impossible to sleep and the days and nights have their own sickly cycle, blinding sun all day and the weird car beams and shadows sliding sick and slow at night and all the time the noise. Jane Burton is nauseous practically the whole time. Nobody can sleep so they keep taking more speed to keep going, psychic energizers like Ritalin, anything, and then smoke more grass to take the goddamn tachycardiac edge off the speed, and acid to make the whole thing turn into something else. Then it all starts swinging back and forth between grueling battering lurching flogging along the highway—and unaccountable delays, stopped, unendurable frustration by the side of the road in the middle of nowhere while the feeling of no-sleep starts turning the body and the skull into a dried-out husk inside with a sour greasy smoke like a tenement fire curdling in the brainpan. They have to pull into gasoline stations to go to the bathroom, cop a urination or an egestion—keep regular, friends—but 12—how many, 14?—did we lose somebody—did we pick up somebody—climbing out of this bus, which is weird-looking for a start, but all these weird people are too much, clambering out—the service station attendant and his Number One Boy stare at this—Negro music is blaring out of the speakers and these weird people clamber out, half of them in costume, lurid shirts with red and white stripes, some of them with weird paint on their faces, like comic-book Indians, with huge circles under their eyes, eyes red, noses not blue, not nearly blue enough, but eyes red—all trooping out toward the Clean Rest Rooms, already queuing up, practically—

"Wait a minute," the guy says. "What do you think you're doing?"

"Fill 'er up!" says Kesey, very soft and pleasant. "Yes, sir, she's a big bus and she takes a lotta gas. Yep."

"I mean what are *they* doing?"

"Them? I 'spect they're going to the bathroom. Ay-yup, that big old thing's the worst gas-eater you ever saw"—all the time motioning to Hagen to go get the movie camera and the microphone.

"Well, can't all those people use the bathrooms."

"All they want to do is go to the bathroom"—and now Kesey takes the microphone and Hagen starts shooting the film—*whirrrrrrrrrrrrrrrrr*—but all very casual as if, well, sure, don't *you* record it all, every last morsel of friendly confrontation whenever you stop on the great American highway to cop a urination or two? or a dozen?

"Well, now, listen! You ain't using the bathrooms! You hear me, now! You see that motel back there? I own that motel, too, and we got one septic tank here, for here and there, and you're not gonna overflow it for me. Now git that thing out of my face!"

—Kesey has the microphone in the guy's face, like this is all for the six o'clock news, and then he brings the microphone back to his face, just like the TV interview shows, and says,

"You see that bus out there? Every time we stop to fill 'er up we have to lay a *whole lot* of money on somebody, and we'd like it to be you, on account of your hospitality."

"It's an unaccountable adventure in consumer spending," says Babbs.

"Get those cameras and microphones out of here," the guy says. "I'm not afraid of you!"

"I should hope not," says Kesey, still talking soft and down-home. "All that money that big baby's gonna drink up. Whew!"

Sheerooooooo—all this time the toilets are flushing, this side and that side and the noise of it roars and gurgles right through the cinder block walls until it sounds like there's nothing in the whole wide open U.S. of A. except for Clean Rest Room toilets and Day-Glo crazies and cameras and microphones from out of nowhere, and the guy just caves in under it. He can't fit it into his movie of Doughty American Entrepreneur—*not no kind of way*—

"Well, they better make it fast or there's going to be trouble around here." And he goes out to fill 'er up, this goddamn country is going down the drain.

But they don't speed it up. Walker is over to the coin telephone putting in a call to Faye back in La Honda. Babbs is clowning around out on the concrete apron of the gas station with Gretchen Fetchin. Jane Burton feels bilious—the idea is to go to New York, isn't it? even on a 1939 school bus it could be done better than this. What are we waiting, waiting, waiting, waiting for, playing games with old crocks at gas stations. Well, we're waiting for Sandy, for one thing. Where in the hell is Sandy. But Sandy—he hasn't slept in days and he has an unspecific urge to *get off the bus*—but not to sleep, just to get off—for—what?—be-fore:::::what? And Sandy is back over at the motel, inspecting this electropink slab out in the middle of nowhere—somebody finally finds him and brings him back. Sandy is given the name Dismount in the great movie.

"There are going to be times," says Kesey, "when we can't wait for somebody. Now, you're either on the bus or off the bus. If you're on the bus, and you get left behind, then you'll find it again. If you're off the bus in the first place—then it won't make a damn." And nobody had to have it spelled out for them. Everything was becoming allegorical, understood by the group mind, and especially this: "You're either on the bus . . . or off the bus."

EXCEPT FOR HAGEN'S GIRL, THE BEAUTY WITCH. IT SEEMS LIKE she never even gets off the bus to cop a urination. She's sitting back in the back of the bus with nothing on, just a blanket over her lap and her legs wedged back into the corner, her and her little bare breasts, silent, looking exceedingly witch-like. Is she on the bus or off the bus? She has taken to wearing nothing but the blanket and she sheds that when she feels like it. Maybe that is her thing and she is doing her thing and *wailing with it* and the bus barrels on off, heading for Houston, Texas, and she becomes Stark Naked in the great movie, one moment all conked out, but with her eyes open, staring, the next laughing and coming on, a lively Stark Naked, and they are all trying to just snap their fingers to it but now she is getting looks that have nothing to do with the fact that she has not a thing on, hell, big deal, but she is now waxing extremely freaking ESP. She keeps coming up to somebody who isn't saying a goddamn thing and looking into his eyes with the all-embracing look of total acid understanding, our brains are one brain, so let's *visit,* you and I, and she says: "Ooooooooh, you really *think* that, I know what you mean, but do you-u-u-u-u-u-u-ueeeeeeeeeeeeeeeeeeeeeeee"—finishing off in a sailing tremulo laugh as if she has just read your brain and it is the weirdest of the weird shit ever, your brain eeeeeeeeeeeeeeeeeeeeeeeeeeeeeeeeeeeeeeeeeeeeeee—

STARK-NAKED

in a black blanket—
    Reaching out for herself,
she woke up one morning to
find herself accosted on all
sides by   LARGE
              MEN
surrounding her threatening her
with their voices, their presence, their always
desire reaching inside herself
and touching her obscenely upon her
desire and causing her to laugh
and
        LAUGH
                with the utter
                ridiculousness
                of it . . .

—but no one denied her a moment of it, neither the conked-out bug-eyed paranoia nor the manic keening coming on, nobody denied her, and she could wail, nobody tried to cool that inflamed brain that was now seeping out Stark Naked into the bouncing goddamn—*stop it!*—currents of the bus throgging and roaring 70 miles an hour into Texas, for it was like it had been ordained, by Kesey himself, back in San Juan Capistrano, like there was to be a reaction scale in here, from negative to positive, and no one was to rise up negative about anything, one was to go positive with everything—*go with the flow*—everyone's cool was to be tested, and to shout No, no matter what happened, was to fail. And hadn't Kesey passed the test first of all? Hadn't Babbs taken Gretchen Fetchin, and did he come back at either one of them uptight over that? And wasn't it Walker who was calling La Honda from the Servicenters of America? All true, and go with the flow. And they went with the flow, the whole goddamn flow

of America. The bus barrels into the superhighway toll stations
and the microphones on top of the bus pick up all the clacking
and ringing and the mumbling by the toll-station attendant and
the brakes squeaking and the gears shifting, all the sounds of the
true America that are screened out everywhere else, it all came
amplified back inside the bus, while Hagen's camera picked up
the faces, the faces in Phoenix, the cops, the service-station own-
ers, the stragglers and the strugglers of America, all laboring in
their movie, and it was all captured and kept, piling up, inside
the bus. Barreling across America with the microphones picking
it all up, the whole roar, and microphone up top gets eerie in a
great rush and then *skakkkkkkkkkkkkk* it is ripping and roaring
over asphalt and *thok* it's gone, no sound at all. The microphone
has somehow ripped loose on top of the bus and hit the roadway
and dragged along until it snapped off entirely—and Sandy can't
believe it. He keeps waiting for somebody to tell Cassady to stop
and go back and get the microphone, because this was something
Sandy had rigged up with great love and time, it was his *thing,*
his part of the power—but instead they are all rapping and
grokking over the sound it made—"Wowwwwwwwww! Did
you—wowwwwwwww"—as if they had synched into a never-
before-heard thing, a unique thing, the sound of an object, a microphone, hitting the American asphalt, the open road at 70 miles
an hour, like if it was all there on tape they would have the instant, the moment, of anything, *anyone* ripped out of the flow and
hitting the Great Superhighway at 70 miles an hour—and they
had it on tape—and played it back in variable lag skakkkkkk-
akkkk-akkkk-akkkoooooooooooo.

ooooooooooooooooooooooooo—Stark Naked waxing weirder
and weirder, huddled in the black blanket shivering, then out,
bobbing wraith, her little deep red aureola bobbing in the crazed
vibrations—finally they pull into Houston and head for Larry
McMurtry's house. They pull up to McMurtry's house, in the
suburbs, and the door of the house opens and out comes Mc-
Murtry, a slight, slightly wan, kindly-looking shy-looking guy,

ambling out, with his little boy, his son, and Cassady opens the door of the bus so everybody can get off, and suddenly Stark Naked shrieks out: "Frankie! Frankie! Frankie! Frankie!"— this being the name of her own divorced-off little boy—and she whips off the blanket and leaps off the bus and out into the suburbs of Houston, Texas, stark naked, and rushes up to McMurtry's little boy and scoops him up and presses him to her skinny breast, crying and shrieking, "Frankie! oh Frankie! my little Frankie! oh! oh! oh!"—while McMurtry doesn't know what in the name of hell to do, reaching tentatively toward her stark-naked shoulder and saying, "Ma'am! Ma'am! Just a minute, ma'am!"—

—while the Pranksters, spilling out of the bus—stop. The bus is stopped. No roar, no crazed bounce or vibrations, no crazed car beams, no tapes, no microphones. Only Stark Naked, with somebody else's little boy in her arms, is bouncing and vibrating.

And there, amid the peaceful Houston elms on Quenby Road, it dawned on them all that this woman—which one of us even knows her?—had completed her trip. She had gone with the flow. She had gone stark raving mad.

chapter VII

Unauthorized Acid

STARK NAKED; STARK NAKED; SILENCE; BUT, WELL . . . That this or a couple of other crackups in the experience of the Pranksters had anything to do with that goofy baboon, Dope, was something that didn't cross the minds of the Pranksters at that point. *Craziness* was not an absolute. They had all voluntarily embarked upon a trip and a state of consciousness that was "crazy" by ordinary standards. The trip, in fact the whole deal, was a risk-all balls-out plunge into the unknown, and it was assumed merely that more and more of what was already inside a person would come out and expand, gloriously or otherwise. Stark Naked had done her thing. She roared off into the void and was picked up by the cops by and by, and the doors closed in the County psychiatric ward, and that was that, for the Pranksters were long gone.

The trip had started out as a great bursting forth out of the forest fastness of La Honda, out into an unsuspecting America. And for Sandy, anyway, that was when the trip went best, when the

Pranksters were out among them, and the citizens of the land were gawking and struggling to summon up the proper emotion for this—what in the name of God are the ninnies *doing*. But the opposite was happening, too. On those long stretches of American superhighway between performances the bus was like a pressure cooker, a crucible, like one of those chambers in which the early atomic scientists used to compress heavy water, drive the molecules closer and closer together until the very atoms exploded. On the bus all traces of freakiness or competition or bitterness or whatever were intensified. They were right out front, for sure.

Jane Burton, who was now known as Generally Famished, and Sandy—Dis-mount—took to going off whenever they could, like in Houston, for a square meal. Square on every level, Tonto. They would just go right into one of those Square American steak houses with the big plate-glass window with the corny little plastic windmill in the window advertising Heineken's Beer and the Diners Club and American Express stickers on the plate-glass door and go in and have a square steak and square French fries and boiled bland peas and carrots and A-1 sauce. Jane, now ravaged from lack of sleep, and ravenously hungry, generally famished, or slightly bilious the whole time, wondering what the hell they were now doing on the southern rim of the United States when New York was way up there. Sandy—with this subliminal urge to get off the bus, and yet be *on the bus*—on *that* level—and neither of them knowing what to make of Kesey—always Kesey . . .

AND THE HEAT. FROM HOUSTON THEY HEADED EAST THROUGH the Deep South, and the Deep South in July was . . . lava. The air rushing into the open windows of the bus came in hot and gritty like invisible smoke, and when they stopped, it just rolled over them, pure lava. The rest in Houston didn't do too much good, because the heat just started it all again, nobody slept, and it was like all you could do to cut through the lava with speed and grass and acid.

New Orleans was a relief, because they got out and walked around the French Quarter and down by the docks in their red and white striped shirts and Day-Glo stuff and the people freaked over them. And the cops came while they were down by the docks, which was just comic relief, because by now the cops were a piece of cake. The city cops were no more able to keep their Cop Movie going than the country cops. Hassler talked sweet to them like the college valedictorian and Kesey talked sweet and down-home and Hagen filmed it all like this was some crazed adventure in cinema verité and the cops skedaddled in a herd of new Ford cruisers with revolving turret lights. Sayonara, you all.

They just kept walking around New Orleans in their striped shirts and wearing shorts, and they could all see Kesey's big muscular legs, like a football player's, striding on up ahead like he owned the place, like they all owned the place, and everybody's spirits picked up. So they head out to Lake Pontchartrain, on the northern edge of New Orleans. They all took acid, but a small dose, about 75 micrograms—everybody happy and high on acid, and rock 'n' roll records blaring, Martha and the Vandellas and Shirley Ellis, all that old stuff pounding away. Lake Pontchartrain is like a great big beautiful spacious—space!—park on the water. They pull the bus up in a parking area and there are nice trees round and all that endless nice water and they put on their bathing suits. Walker, who has a hell of a build, puts on a pair of red, yellow, and black trunks, and Kesey, who has a hell of a build, puts on a pair of blue and white trunks, and Zonker, who has a hell of a build, only leaner, puts on a pair of orange trunks, and the blue of the water and the scorched-out green of the grass and the leaves and—a little breeze?—it is all swimming in front of their old acid eyes like a molten postcard—water! What they don't know is, it is a segregated beach, for Negroes only. The spades all sitting there on benches sit there staring at these white crazies coming out of a weird bus and heading for New Or-leans 30th-parallel Deep South segregated water. Zonker is really zonked this time, and burning up with the heat, about 100 degrees, and he dives in and swims out a ways and pretty soon he sees he is surrounded by deep orange men, Negroes, all treading water around him and giving him rotten looks. One of them has a gold tooth in the front with a star cut out in it, so that a white enamel star shows in the middle of the gold, and the gold starts flashing out at him in the sun—*cheeeakkk*—in time with his heartbeat which is getting faster all the time, these goddamn flashes of gold and white star after-images, and the Golden Mouth says, "Man, there sure is a lotta trash in the water today."

"You ain't shittin', man," says another one of them.

"Lotta fuckin' trash, man," says another one, and so on.

Suddenly Golden Mouth is speaking straight to Zonker: "What's all this trash doing in the water, man?"

Zonker is very nonplused, partly because the whole day has turned orange on him, because of the acid—orange trunks, orange water, orange sky, orange menacing spades.

"Boy, what you doing here!" Golden Mouth says very sharp all of a sudden. Orange and big and orange hulking fat back big as an orange manta ray. "Boy, you know what we gonna do? We gonna cut yo' little balls off. We gonna take you up on that beach and *wail* with you!"

"Heh-hehhhhhhhhhhhh!" The others start this wailing moaning laugh.

For some reason, however, this makes Zonker smile. He can feel it spreading across his face, like a big orange slice of orange sugar-jelly candy and he is suspended there treading water and grinning while the Golden Mouth flashes and flashes and flashes.

Then the Golden Mouth says, "Well, it sure is *some kinda trash,*" and starts laughing, only amiably this time, and they all laugh, and Zonker laughs and swims back to shore.

By this time a big crowd of Negroes has gathered around the mad bus. Funky music is blasting off the speakers, a Jimmy

Smith record. Zonker gets on the bus. It seems like thousands of Negroes are dancing around the bus, doing rock dances and the dirty boogie. Everything is orange and then he looks at the writhing mass of Negroes, out every window, nothing but writhing Negroes mashed in around the bus and writhing, and it all starts turning from orange to brown. Zonker starts getting the feeling he is inside an enormous intestine and it is going into peristaltic contractions. He can feel the whole trip turning into a horrible bummer. Even Kesey, who isn't afraid of anything, looks worried. "We better get out of here," Kesey says. But squeezed out?—in bummer brown peristaltic contractions? Luckily for Zonker, maybe for everybody, the white cops turn up at that point and break up the crowd and tell the white crazies to drive on, this is a segregated beach, and for once they don't pile out and try to break up the Cop Movie. They go with the Cop Movie and get their movie out of there.

ON INTO THE FLATLANDS OF MISSISSIPPI AND ALABAMA, Biloxi, Mobile, U.S. Route 90, the flatlands and the fields and the heat doesn't let up ever. They are heading for Florida. Sandy hasn't slept in days:::::how many:::::like total insomnia and everything is *bending* in curvy curdling lines. Sun and flatlands. So damned hot—and everything is getting torn into opposites. The dead-still heat-stroked summertime deep Southland—and Sandy's heart racing at a constant tachycardia and his brain racing and reeling out and so essential to . . . *keep moving, Cassady!* . . . but there are two Cassadys. One minute Cassady looks 58 and crazy—*speed!*—and the next, 28 and peaceful—*acid*—and Sandy can tell the peaceful Cassady in an instant, because his nose becomes . . . long and smooth and almost patrician, whereas the wild Cassady looks beat-up. And Kesey—*always Kesey!* Sandy looks . . . and Kesey is old and haggard and his face is lopsided . . . and then Sandy looks and Kesey is young, serene, and his face is lineless, and round and smooth as a

baby's as he sits for hours on end reading comic books, absorbed
in the plunging purple Steve Ditko shadows of Dr. Strange at-
tired in capes and chiaroscuro, saying: "How could they have
known that this gem was merely a device to bridge dimensions!
It was a means to enter the dread purple dimension—from our
own world!" Sandy may wander . . . off the bus, but it remains all
Kesey. Dr. Strange! Always seeing two Keseys. Kesey the
Prankster and Kesey the organizer. Going through the steams of
southern Alabama in late June and Kesey rises up from out of the
comic books and becomes Captain Flag. He puts on a pink kilt,
like a miniskirt, and pink socks and patent-leather shoes and
pink sunglasses and wraps an American flag around his head like
a big turban and holds it in place with an arrow through the back
of it and gets up on top of the bus roaring through Alabama and
starts playing the flute at people passing by. The Alabamans
drawn into the PINK DIMENSION do a double-freak take for
sure and it is *Too Much!* as George Walker always says, too mul-
lyfogging much. They pull into a gas station in Mobile and half
the Pranksters jump out of the bus, blazing red and white stripes
and throwing red rubber balls around in a crazed way like a
manic ballet of slick Servicenter flutter decoration while the guy
fills up the tank, and he looks from them to Captain Flag to the
bus itself, and after he collects for the gas he looks through the
window at Cassady in the driver's seat and shakes his head and
says:

"No wonder you're so nigger-heavy in California."
FORNIA-FORNIA-FORNIA-FORNIA-FORNIA-FOR-
NIA-FORNIA-FORNIA as it picked up inside the bus in vari-
able lag, and that breaks everybody up.

That was when it was good . . . grinding on through Alabama,
and then suddenly, to Sandy, Kesey is old and haggard and the
organizer. Sandy can see him descending the ladder down from
the roof of the bus and glowering at him, and he knows—intersubjectivity!—that Kesey is thinking. You're too detached,
Sandy, you're not out front, you may be sitting right here grind-

ing and roaring through Alabama but you're ... off the bus ...
And he approaches Sandy, hunched over under the low ceiling of
the bus, and to Sandy he looks like an ape with his mighty arms
dangling, like The Incredible Hulk, and suddenly Sandy jumps
up and crouches into an ape position, dangling his arms and
mimicking him—and Kesey breaks into a big grin and throws
his arms around Sandy and hugs him—

He approves! Kesey approves of me! At last I have re*sponded*
to something, brought it all out front, even if it is resentment,
done something, done my thing—and in that very action, just as
he taught, it is gone, the resentment ... and I am back on the bus
again, synched in ...

Always Kesey! And in that surge of euphoria—*Kesey approves!*—Sandy knew that Kesey was the key to whatever was
going right and whatever was going wrong on this trip, and nobody, not one of them who ever took this trip, got in this movie,
would ever have even the will to walk up to Kesey and announce
irrevocably: I am off the bus. It would be like saying, I am off
this ... Unspoken Thing we are into ...

PENSACOLA, FLORIDA. 110 DEGREES. A FRIEND OF BABBS HAS A
little house near the ocean, and they pull in there, but the ocean
doesn't help at all. The heat makes waves in the air, like over a
radiator. Most of the Pranksters are in the house or out in the
yard. Some of the girls are outside the bus barbecuing some meat.
Sandy is by himself inside the bus, in the shade. The insomnia is
killing him. He has got to get some sleep or keep moving. He
can't stand it in here stranded in between with his heart pounding. He goes to the refrigerator and takes out the orange juice.
The acid in New Orleans, the 75 micrograms, wasn't enough. It's
like he hasn't had a good high the whole trip, nothing ... blissful. So he hooks down a big slug of Unauthorized Acid and sits
back.

He would like something nice and peaceful, closed in softly

alone on the bus. He puts on a set of earphones. The left ear-
phone is hooked into a microphone inside the house and picks up
Kesey's cousin Dale playing the piano. Dale, for all his country
ways, has studied music a long time and plays well and the notes
come in like liquid drops of amethyst vibrating endlessly in
the . . . acid . . . atmosphere and it is very nice. The right ear-
phone is hooked into a microphone picking up the sounds outside the house, mainly the barbecue fires crackling. So Dale
concerto and fire crackling in these big padded earphones closed
in about his head . . . only the sounds are somehow sliding out of
control. There is no synch. It is as if the two are fighting for his
head. The barbecue crackles and bubbles in his head and the
amethyst droplets crystallize into broken glass, and then tin, a tin
piano. The earphones seem to get bigger and bigger, huge
padded shells about to enclose his whole head, his face, his
nose—amok sound overpowering him, as if it is all going to end
right here inside this padded globe—*panic*—he leaps up from the
seat, bolts a few feet with the earphones still clamped on his skull,
then rips them off and jumps out of the bus—Pranksters everywhere in the afternoon sun, in red and white striped shirts. Babbs
has the power and is directing the movie and is trying to shoot
something—Acid Piper. Sandy looks about. Nobody he can tell
it to, that he has taken acid by himself and it is turning into a
bummer, he can't bring this out front . . . He runs into the house,
the walls keep jumping up so goddamn close and all the angles
are under extreme stress, as if they could break. Jane Burton is
sitting alone in the house, feeling bilious. Jane is the only person
he can tell.

"Jane," he says, "I took some acid . . . and it's really weird . . ."
But it is such an effort to talk . . .

The heat waves are solidifying in the air like the waves in a
child's marble and the perspectives are all berserk, walls rushing
up then sinking way back like a Titian banquet hall. And the
heat—Sandy has to do something to pull himself together, so he
takes a shower. He undresses and gets in the shower and . . . flute

music, Babbs! flute music comes spraying out of the nozzle and the heat is inside of him, it is like he can look down and see it burning there and he looks down, two bare legs, a torso rising up at him and like he is just noticing them for the first time. They exist apart from, like another human being's, such odd turns and angles they take amid the flute streams, swells and bony processes, like he has never seen any of this before, this flesh, this stranger. He groks over that—only it isn't a stranger, it is his . . . mother . . . and suddenly he is back in this body, only it is his mother's body—and then his father's—he has become his mother and his father. No difference between I and Thou inside this shower of flutes on the Florida littoral. He wrenches the water off, and it stops the flute. He is himself again—hide from the panic—no, *gotcha*—and he pulls on his clothes and goes back out in the living room. Jane is still sitting there. Talk, christ, to some-body—Jane!—but the room goes into the *zooms*, wild lurches of perspective, a whole side of the room zooming right up in front of his face, then zooming back to where it was—Jane!—Jane in front of his face, a foot away, then way back over there on the sofa, then zooming up again, all of it rocketing back and forth in the hulking heat—"Sandy!"—somebody is in the house looking for him, Hagen? who is it?—seems Babbs wants him in the movie. Red-and-white striped Pranksters burning in the sun. Seems Babbs has an idea for a section of the movie. In this scene Babbs is the Pied Piper, tootling on a flute, and all the red-and-white striped children are running after him in colorful dances. They hand Sandy a Prankster shirt, which he doesn't want. It is miles too big. It hangs on him in this sick loose way like he is des-iccating in the sun. Into the sun—the shirt starts flashing under his face in the sun in explosive beams of sunball red and sunball silver-white as if he is moving through an aura of violent beams. Babbs gives him his cue and he starts a crazy dance out by a clothesline while the camera whirrs away. He can feel the crazy look come over his face and feel his eyeballs turning up and white with just vague flashes of red and silver-white exploding in under his eyelids . . . and the freaking heat, dancing like a crazy in the sun, and he goes reeling off to one side.

It becomes very important that nobody know he has taken Unauthorized Acid. He can trust Jane . . . This is not very out front, but he must remain very cool. Chuck Kesey is marching around the yard blowing a tuba, going *boop boop a boop boop* very deep and loud, then he comes by Sandy and looks at him and smiles over the mouthpiece and goes *bup bup a bup bup,* very tender and soft and—intersubjectivity!—he *knows* and *under-stands*—and that is nice because Chuck is one of the nicest people in the world and Sandy can trust him. If only he can remain cool . . .

There is a half pound of grass in a tin can by the bus and Sandy gets down on all fours to help and starts digging his playing in the sun, and he somehow kicks over the can and the grass spills all over this silty brown dirt. Everybody is upset and Hagen gets down to try to separate the grass from the dirt, and Sandy gets down on all fours to help and starts digging his fingers into the dirt to try to dig out the grass, only as he starts digging, the dirt gets browner and browner as he digs, and he starts grooving over the brownness of it, so brown, so deep, so rich, until he is digging way past the grass, on down into the ground, and Hagen says,

"Hey! What the hell's the matter with you?"

And Sandy knows he should just come out with it and say, I'm stoned man, and this brown is a groove, and then it would be all out front and over with. But he can't bring himself to do it, he can't bring himself all the way out front. Instead, it gets worse.

Kesey comes over with a football and a spray can of Day-Glo. He wants Sandy to spray it Day-Glo, and then he and Babbs and some others are going to take it out near the water at dusk and pass the Day-Glo ball around, and Sandy starts spraying it, only it's all one thing, the ball and Kesey's arm, and he is spraying Kesey's arm in the most dedicated, cool way, and Kesey says:

"Hey! What the hell's the matter with you—"

And as soon as he says it, he *knows,* which is suddenly very bad.

"I'm . . . stoned," says Sandy. "I took some acid, and I . . . took too much and it's going very bad."

"We wanted to save that acid for the trip back," Kesey says. "We wanted to have some for the Rockies."

"I didn't take *that much*"—he's trying to explain it, but now a Beatles record is playing over the loudspeaker of the bus and it's raining into his head like needles—"but it's bad."

Kesey looks exasperated, but he tries some condolence. "Look—just stay with it. Listen to the music—"

"Listen to the *music!*" Sandy yells. "Christ! Try and stop me!"

Kesey says very softly: "I know how you feel, Sandy. I've been there myself. But you just have to stay with it"—which makes Sandy feel good: *he's with me.* But then Kesey says, "But if you think I'm going to be your guide for this trip, you're sadly mistaken." And he walks off.

Sandy starts feeling very paranoid. He walks off, away from the house, and comes upon some sort of greeny glade in the woods. Babbs and Gretchen Fetchin are lying on the ground in the shade, just lazing on it, but Babb's legs shift and his arms move and Gretch's legs shift, and Sandy sees . . . Babbs and Gretch in a *pond,* swimming languidly. He knows they are on ground, and yet they are *in the water*—and he says,

"How is it?"

"Wet!" says Babbs.

—and—marvelous—it is very nice—as if Babbs knows exactly what is in his mind—*synch*—and is going to swing with it. We are all one brain out here and we are all on the bus, after all. And suddenly there in the Florida glade it is like the best of the whole Prankster thing all over again.

HE CAME BACK TO THE HOUSE AT DARK, INTO THE YARD, AND there were a million stars in the sky, like tiny neon bulbs, and you could see them between the leaves of the trees, and the trees seemed to be covered with a million tiny neon bulbs, and the bus, it broke up into a sculpture of neon bulbs, millions of them massed together to make a bus, like a whole nighttime of neon dust, with every particle a neon bulb, and they all vibrated like a huge friendly neon cicada universe.

He goes down to the water where the Pranksters all are, a little inlet, and it is dark and placid and he gets in and wades out until the water laps almost even with his mouth, which makes it very secure and warm and calm and nice and he looks at the stars and then at a bridge in the distance. All he can see of the bridge is the lights on it, swooping strands of lights, rising, rising, rising—and just then Chuck Kesey comes gliding toward him through the water, smiling, like a great friendly fish. Chuck *knows* and it is very nice—and the lights of the bridge keep rising, rising, until they merge with the stars, until there is a bridge leading right up into heaven.

VIII

Tootling the Multitudes

IN GEORGIA THEY PULLED OVER TO THE SIDE OF THE HIGH-way at a rest area, by a lake. Old Brother John put on a Robin Hood hat and sang a lot of salty songs and got the MDT Award, Most Disgusting Trip. Babbs nailed a baby doll up on a post and painted it Day-Glo and nailed a lot of nails through it and burnt it, and he got an MDT Award, too. Then something happened that made Sandy very happy. He got the idea of spraying his hand in Day-Glo designs and getting in the water and then rushing up out of the water with his hand stretched out toward Hagen's movie camera so the film would show an enormous Day-Glo hand rushing up in frantic foreshortening. Everybody grooved on that and started doing it, and Sandy felt like he now shared part of the power. Everybody started painting one hand Day-Glo and opening it and sticking one vast vibrating Day-Glo palm out at the straight world floating by comatose...

Kesey held another briefing, and without anybody having to say anything, they all began to feel that the trip was becoming a . . . mission, of some sort. Kesey said he wanted them all to do their thing and be Pranksters, but he wanted them to be deadly competent, too. Like with the red rubber balls they were always throwing around when they got out of the bus. The idea of the red rubber balls was that every Prankster should always be ready to catch the ball, even if he wasn't looking when it came at him. They should always be that alert, always that alive to the moment, always that deep in the whole group thing, and be deadly competent.

Well, one Prankster who was proving out deadly competent was Cassady. They highballed on up the Eastern seaboard to New York, and highballing was about it. Cassady had never been in better form. By this time everybody who had any reservations about Cassady had forgotten it. Cassady had been a rock on this trip, the totally dependable person. When everybody else was stroked out with fatigue or the various pressures, Cassady could still be counted on to move. It was as if he never slept and didn't need to. For all his wild driving he always made it through the last clear oiled gap in the maze, like he knew it would be there all the time, which it always was. When the bus broke down, Cassady dove into the ancient innards and fixed it. He changed tires, lugging and heaving and jolting and bolting, with his fantastic muscles popping out striation by striation and his basilic veins gorged with blood and speed.

Coming up over the Blue Ridge Mountains everybody was stoned on acid, Cassady included, and it was at that moment that he decided to make it all the way down the steepest, awfulest windingest mountain highway in the history of the world without using the brakes. The lurid bus started barreling down the Blue Ridge Mountains of Virginia. Kesey was up on top of the bus to take it all in. He was up there and he could feel the motion of the thing careening around the curves and the road rippling and writhing out in front of him like someone rippling a bullwhip. He felt totally synched with Cassady, however. It was as if, if he were panicked, Cassady would be panicked, panic would rush through the bus like an energy. And yet he never felt panic. It was an abstract thought. He had total faith in Cassady, but it was more than faith. It was as if Cassady, at the wheel, was in a state of satori, as totally into this very moment, Now, as a being can get, and for that moment they all shared it.

THEY REACHED NEW YORK IN THE MIDDLE OF JULY, AND THEY were like horses in the home stretch. Everybody felt good. They tooled across 42nd Street and up Central Park West with the speakers blaring and even New York had to stop and stare. The Pranksters gave them the Day-Glo glad hands, Kesey and Babbs got up on top of the bus with their red-and-white striped shirts on and tootled the people. This tootling had gotten to be a thing where you got on top of the bus and *played people* like they were music, the poor comatose world outside. If a guy looked at you fat and pissed off, you played on the flute in dying elephant tones. If a woman looked up nervous and twittering, you played nervous and twittering. It was saying it right to their faces, out front, and they never knew what to do. And New York—what a dirge New York was. The town was full of solemn, spent, irritable people shit-kicking their way down the sidewalks. A shit kicker is a guy with a frown on and his eyes on the ground, sloughing forward with his shoes scuffing the pavement like he's kicking horseshit out of the way saying oh that this should happen to me. The shit kickers gave them many resentful looks, which was the Pranksters' gift to the shit kickers. They could look up at the bus and say *those* are the bastids who are causing it, all the shit. They pulled into the big driveway out front of the Tavern on the Green, a big restaurant in Central Park, and tootled the people there. One way or another they were drawing the whole freaking town into their movie, and Hagen got it all on film.

One of the old Perry Lane crowd, Chloe Scott, had arranged to get them an apartment of some friends of hers who were away for the summer, up on Madison Avenue at 90th Street. They parked the bus out front and had a time for themselves. Cassady looked up all his old pals from the *On the Road* days. Two of them were Jack Kerouac and Allen Ginsberg.

They gave a party up at the apartment at Madison and 90th and Kerouac and Ginsberg were there. A guy also showed up saying, Hi, I'm Terry Southern and this is my wife Carol. He was a pretty funny guy and talked a blue streak most amiably. It was a week before they found out he wasn't Terry Southern and didn't even look like him. It was just some guy's little freaky prank and they were glad they had gone ahead and wailed with it. Kesey and Kerouac didn't say much to each other. Here was Kerouac and here was Kesey and here was Cassady in between them, once the mercury for Kerouac and the whole Beat Generation and now the mercury for Kesey and the whole—what?—something wilder and weirder out on the road. It was like hail and farewell. Kerouac was the old star. Kesey was the wild new comet from the West heading christ knew where.

Sometimes a Great Notion came out and the reviews ran from the very best to the very worst. In the daily New York *Herald Tribune,* Maurice Dolbier said: "In the fiction wilderness, this is a towering redwood." Granville Hicks said: "In his first novel, *One Flew Over the Cuckoo's Nest,* Ken Kesey demonstrated that he was a forceful, inventive and ambitious writer. All of these qualities are exhibited, in even higher degree, in *Sometimes a Great Notion.* Here he has told a fascinating story in a fascinating way." John Barkham of the *Saturday Review* said: "A novelist of unusual talent and imagination . . . a huge, turbulent tale . . ." *Time* said it was a big novel—but that it was overwritten and had failed. Some of the critics seemed put out with the back-woodsy, arch, yep-bub-golly setting of the novel and the unusual theme of the heroic strikebreaker and the craven union men. Leslie Fiedler wrote an ambivalent review in the Herald Tribune's *Book Week,* but in any case it was a long, front-page review by a major critic. *Newsweek* said the book "rejects the obligations of art and therefore ends up as a windy, detailed mock-epic barrel-chested counterfeit of life." Orville Prescott in *The New York Times* called it "A Tiresome Literary Disaster" and said: "His monstrous book is the most insufferably pretentious and the most totally tiresome novel I have had to read in many years." He referred to Kesey as "a beatnik type" who had been the model for Dean Moriarty in Kerouac's *On the Road,* confusing Kesey with Cassady. The Pranksters got a good laugh over that. The old guy was mixed up and . . . maybe put out by the whole thing of the bus and the big assault upon New York: *stop the Huns . . .*

But the hell with it. Kesey was already talking about how writing was an old-fashioned and artificial form and pointing out, for all who cared to look . . . the bus. The local press, including some of the hipper, smaller sheets, gave it a go, but nobody really comprehended what was going on, except that it was a party. It was a party, all right. But in July of 1964 not even the hip world in New York was quite ready for the phenomenon of a bunch of people roaring across the continental U.S.A. in a bus covered with swirling Day-Glo mandalas aiming movie cameras and microphones at every freaking thing in this whole freaking country while Neal Cassady wheeled the bus around the high curves like Super Hud and the U.S. nation streamed across the windshield like one of those goddamned Cinemascope landscape cameras that winds up your optic nerves like the rubber band in a toy airplane and let us now be popping more speed and acid and smoking grass as if it were all just coming out of Cosmo the Prankster god's own local-option gumball machines—

Cosmo!

Furthur.

The Crypt Trip

IF THERE WAS ANYBODY IN THE WORLD WHO WAS GOING TO comprehend what the Pranksters were doing, it was going to be Timothy Leary and his group, the League for Spiritual Discovery, up in Millbrook, New York. Leary and his group had been hounded out of Harvard, out of Mexico, out of here, out of there, and had finally found a home in a big Victorian mansion in Millbrook, on private land, an estate belonging to a wealthy New York family, the Hitchcocks. So the bus headed for Millbrook.

They headed off expecting the most glorious reception ever. It is probably hard at this late date to understand how glorious they thought it was going to be. The Pranksters thought of themselves and Leary's group as two extraordinary arcane societies, and the only ones in the world, engaged in the most fantastic experiment in human consciousness ever devised. The thing was totally new. And now the two secret societies bearing this new-world energy surge were going to meet.

The Pranksters entered the twisty deep green Gothic grounds of Millbrook with flags flying, American flags all over the bus, and the speakers blaring rock 'n' roll, on in over the twisty dirt road, through the tangled greeny thickets, past the ponds and glades, like a rolling yahooing circus. When they got in sight of the great gingerbread mansion itself, all towers and turrets and jigsaw shingles, Sandy Lehmann-Haupt started throwing green smoke bombs off the top of the bus, great booms and blooms of green smoke exploding off the sides of the bus like epiphytes as the lurid thing rolled and jounced around the curves. We are here! We are here!

The Pranksters expected the Learyites to come rolling out of the house like the survivors of the siege of Khartoum. Instead—a couple of figures there on the lawn dart back into the house. The Pranksters stop in front and there is just the big house sitting there sepulchral and Gothic—and them jumping off the bus still yahooing and going like hell. Finally a few souls materialize. Peggy Hitchcock and Richard Alpert and Susan Metzner, the wife of Dr. Ralph Metzner, another leading figure in the Leary group. Alpert looks the bus up and down and shakes his head and says, "Ke-n-n-n Ke-e-e-esey . . ." as if to say I might have known that you would be the author of this collegiate prank. They are friendly, but it is a mite . . . *cool* here, friends. Maynard Ferguson, the jazz trumpet player, and his wife, Flo, are there, and they groove over the bus, but the others . . . there is a general . . . *vibration* . . . of: We have something rather deep and meditative going on here, and you California crazies are a sour note.

Finally, Peggy Hitchcock invites some of them over to her house, a big modern house, known as The Bungalow, off from the gingerbread manse. Babbs is one of them. Babbs and the Pranksters are not ready for a lazy afternoon in the country, meditative or not. Inside The Bungalow, Babbs came upon a big framed photograph on the wall, looking like a Yale class picture from the year '03, a lot of young fellers seated, in tiers, in a clump and staring full-face at the camera.

"There's Cassady!" says Babbs.

"There's Hassler!"

"There's Kesey!"

"There's Sandy!"

They found every single man on the bus in the picture, while the Learyites looked on, tolerantly, and Babbs got the idea of "The Pranksters' Ancestral Mansion."

The Learyites were going to take them on a tour of the great gingerbread mansion, but it became Babbs's tour. He started leading it.

"Now ladies and gentlemen," he said, "we are embarked upon the first annual tour of the Pranksters' Ancestral Mansion. Now over here you may regard"—he points to a big lugubrious oil portrait, or something of the sort, up on the wall—"one of the Pranksters' great forefathers, sire and scion of the fabulous line, the fabulous lion, Sir Edward the Freak. Sir Edward the Freak, a joke in his own time. I've heard if he got aroused, he would freak a whole block of city, Sir Edward the Freak—"

—and so on, while the Learyites tagged along, looking more and more dour, as if they sensed disaster, Babbs looking more and more animated, rapping off everything, the ancestral staircase, the ancestral paneling, the ancestral fireplace, his rheostat eyes turning up to 300 watts—

—then down to one of the four "meditation centers," little sanctums where the Learyites retreated for the serious business of meditation upon inner things—

"—and now, for this part of our tour, the Crypt Trip—" And the Pranksters started rapping off the Crypt Trip, while Babbs entered into a parody rendition of *The Tibetan Book of the Dead*. This was one of the Learyites' most revered texts. "This is where we take our followers to hang them up when they're high," says Babbs, "the Crypt Trip." The clear message was Fuck you, Millbrook, for your freaking frostiness.

Other Pranksters were out playing under a little waterfall in the woods. Zonker's girl friend Kathy, whom he had picked up in New York, sat under the waterfall and the water pasted her bikini, or her bra and panties, or whatever it was she had on, pasted it most nicely to her body and Hagen filmed it. She became Sensuous X in the great movie.

Where was Leary? Everyone was waiting for the great meeting of Leary and Kesey.

Well, word came down that Leary was upstairs in the mansion engaged in a very serious experiment, a three-day trip, and could not be disturbed.

Kesey wasn't angry, but he was very disappointed, even hurt. It was unbelievable—this was Millbrook, one big piece of uptight constipation, after all this.

The Pranksters made a few more stabs at getting things going around Millbrook, but it seemed like everybody in the place was retreating to some corner or other. Finally they pulled out. Before they left, Kesey asked Alpert if he could get them some more acid. He said he couldn't, but he could give them some morning-glory seeds. Morning-glory seeds. The idea of morning-glory seeds sloshing around in your belly like a ptomaine bean bag while the bus bounced and shook and swayed and leaned out on the curves was more than a body could bear. So thanks anyway, and sayonara, you all, League for Spiritual Discovery.

chapter X

Dream Wars

ON THE TRIP BACK WEST THEY TOOK THE NORTHERN ROUTE, through Ohio, Indiana, Illinois, Wisconsin, Minnesota, South Dakota—

South Dakota! 191 miles in South Dakota . . .

—which made it all cooler, for a start . . . In fact, the trip back was a psychic Cadillac, a creamy groove machine, and they soon found themselves grooving in a group mind. Now they could leave behind all the mind-blown freaky binds and just keep going Furthur! on the bus. For example, Zonker meant to stay in New York but he went back with them. He couldn't break off from the group mind takeoff that had begun, the Unspoken Thing, the all-in-one . . . He brought with him his gorgeous blond telepathic girl friend Kathy, who felt at once the careening, crazydreaming, creamy bobbing rhythm of the bus and became at once recklessly and infectiously and insenescibly and ultra-infra-sexily one of them: most sinuous Prankstress in their ranks. The Pranksters named her Sensuous X, glowing girl friend resolutely going . . . Furthur . . . Kesey laid eyes on the Sensuous horizon—loved it! On the bus. Next, she became Zonker's sensuous ex—lost her! On the bus. At first Zonker's mad, feels he's been had—affront! But then thanks to his feeling for the Prankster experiment, he sees nothing to resent. There can be no hard feelings when one is dealing totally out front on the bus.

There was very little LSD left, so they were taking mostly speed and grass, soaring through the Northlands, on Speed. For Sandy—at Millbrook a Main Guru had taken Sandy and Jane aside and confided: It would be good if you took the Millbrook trip alone . . . meaning, probably, without your obstreperous companions, i.e., off the bus, and Sandy had . . . *Dis-Mounted* again and returned to Millbrook, with Jane, and the Main Guru turned him on to DMT, a 30-minute trip like LSD but with a fierce roan-mad intensity—fragments! Sandy had a mad sense of the world torn apart into stained-glass shards behind his eyelids. No matter what he did, eyes open, eyes shut, the world erupted into electric splinters and the Main Guru said, "I wish to enter your metaphysical soul." But to Sandy—paranoia!—he seemed like a randy-painted lulu bent on his rectococcygeal shoals, a randy boy-enjoyer, while the world exploded and there was no antidote for this rocketing, rocketing, rocketing, rocketing . . . They returned to New York and Jane disembarked from the bus, stayed behind, but Sandy felt impelled to ride it out on the bus with the rest of the Pranksters, heading west, rocketing, rocketing, rocketing, rocketing Furthur . . . And now in the Midwest it was as if the DMT trip at Millbrook had been the last stage of a rocket and his whole psyche was now committed to speed and motion, and it was necessary to keep soaring through the Northlands. Certain vibrations of the bus would trip his brain somehow and suddenly bring back the sensation of the rocketing DMT trip and it would be necessary to speed up and *keep moving.* The sweet wheatfields and dairy lands of America would be sailing by beauty rural green and curving, and Sandy is watching the serene beauty of it . . . and then he happens to look into the big rear-view mirror outside the bus and—the fields are—in flames ::::::: curve and curdle straight up in hideous orange flames ::::: So he whips his head around and looks way back as far as he can see and over over to the horizon and it is nothing but flat and sweet and green again, sailing by serene. Then he looks back into the mirror—and the flames shoot up again, soaring, corn and lespedeza turning brown like burning color film when the projector is too hot and bursting into flames, corn, wheat, lespedeza turning into brown scouring rush, death camass, bloodwort, wild iris, blue flag, grease wood, poison sucklyea, monkshood mandrake, moonseed, fitweed, locoweed, tumble mustard, spurge nettle, coyote tobacco, crab's eye bursting into flames—*a sea of flames*—a mirror with a sea of flames, Narcissus, Moon, twins, thesis and anti-thesis, infirmity of life, as if he is forced to endure at any moment the visual revelation of a paleopsychic mystery—and Sandy looks away and forces himself not to look toward the rearview mirror and once again just sun and the green belly of America sailing by . . .

. . . serene. Certain things worked smoothly on every level. They knew how to run the bus better, for one thing, even though Cassady had had to go back ahead of time by car with Hassler, who had to report back to Fort Ord. The Pranksters took turns driving. Getting food, copping urinations, shooting the movie, making tapes—they managed it all like a team. Once a few minor personal hassles were worked out—out front—and the bus crossed the Mississippi, and they were way out West—then it all merged into the Group Mind and became very psychic . . .

Intersubjectivity!

. . . Sandy himself wheeling the bus through dour Roosian South Dakota with cold shadows sweeping over the green and golden grasslands. No sea of flames now, just a green and gold sea, serene, coming from out of the stream of the Northlands themselves—and sleep means nothing, because there is no time, only Now, a perfect experience in the perfect momentum set perfectly by his foot on the accelerator—for 191 miles he drove, by the speedometer. Then he goes to the back of the bus and there up on the ceiling is a map of the U.S. pasted up there, and—see!—there is a red line on the map, leaping out on, and it is exactly those 191 miles he drove, glowing on the ceiling of the bus. He looks around, starts asking, very excited—and Sensuous X said she made the line—

"Why!"

Sensuous doesn't know. No why to it. She just had the crayon and that was where the line went—

—but no need to explain. Telepathic Kathy! Just one line, one current, running through the entire bus. Group Mind, and Cosmic Control, on the bus . . .

Then the bus heads up into Canada, to Calgary, to catch the Calgary Stampede. The unquenchable Hagen of the Screw Shack prowls the Stampede for ginch ahoof and comes back to the bus with nice little girl with lips as raunchy as a swig of grape soda, tender in age but ne'mind, ready to go, and she is on the bus, christened Anonymous, down to her bra and panties, which she prefers. The call goes out to the Canadian Royal Mounties for the runaway, or stowaway, the little girl from the Stampede, and they stop the bus in the road check—

—Why, come right on in, officers, take a look around—

—while Hagen grinds the camera at them—

—while the Head Mountie rereads the long description, five feet two, dark hair, etc., and checks out Sensuous X and Gretch and Anonymous in the window—

—Anonymous reads the description over the Mountie's shoulder, perched up at the window, and laughs merrily at such a funny-sounding girl—she by now having her face all painted up in Prankster designs and half her grape-soda body as well so that she doesn't look too much like the pretty helpless waif Grandma described to the Mounties, and the Mounties wave them by and peer on down the road for the next.

Next down to Boise, Idaho, and everywhere Kesey and Babbs

up top the bus with flutes, mercilessly tootling the people of America as they crowd around the bus and getting pretty good at it even. Winces here and there as some little cringing shell in the population pinioned in his crispy black shiny shoes knows, no mistake, that it is *him* they have singled out—they are playing my song, the desperate sound track from my movie—and Kesey and Babbs score again and again, like the legendary Zen archers, for they no longer play their music *at* people but *inside* them. They play inside them, oh merciless flow. And many things are clear in the flow. They are above the multitudes, looking down from the Furthur heights of the bus, and the billion eyes of America glisten at them like electric kernels, and yet the Pranksters are grooving with this whole wide-screen America and going with its flow with American flags flying from the bus and taking energy, as in solar heat, from its horsepower and its neon and there is no limit to the American trip. Bango!—that's it!—the trouble with Leary and his group is that they have turned *back*. But of course! They have turned back into that old ancient New York intellectual thing, ducked back into the romantic past, copped out of the American trip. New York intellectuals have always looked for . . . another country, a fatherland of the mind, where it is all better and more philosophic and purer, gadget-free, and simpler and pedigreed: France or England, usually—oh, the art of living, in France, boys. The Learyites have done the same thing, only with them it's—India—the East—with all the ancient flap-doodle of Gautama Buddha or the Rig-Veda blowing in like mildew, and Leary calls for blue grass growing in the streets of New York, and he decrees that everyone should have such a dwelling place of such pristine antique décor, with everyone hunkered down amid straw rugs and Paisley wall hangings, that the Gautama Buddha himself from 485 B.C. could walk in and feel at home instantly. Above all, keep quiet, for God's sake, hold it down, whisper, moan, mumble, meditate, and for chrissake, no *gadgets*—no tapes, video tapes, TV, movies, Hagstrom electric basses, variable lags, American flags, no neon, Buick

Electras, mad moonstone-faced Servicenters, and no manic buses, f'r chrissake, soaring, doubledyclutch doubledyclutch, to the Westernmost edge—

And in Boise they cut through a funeral or wedding or something, so many dressed-up people in the sun gawking at Pranksters gathered at a fountain and all cutting up in the sunspots, and a kid—they have tootled *his song,* and he likes it, and he runs for the bus and they all pile on and pull out, just ahead of him, and he keeps running for the bus, and Kesey keeps slowing down and then pulling out just out of his reach, six or eight blocks this way, and then they speed up for good, and they can still see him floating away in the background, his legs still running, like a preview—

—allegory of life!—

—of the multitudes who very shortly will want to get on the bus . . . themselves . . .

> Back at Kesey's in La Honda,
> Deep into the rusky-dusky neon dusty,
> More synched in than
> They had ever been,
> Deep into the Unspoken Thing,
> The Pranksters now aligned
> Along a sheerly dividing line:
> Before the bus and
> After the bus,
> On the bus or
> Off the bus,
> A sheerly Diluvial divide:
> Did you take the Epoch Ride?
> One-way ticket into the nirvana thickets
> Of the *ex* redwood *cathedra* Unspoken Thing.
> Most peaceful synching in,
> Serene bacchanal
> For all . . .

. . . except Sandy. For Sandy, the bus had stopped but he hadn't. It was as if the bus had hit a wall and he had shot out the window and was living in the suspended interminable moment before *he* hit—what? He didn't know. All he knew was that there would be a crash unless the momentum of the Pranksters suddenly resumed and caught up with him the way the Flash, in the Pranksters' ubiquitous comic books, caught speeding bullets by streaking at precisely their speed and reaching out and picking them up like eggs . . .

Sandy went about wide-eyed and nervous, an endless ratchet of activity that no one quite comprehended at first. The bus was parked out in front of the log house and Kesey would be inside the bus doing something and Sandy, outside the door, would suddenly begin arguing with him over some esoteric point of the sound system. Kesey was keeping the tapes on a hick level, he was saying. Kesey was, like, rustling cellophane in front of a microphone for "fire," and so forth and so on. So many complaints! Until Kesey puts his arms up on the walls of the bus in the Christ on the Cross gesture—which is precisely what one of Sandy's brothers used to do when he started complaining—and this drives Sandy into a rage and he yells *Fuck you!* and gives Kesey the finger. Kesey streaks out of the door of the bus and pins Sandy up against the side of the bus—and it is all over as fast as that. Sandy is overwhelmed. He has never seen Kesey use his tremendous strength against anyone before, and it is overwhelming, the idea of it even. But it is all over in no time. Kesey is suddenly calm again and asks Sandy to come with him to the backhouse, the shack by the creek. He wants to talk to him.

So they go out there and Kesey talks to Sandy about Sandy's attitude. Sandy is still *Dis-mount,* still getting off the bus continually, and why? You don't understand, says Sandy. You don't understand my dis-mounting. It's like climbing a mountain. Would you rather climb the mountain or have a helicopter deposit you on the top? The continual climb, the continual *remounting,*

makes it a richer experience, and so on. Kesey nods in a somewhat abstracted way and says O.K., Sandy . . .

But Sandy feels paranoid . . . what do they *really* think of him?
What are they planning? What insidious prank? He can't get it
out of his mind that they are building up to some prank of enormous proportions, at his expense. A Monstrous Prank . . . He
can't sleep, his brain keeps going at the furious speed of the bus
on the road, like an eternal trip on speed.

Then Kesey devised a game called "Power." He took a dart-
board and covered it with Masonite and put a spinner in the middle and marked off spoke lines forming one section for each
Prankster. Each person's Prankster name was written in his section, Intrepid Traveler for Babbs, Mal Function for Hagen,
Speed Limit for Cassady, Hassler for Ron Bevirt, Gretchen
Fetchin for Paula—in truth, her old name and persona were
gone entirely and she was now a new person known as Gretchen
Fetchin or Gretch. Sandy looked and in his section it said: "dis-
MOUNT," with the heavy accent on Mount, even as he had explained it to Kesey in the backhouse. He was overwhelmed with
relief and gratitude. Kesey *knew!* Kesey understood! He was
back in the bus.

Everybody was to write out some "tasks" on slips of paper and
they would all be put in a big pile. Then the spinner was spun,
and if it landed on you, you reached into the pile and pulled out
a "task," which you then had to do, and the others gave you
points according to how well you had done the task, on a scale of
one to five points, five being the best. A lot of the tasks were very
pranked-up, like "put on an article of somebody else's clothing."
There was a scoreboard and everybody moved his counter up the
scoreboard as he picked up points. Everybody made his own
counter. Sandy was making his out of Sculpt Metal. He stretched
it to a long spidery length, then suddenly compressed it into an
ugly wad, because that was the way he was beginning to feel. So
Page picked it up and made a nice little form out of it, like a

bridge, and everybody said that's the way it should be done—and Sandy feels the paranoia coming back . . .

The prize for winning was: Power. Thirty minutes of absolute power in which your word was law and everyone had to do whatever you wanted. Very allegorical, this game. By and by Babbs won a game and he ordered everybody to bring everything they possessed into the living room. Everybody went forth and hauled in all their stuff, out to the bedrooms, tents, Kampers, sleeping bags, the bus, and brought in a ragamuffin mountain of clothes, shoes, boots, toys, paint pots, toothbrushes, books, boxes, capsules, stashes, letters, litter, junk. It was all piled up in the center of the room, a marvelous Rat mountain of junk. "Now," said Babbs, "we redistribute the wealth." And he would hold up some piece of it and say, "Who wants one 1964 Gretchen Fetchin toothbrush?" and somebody would hold up his hand and it would go to him and somebody else would catalogue it all solemnly on a legal pad.

Then the pointer hits Sandy and he picks up a task, a slip of paper. It is in Gretch's handwriting, and it says: "Go out and build a fire." He reads it out loud and just keeps staring at it. Then they all stare at him, waiting for him to get up and go out and build a fire, and he feels them staring and then he *knows*—it is a very clever plot to get him out of the house, get him outside in the dark, and then pull the Monstrous Prank—

And he starts blurting it all out. *I can't do it. Can't you see how it is? It's getting awful—I can't sleep and everything is like this:*

He lays the fingers of one hand over the fingers of the other, forming a trellis pattern, and peers through the spaces in between to show how everything keeps breaking up, fragmenting, his whole field of vision, ever since the DMT trip at Millbrook, and the sea of flames and the paranoia, the everlasting paranoia, he blurts it all out, everything that is hanging him up and rocketing him toward—what?

And suddenly it is very quiet in the log house. Every Prankster eye is upon him, absorbed, giving him total . . . Attention, He has come all the way out front. The furious motion stops, and he suddenly feels :::: peace.

"How many points do we give him?" says Kesey.

And around the circle everyone says "Five!" "Five!" "Five!" "Five!" "Five!"—

"Three," says Gretch, who had written the task in the first place—and Sandy—a small microgram of paranoia creeps back in like a mite . . .

THE PRANKSTERS NOW REALIZED THAT SANDY WAS IN A BAD way. Kesey had a saying, "Feed the hungry bee." So the Pranksters set about showering . . . Attention on Sandy, to try to give him a feeling of being at the cool center of the whole thing. But he kept misinterpreting their gestures. Why are they staring? His insomnia became more and more severe. One night he walked down the road to the housing development, Redwood Terrace, to try to borrow some Sominex. He was just going to walk up to a door in the middle of the night and knock and ask for some Sominex. Somehow he had the old New York apartment-house idea that you walk down the hall and borrow a cup of sugar, even if you don't know the people. So he starts knocking on doors and asking for Sominex. Of course, they all either panic and shut the door or tell him to fuck off. The people of Redwood Terrace were a little paranoid themselves by this time about the crazies down the road at Kesey's.

By day it was no better. As his insomnia got worse, he started having more fragmented vision and finally . . . he looks at the wild-painted bus and the lurid chaos of the swirls changes into . . . the tunnel! A tunnel they had gone through, a long tunnel, in which he had been possessed by intense claustrophobia and the paranoid certainty that they would never emerge from the tunnel, and now the tunnel appears on the side of the bus in horrifying detail. He turns away . . . there is the cool limelit bower, cathedral in the redwoods, serenity . . . he turns back to the bus slowly :::::::: It is still there! The tunnel! ::::: The bus! ::::: Now painted as if by a master, a very Titian :::: An Hieronymus Bosch :::: A Matthias Grünewald :::: With the most horrifying scenes of my life.

salvation? kesey announces they are getting back on the bus—moving again—and going up to Esalen Institute up in Big Sur, four hours drive to the south. Esalen was an "experiment in living," as they say, a sort of Roughin-it resort perched on a cliff about 1,000 feet above the Pacific. A very dramatic piece of Nature, in the nineteenth-century seascape fashion. Waves crashing way down below and sparkling air way up here and a view of half the world, mountains, ocean, sky, the whole show, in a word, for which Big Sur is famous. There was a lodge and a swimming pool and a stretch of greensward out to the edge of the cliff and some hot sulphur springs about 100 yards away, also perched on the side of a cliff, in which one could bathe and gaze out over the eternal ocean. Behind the lodge were rows of tiny cabins and a few trailers. These were for the clientele. The clients—well, to put it simply, Esalen was a place where educated middle-class adults came in the summer to try to get out of The Rut and wiggle their fannies a bit.

The main theoretician at Esalen was a Gestalt psychologist named Fritz Perls. Perls was a great goateed man in his seventies who went about in a jump suit made of blue terrycloth. He had the air of a very learned, dignified, and authoritative blue bear. Perls was the father of the Now Trip. His theory was that most people live fantasy lives. They live totally in the past or in terms of what they expect in the future, which amounts to fear, generally. Perls tried to teach his patients, pupils, and the clients at Esalen to live Now for a change, in the present, to become aware of their bodies and all the information their senses brought them, to shelve their fears and seize the moment. They went through "marathon encounters," in which a group stayed together for days and brought everything out front, no longer hiding behind custom, saying what they really felt—shouts, accusations, embraces, tears—a perfect delight, of course: "You want to know what I really think of you . . ." One of the exercises at Esalen was the Now Trip exercise, in which you try to catalogue the information your senses are bringing you in the present moment. You make a rapid series of statements beginning with the word "Now": "Now I feel the wind cooling the perspiration on my forehead . . . Now I hear a bus coming up the drive in low gear . . . Now I hear a Beatles record playing over a loudspeaker . . ."

A bus? A Beatles record? The Pranksters are here, Now Trippers. Kesey had been invited to Esalen to conduct a seminar entitled "A Trip with Ken Kesey." Nobody had quite counted on the entire fully wired and wailing Prankster ensemble, however. The clientele at Esalen had come a long way in a few weeks and many were beginning to peek over the edge of The Rut. And what they saw . . . it could be scary out there in Freedomland. The Pranksters were friendly, but they glowed in the dark. They pranked about like maniacs in the serene Hot Springs. Precious few signed up for a trip with Ken Kesey, even in seminar form.

Sandy, meanwhile, was swinging wildly from feelings of paranoia to feelings of godly . . . Power. And the trip was always the bus. One moment it was covered with the Hieronymus Bosch scenes of his most private Hell. The next—he controls the bus. One night he discovers he can unpaint the bus just by staring at it. He has psychokinetic powers. His stare bears the power of life or death. The waves crash below the Esalen cliff—and he stares at the bus and . . . *unpaints it*. He strips one whole side down to its original sunny school-bus yellow. The whole Prankster overlay is gone. A trick of the mind? He looks away, out over the Pacific and at the stars—then swings back suddenly toward the bus :::::
IT IS STILL UNPAINTED :::: STILL VIRGIN SCHOOL-BUS YELLOW.

He has the power—but can it ward off the Monstrous Prank? The Pranksters take the bus into Monterey to see a movie, *The*

Night of the Iguana. He sits in the back of the bus, so he can watch them. If any of them tries anything, with one stare he can . . . They go into the theater and he lags behind, then sits several rows behind them. To keep an eye out . . . There is a *Tom and Jerry* cartoon on the screen. The mouse, Jerry, tricks the cat, Tom, and the cat goes off a cliff and *hits,* flattened in an explosion of eyeballs, thousands of eyeballs. Everyone is laughing, but to Sandy it is sickening, incredibly brutal. He jumps up and runs out of the theater and wanders around Monterey for an hour and a half or so. Then he wanders back to the theater, and Hagen is standing outside.

"Where the hell have you been? Kesey is looking all over for you."

Sandy runs back into the theater. *Kesey!* He looks up on the screen—and the mouse, Jerry, tricks the cat, Tom, and the cat goes off a cliff and *hits,* flattened in an explosion of eyeballs, thousands of eyeballs . . . Sandy flees again. Kesey is now waiting outside. He coaxes Sandy on to the bus and they head back to Esalen.

Back in Esalen, in his cabin, Sandy falls half asleep into . . . DREAM WARS! It is his Power vs. Kesey's, like Dr. Strange vs. Aggamon, and one of them will kill the other in the Dream War . . . He exerts the utmost psychic energy . . . opens his eyes and makes out a machine in the cabin—a heater? It *looks* like a heater but it is Kesey's death instrument, and in that moment the thermostat turns on the machine and a tiny red light comes on—Kesey's ray gun—has triumphed, *killed* him, and Sandy falls off the bed, dead, lying on the floor, and he leaves his body in astral projection and sails out over the Pacific, out from the Esalen cliff, out for 40 or 50 miles, soaring, and the wind goes in gusts, *huhhhh-hhnnnh, huhhhhhhhhhhnnnh, huhhhhhhhhhnnnh,* and he is the wind, not even a compact spirit flying but a totally diffuse being, dissolved in the upper ethers, and he can see the whole moonlit ocean and Esalen way back there. Then he comes to, and he is on the floor of the cabin, breathing hard, *huhhhhhhhhhnnnh, huhhhh-hhhhhnnh, huhhhhhhhhnnnh.*

"San-dy! San-dy! San-dy!"—daylight, and they're outside the cabin, calling him, the Pranksters . . . what Monstrous Prank?—

In fact, Kesey had instructed the Pranksters to give Sandy total Attention to try to bring him around, to put him at the center of everything. Sandy comes out, sees them staring but takes it for glowers and aggression . . . Nevertheless—on to the bus, and they ride out along Big Sur in the sunlight. Kesey and the Pranksters have prepared a long *Sandy* document, twelve pages of text and drawings, very fanciful, like a psychic brief, bringing all of Sandy's fears out front and dispelling them in camaraderie—and it begins to work. Then as they roll along the cliff highway Kesey takes Sandy up on top of the bus for a Now Trip. They sit up there in the sun with the wind streaming by and Kesey is grooving off the designs on the hood of the bus: "Now I see the green snake form going into the red and the edge of it melts into . . ." and so forth, and Sandy grooves off Kesey's Now Trip—Kesey!—Total Attention!—and it is like he is coming around at last, he feels *on the bus again.* And then he decides to take Kesey on a Now Trip, sailing along the cliff highway. "Now," says Sandy, "I see the ocean like a sheet of ice slanting in toward the shore . . . Now I see three suns . . ."—in truth! the vibration of the bus has thrown him into the DMT reaction. He gets a triple image from the vibration and shaking of the bus, but instead of refocusing on one sun, he keeps seeing three. Kesey looks up at the sky, and says, "Yeah, yeah," grooving with it, which makes Sandy feel very good . . .

But then nighttime. "San-dy! San-dy!" They're trying to coax him out of the cabin again. For—what? Why, the Monstrous Prank, naturally, but . . . he has Power. Outside—they have candles, the Pranksters do, and they're beginning a candlelight march down a path in a ravine that cuts down through the cliff, all the way to the water's edge. For—what? Why, the Monst—But then Kesey's wife, Faye, comes up very silent and smiling and loving and gives him a candle and lights it, and Faye is like complete honesty and love, so he starts off, following them down the path, holding candles, while the surf booms up the ravine from below. Why do they want him to join this spooky procession? Why, for the most Monstrous Prank of all—to *kill* him at the water's edge, but *he* has the power—the candle dims in the wind, and then comes back up, burning full—but it is not the wind, it is Sandy—he can make it shrink and dim down just by staring at it, psychokinesis, then draw it back up, all with his mind, he can control the flame utterly, and it can control him, for they are one and the same, *God,* and he trudges down the ravine, becoming more and more powerful—but a girl named Lola has stopped ahead of him. He draws closer and she has a candle and is tilting it so that the wax drips on her fingers and she is grooving over the wax dripping over her fingers and grinning, and her hand, in wax, turns white and dead, a skeleton, and her grin, lit from beneath by the candle, turns waxy and zombie—THE DEATH STARTS HERE—and Sandy bolts, charging back up the ravine—

—not knowing that the whole procession had been set up as a ceremony of love, a love trip, for him, to bring him around, a candlelit celebration of Sandy down by the water—

—but he is long gone, running down the cliff highway now, toward Monterey, running until his lungs give out, then walking, then running up to the lights in the houses on the cliffs over the water, Big Sur summer places, and knocking on the door, screaming incoherently about jumping off the cliffs; until the police come. Gotcha! Which is a joke, because he can annihilate them any moment he chooses, with a psychokinetic ray—

They put him in the back seat, streaking down Route 1 toward Monterey, wheeling around the curves, faster and faster—

"Don't go so fast!" Sandy says.

"What?"

"Don't go so fast!"

"Listen," the cop says. "I'll slow down if you stop staring at the back of my head."

"Ahhhhhh."

"Look out the window or something. Look at the scenery. Stop staring at the back of my head."

So he takes his eyes out of the back of the cop's skull. Two fever hole depressions. Another moment—

THE MONTEREY POLICE HELD HIM IN THE JAIL IN MONTEREY until his brother Chris could get there from New York. Chris ran into Kesey at the jail. We've got to get him out of here, said Kesey. What do you mean? We've got to get him back where he belongs, with the Pranksters. Chris took Sandy back to New York for treatment. It was a long time before Chris knew what in the hell Kesey had been talking about.

The Unspoken Thing

HOW TO TELL IT! . . . THE CURRENT FANTASY . . . I NEVER heard any of the Pranksters use the word *religious* to describe the mental atmosphere they shared after the bus trip and the strange days in Big Sur. In fact, they avoided putting it into words. And yet—

They got on the bus and headed back to La Honda in the old Big Sur summertime, all frozen sunshine up here, and no one had to say it: they were all deep into some *weird shit* now, as they would just as soon call it by way of taking the curse . . . off the Unspoken Thing. Things were getting very *psychic*. It was like when Sandy drove 191 miles in South Dakota and then he had looked up at the map on the ceiling of the bus and precisely those 191 miles were marked in red . . . Sandy : : : : : back in Brain Scan country the White Smocks would never in a million years comprehend where he had actually been . . . which was where they all were now, also known as Edge City . . . Back in Kesey's log house in La Honda, all sitting around in the evening in the main

room, it's getting cool outside, and Page Browning: *I think I'll
close the window*—and in that very moment another Prankster
gets up and closes it for him and smi-i-i-i-les and says nothing . . .
The Unspoken Thing—and these things keep happening over
and over. They take a trip up into the High Sierras and Cassady
pulls the bus off the main road and starts driving up a little
mountain road—see where she goes. The road is so old and de-
serted the pavement is half broken up and they keep climbing
and twisting up into nowhere, but the air is nice, and up at the
top of the grade the bus begins bucking and gulping and won't
pull any more. It just stops. It turns out they're out of gas, which
is a nice situation because it's nightfall and they're stranded totally hell west of nowhere with not a gas station within thirty,
maybe fifty miles. Nothing to do but stroke themselves out on the
bus and go to sleep . . . hmmmmmm . . . scorpions with boots on
red TWA Royal Ambassador slumber slippers on his big Stinger
Howard Hughes in a sleeping bag on the floor in a marble pent-
house in the desert

Dawn

All wake up to a considerable fetching and hauling and grinding up the grade below them and over the crest comes a

Chevron

gasoline tanker, a huge monster of a tanker. Which just stops
like they all met somewhere before and gives them a tankful of
gas and without a word heads *on* into the Sierras toward absolutely

Nothing

Babbs—*Cosmic control, eh Hassler!*

And Kesey—*Where does it go? I don't think man has ever been
there. We're under cosmic control and have been for a long long time,
and each time it builds, it's bigger, and it's stronger. And then you find
out . . . about Cosmo, and you discover that he's running the show . . .*

The Unspoken Thing; Kesey's role and the whole direction
the Pranksters were taking—all the Pranksters were conscious of
it, but none of them put it into words, as I say. They made a point

of not putting it into words. That in itself was one of the unspoken rules. *If you label it* this, *then it can't be* that ... Kesey took
great pains not to make his role explicit. He wasn't the authority,
somebody else was: "Babbs says ..." "Page says ..." He wasn't
the leader, he was the "non-navigator." He was also the non-
teacher. "Do you realize that you're a teacher here?" Kesey says,
"Too much, too much," and walks away ... Kesey's explicit
teachings were all cryptic, metaphorical; parables, aphorisms:
"You're either on the bus or off the bus." "Feed the hungry bee,"
"Nothing lasts," "See with your ears and hear with your eyes,"
"Put your good where it will do the most," "What did the mirror
say? It's done with people." To that extent it was like Zen Buddhism, with the inscrutable koans, in which the novice says,
"What is the secret of Zen?" and Hui-neng the master says,
"What did your face look like before your parents begat you?"
To put it into so many words, to define it, was to limit it. If it's
this, then it can't be *that* ... Yet there it was! Everyone had his
own thing he was working out, but it all fit into the group thing,
which was—"the Unspoken Thing," said Page Browning, and
that was as far as anyone wanted to go with words.

For that matter, there was no theology to it, no philosophy, at
least not in the sense of an *ism.* There was no goal of an improved
moral order in the world or an improved social order, nothing
about salvation and certainly nothing about immortality or the
life hereafter. Hereafter! That was a laugh. If there was ever a
group devoted totally to the here and now it was the Pranksters.
I remember puzzling over this. There was something so ... *religious* in the air, in the very atmosphere of the Prankster life, and
yet one couldn't put one's finger on it. On the face of it there was
just a group of people who had shared an unusual psychological
state, the LSD experience—

But exactly! The *experience*—that was the word! and it began
to fall into place. In fact, none of the great founded religions,
Christianity, Buddhism, Islam, Jainism, Judaism, Zoroastrianism, Hinduism, none of them began with a philosophical frame-

work or even a main idea. They all began with an overwhelming *new experience,* what Joachim Wach called "the experience of the holy," and Max Weber, "possession of the deity," the sense of being a vessel of the divine, of the All-one. I remember I never truly understood what they were talking about when I first read of such things. I just took their weighty German word for it. Jesus, Mani, Zoroaster, Gautama Buddha—at the very outset the leader did not offer his circle of followers a better state hereafter or an improved social order or any reward other than a certain "psychological state in the here and now," as Weber put it. I suppose what I never really comprehended was that he was talking about an actual mental experience they all went through, an *ecstasy,* in short. In most cases, according to scriptures and legend, it happened in a flash. Mohammed fasting and meditating on a mountainside near Mecca and—*flash!*—ecstasy, vast revelation and the beginning of Islam. Zoroaster hauling haoma water along the road and—*flash!*—he runs into the flaming form of the Archangel Vohu Mano, messenger of Ahura Mazda, and the beginning of Zoroastrianism. Saul of Tarsus walking along the road to Damascus and—*flash!*—he hears the voice of the Lord and becomes a Christian. Plus God knows how many lesser figures in the 2,000 years since then, Christian Rosenkreuz and his "God-illuminated" brotherhood of Rosicrucians, Emanuel Swedenborg whose mind suddenly "opened" in 1743, Meister Eckhart and his disciples Suso and Tauler, and in the twentieth-century Sadhu Sundar Singh—with—*flash!*—a vision at the age of 16 and many times thereafter; ". . . often when I come out of ecstasy I think the whole world must be blind not to see what I see, everything is so near and clear . . . there is no language which will express the things which I see and hear in the spiritual world . . ." Sounds like an acid head, of course. What they all saw in . . . a flash was the solution to the basic predicament of being *human,* the personal *I, Me,* trapped, mortal and helpless, in a vast impersonal *It,* the world around me. Suddenly!—All-in-one!—flowing together, *I* into *It,* and *It* into *Me,* and in that flow I perceive a power, so near and so clear, that the whole world is blind to. All the modern religions, and the occult mysteries, for that matter, talk about an Other World—whether Brahma's or the flying saucers'—that the rational work-a-day world is blind to. The—*so called!* friends—rational world. If only *they,* Mom&Dad&Buddy&Sis, dear-but-square ones, could but know the *kairos,* the supreme moment... The historic *visions* have been explained in many ways, as the result of epilepsy, self-hypnosis, changes in metabolism due to fasting, or actual intervention by gods—or drugs: Zoroastrianism began in a grand bath of haoma water, which was the same as the Hindu soma, and was unquestionably a drug. *The experience!*

And following *the experience*—after I got to know the Pranksters, I went back and read Joachim Wach's paradigm of the way religions are founded, written in 1944, and it was almost like a piece of occult precognition for me if I played it off against what I knew about the Pranksters:

Following a profound new experience, providing a new illumination of the world, the founder, a highly charismatic person, begins enlisting disciples. These followers become an informally but closely knit association, bound together by the new experience, whose nature the founder has revealed and interpreted. The association might be called a circle, *indicating that it is oriented toward a central figure with whom each of the followers is in intimate contact. The followers may be regarded as the founder's companions, bound to him by personal devotion, friendship and loyalty. A growing sense of solidarity both binds the members together and differentiates them from any other form of social organization. Membership in the circle requires a complete break with the ordinary pursuits of life and a radical change in social relationships. Ties of family and kinship and loyalties of various kinds were at least temporarily relaxed or severed. The hardships, suffering and persecution that loomed for those who cast their lot with the group were counterbalanced by their high hopes and firm expectations* ... and so on. And of the founder himself: he has "visions, dreams, trances, frequent ecstasies" ... "unusual sensitiveness and an intense emotional life" ... "is ready to interpret manifestations of the divine" ... "there is something elemental about [him], an uncompromising attitude and an archaic manner and language" ... "He appears as a renewer of lost contracts with the hidden powers of life" ... "does not usually come from the aristocracy, the learned or refined; frequently he emerges from simpler folk and remains true to his origin even in a changed environment" ... "speaks cryptically, with words, signs, gestures, many metaphors, symbolic acts of a diverse nature" ... "illuminates and interprets the past and anticipates the future in terms of the *kairos* (the supreme moment)"—

The *kairos!*—the *experience!*

—in one of two ways, according to Max Weber: as an "ethical" prophet, like Jesus or Moses, who outlines rules of conduct for his followers and describes God as a super-person who passes judgment on how they live up to the rules. Or as an "exemplary" prophet, like Buddha: for him, God is impersonal, a force, an energy, a unifying flow, an All-in-one. The exemplary prophet does not present rules of conduct. He presents his own life as an example for his followers ...

In all these religious circles, the groups became tighter and tighter by developing their own symbols, terminology, life styles, and, gradually, simple cultic practices, *rites,* often involving music and art, all of which grew out of the *new experience* and seemed weird or incomprehensible to those who have never had it. At that point they would also ... "develop a strong urge to extend the message to all people."

... all people ... Within the religious circle, status was always a simple matter. The world was simply and sheerly divided into "the aware," those who had had the experience of being vessels of the divine, and a great mass of "the unaware," "the unmusical," "the unattuned." Or: *you're either on the bus or off the bus.* Consciously, the Aware were never snobbish toward the Unaware, but in fact most of that great jellyfish blob of straight souls looked like hopeless cases—*and the music of your flute from up top the bus*

just brought them up tighter. But these groups treated anyone who
showed possibilities, who was a potential brother, with generous
solicitude . . .

. . . THE POTENTIALLY ATTUNED . . . BEAUTIFUL PEOPLE
started showing up at Kesey's in La Honda, and no one was
turned away. They could stay there, live there, if they . . . seemed
attuned. Mountain Girl was waiting out front of Kesey's house
when the bus came around the last bend on Route 84 and into the
redwood gorge. Mountain Girl was a big brunette with a black
motorcycle, wearing a T-shirt and dungarees. She was only 18
but big, about five-foot-nine, and heavy; and loud and sloppy, as
far as that went. But it was funny . . . she had beautiful teeth and
a smile that lit up one's gizzard . . . Her name was Carolyn
Adams, but she became Mountain Girl right away. As far as I
know, nobody ever called her anything else after that, until the
police got technical about it nine months later with her and
eleven other Pranksters . . .

Cassady had turned Mountain Girl on to Kesey's place. She
had been working as a technician in a biological laboratory in
Palo Alto. She had a boyfriend who—well, he probably thought
of himself as a "beatnik" in his square hip way. Only he never did
anything, this boyfriend of hers. They never went anywhere.
They never went out. So she went out by herself. She ended up
one night in St. Michael's Alley, one of Palo Alto's little boho
rookeries, at a birthday party for Cassady. Cassady said over the
mountain and down under the redwoods was where it was at.

Mountain Girl was a big hit with the Pranksters from the very
start. She seemed always completely out front, without the slightest prompting. She was one big loud charge of vitality. Here
comes Mountain Girl—and it was a thing that made you pick up,
as soon as you saw her mouth broaden into a grin and her big
brown eyes open, open, open, open until they practically exploded like sunspots in front of your eyes and you knew that

wonderful countryfied voice was going to sing out something
like:

"Hey! Guess what we're gonna do! We were just up to
Baw's"—the general store—"and we're gonna git some seeds and
plant some grass in Baw's window box! Can't you see it! The
whole town's gonna git turned on in six months!"—and so on.

But underneath all the gits and gonnas, she turned out to be
probably the brightest girl around there, with the possible ex-
ception of Faye. Faye said very little, so it was a moot point.
Mountain Girl turned out to be from a highly respectable upper-
middle-class background in Poughkeepsie, N.Y., a family of
Unitarians. In any case, she caught on to everything right away.
She was decisive and had all the nerve in the world. Also she was
getting more beautiful every day. All it took was a few weeks of
the rice and stew and irregular eating around Kesey's, the old in-
voluntary macrobiotic diet, so to speak, and she started thinning
out and getting beautiful. None of this was lost on Kesey. He was
the Mountain Man and she was the Mountain Girl. She was just
right for him . . .

Mountain Girl moved into a tent up on a little plateau on the
hill behind the house, under the redwoods. Page Browning had
a tent up there, too. So did Babbs and Gretch. Mike Hagen had
his Screw Shack. The Screw Shack was a very stellar—*Mal
Function!*—Hagen production. None of the boards lay true and
none of the nails ever quite made it all the way in. The boards
seemed to be huddled together in a tentative agreement. One day
Kesey took a hammer and hit a single nail on the peak of the
shack and the whole shack fell down.

"Nothing lasts, Hagen!" yelled Mountain Girl, and her laugh
boomed through the redwoods.

And the Hermit's Cave . . . One day Faye looked out the
kitchen window and there was a little creature at the foot of the
hill behind the house, peering out from the edge of the woods
like a starved animal. He was a small, thin kid, barely five feet
tall, but he had a huge black beard, like some Ozark g-nome in

Barney Google. He just stood there with these big starveling eyes bugging out of his wild black shag, looking at the house. Faye brought him out a plate of tuna fish. He took it without saying anything and ate it; and never left. The Hermit!

The Hermit hardly ever said anything, but he turned out to be perfectly literate, and he would talk to people he trusted, like Kesey. He was only 18. He had lived with his mother somewhere around La Honda. He had had a lot of trouble in school. He had had a lot of trouble everywhere. He was the Oddball. Finally he took off for the woods and lived up there barefoot, just wearing a shirt and Levi's, killing animals and spearing fish for food. People caught glimpses of him now and again and high-school kids used to try to hunt him down and demolish his lean-tos and otherwise torment him. His wandering had brought him up to the woods up behind Kesey's house, a wild stretch that had been designated "Sam McDonald Park" but never cleared.

The Hermit built himself a Hermit's Cave down in a pit in a dark green moldy mossy gully that dropped off the path up into the woods. He filled it with objects that winked and blinked and cooed. He was also keeper of the communal acid stash down there in the cave. And he had other secrets, such as his diaries . . . the Hermit Memoirs, in which real life and his Hermit fantasy ran together in wriggling rivers of little boys and lost hunters whom only the Hermit could rescue . . . Nobody ever knew his real name at all until a few months later when, as I say, the police would get technical about it . . .

Then Babbs discovered Day-Glo, Day-Glo paint, and started painting it up the very trunks of the redwoods, great zappers of green, orange, yellow. Hell, he even painted the leaves, and Kesey's place began to glow at night. And resound. More and more people were showing up for long or short stays. Cassady brought in a Scandinavian-style blonde who was always talking about hangups. Everybody had hangups. She became June the Goon. Then a girl who wore huge floppy red hats and granny glasses, the first anybody had ever seen. She became Marge the Barge.

Then a sculptor named Ron Boise, a thin guy from New England with a nasal accent like Titus Moody, only a Titus Moody who spoke the language of Hip: "Man, like, I mean, you know," and so on. Boise brought in a sculpture of a hanged man, so they ran it up a tree limb with a hangman's noose. He also built a great Thunderbird, a great Thor-and-Wotan beaked monster with an amber dome on its back and you could get inside of it. Inside were some mighty wire strings, which you could pull, which they did, and the Thunderbird twanged out across the gorge like the mightiest vibrating bass beast in the history of the world. Then he brought in a Kama Sutra sculpture, a huge sheetmetal man with his face in the sheetmetal groin of a big sheetmetal babe. She had her left leg sticking up in the air. It was hollow and Babbs ran a hose up it and turned the water on and it spurted out, so they left it running, eternally spurting. It looked like she was having an eternal orgasm out of her left foot.

And . . . *Sssss—ssss—ssss*—Bradley. Bradley, Bradley Hodgeman, had been a college tennis star. He was short but very muscular. He turned up—or came on, Bradley was always coming on—acting so weird, people would stand there and look at him, even at Kesey's. He talked in clots of words, "Fell down by the wino station—insoluble flying objects, nitrate—creasey greens by the back porch—Ray Bradbury interlining of the lone chrome nostril, you understand"—sidling through the room with a nonspecific grin on and his hair combed down over his face like a surfer, his back hunched over, and then going into a stopped-up laugh, *Sssss—ssss—ssss—ssss*—until somebody would try to break up his sequence by asking him how was the tennis playing going these days and he would widen his grin and open his eyes to a horizon of vast significance and say, "One day I hit the ball up in the air . . . and it *never came down* . . . *Sssss—ssss—ssss—ssss* . . ."

ACTUALLY, THERE WERE A LOT OF KIDS IN THE EARLY 1960s who were . . . yes; *attuned.* I used to think of them as the Beauti-

ful People because of the Beautiful People letters they used to
write their parents. They were chiefly in Los Angeles, San Francisco, and New York City, these kids. They had a regular circuit
they were on, and there was a lot of traffic from city to city. Most
of them were from middle-class backgrounds, but not upper
bourgeois, more petit bourgeois, if that old garbanzo can stand
being written down again—homes with Culture but no money
or money but no Culture. At least that was the way it struck me,
judging by the Beautiful People I knew. Culture, Truth, and
Beauty were important to them . . . "Art is a creed, not a craft," as
somebody said . . . Young! Immune! Christ, somehow there was
enough money floating around in the air so that one could do this
thing, live together with other kids—Our own thing!—from our
own status sphere, without having to work at *a job,* and live on
our own terms—Us! and people our age!—it was . . . *beautiful,* it
was a . . . *whole feeling,* and the straight world never understood
it, this thing of one's status sphere and how one was only nine-
teen, twenty, twenty-one, twenty-two or so and not starting out
helpless at the bottom of the ladder, at all, because the hell with
the ladder itself—one was already up on a . . . level that the
straight world was freaking *baffled* by! Straight people were always trying to figure out what is *wrong* here—never having had
this feeling themselves. Straight people called them beatniks. I
suppose the Beautiful People identified with the Beat Generation
excitement of the late 1950s, but in fact there was a whole new
motif in their particular bohemian status sphere: namely, psychedelic drugs.

El . . . Es . . . Dee . . . se-cret-ly . . . Timothy Leary, Alpert, and
a few chemists like Al Hubbard and the incognito "Dr. Spauld-
ing" had been pumping LSD out into the hip circuit with a truly
messianic conviction. LSD, peyote, mescaline, morning-glory
seeds were becoming the secret new *thing* in the hip life. A lot of
kids who were into it were already piled into amputated apartments, as I called them. The seats, the tables, the beds—none of
them ever had legs. Communal living on the floor, you might say,

although nobody used terms like "communal living" or "tribes" or any of that. They had no particular philosophy, just a little left-over Buddhism and Hinduism from the *beat* period, plus Huxley's theory of opening doors in the mind, no distinct life style, except for the Legless look ... They were ... well, *Beautiful People!*—not "students," "clerks," "salesgirls," "executive trainees"—Christ, don't give me your occupation-game labels! we are Beautiful People, ascendent from your robot junkyard :::::: and at this point they used to sit down and write home the Beautiful People letter. Usually the girls wrote these letters to their mothers. Mothers all over California, all over America, I guess, got to know the Beautiful People letter by heart. It went:

"Dear Mother,

"I meant to write to you before this and I hope you haven't been worried. I am in [San Francisco, Los Angeles, New York, Arizona, a Hopi Indian Reservation!!!! New York, Ajijic, San Miguel de Allende, Mazatlán, Mexico!!!!] and it is really beautiful here. It is a beautiful scene. We've been here a week. I won't bore you with the whole thing, how it happened, but I really tried, because I knew you wanted me to, but it just didn't work out with [school, college, my job, me and Danny] and so I have come here and it a really beautiful scene. I don't want you to worry about me. I have met some BEAUTIFUL PEOPLE and ..."

... and in the heart of even the most unhip mamma in all the U.S. of A. instinctively goes up the adrenal shriek: beatniks, bums, spades—*dope.*

AT KESEY'S THE DAYS BEGAN—WHEN? THERE WERE NO clocks around and nobody had a watch. The lime light would be sparkling down through the redwoods when you woke up. The first sounds, usually, would be Faye calling the children—"Jed! Shannon!"—or a cabinet door slamming in the kitchen or a pan being put down on the drainboard. Faye the eternal—Then maybe a car coming over the wooden bridge and parking in the dirt area out front of the house. Sometimes it would be one of the regulars, like Hagen, coming back. He was always going off somewhere. Sometimes it would be the everlasting visitors, from god knows where, friends of friends of friends, curiosity seekers, some of them, dope seekers, some of them, kids from Berkeley, you could never tell. People around the house would just start to be getting up. Kesey emerges in his undershorts, walks out front to the creek and dives in that mothering cold water, by way of shocking himself awake. George Walker is sitting on the porch with just a pair of Levi's on, going over his muscles, his arms, shoulders and torso and all the muscles, with his hands, looking for flaws, picking off hickies, sort of like the ministrations of a cat. There would be a great burst of activity in the late afternoon, people working on various projects, the most complicated of which, endless, it seemed like, was The Movie.

The Pranksters spent much of the fall of 1964, and the winter, and the early spring of 1965, working on . . . The Movie. They had about forty-five hours of color film from the bus trip, and once they got to going over it, it was a monster. Kesey had high hopes for the film, on every level. It was the world's first acid film, taken under conditions of total spontaneity barreling through the heartlands of America, recording all *now,* in the moment. The current fantasy was . . . a total breakthrough in terms of expression . . . but also something that would amaze and delight many multitudes, a movie that could be shown commercially as well as in the esoteric world of the heads. But The Movie was a monster, as I say. The sheer labor and tedium in editing forty-five hours of film was unbelievable. And besides . . . much of the film was out of focus. Hagen, like everybody else, had been soaring half the time, and the bouncing of the bus hadn't helped especially—*but that was the trip!* Still . . . Also, there were very few establishing shots, shots showing where the bus was when this or that took place. But who needs that old Hollywood thing of long shot, medium shot, closeup, and the careful cuts and wipes and pans and dolly in and dolly out, the old bullshit.

Still . . . plunging in on those miles of bouncing, ricocheting, blazing film with a splicer was like entering a jungle where the greeny vines grew faster than you could chop them down in front of you.

The film had already cost a staggering sum, about $70,000, mostly for color processing. Kesey had put everything he had gotten from his two novels plus the play adaptation of *One Flew Over the Cuckoo's Nest* into Intrepid Trips, Inc. His brother, Chuck, who had a good creamery business in Springfield, Oregon, invested to some extent. George Walker's father had set up a trust fund for him, with strings on it, but he contributed when he could. By the end of 1965, according to Faye's bookkeeping, Intrepid Trips, Inc., had spent $103,000 on the various Prankster enterprises. Living expenses for the whole group ran to about $20,000 for the year, a low figure considering that there were seldom fewer than ten people around to be taken care of and usually two or three vehicles. Food and lodging were all taken care of by Kesey.

A pot of money at the front door—There was a curious little library building up on the shelves in the living room, books of science fiction and other mysterious things, and you could pick up almost any of these books and find truly strange vibrations. The whole thing here is so much like . . . *this* book on Kesey's shelf, Robert Heinlein's novel, *Stranger in a Strange Land*. It is bewildering. It is as if Heinlein and the Pranksters were bound together by some inexplicable acausal connecting bond. This is a novel about a Martian who comes to earth, a true Superhero, in fact, born of an Earth mother and father after a space flight from Earth to Mars, but raised by infinitely superior beings, the Martians. Beings on other planets are always infinitely superior in science-fiction novels. Anyway, around him gathers a mystic brotherhood, based on a mysterious ceremony known as watersharing. They live in—*La Honda!* At *Kesey's!* Their place is called the Nest. Their life transcends all the usual earthly games of status, sex, and money. No one who once shares water and partakes of life in the Nest ever cares about such banal competitions again. There is a pot of money inside the front door, provided by the Superhero . . . Everything is totally out front in the Nest—no secrets, no guilt, no jealousies, no putting anyone down for anything: ". . . a plural marriage—a group theogamy . . . Therefore whatever took place—or was about to take place . . . was not public but private. 'Ain't nobody here but us gods'—so how could anyone be offended? Bacchanalia, unashamed swapping, communal living . . . everything."

Kesey by now had not only the bus but the very woods wired for sound. There were wires running up the hillside into the redwoods and microphones up there that could pick up random sounds. Up in the redwoods atop the cliff on the other side of the highway from the house were huge speakers, theater horns, that could flood the entire gorge with sound. Roland Kirk and his half a dozen horns funking away in the old sphenoid saxophone sinus cavities of the redwoods.

Dusk! Huge stripes of Day-Glo green and orange ran up the soaring redwoods and gleamed out at dusk as if Nature had said at last, Aw freak it, and had freaked out. Up the gully back of the house, up past the Hermit's Cave, were Day-Glo face masks and boxes and machines and things that glowed, winked, hummed, whistled, bellowed, and microphones that could pick up animals, hermits, anything, and broadcast them from the treetops, like the crazy gibbering rhesus background noises from the old Jungle Jim radio shows. *Dusk!* At dusk a man could put on something like a World War I aviator's helmet, only painted in screaming Day-Glo, and with his face painted in Day-Glo constellations, the bear, the goat, a great walking Day-Glo hero in the dusky rusky forests, and he could orate in the deep of the forest, up the hill, only in spectral tones, like the Shadow, any old message, something like: *"This is control tower, this is control tower, clear Runway One, the cougar microbes approach, bleeding antique lint from every pore and begging for high octane, beware, be aware, all ye who sleep in barracks on the main strip, the lumps in your mattress are carni-*

vore spores, venereal butterflies sent by the Combine to mothproof your brain, a pro-kit in every light socket—Plug up the light sockets! The cougar microbes are marching in like army ants . . ."—happy to know that someone, somebody, might answer from the house, or some place, over another microphone, booming over the La Honda hills: *"May day, May day, collapse the poles at every joint, hide inside your folding rules, calibrate your brains for the head count . . ."* And Bob Dylan raunched and rheumed away in the sphenoids or some damned place—

By nightfall the Pranksters are in the house and a few joints are circulating, saliva-liva-liva-liva-liva, and the whole thing is getting deeper into the *moment,* as it were, and people are working on tapes, tapes being played back, stopped, rewound, played again, a click on the plastic lever, stopped again . . . and a little speed making the rounds—such a lordly surge under the redwoods!—tablets of Benzedrine and Dexedrine, mainly, and you take off for a burst of work and rapping into the night . . . experiments of all sorts favored here, like putting contact microphones up against the bare belly and listening to the enzymes gurgling. Most Prankster bellies go *gurgle-galumph-blub* and so on, but Cassady's goes *ping!—dingaping!—ting!* as if he were wired at 78 rpm and everyone else is at 33 rpm, which seems about right. And then they play a tape against a television show. That is, they turn on the picture on the TV, the *Ed Sullivan Show,* say, but they turn off the sound and play a tape of, say, Babbs and somebody rapping off each other's words. The picture of the *Ed Sullivan Show* and the words on the tape suddenly force your mind to reach for connections between two vastly different orders of experience. On the TV screen, Ed Sullivan is holding Ella Fitzgerald's hands with his hands sopped over her hands as if her hands were the first robins of spring, and his lips are moving, probably saying, "Ella, that was wonderful! Really wonderful! Ladies and gentlemen, another hand for a great, great lady!" But the voice that comes out is saying to Ella Fitzgerald—*in perfect synch*—*"The lumps in your mattress are carnivore spores, venereal*

*butterflies sent by the Combine to mothproof your brain, a pro-kit in
every light socket—Ladies and gentlemen, Plug up the light sockets!
Plug up the light sockets! The cougar microbes are marching in . . ."*

Perfect! The true message!—

—although this kind of weird synchronization usually struck
outsiders as mere coincidence or just whimsical, meaningless in
any case. They couldn't understand why the Pranksters grooved
on it so. The inevitable confusion of the unattuned—like most of
the Pranksters' unique practices, it derived from the LSD experience and was incomprehensible without it. Under LSD, if it really went right, *Ego* and *Non-Ego* started to merge. Countless
things that seemed separate started to merge, too: a sound became . . . *a color!* blue . . . colors became smells, walls began to
breathe like the underside of a leaf, with one's own breath. A curtain became a column of concrete and yet it began rippling, this
incredible concrete mass rippling in harmonic waves like the
Puget Sound bridge before the crash and you can *feel* it, the entire harmonics of the universe from the most massive to the
smallest and most personal—*presque vu!*—all flowing together in
this very moment . . .

This side of the LSD experience—the *feeling!*—tied in with
Jung's theory of synchronicity. Jung tried to explain the meaningful coincidences that occur in life and cannot be explained by
cause-and-effect reasoning, such as ESP phenomena. He put
forth the hypothesis that the unconscious perceives certain archetypical patterns that elude the conscious mind. These patterns, he
suggested, are what unite subjective or psychic events with objective phenomena, the *Ego* with the *Non-Ego,* as in psychosomatic medicine or in the microphysical events of modern physics
in which the eye of the beholder becomes an integral part of the
experiment. Countless philosophers, prophets, early scientists,
not to mention alchemists and occultists, had tried to present the
same idea in the past, Plotinus, Lao-tse, Pico della Mirandola,
Agrippa, Kepler, Leibniz. Every phenomenon, and every person,
is a microcosm of the whole pattern of the universe, according to

this idea. It is as if each man were an atom in a molecule in a fingernail of a giant being. Most men spend their lives trying to understand the workings of the molecule they're born into and all they know for sure are the cause-and-effect workings of the atoms in it. A few brilliant men grasp the structure of the entire fingernail. A few geniuses, like Einstein, may even see that they're all part of a finger of some sort—So *space* equals *time, hmmmmmm* . . . All the while, however, many men get an occasional glimpse of another fingernail from another finger flashing by or even a whole finger or even the surface of the giant being's face and they realize instinctively that this is a part of a pattern they're all involved in, although they are totally powerless to explain it by cause and effect. And *then*—some visionary, through some accident—

—*ac*cident, Mahavira?—

—through some quirk of metabolism, through some *drug* perhaps, has his doors of perception opened for an instant and he almost sees—*presque vu!*—the entire being and he knows for the first time that there is a whole . . . *other pattern* here . . . Each moment in his life is only minutely related to the cause-and-effect chain within his little molecular world. Each moment, if he could only analyze it, reveals the entire pattern of the motion of the giant being, and his life is minutely synched in with it—

—AND WHEN THE CHEVRON TANKER FOLLOWS THE BUS INTO . . . NOWHERE . . . ONE GETS A GLIMPSE OF THE PATTERN, A NEW LEVEL . . . MANY LEVELS HERE . . .

The Pranksters never talked about synchronicity by name, but they were more and more attuned to the principle. Obviously, according to this principle, man does not have free will. There is no use in his indulging in a lifelong competition to change the structure of the little environment he seems to be trapped in. But one could *see* the larger pattern and move *with* it—*Go with the flow!*—and accept it and rise above one's immediate environment and even alter it by accepting the larger pattern and grooving with it—*Put your good where it will do the most!*

Gradually the Prankster attitude began to involve the main things religious mystics have always felt, things common to Hindus, Buddhists, Christians, and for that matter Theosophists and even flying-saucer cultists. Namely, the *experiencing* of an Other World, a higher level of reality. And a perception of the cosmic unity of this higher level. And a feeling of timelessness, the feeling that what we know as time is only the result of a naïve faith in causality—the notion that A in the past *caused* B in the present, which will *cause* C in the future, when actually A, B, and C are all part of a pattern that can be truly understood only by opening the doors of perception and experiencing it . . . in this moment . . . this supreme moment . . . this *kairos*—

For a long time I couldn't understand the one Oriental practice the Pranksters liked, the throwing of the *I Ching* coins. The *I Ching* is an ancient Chinese text. The Book of Changes, it is called. It contains 64 oracular readings, all highly metaphorical. You ask the *I Ching* a question and throw three coins three times and come up with a hexagram and a number that points to one of the passages. It "answers" your question . . . yes; but the *I Ching* didn't seem very Pranksterlike. I couldn't fit it in with the Pranksters' wired-up, American-flag-flying, Day-Glo electropastel surge down the great American superhighway. Yet—of course! The *I Ching* was supremely the book of *Now,* of the moment. For, as Jung said, the way the coins fall is inevitably tied up with the quality of the entire moment in which they fall, the entire pattern, and "form a part of it—a part that is insignificant to us, yet most meaningful to Chinese minds" . . . these things

THAT ONLY LUCKY DOGS AND MERRY PRANKSTERS HEAR—and so many mysteries of *the synch* from that time on . . . There is another book in the shelf in Kesey's living room that everybody seems to look at, a little book called *The Journey to the East,* by Hermann Hesse. Hesse wrote it in 1932 and yet . . . *the synch!* . . . it is a book about . . . exactly . . . the Pranksters! and the great bus trip of 1964! "It was my destiny to join in a great experience," the book began. "Having had the good fortune to belong to the

League, I was permitted to be a participant in a unique journey."
It goes on to tell about a weird, circuitous journey across Europe,
toward the East, that the members of this League took. It began,
supposedly, as just a journey, to get from here to there, but gradually it took on a profound though unclassifiable meaning: "My
happiness did indeed arise from the same secret as the happiness
in dreams; it arose from the freedom to experience everything
imaginable simultaneously, to exchange outward and inward
easily, to move Time and Space about like scenes in a theater.
And as we League brothers traveled throughout the world without motor-cars or ships, as we conquered the war-shattered
world by our faith and transformed it into Paradise, we cre-
atively brought the past, the future and the fictitious into the
present moment." The present moment! Now! The *kairos!* It was
like the man had been on acid himself and was *on the bus.*

EVERY FRIDAY NIGHT THEY HELD A BRIEFING. BRIEFING WAS
Babbs's term, from his military days in Vietnam. Faye fixes some
supper of rice and beans and meat, kind of a stew, and they all go
into the kitchen and dig into the pots and put some on a plate and
eat. A few joints are circulating around, saliva-liva-liva-liva-liva.
Then they all go up to one of the tents on the plateau, Page's, and
they all crowd in there, sitting this way and that with their legs
pulled up under their chins and they start throwing out this and
that subject for discussions. Curiously, this is like summer camp,
on one level, the Honor Council meeting out in the woods after
supper, everything smelling of charred firewood and canvas
damp with dew, and crickets and cicadas sounding off and people slapping their ankles from mosquitoes and bugs and shit. On
the other hand, the smell of new-mown grass burning and . . . the
many levels . . . aren't particularly summer camp. They usually
wait for Kesey to start off. He usually starts off with something
specific, something he's seen, something he's been doing . . . and
builds up to what he's been thinking.

He starts talking about the lag systems he is trying to work out with tape recorders. Out in the backhouse he has variable lag systems in which a microphone broadcasts over a speaker, and in front of the speaker is a second microphone. This microphone picks up what you just broadcast, but an instant later. If you wear earphones from the second speaker, you can play off against the sound of what you've just said, as in an echo. Or you can do the things with tapes, running the tape over the sound heads of two machines before it's wound on the takeup reel, or you can use three microphones and three speakers, four tape recorders and four sound heads, and on and on, until you get a total sense of the lag . . .

A person has all sorts of lags built into him, Kesey is saying. One, the most basic, is the sensory lag, the lag between the time your senses receive something and you are able to react. One-thirtieth of a second is the time it takes, if you're the most alert person alive, and most people are a lot slower than that. Now, Cassady is right up against that $1/30$th of a second barrier. He is going as fast as a human can go, but even he can't overcome it. He is a living example of how close you can come, but it can't be done. You can't go any faster than that. You can't through sheer speed overcome the lag. We are all of us doomed to spend our lives watching a *movie* of our lives—we are always acting on what has just finished happening. It happened at least $1/30$th of a second ago. We think we're in the present, but we aren't. The present we know is only a movie of the past, and we will really never be able to control the present through ordinary means. That lag has to be overcome some other way, through some kind of total breakthrough. And there are all sorts of other lags, besides, that go along with it. There are historical and social lags, where people are living by what their ancestors or somebody else perceived, and they may be twenty-five or fifty years or centuries behind, and nobody can be creative without overcoming all those lags first of all. A person can overcome that much through intellect or theory or study of history and so forth and get pretty much into the present that way, but he's still going to be up against one of the worst lags of all, the psychological. Your emotions remain behind because of training, education, the way you were brought up, blocks, hangups and stuff like that, and as a result your mind wants to go one way but your emotions don't—

Cassady speaks up: "Blue noses, red eyes, and that's all there is to say about that." And, for once, he stops right there.

But of course!—*the whole emotional lag*—and Cassady, voluble King Vulcan himself, has suddenly put it all into one immediate image, like a Zen poem or an early Pound poem—*hot little animal red eyes* bottled up by *cold little blue nose hangups*—

Cassady's disciple, Bradley, says: "God is red"—and even *he* stops right there. The sonofabitch is *on* for once—it is all compacted into those three words, even shorter than Cassady's line, like Bradley didn't even have to think it out, it just came out, a play on the phrase *God is dead,* only saying, for those of us on to the analogical thing, God is not dead, God is red, God is the bottled-up red animal inside all of us, whole, all-feeling, complete, out front, only it is made dead by all the lags—

Kesey giggles slightly and says, "I think maybe we're really synched up tonight"—

Somebody starts talking about some kid they know who has been busted for possession, of grass, and the cops said something to him and he said something back and the cops started beating on him. Everybody commiserates with the poor incarcerated bastard and they comment on the unfortunate tendency cops have of beating up on people, and Babbs says,

"Yeah! Yeah! Right! Right! Right!—but that's in his movie."

In his movie—*right right right*—and they all grok over that. *Grok*—and then it's clear, without anybody having to say it. Everybody, everybody everywhere, has his own movie going, his own scenario, and everybody is acting his movie out like mad, only most people don't know that is what they're trapped by, their little script. Everybody looks around inside the tent and nobody says it out loud, because nobody has to. Yet everybody knows at once ::::: somehow this ties in, *synchs,* directly with what Kesey has just said about the movie screen of our perceptions that closes us out from our own reality ::::: and somehow *synchs* directly, at the same time, in this very moment, with the actual, physical movie, The Movie, that they have been slaving over, the great morass of a movie, with miles and miles of spiraling spliced-over film and hot splices billowing around them like so many intertwined, synched, but still chaotic and struggling human lives, theirs, the whole fucking world's—*in this very moment*—Cassady in his movie, called *Speed Limit,* he is both a head whose thing is speed, meaning amphetamines, and a unique being whose quest is Speed, faster, goddamn it, spiraling, jerking, kicking, fibrillating tight up against the $1/30$ of a second movie-screen barrier of our senses, trying to get into... *Now*—

—Mountain Girl's movie is called *Big Girl,* and her scenario stars a girl who grew up being the big surging powerful girl in genteel surroundings, oh, *fin de siècle* Poughkeepsie, N.Y., oh Vassar scholars, and who didn't fit into whatever they had in mind for delicate girls in striped seersucker jumpers in faint ratcheting watersprinkler sun jewels on the water drops on the green grass Poughkeepsie, a big girl who's got to break out and she gets good and loud and brassy to come on stronger in this unequal contest—and later in the plot finds out she is bigger in quite another way, and bright, and beautiful...

...One looks around, and one sees the Hermit, huddled up here inside the tent, Hermit whom all love but he gets on nerves—why?—and they say Fuck off, Hermit, after which they regret it, and his movie is called *Everybody's Bad Trip.* He is everybody's bad trip, he takes it upon himself, he takes your bad trip for you, the worst way you thought it could happen—

And Page, with his black jacket with the Iron Cross on it, his movie is called—of course!—*Zea-lot.* It is as if everyone in here, smelling the burning grass, suddenly remembers a dream Page told them he had while he was sleeping on a cot in a jail in Arizona for, er, turning the citizens on to Dimensional Kreemo, yes, well—in this dream a young man named Zea-lot came to town, dressed in black, and he inflamed the citizens into doing all the secret fiend things they most dreaded letting themselves do, like staving in the windows of the Fat Jewelry Co., Inc., and sco-o-o-o-o-o-o-ping it up, like jumping little high-assed mulatto wenches, doing all the forbidden things, led on, encouraged, onward, upward, by the burning shiny black horseman, Zea-lot—after which, in the freaking cold blue morning after, they all look at each each—*who did this?*—who did all this dope-taking and looting and shafting?—what in the name of God came over us?—what came over this town?—well—*shit!*—it wasn't us, it was him, he infected and inflamed our brains, that damned snake, *Zea-lot*—and they charge down the street alternately beating their breasts and their bald heads, yelling for the hide of Zea-lot, crying out his name as the ultimate infamy—while Zea-lot just rides off nonchalantly into the black noon, and they just have to watch his black back and the black ass of his horse receding over the next hill, taking the crusade on to . . . . turn on . . . the next town . . .

. . . yes . . .

"Yeah, we're really synched up tonight."

—and, of course, everyone in this tent looks at Kesey and wonders. What is his movie? Well, you might call it *Randle McMurphy,* for a start. McMurphy, goading, coaxing, leading everybody on to give themselves a little bigger movie, a little action, moving the plot from out of deadass snug harbor. There's a hell of a scene going for you, bub, out here in Edge City. But don't even stop there—

—and all those things are keeping us out of the present, Kesey is saying, out of our own world, our own reality, and until we can get into our own world, we can't control it. If you ever make that breakthrough, you'll know it. It'll be like you had a player piano, and it is playing a mile a minute, with all the keys sinking in front of you in fantastic chords, and you never heard of the song before, but you are so far into the thing, your hands start going along with it exactly. When you make that breakthrough, then you'll start controlling the piano—

—and extend the message to all people—

chapter

XII

The Bust

WHEREAS La Honda's Wilde Weste lode
Seems to be owed to the gunslinging Younger
   Brothers;
and
WHEREAS They holed up in town
And dad-blamed but they found a neighborly way
To pay for their stay; and
WHEREAS They built a whole modern store, those notorious
   mothers;
But them was the Younger Brothers,
Mere gunslingers; and
WHEREAS Now this Kesey
And his Merry Humdingers down the road—
God-damn Wild West ob-scene
Crazies and dope fiends
And putrescent beatniks
Paint the treetrunks phosphorescent; and

WHEREAS   They beat on tin drums with sticks
          And roots while a tin man
          With a tin tenderloin
          Buries his smile in the tin groin
          Of a tin bitch ejaculating through a bunion; and
WHEREAS   The crazies go cooing, keening, itchy-gooning
          Ululating and yahooing
          Worse than gunslingers; and
WHEREAS   We know what the ninnies are doing—
YOU ARE HEREBY EMPOWERED ::::::::::::

By now the Pranksters had built up so much momentum they begin to feel immune even to a very obvious danger, namely, the cops.

The citizens of La Honda were becoming more and more exercised about Kesey and the Pranksters, and so were the San Mateo County sheriff and federal narcotics officials. Not knowing what the hell accounted for the crazy life at Kesey's place, they apparently assumed there was some hard drug use going on—heroin, cocaine, morphine. Late in 1964 they put Kesey's place under surveillance. The Pranksters knew about it and used to play games with the cops. The main federal narcotics agent in the area was a San Francisco Chinese, Agent William Wong. The Pranksters made a huge sign and put it up on the house:

WE'RE CLEAN, WILLIE!

It was fun, the cop game. The cops would be out in the woods at night, along the creek, and one of them would step into the creek and get his feet wet and say something. The Pranksters would pick all this up on the remote mikes in the woods, whereupon the voice of Mountain Girl, broadcasting from inside the cabin, would jeer out over an amplifier up in the redwoods: "Hey! Why don't you come in the house and dry off your feet, you cops! Quit playing the cop game and come in and git some nice hot coffee!"

The cops were just playing their eternal cop game. That's all it seemed like to the Pranksters.

About April 21, 1965, the Pranksters got a tip that a warrant had been drawn up and the cops were going to raid. Delightful! The cops were really going to play their game right up to their BB gun eyeballs. The Pranksters put up a great sign at the front gate

No Admittance. Five-Day Countdown in Progress

as if they were embarked upon the damnedest, most awfulest dope orgy brain blowout in the history of the world. In fact, they set about making the premises clean. On the third day of the countdown, April 23, 1965, 10:50 p.m., the raid came. Oh God, there was never a better game played by any cops. Here they were, the absolute perfect cop-game cops, the sheriff, seventeen deputies, Federal Agent Wong, eight police dogs, cars, wagons, guns, posses, ropes, walkie-talkies, bullhorns—Cosmo! the whole freaking raid scene—and right up to the end the Pranksters played it as they saw it: namely, as a high farce, an *opéra bouffe*. The cops claimed they caught Kesey trying to flush a batch of marijuana down the toilet. Kesey claimed he was only in there painting flowers on the toilet bowl. The bathroom was already a madhouse collage of photos, clippings, murals, mandalas, every weird thing in the world, like an indoor version of the bus, and the cops crashed in and Agent Wong grabbed Kesey from behind. Kesey was later booked on a charge of resisting arrest, among other charges, to which he said that he had been in the bathroom and some unidentified male came up and embraced him from behind, and so naturally he slugged him. It was a laugh and a half. Kesey's resistance, he said, upended Wong and hurtled him into the bathtub on top of Page Browning, who was taking a bath. Browning was arrested for resisting arrest, too. It was too much.

Even after the raiders had everybody in there, thirteen people,

lined up against the walls, and were searching them for drugs, it
was just the most wacked-out cop game anybody had ever seen
any cops play. One of the raiders reached into Mike Hagen's
pocket, and when he drew his hand out, it held a vial of some
clear liquid, whereupon all the Pranksters started shouting:
"Hey! Play fair! Play fair! Be fair cops! Play hard but play
fair"—and so on. The vial, whatever it was or was supposed to
be, was never heard of again. In a tool box outside, the raiders
found a hypodermic syringe full of some kind of liquid—which
turned out to be Three-in-One Oil for oiling the tape-recorder
mechanisms—and Kesey and twelve others, including Babbs,
Gretch, Hagen, Walker, Mountain Girl, Page, Cassady, and the
Hermit, were booked on many charges, including possession of
marijuana and narcotics paraphernalia (the syringe), resisting arrest and impairing the morals of minors (Mountain Girl and the
Hermit). Even then, the whole thing became not much more
than the cop-and-jailhouse-and-judge-and-lawyer game, with
such high moments as when they all got bailed out and emerged
from the jail in San Mateo and the Hermit's mother appeared.
Hermit, they discovered from the police blotter, was named An-
thony Dean Wells. Nobody had ever asked him what his name
was. Anyway, his mother slapped Kesey across the face with a paperback edition of *One Flew Over the Cuckoo's Nest* and screamed,
"Go back to your cuckoo pad! You should have stayed in the nest
instead of flying over it, you big cuckoo!"

Well, the whole thing was too much. When the cops booked
them, Babbs gave his occupation as "movie producer," and
Mountain Girl said she was a "movie technician." So Babbs
solemnly appeared in the local newspapers as the big movie producer caught in the raid along with the big novelist, Kesey. It was
something. The San Francisco newspapers took a very lively in-
terest in the case and sent people out to interview Kesey within
the Dope Den, and word of the Prankster life style was made
public, however obliquely, for the first time.

The publicity couldn't have been better, at least in terms of the hip-intellectual circles where the Pranksters might hope to have some immediate influence. Accusing somebody of possession of marijuana was like saying "I saw him take a drink." Kesey was referred to as a kind of "hipster Christ," "a modern mystic," after the model of Jack Kerouac and William Burroughs. As all could plainly read in the press, Kesey had gone even further. He had stopped writing. He was now working on a vast experimental movie entitled—the newspapers solemnly reported—*Intrepid Traveler and His Merry Pranksters Leave in Search of a Cool Place.* "Writers," he told a reporter, "are trapped by artificial rules. We are trapped in syntax. We are ruled by an imaginary teacher with a red ball-point pen who will brand us with an A-minus for the slightest infraction of the rules. Even *Cuckoo* seems like an elaborate commercial."

LSD was never mentioned in all this. Kesey came off chiefly as a visionary who had forsaken his riches and his career as a novelist in order to explore new forms of expression. In the California press he graduated from mere literary fame to celebrity. If the purpose of the raid was to stamp out dopeniks—the cop game couldn't have backfired more completely.

After Kesey and the Pranksters got out on bail, the legal wrangling went on interminably—but they all stayed free. Kesey had a team of aggressive, bright young lawyers working on the case, Zonker's brother-in-law Paul Robertson in San Jose, and Pat Hallinan and Brian Rohan from San Francisco. Hallinan was the son of Vincent Hallinan, the lawyer, a famous champion of the underdog. By and by the charges were dropped against everybody but Kesey and Page Browning, and even they ended up with only one charge lodged against them, possession of marijuana. They trooped down to Redwood City, the San Mateo County Seat, fifteen times during the last eight months of 1965, by Rohan's count. It was interminable, but they all stayed free . . .

Yes! And heads, kids, kooks, intellectual tourists of all sorts, started heading for Kesey's in La Honda.

Even Sandy Lehmann-Haupt returned. About a year had

gone by and he was O.K. again and he flew into San Francisco. Kesey and four or five other Pranksters drove to the San Francisco Airport to meet him. As they drove back to La Honda, Sandy cheerfully gave a brief account of what had happened to him in Big Sur before he split like he did.

"—then I started having dream wars ... with somebody," said Sandy. He didn't want to say who.

"Yeah, I know," said Kesey. "With me."

He knew!

And the mysto fogs began to roll in again off the bay ...

NORMAN HARTWEG AND HIS FRIEND EVAN ENGBER DROVE UP to La Honda from Los Angeles with the idea of doing the Tibetan thing for a few weeks and seeing what it was all about. That was pretty funny, the idea of doing the Tibetan thing at Kesey's. Nevertheless, that was Norman's idea. Norman was a 17-year-old playwright from Ann Arbor, Michigan. He was a thin guy, five feet seven, with a thin face and sharp features and a beard. But his nose tilted up slightly, which gave him a boyish look. He was eking out a living by writing a column for the Los Angeles *Free Press,* a weekly, the L.A. counterpart of the *Village Voice,* and working on avant-garde films, and living in a room underneath the dance floor of a discotheque on the Sunset Strip. He had run into Kesey's friend Susan Brustman and then into Kesey himself, and Kesey had invited him up to La Honda to edit The Movie and ... partake of the life ... Somehow Norman got the idea the people at Kesey's were like, you know, monks, novitiates; a lot of meditating with your legs crossed, chanting, eating rice, feeling vibrations, walking softly over the forest floor and thinking big. Why else would they be out in the woods in the middle of nowhere?

So Norman drove up from L.A. with Evan Engber, who was a theater director, occasionally, and, later, a member of Dr. West's Jug Band, and, as a matter of fact, the husband of Yvette

Mimieux the movie actress. They drove up the coastal route, California Route 1, then cut over Route 84 at San Gregorio and on up into the redwood forests; around a bend, and they're at Kesey's. But jesus, somehow it doesn't look very Tibetan. It isn't the hanged man in the tree so much, or the statue of a guy eating it. Hell, there are no flies on the Tibetans. It is more the odd detail here and there. Kesey's mailbox, for example, which is red, white, and blue, the Stars and Stripes. And a big framed sign on top of the house: WE WUZ FRAMED. And the front gate, across the wooden bridge. The gate is made of huge woodcutter's saw blades and has a death mask on it—and a big sign, about 15 feet long, that reads: THE MERRY PRANKSTERS WELCOME THE HELL'S ANGELS. Music is blasting out of some speakers on top of the house, a Beatles record—*Help, I ne-e-e-ed somebody*—

At that moment, that very moment, Engber gets a stabbing pain in his left shoulder.

"I don't know what it is, Norman," he says, "but it's killing me."

They drive on in across the bridge and get out and go into the house looking for Kesey. Brown dogs belly through the flea clouds outside the house, coughing fruit flies. Engber clutches his shoulder. Inside, bright green-and-gold light streams in through the French doors onto the damnedest clutter. There are big pipes hanging down from the rafters in the main room, a whole row of them, like some enormous vertical xylophone. Also dolls, dolls hanging from the rafters, re-assembled dolls, dolls with the heads sticking out of a hip joint, a leg out of the neck joint, arm out of other leg joint, leg out of shoulder joint, and so on, and a Day-Glo navel. Also balloons, also Chianti bottles stuck on the rafters at weird angles somehow, as if they had been in the very process of falling to the floor and suddenly they froze there. And on the floor, on the chairs, on tables, on the couch, toys, and tape recorders, and pieces of tape recorders, and pieces of pieces of tape recorders, and movie equipment, and pieces of pieces of pieces of movie equipment, and tapes and film running all over the place, plaited in among wires and sockets, all of it in great spiral tangles, great celluloid billows, and a big piece of a newspaper headline cut out and stuck up on the wall: HAIL TO ALL EDGES . . .

In the midst of all this, sitting toward the side, is a gangling girl, looks very Scandinavian, idling over a guitar, which she can't play, and she looks up at Norman and says:

"We've all got hangups . . . and we've got to get rid of them."

Yeah . . . yeah . . . I guess that's right. There . . . on the other side here is a little figure with an enormous black beard. The little g-nome looks up at Norman. His eyes narrow and he breaks into a vast inexplicable grin, looking straight at Norman and then Engber, and then he goes scuttling out the door, snuffling and giggling to himself. Yeah . . . yeah . . . I guess that's right, too.

"I don't know what the hell has happened to me," says Engber, clutching his shoulder, "but it's getting worse."

Norman keeps walking back through the house until he hits a bathroom. Only it is a madhouse of a bathroom. The walls, the ceilings, everything, one vast collage, lurid splashes of red and orange, lurid ads and lurid color photos from out of magazines, pieces of plastic, cloth, paper, streaks of Day-Glo paint, and from the ceiling and down one wall a wild diagonal romp of rhinoceroses, like a thousand tiny rhinoceroses chasing each other through Crazy Lurid Land. Over the top part of the mirror over the sink is a small death mask painted in Day-Glo. The mask hangs from a hinge. Norman lifts it up and underneath the mask is a typewritten message pasted on the mirror:

"Now that I've got your attention . . ."

Norman and Engber go out back and head up the path that leads into the woods, to look for Kesey. Up past screaming Day-Glo tree trunks and tents here and there and some kind of weird cave down in a gully with Day-Glo objects glowing in the mouth of it and then into deep green glades under the redwoods with the lime light filtering through—and they keep coming upon weird objects. Suddenly, a whole bed, an old-fashioned iron bedstead, a mattress, a cover, but all glowing with mad stripes and swirls of orange, red, green yellow Day-Glo. Then a crazed toy horse in a tree trunk. Then a telephone—a *telephone*—sitting up on a tree stump, glowing in the greeny deeps with beautiful glowing cords of many colors coming out of it. Then a TV set, only with mad Day-Glo designs painted on the screen. Then into a clearing, a flash of sunlight, and down the slope, here comes Kesey. He looks twice as big as the time Norman saw him in L.A. He has on white Levi's and a white T-shirt. He walks very erect and his huge muscled arms swing loose. The redwoods soar all around.

Norman says, "Hello—"

But Kesey just nods slightly and smiles very faintly as if to say, You said you'd be here and here you are. Kesey looks around and then down the slope toward the tent plateaus and the house and the highway and says:

"We're working on many levels here."

Engber clutches his shoulder and says:

"I don't know what this thing is, Norman, but it's killing me. I've got to go back to L.A."

"Well, O.K., Evan—"

"I'll come back up when I get over it."

Norman kind of knew he wouldn't, and he didn't, but Norman wanted to stick around.

ALL RIGHT, FILM EDITOR, ARTICLE WRITER, PARTICIPANT-Observer, you're here. On with your . . . editing writing observing. But somehow Norman doesn't start cutting film or writing his column. Almost immediately the strange atmosphere of the place starts rolling over him. There is an atmosphere of—how can one describe it?—we are all *on* to something here, or *into* something, but no one is going to put it into words for you. Put it into words—one trouble right away is that he finds it very hard to get into the conversations here in the house in the woods. Everyone is very friendly and most of them are outgoing. But

they are all talking about—how can one describe it?—about . . .
life, things that are happening around there, things they are doing—or about *things* of such an abstract and metaphorical nature
that he can't fasten them, either. Then he realizes that what it really is is that they are interested in none of the common intellectual currency that makes up the conversations of intellectuals in
Hip L.A., the standard topics, books, movies, new political movements—For years he and all his friends have been talking about
nothing but intellectual products, ideas, concoctions, brain candy,
shadows of life, as a substitute for living; yes. They don't even use
the usual intellectual words here—mostly it is just *thing.*

Cassady's *thing* is—christalmighty, Cassady—and it is with
Cassady that he gets the first sense of the daily allegory at Kesey's,
allegorical living, every action a demonstration of a lesson of
life—like Cassady's Gestalt Driving—but that is *your* term . . .
Whenever there is any driving to be done, Cassady does it. That
is Cassady's thing, or his thing on one level. They drive up the
mountain, up to Skylonda, atop Cahill Ridge, for something.
Coming back, down the mountain, Norman is in the back seat,
two or three others are sitting front and back, and Cassady is
driving. They start hauling down the mountain, faster and faster,
the trees snapping by like in some kind of amusement park ride,
only Cassady isn't looking at the road. Or holding onto the
wheel. His right hand is flipping the dial on the radio. One rock
'n' roll number blips out here—*I'm nurding ut noonh er-
lation*—then another one here on the dial—*vronnnh ba-bee
suckoo pon-pon*—all the time Cassady is whamming out the beat
on the steering wheel with the heel of his left hand and the whole
car seems to be shuddering with it—and his head is turned completely around looking Norman squarely in the eye and grinning
as if he is having the most congenial delightful conversation with
him, only Cassady is doing all the talking, an incredible oral fibrillation of words, nutty nostalgia—"a '46 Plymouth, you understand, gear shift like a Dairy Queen pulled up side a '47 Chrysler
jumpy little marshmallow fellow in there had a kickdown gear

was gonna ossify the world, you understand"—all to Norman with the happiest smile in the world—

You crazy fool—the truck—

—at the last possible moment somehow Cassady fishtails the car back onto the inside of the curve and the truck shoots by clean black shot like a great 10-ton highballing tear drop of tar—Cassady still talking, hanging on the steering wheel, pounding and rapping away. Norman terrified; Norman looks at the others to see if—but they're all sitting there throughout the whole maniacal ride as if nothing out of the ordinary has happened at all.

And maybe that's it—the first onset of Ahor paranoia hits—maybe that's it, maybe he has been sucked into some incredible trap by a bunch of dope-taking crazies who are going to toy with him, for what reason I do not—

Back at the house he decides to get into his role of Journalist Reporter Observer. At least he will be doing something and be *outside,* sane, detached. He starts asking about this and that, about Cassady, about Babbs, about the ineffable *things,* about why—

Mountain Girl explodes suddenly.

"Why! Why! Why! Why! Why! Why! Why!" she says, throwing up her hands and shaking her head, with such an air of authority and conviction that he is crushed.

Later Kesey comes in and happens to say in the course of something—"Cassady doesn't have to think any more"—then he walks away. It is as if for some reason he is furnishing Norman with part of the puzzle.

Kesey keeps doing this kind of thing. As if by radar, Kesey materializes at the critical moment, in the cabin, out front, in the backhouse, up in the woods. The crisis may be somebody's personal thing or some group thing—suddenly Kesey pops up like Captain Shotover in Shaw's play *Heartbreak House,* delivers a line—usually something cryptic, allegorical, or merely descriptive, never a pronouncement or a judgment. Half the time he quotes the wisdom of some local sage—Page says, Cassady says,

Babbs says—*Babbs says, if you don't know what the next thing is, all you have to*—and just as suddenly he's gone.

For example—well, it always seems like there's no dissension around here, no arguments, no conflict, in spite of all these different and in some cases weird personalities ricocheting around and rapping and carrying on. Yet that is only an illusion. It is just that they don't have it out with one another. Instead, they take it to Kesey, all of them forever waiting for Kesey, circling around him.

One kid, known as Pancho Pillow, was a ball-breaker freak. He has to break your balls by coming on obnoxious in any way he could dream up, after which you were supposed to reject him, after which he could feel hurt and blame you for . . . *all*. That was his movie. One night Pancho is in the house with a book about Oriental rugs, full of beautiful color plates, and he is rapping on and on about the beautiful rugs—

"—like, man, I mean, these cats were turned on *ten centuries* ago, the whole thing, they had mandalas you never *dreamed* of—right?—look here, man, I want to blow your mind for you, just one time—"

—and he sticks the book under some Prankster's nose—here's a beautiful color picture of an Isfahan rug, glowing reds and oranges and golds and starlike vibrating lines all radiating out from a medallion at the center—

"No thanks, Pancho, I already had some."

"Come on, man! I mean, like, I gotta *share* this thing, I gotta *make* you see it, I can't keep this whole thing to myself! Like, you know, I mean, I want to *share* it with you—you dig?—now you look at this one—"

And so on, shoving the goddamn book at everybody, waiting for somebody to tell him to go fuck himself, at which point he can stalk out, fulfilled.

Feed the hungry bee—but christ, this ball breaker is too much. So now all the Pranksters *endure,* waiting for one thing, waiting for Kesey to turn up. By and by the door opens and it's Kesey.

"Hey man!" Pancho says and rushes up to him. "You gotta look at these things I found! I gotta turn you on to this, man! I mean, I really got to, because it will fucking *blow your mind!*" and he sticks the book in Kesey's face.

Kesey just looks down at the picture of the Isfahan or the Shiraz or the Bakhtiari or whatever it is, as if he is studying it. And then he says, softly, in the Oregon drawl,

"Why should I take your bad trip?"

—without looking up, as if what he is saying has something to do with this diamond medallion here or this border of turtles and palms—

"Bad trip!" Pancho screams. "What do you mean, bad trip!" and he throws the book to the floor, but Kesey is already off into the back of the house. And Pancho knows his whole thing is, in fact, not sharing beauty rugs at all, but simply his bad trip, and *they* all know that's what it's all about, and he *knows* they know it, and the whole game is over and so long, Pancho Pillow.

AND YET IT BEGAN TO SEEM TO NORMAN THAT EVEN PANCHO was further into the group thing than he was. He felt useless. He never got to edit the movie. Kesey and Babbs would just say do some cutting. But he wanted to see the whole film first, a whole run-through, so he could see where it was going. It was the same with the group. He wanted to run the whole group back through his personal editing machine and see what the whole picture looked like and what the goal was. All the while it seemed like they were probing him, probing him, probing him for weaknesses. Bradley, of all people, blew up at him one morning, started calling him everything he could think of, apparently trying to stir him up. Norman was reading a Sanskrit textbook at the time, trying to learn the alphabet. He figured he might as well do that, since he wasn't doing anything else. He was also smoking a cigarette. Bradley starts in.

"Every time you read a book or smoke a cigarette," he yells, "you're *hitting me*. Look at Pancho. Pancho's working. Pancho is writing poetry all the time, and every day he brings me a poem—"

—which is ridiculous, Pancho's poems are *so* bad. In fact, it is so ridiculous Bradley breaks into a smile over it. Nevertheless, the point has been made. Which is that Norman is lazy, "personal." Reading is something that just gives pleasure to the reader. It is not for the group. Also smoking—a thing that begets nothing but itself. So he is telling Norman that he is lazy and not contributing. *Which is true. He is right.* But he wants to start a fight over it or something. This amuses Norman and he laughs at Bradley—*Bradley*—and yet even though it is only Bradley, it seems like an indication of how the rest feel. Otherwise Bradley probably never would have said anything. Norman becomes quieter and quieter, like a clam. And it seemed as if they laughed at him—

"Not *at* you—*with* you," Kesey kept telling him, trying to josh him out of all his hangups and inferiorities.

But the only thing that really helped was having Paul Foster turn up.

Foster was a tall, curly-headed guy in his late twenties with a terrible stutter. He was a mathematician and had been working in Palo Alto as a computer programmer, making a lot of money, apparently. Then he started hanging out with some musicians and they turned him on to a few . . . mind-expanders, and now Foster's life seemed to alternate between stretches of good straight computer programming, during which he wore a necktie and an iridescent teal-green suit of Zirconpolyesterethylene and was a formidable fellow in the straight world, and stretches of life with . . . Speed, the Great God Rotor, during which he wore his Importancy Coat. This was a jacket he had turned into a collage. It had layers and layers of ribbons and slogan buttons and reflectors and Cracker Jack favors all over it, piled up and flapping in the breeze until it looked like a lunatic billowsleeve coat from out of the court of Louis XV. He moved into the tree. Sandy had built

a house in the tree, a platform with a tent on it. Paul built one under it; O.K., a duplex tree house. Paul Foster came in with just an
enormous amount of stuff, all this stuff. He brought it all in and
he set up housekeeping in the tree. He put a window up in the
tree, and a gate, and bookshelves. He had strange books. An encyclopedia, only it was an 1893 encyclopedia, and books on the
strangest languages, Tagalog, Urdu, and apparently he knew
something about all these languages . . . and more and more *stuff*.
He had a huge sack of googaws that he would carry around, of the
weirdest stuff, bits of glittering glass and tin and transistor-radio
shells, just the shells, and nails and screws and tops and tubes, and
inside his sack of weird junk was a little sack that was a miniature
of the big sack and contained *tiny* weird junk . . . and you got the
idea that somehow, somewhere in there was a *very* tiny little sack
that contained *very* tiny weird junk, and that it went on that way
into infinity . . . He also had a lot of pens, some of them felt-nib
pens with colors, and he sat up in the tree house while the old restless Roto-rooter, the good god Speed, scoured puns, puns, puns,
puns, puns from out of the walls of his skull and he fashioned
signs like one he put at the entrance of the place, where the driveway turned in to the bridge from Route 84, a sign reading: "No
Left Turn Unstoned." Then people would come and he'd entertain them up in his tree house, and at night you would see it lit up
like some mad thing, gleaming with Dali-Day-Glo swoops, and
he would be up there drawing, drawing, drawing, drawing, or
working on a huge mad scrapbook he had . . .

Norman and Paul Foster had a lot in common. They were
both fairly good artists, they both had a certain fund of erudition
erudition erudition. Foster, with his terrible stutter, valued privacy in the midst of it all, just as Norman did. Of course, Foster
was proving himself a Prankster far faster than Norman was. It
was a strange thing about that. There were no rules. There was
no official period of probation, and no vote on is he or isn't he one
of us, no blackballing, no tap on the shoulders. And yet there was
a period of proving yourself, and everyone knew it was going on

and no one ever said a word about it. In any case, Norman could talk to Foster, and that made all the difference. He didn't feel so desperately lonely any more. Also he suddenly saw that it wasn't just him—the Pranksters probed everybody, to make them bring their hangups out front to the point where they could act totally out front, live in the moment, spontaneously, and if needling was what it took to bring you that far—

Foster is coming on, in the house, with these wild logical conundrums he had, only stuttering something awful:

—Sup-puh-puh-puh-*pose* that that everything you per-per-per-perceive is only a . . ."—some long involved thing, and Mountain Girl breaks in:

—B-b-b-b-b-but, P-P-P-P-P-Paul, I don't git the p-p-p-p-p-point about all this per-per-per-per-per-per-ception. I try to git it, b-b-b-b-b-b-but all I git is the w-w-w-w-w-w-words. How 'bout goin' over it ag-gih-gih-gih-gih-gih-gih-gih-gih-gih-gih-gih-gih -gih-*gihn!*"

Foster can't believe this performance. He stands there frozen with his eyes bugging out, bugging out, bugging out, bugging out bigger and bigger until he explodes:

"Is that supposed to be funny! You've got a worse hangup than stuttering, Mountain Girl! You've got a fat mouth and you don't know what to use it for! Ugly—that's your trip, the ugly trip! Well, all I know is—"

"Yuh see!" Mountain Girl says. She is grinning, triumphant practically laughing and clapping her hands, she is so pleased with the results. "When you git mad, you don't stutter!"

Foster freezes again. He stares at her. Then he wheels around and walks out the door without saying another word.

The funny part is, she's right.

WHAT WAS IT? . . . IT WAS LIKE . . . WELL, YES! *GROUP THERAPY,* like a marathon encounter in group therapy, in which everybody is together for days, probing everybody's weaknesses, bringing everything out front. Only this was group therapy not for the middle-aged and fucked-up but for the Young! and Immune!—as if they were not patching up wrecks but tooling up the living for some incredible breakthrough, *beyond* catastrophe. Since time was, the serious concerns of man have always been fights against catastrophe, against sickness, war, poverty, enslavement, always the horsemen of the Apocalypse riding. But what to do in that scary void *beyond catastrophe,* where all, supposedly, will be possible—and Norman happens upon another of those strange, prophetic books on Kesey's shelf, Arthur Clarke's *Childhood's End,* in which . . . the Total Breakthrough generation is born on Earth and as mere infants they show powers of mind far beyond their parents' and they go off into a colony by themselves, not as individuals, however, but as one great colonial being, in the biological sense of the colonial animal, until, at last, the Earth, its mission complete, convulses, starts coming apart, and they, the children: "Something's starting to happen. The stars are becoming dimmer. It's as if a great cloud is coming up, very swiftly, all over over all the sky. But it isn't really a cloud. It seems to have some sort of structure—I can glimpse a hazy network of lines and bands that keep changing their position. It's almost as if the stars are tangled in a ghostly spider's web. The whole network is beginning to glow, to pulse with light, exactly as if it were alive . . . There's a great burning column, like a tree of fire, reaching above the western horizon. It's a long way off right around the world. I know where it springs from: *they're* on their way at last, to become part of the Overmind. Their probation is ended: they're leaving the last remnants of matter behind . . . The whole landscape is lit up—it's brighter than day—reds and golds and greens are chasing each other across the sky—oh, it's beyond words, it doesn't seem fair that I'm the only one to see it—I never thought such colors—"

In short, zonked out of their ever-loving gourds, man, and heading out toward . . . Edge City, absolutely, and we're truly synched tonight.

—but no water spouts of Académie Française cherubim and water babies here, and no reverent toga-linen-flapping Gautama Buddha Orientals breathing out the spent Roquefort breath of spiritual detachment. Instead, somehow they're going to try it right down the main highway, eight lanes wide, heron-neck arc lamps rising up as far as the eye can see, and they will broadcast on all frequencies, waving American flags, turning up the Day-Glo and the neon of 1960s electro-pastel America, wired up and amplified, 327,000 horsepower, a fantasy bus in a science-fiction movie, welcoming all on board, no matter how unbelievably Truck Stop Low Rent or raunchy—

chapter XIII

The Hell's Angels

I DOUBT IF ANY OF THE PRANKSTERS TRULY UNDERSTOOD Mountain Girl, except for Kesey. Most of the time she was so 100 percent out front, coming on loud and clear and candid as a Mack truck, it never occurred to anybody that a whole side of her was hidden. Except for Kesey, as I say. Sometimes Kesey and Mountain Girl would disappear into the backhouse and lie on mattresses and just talk, Kesey rapping on about how he felt about all sorts of things, life, fate, Now—while Mountain Girl—one thought of hers making sorties through the soft word flow coming from Kesey on the mattress there—yes, well, and she told Kesey as frankly as she could about the last four or five years of her life. Kesey didn't understand completely. Namely, she was sometimes lonely as hell.

Lonely? Why, for chrissake, Mountain Girl came swinging into every situation like on a vine, like Sheena, Queen of the Jungle. She was high in the Prankster hierarchy already. Nobody was closer to Kesey than Mountain Girl, not even Faye, it often seemed. But there it was: Kesey ... Kesey was essential to Mountain Girl's whole life with the Pranksters. Without him, and Hassler, a weird loneliness could take over ... Hassler was the only other person she could talk to. Without Hassler— But it can be tense underneath in a commune, beautiful on one level, but you have to be willing to force it a little to keep it that way.

It is really funny. This afternoon the sprinklers are ratcheting away all sprinkly and starchy on the lawns of Poughkeepsie. In August the sun causes such brown spots where the trees don't shade it, you understand. Well, freak that. The solution, Doctor, happens to be named Kesey. This sound now, Doctor, rising above the ratcheting, would probably throw your poor little thready heart into fibrillation. It's like a locomotive coming through the redwood trees around the bends down Route 84 from Skylonda. The Hell's Angels in running formation, to be exact, scores of the monsters, on Harley-Davidson 74s. Miss Carolyn Adams of Poughkeepsie, N.Y., is about to look this primordial menace in the face and bark bullshit commands at the Hell's Angels, which they obey, since the sunspots exploding in their eyes bedazzle the monsters. The energy flows from Kesey, Doctor, and there is not one goddamn thing to git your little heart scared of.

KESEY MET THE HELL'S ANGELS ONE AFTERNOON IN SAN Francisco through Hunter Thompson, who was writing a book about them. It turned out to be a remarkable book, as a matter of fact, called *Hell's Angels, a Strange and Terrible Saga*. Anyway, Kesey and Thompson were having a few beers and Thompson said he had to go over to a garage called the Box Shop to see a few of the Angels, and Kesey went along. A Hell's Angel named Frenchy and four or five others were over there working on their motorcycles and they took to Kesey right away. Kesey was a stud who was just as tough as they were. He had just been busted for marijuana, which certified him as Good People in the Angels' eyes. They told him you can't trust a man who hasn't done time, and Kesey was on the way to doing time, in any case. Kesey said later that the marijuana bust impressed them but they couldn't have cared less that he was a novelist. But they knew about that, too, and here was a big name who was friendly and interested in them, even though he wasn't a queer or a reporter or any of those other creep suck-ups who were coming around that summer.

And a great many were coming around in the summer of 1965. The summer of 1965 had made the Hell's Angels infamous celebrities in California. Their reputation was at its absolutely most notorious all-time highest. A series of incidents—followed by an amazing series of newspaper and magazine articles, *Life* and the *Saturday Evening Post* among them—had the people of the Far West looking to each weekend in the Angels' life as an invasion by baby-raping Huns. Intellectuals around San Francisco, particularly at Berkeley, at the University of California, were beginning to romanticize about the Angels in terms of "alienation" and "a generation in revolt," that kind of thing. People were beginning to get in touch with Thompson to see if he couldn't arrange for them to meet the Angels—not the whole bunch, Hunter, maybe one or two at a time. Well, Kesey didn't need any one or two at a time. He and the boys took a few tokes on a joint, and the Hell's Angels were on the bus.

The next thing the citizens of La Honda knew, there was a huge sign at the Kesey place—15 feet long, three feet high, in red white and blue.

THE MERRY PRANKSTERS
WELCOME THE HELL'S ANGELS

Saturday, August 7, 1965, was a bright clear radiant limelit summer day amid God's handiwork in La Honda, California. The citizens were getting ready for the day by nailing shut their doors. The cops were getting ready by revving up a squad of ten patrol cars with flashing lights and ammunition. The Pranksters were getting ready by getting bombed. They were down there in the greeny gorge, in the cabin and around it, under the red-woods, getting bombed out of their gourds. They had some good heavy surges of God-given adrenaline going for them, too. No-body ever came right out front and said it, but this happened to be the real-life Hell's Angels coming, about forty of them, on a full-fledged Angels' "run," the sort of outing on which the An-gels did their thing, their whole freaking thing, *en* mangy raunchy head-breaking fire-pissing rough-goddamn-housing *masse*. The Pranksters had a lot of company for the occasion. It was practically like an audience, all waiting for the stars to ap-pear. A lot of the old Perry Lane crowd was there, Vic Lovell, Ed McClanahan, and the others. Allen Ginsberg was there and so was Richard Alpert and a lot of San Francisco and Berkeley in-tellectuals. *Tachycardia,* you all—but Kesey was calm and even laughing a little, looking strong as an ox in his buckskin shirt, the Mountain Man, and he made it all seem right and inevitable, an inevitable part of the flow and right now in this moment. Hell, if the straight world of San Mateo County, California, had decided to declare them all outlaws over an innocuous thing like mari-juana, then they could freaking well go with the flow and show them what the saga called Outlaw was really like. The Angels brought a lot of things into synch. Outlaws, by definition, were people who had moved off of dead center and were out in some kind of Edge City. The beauty of it was, the Angels had done it like the Pranksters, by choice. They had become outlaws first— to *explore,* muvva—and then got busted for it. The Angels' trip was the motorcycle and the Pranksters' was LSD, but both were in an incredible entry into an orgasmic moment, *now,* and within forty-eight hours the Angels would be taking acid on board, too. The Pranksters would be taking on . . . Ahor, the ancient horror, the middle-class boy fear of Hell's Angels. *Hell's Angels,* in the dirty flesh, and if they could bring that dark deep-down thing into their orbit—

Kesey! What in the freaking—tachycardia, you all . . .

Bob Dylan's voice is raunching and rheuming in the old jack-legged chants in huge volume from out the speakers up in the redwood tops up on the dirt cliff across the highway—*He-e-e-ey Mis-ter Tam-bou-rine Man*—as part of Sandy Lehmann-Haupt's Non-Station KLSD program, the indomitable disco-freak-jockey Lord Byron Styrofoam himself, Sandy, broadcasting over a microphone in a cabin and spinning them for you—Cassady revved up so tight it's like mechanical speed man sprocket—Mountain Girl ready—*Hey, Kesey!*—Hermit grin—Page ablaze—men, women, children, painted and in costume—ricochet around the limelit dell—*Arggggggghhhhh*—about 3 P.M. they started hearing it.

It was like a locomotive about ten miles away. It was the Hell's Angels in "running formation" coming over the mountain on Harley-Davidson 74s. The Angels were up there somewhere weaving down the curves on Route 84, gearing down—*thraggggggggggh*—and winding up, and the locomotive sound got louder and louder until you couldn't hear yourself talk any more or Bob Dylan rheumy and—*thraaaaaaaggggghhh*—here they came around the last curve, the Hell's Angels, with the bikes, the beards, the long hair, the sleeveless denim jackets with the death's head insignia and all the rest, looking their most royal rotten, and then one by one they came barreling in over the wooden bridge up to the front of the house, skidding to a stop in explosions of dust, and it was like a movie or something—each one of the out-laws bouncing and gunning across the bridge with his arms spread out in a tough curve to the handlebars and then skidding to a stop, one after another after another.

The Angels, for their part, didn't know what to expect. No-body had ever invited them anywhere before, at least not as a gang. They weren't on many people's invitation lists. They fig-

ured they would see what was there and what it was all about, and
they would probably get in a hell of a fight before it was all over,
and heads would break, but that was about par for the course anyway. The Angels always came into alien situations black and
wary, sniffing out the adversary, but that didn't even register at
this place. So many people were already so high, on something, it
practically dissolved you on the spot. The Pranksters had what
looked like about a million doses of the Angels' favorite
drug—beer—and LSD for all who wanted to try it. The beer
made the Angels very happy and the LSD made them strangely
peaceful and sometimes catatonic, in contrast to the Pranksters
and other intellectuals around, who soared on the stuff.

June the Goon gave a Hell's Angel named Freewheeling
Frank some LSD, which he thought was some kind of souped-
up speed or something—and he had the most wondrous experience of his life. By nightfall he had climbed a redwood and was
nestled up against a loudspeaker in a tree grooving off the sounds
and vibrations of Bob Dylan singing "The Subterranean Home-
sick Blues."

Pete, the drag racer, from the San Francisco Hell's Angels,
grinned and rummaged through a beer tub and said, "Man, this
is nothing but a goddamn wonderful scene. We didn't know
what to expect when we came, but it turned out just fine. This
time it's all ha-ha, not thump-thump." Soon the gorge was booming with the Angels' distinctive good-time lots-a-beer belly
laugh, which goes: Haw!—Haw!—Haw!—Haw!—Haw!—
Haw!

Sandy Lehmann-Haupt, Lord Byron Styrofoam, had hold of
the microphone and his disco-freak-jockey rapping blared out of
the redwoods and back across the highway: "This is Non-Station
KLSD, 800 micrograms in your head, the station designed to
blow your mind and undo your bind, from up here atop the redwoods on Venus!" Then he went into a long talking blues song
about the Hell's Angels, about fifty stanzas worth, some of it ob-
scure acid talk, some of it wild legends, about squashing turtles

on the highway, nutty stuff like that, and every stanza ending with the refrain:

> *Oh, but it's great to be an Angel,*
> *And be dirty all the time!*

What the hell—here was some wild-looking kid with the temerity to broadcast out over the highways of California that Angels were dirty all the time—but how the hell could you resist, it was too freaking madly manic—and pretty soon the Angels and everybody else were joining in the chorus:

> *Oh, but it's great to be an Angel,*
> *And be dirty all the time!*

Then Allen Ginsberg was in front of the microphone with finger cymbals on each hand, dancing around with a beard down to his belly and chanting Hindu chants into the microphone booming out over California, U.S.A., *Hare krishna hare krishna hare krishna hare krishna*—what the mollyfock is hairy krishna—who is this hairy freak—but you can't help yourself, you got to groove with this cat in spite of yourself. Ginsberg really bowled the Angels over. He was a lot of things the Angels hated, a Jew, an intellectual, a New Yorker, but he was too much, the greatest straightest unstraight guy they ever met.

> *And be dirty all the time!*

The filthy kooks—by nightfall the cops were lined up along the highway, car after car, just across the creek, outside the gate, wondering what the fock. The scene was really getting weird. The Pranksters had everything in their electronic arsenal going, rock 'n' roll blazing through the treetops, light projections streaming through the gorge, Station KLSD blazing and screaming over the cops' heads, people in Day-Glo regalia blazing and lurching in the gloom, the Angels going *Haw—Haw—Haw—Haw,* Cassady down to just his hell of a build, nothing else, just his hell of a build, jerking his arms out and sprocketing around under a spotlight on the porch of the log manse, flailing a beer bottle around in one hand and shaking his other one at the cops:

"You sneaky motherfuckers! What the fuck's wrong with you! Come on over here and see what you get . . . goddamn your shit-filled souls anyway!"—laughing and jerking and sprocket-ing—"Don't fuck with me, you sons of shit-lovers. Come on over. You'll get every fucking thing you deserve."

The hell of it, men, is here is a huge obscene clot of degrada-tion, depradation and derogation proceeding loose and crazed on the hoof before our very eyes, complete with the very Hell's An-gels, and there is nothing we can do but contain it. Technically, they might have been able to move in on the grounds of Cassady's exposing himself or something of the sort, but no real laws were being broken, except every law of God and man—but sheer con-tainment was looking like the best policy. Moving in on those crazies even with ten carloads of armed cops for a misdemeanor like lewd display—the explosion was too grotesque to think of. And the cops' turret lights revolved and splashed against the dirt cliff in a red strobe light effect and their car-to-headquarters ra-dios were wide open and cracking out with sulphurous 220-volt electric thorn baritones and staticky sibilants—*He-e-e-ey Mis-ter Tam-bou-rine Man*—just to render the La Honda gorge totally delirious.

Meanwhile, the Angels were discovering the goddamnedest thing. Usually, most places they headed into on their runs, they tested people's cool. What are *you* looking at, mother. As soon as the shock or naked terror registered, they would be happy. Or if there was no shock and terror but instead somebody tried some brave little shove back, then it was time to break heads and tear everybody a new asshole. But these mollyfocking Pranksters were test-proof. The Angels didn't know what permissive was until they got to Kesey's. *Go with the flow!* The biggest baddest toughest most awfulest-looking Hell's Angel of them all was a big monster named Tiny. The second biggest baddest toughest most-awfulest-looking Hell's Angel was a big raw-boned guy named Buzzard, dark-looking, with all this dark hair and a beard, all shaggy and matted and his nose came out like a beak and his Adam's apple hung down about a foot, and he was just like an enormous buzzard. Tiny and Buzzard had a thing of coming up to each other when they were around non-Angels and sticking out their tongues and then licking each other's tongues, a big sloppy lap it up, just to shake up the squares, it really jolted them—so they came up right in front of this tall broad of Kesey's, Mountain Girl, and la-a-a-a-a-ap—and they couldn't believe it. She just looked right at them and grinned and exploded sunballs out of her eyes and started laughing at them, *Haw—Haw—Haw,* as if to say in plain language: What a bullshit thing. It was freaking incredible. Then some of them passed a joint around and they passed it to Mountain Girl and she boomed out:

"Hell, no! What the hell you doing putting your dirty mouth on this clean joint for! This is a clean joint and you're putting your dirty mouths on it!" Nobody in living memory had ever refused a toke from a joint passed by Angels, at least not on grounds of sanitation, except this crazy girl who was just bullshitting them blind, and they loved it.

It even got to the point where Mountain Girl saw Tiny heading into the mad bathroom with a couple of beer cans like he is going to hole up in there and drink a couple of cans in peace, but this is the bathroom all the girls around here are using, and Mountain Girl yells out to Sonny Barger, the maximum leader of the Hell's Angels, "Hey, Sonny! Tell this big piece of trash to stay out of our clean bathroom!"—in a bullshit tone, of course—and Sonny picks it up, "Yeah, you big piece of trash! Stay out of the clean bathroom! They don't want you in there!"—and Tiny slinks out the door, outside, in a bullshit slink, but he does it—

And that's it! It's happening. The Hell's Angels are in our movie, we've got 'em in. Mountain Girl and a lot of the Pranksters had hit on the perfect combination with the Angels. They were friendly toward them, maybe friendlier than anybody had been in their lives, but they weren't craven about it, and they took no shit. It was the perfect combination, but the Pranksters didn't even have to think of it as a combination. They just did their thing and that was the way it worked out. All these principles they had been working on and talking about in the isolation of La Honda—they freaking well *worked*.

Go with the flow—and what a flow—these cats, these Pranksters—at big routs like this the Angels often had a second feature going entitled *Who Gets Fucked?*—and it hadn't even gotten to that before some blonde from out of town, one of the guests from way out there, just one nice soft honey hormone squash, she made it clear to three Angels that she was ready to go, so they all trooped out to the backhouse and they had a happy round out there. Pretty soon all the Angels knew about the "new mamma" out in the backhouse and a lot of them piled in there, hooking down beers, laughing, taking their turns, making various critiques. The girl had her red and white dress pushed up around her chest, and two or three would be on her at once, between her legs, sitting on her face in the sick ochre light of the shack with much lapping and leering and bubbling and gulping through furzes of pubic hair while sweat and semen glistened on the highlights of her belly and thighs and she twitched and moaned, not in protest, however, in a kind of drunken bout of God knew what and men with no pants on were standing around, cheering, chiding, waiting for their turn, or their second turn, or the third until she had been fenestrated in various places at least fifty times. Some of the Angels went out and got her ex-husband. He was weaving and veering around, bombed, they led him in there under glare and leer and lust musk suffocate the rut hut they told him to go to it. All silent—shit, this is going too far—but the girl rises up in a blear and asks him to kiss her, which he does, glistening secretions, then he lurches and mounts her and slides it in, and the Angels cheer Haw Haw—

—but that is her movie, it truly is, and we have gone with the flow.

So much beer—which is like an exotic binge for the Pranksters, beer. Mountain Girl and Kesey are up in the limelit bower and the full moon comes down through the treetop silhouettes. They are just rapping in the moonlight, and then Sandy wanders on up there and sits with them, high on acid, and he looks down and the floor of the forest is rippling with moonlight, the ground shimmers and rolls like a stream in the magic bower and they just sit there—a *buzzard!* Buzzard is wandering up the slope toward them and there in the moonlight in the dark in the magic bower he . . . *is* a buzzard, the biggest ever made, the beak, the deathly black, the dopply glottal neck, the shelled back and dangling wings, stringy nodule legs—Kaaawwwwwww!—and Kesey jumps up and starts throwing his arms up at him, like the way you would scare away a buzzard, and says,

"Aaaaagh! a buzzard! Hey! Get away, you're a buzzard! Get this buzzard out of here!"

It's a bullshit gesture, of course—and Buzzard laughs—*Haw! Haw! Haw!*—it is not real, but it is . . . *real,* real buzzard, you can see the whole thing with two minds—Kaw Kaw Kaaawwwww—and Buzzard jumps and flaps his arms—and the whole . . . connection, the *synch,* between the name, the man, the bird, flows together right there, and it doesn't matter whether he is buzzard or man because it has all come together, and they all see it . . .

They all see so much. Buzzard goes, and Sandy goes, and Kesey and Mountain Girl are in the moonlight ripply bower. By and by—where?—Kesey and Mountain Girl—and so much flows together from the lights and the delirium and the staticky sibilants down below, so much is clear, so much flows in rightness, that night, under the full moon, up above the flails and bellows down below—

.   .   .

THE HELL'S ANGELS PARTY WENT ON FOR TWO DAYS AND THE
cops never moved in. Everybody, Angels and Pranksters, had a
righteous time and no heads were broken. There had been one
gang-bang, but the girl was a volunteer. It was her movie. In fact,
for the next six or seven weeks, it was one long party with the
Angels. The news spread around intellectual-hip circles in the
San Francisco-Berkeley area like a legend. In these circles, anyway, it once and for all put Kesey and the Pranksters up above
the category of just another weirdo intellectual group. They had
broken through the worst hangup that intellectuals know—the
real-life hangup. Intellectuals were always hung up with the feeling that they weren't coming to grips with real life. Real life
belonged to all those funky spades and prize fighters and bull-
fighters and dock workers and grape pickers and wetbacks. *Nos-
talgie de la boue.* Well, the Hell's Angels were real life. It didn't
get any realer than that, and Kesey had pulled it off. People from
San Francisco and Berkeley started coming by La Honda more
than ever. It was practically like an intellectual tourist attraction.
Kesey would talk about the Angels.

"I asked Sonny Barger how he picks new members, new Angels, and he told me, 'We don't pick 'em. We *rec*ognize 'em.' "

And everybody grokked over that.

Likely as not, people would find Hell's Angels on the place.
The Angels were adding LSD to the already elaborate list of
highs and lows they liked, beer, wine, marijuana, benzedrine,
Seconal, Amytal, Nembutal, Tuinal. Some of them had terrible
bummers—bummer was the Angels' term for a bad trip on a
motorcycle and very quickly it became the hip world's term for a
bad trip on LSD. The only bad moment at Kesey's came one day
when an Angel went berserk during the first rush of the drug
and tried to strangle his old lady on Kesey's front steps. But he
was too wasted at that point to really do much.

So it was wonderful and marvelous, an unholy alliance, the
Merry Pranksters and the Hell's Angels, and all hours of the day
or night you could hear the Hell's Angels gearing and winding

down Route 84 to Kesey's, and the people of La Honda felt like the plague had come, and wasn't there anything that could be done. More than one of the Pranksters had his reservations, too. The Angels were like a time bomb. So far, so good—one day the Angels even swept and cleaned up the place—but they were capable of busting loose into carnage at any moment. It brought the adrenaline into your throat. The potential was there, too, because if the truth were known, there were just a few of the Pranksters who could really talk to the Angels—chiefly Kesey and Mountain Girl. Mainly it was Kesey. Kesey was the magnet and the strength, the man in both worlds. The Angels respected him and they weren't about to screw him around. He was one of the coolest guys they had ever come across. One day, finally, Kesey's cool came to the test with the Angels and it was a strange moment.

Kesey and the Pranksters and the Angels had taken to going out to the backhouse and sitting in a big circle and doing the Prankster thing, a lot of rapping back and forth and singing, high on grass, and you never knew where it was going to go. Usually it went great. The Angels took to the Prankster thing right away. They seemed to have an immediate intuitive grasp of where it was going, and one time Kesey started playing a regular guitar and Babbs started playing a four-string amplified guitar and Kesey got into a song, off the top of his head, about "the vibrations," a bluesy song, and the Angels joined in, and it got downright religious in there for a while, with everybody singing, "Oh, the vi-bra-tions . . . Oh, the vi-bra-tions . . ."

And then Kesey and a few of the Pranksters and a lot of the Angels, including Sonny Barger of the Oakland Chapter, the maximum leader of all the Angels, were sitting around in the backhouse passing around joints and rapping. The subject was "people who are bullshit."

There are certain people who are bullshit and you can always recognize them, Kesey was saying, and the Angels were nodding yeah, that certainly is right.

"Now you take—," said Kesey, mentioning one of the Angels who was not present. "He's a bullshit person."

A bullshit person—and man—

"Listen, Kesey," says Barger, 100 percent Hell's Angel, "—is an Angel, and nobody—*nobody*—calls an Angel a bullshit person."

—the freaking gauntlet is down. It's like forever and every eye in the place pins on Kesey's face and you can hear the blood squirt in your veins. But Kesey doesn't even blink and his voice doesn't even change one half tone, just the old Oregon drawl:

"But I *know* him, Sonny. If I didn't *know* him, I wouldn't call him a bullshit person."

Yeah—we-e-e-elll—everybody, Angels and Pranksters— well—Kesey *knows* him—there is nothing to do but grok over this statement, and everybody sits there, still, trying to grok over it, and after a second, the moment where heads get broken and fire gets pissed is over—*We-e-ell, ye-ah*—

Two or three days later it occurs to some of the Pranksters that they *still* don't know what the hell Kesey meant when he said that. He *knows* the guy. It doesn't make any sense. It's a concept with no bottom to it—but so what! At the moment he said it, it was the one perfect thing he could have said. Kesey was so totally into the moment, he could come up with it, he could break up that old historic push me, shove you, yeah-sez-who sequence and in an instant the moment, that badass moment, was over.

THE PRANKSTERS GOT PRETTY CLOSE TO SEVERAL OF THE AN- gels as individuals. Particularly Gut and Freewheeling Frank and Terry the Tramp. Every now and then somebody would take one or another of the Angels up into the tree house and give them a real initiation into psychedelics. They had a huge supply of DMT. As somebody once put it, LSD is a long strange journey; DMT is like being shot out of a cannon. There in the tree house, amid the winking googaws, they would give the Angels DMT, and Mountain Girl saw some of them, like Freewheeling Frank, after they came down. They would walk around in no particular direction, listing slightly, the eyes bugged wide open, glazed.

"They were as naked as an Angel is ever gonna git," she told Kesey.

chapter

XIV

A Miracle in Seven Days

Oh, the vi-bra-tions . . .
Oh, the Unitarians . . .
Apostate seminarians . . .
Grok the groovy
Pranksters and Hell's Angels . . .
Whose Angels?—

Why the consternation?
Arise ye antediluvians,
Groove on
The Pranksters and Hell's Angels . . .
Noah's destination
Is where it's at:
Now showing at the Mount Ararat,
Apis the Bull in *Après le déluge,*
Groovy movie with a thousand castoffs:

Whose Angels?—
Hell's Angels . . .
Dear Lord, prepare to blast off
Into the Angel blue.
Oh, the vi-bra-tions . . .

Among those who began to wonder about the mysteries of La
   Honda
Were some Unitarian ministers known as the Young Turks;
Bob Kimball, Dick Weston and Paul Sawyer said freak our
   cerebral cloisters and
Emerge! See how the alleged grass-smoking Kesey's magic
   works.
The Young Turks saw Unitarians becoming ghostly
   seminarians,
Desiccated Kantians cut off from Early Christianity.
Oh, a century ago we were the vangard, routing the redneck
   blackguards
Of Fundamentalism—and today?—the Youth *yawn* at our
   inanity.

Oh, the vi-bra-tions . . .
Oh, the Unitarians . . .
Apostate seminarians . . .
Grok the groovy
Pranksters and Hell's Angels . . .
Whose Angels?—

Sawyer found our Day-Glo heroes on the beach at Pescadero
One sunny afternoon with Allen Ginsberg in his finest bearded
   form.
The scene was charged with energy, yet there was a weird
   serenity

Even when the Hell's Angels pulled in, *rank* but most
   righteously warm.

Now, Sawyer had his teenage daughter along and she feared
   something might . . . *go wrong.*
When Kesey said, *On the bus!* she said, "Daddy, I . . . don't want
   to go."
So his daughter stayed behind, but Sawyer was determined to
   find
The secret of this vibrant communion: Angel Black & Prankster
   Day-Glo.

> Oh, the vi-bra-tions . . .
> Oh, the Unitarians . . .
> Apostate seminarians . . .
> Grok the groovy
> Pranksters and Hell's Angels . . .
> *Whose Angels?*—

Onto the bus! and it was so fine, with Angels hooking down
   great jugs of wine
And grooving on the sunlit ocean like euphoric Nature freaks,
Passing joints and Haw!—Haw!—Hawing! but coursing
   through their raucous bawling—
A precognitive Early Churchly Gnostic note: *Ecstatic Peace!*
Kesey knows precisely what he's about! No motorcycle beatnik
   rout
But a trip more vital than all the Kantian prattle in the world.
He has reached the unreachable! Taught and *learned from* the
   unteachable!
The Young Turks owed it to the Church to give the Prankster
   trip a whirl.

> Oh, the vi-bra-tions . . .
> Oh, the Unitarians . . .

Apostate seminarians . . .
Grok the groovy
Pranksters and Hell's Angels . . .
Whose Angels?—

Why the consternation?
Arise ye antediluvians,
Groove on
The Pranksters and Hell's Angels . . .
Noah's destination
Is where it's at:
Now showing at the Mount Ararat,
Apis the Bull in *Après le déluge,*
Groovy movie with a thousand castoffs:
Whose Angels?—
Hell's Angels . . .
Dear Lord, prepare to blast off
Into the Angel blue.
Oh, the vi-bra-tions . . .

So Kesey was invited to come take part in the annual California Unitarian Church conference at Asilomar, beautiful state
park by the sea in Monterey. The theme this year was: "Shaking
the Foundations."

The fact that Kesey had lately been arrested on a narcotics
charge couldn't have mattered less to the Unitarians assembled
on the greeny glades of Asilomar by the sea, not even the older
ones. The Unitarians had a long tradition of liberalism in such
matters and, in fact, were in the vanguard of the civil-rights
movement in California. There was a good deal of civil disobedi-
ence and scrapes with the police in that fight; yes, sir. But *this* . . .
. . . *this* . . . The Unitarians were assembled there in Intellectual Sport Shirt multitudes—intellectuals Roughing-it, you understand, in short-sleeved sport shirts and casual Stretcheez
trousers with roomy bottoms and waists up about the rib cage,

drawing, casually, on pipes. And here came Kesey. But not alone, it so happened. He arrived on the bus, in a blur of Day-Glo swirls, with Pranksters in costume flapping out of every portal. Among the middle-aged Unitarians, ministers and laymen, tamping down their pipes for a nice relaxed Sport Shirt week, there was consternation written on practically every face as they watched the bizarre vehicle pitching and rolling into the camp grounds. Things were . . . up tight from the moment they got there.

I guess this is kind of rubbing their noses in it, thought Kesey. *The Unitarians are people who stand up for the right to dissent and non-conformity and a lot of other good things, and we're rubbing their noses in it—a bunch of dope fiends, a couple of ex-convicts, one homosexual, men and women living on a bus . . .*

But the Unitarian . . . Youth, the teenagers weren't up tight at all. They flocked around the bus as soon as it got there. Which only wound their parents up tighter, of course. By nightfall the Unitarian Church in California was divided into two camps: on the bus and off the bus.

Kesey's very first appearance on the rostrum got three-fourths of the Sport Shirts so up tight, the conference was ready to fly apart. The main programs were held in a rustic summer-theater-type building on the camp grounds. Kesey appeared at the rostrum in a glowing Yin-Yang jacket. It was an iridescent jacket with a huge Yin-Yang symbol painted on the back in red, white, and blue.

"We're going to be here seven days," said Kesey, "so we're going to try to work a miracle in seven days—"

—and not by talking about it, bub, but by doing it, all of us together, and not by me talking *at* you, either, but by all of us doing our thing out front and wailing with it.

Many of the women at the conference began to look, rapt, at this rugged, virile man of action who now manned the pulpit. The Sports Shirts did not fail to take note of that rapt gleam on their chops, either.

Paul Sawyer, in the front row, was aware of the tension building up; but so far, all to the good. "Shake the Foundations" was the name of the conference, and so let it be. Sawyer was sitting next to Mountain Girl. What an amazing creature!—sitting next to him here in a vast purple robe. By a remarkable coincidence—coincidence?—she had been brought up as a Unitarian herself and had been a member of the real hope of the church, the LRY, the Liberal Religious Youth. And now—but had she really strayed far from what the LRY *ought* to be? It was debatable . . .

Onstage, Kesey, not talking in any formal way, more like *performing,* working magic—telling of the kind of symbols we use and the games we're in, and how you can't really know what an emotion is until you've experienced both sides of it, whereupon he seizes the big American flag up on the stage and *steps on it,* grinds it into the floor—

—huge gasp from the crowd, many of whom are teenagers—

Sawyer is already into the thing, and he sees what Kesey is trying to do—don't just describe an emotion, but arouse it, make them experience it, by manipulating the symbol of the emotion, and sometimes we have to come into awareness through the back door. Sawyer hears *sobs,* wheels around in his seat, sees a group of teenagers behind him, from Salt Lake City, looks into their faces, reads the horror that fills them—*The Flag!*—then feels the manic energy from the crazed thing that has been packed into these children even at this age like a time warp vibration from the Salem witch hysteria, the primordial cry of *Die, Infidel*—and yet he can't leave them with that. So he rises up and faces the crowd and says,

—Now wait a minute. That flag is a symbol we attach our emotions to, but it isn't the emotion itself and it isn't the thing we really care about. Sometimes we don't even realize what we really care about, because we get so distracted by the symbols. I remember when I was at school, we used to sing *America the Beautiful* and somebody would walk down the aisle carrying the flag. I always wanted to be the one who carried the flag down the aisle but I never was. Now, what was I really feeling? Patriotism? Or was it—

But he doesn't get to finish. A voice cries: "Do it!"

—what?

"Do it!" It's Mountain Girl, beaming at him from her folds of purple, quite delighted with the turn of events.

Before he knows it, he is leading them all in the singing of *America the Beautiful,* and *O beau-ti-ful for spa-cious skies* rings out in the hall—as he holds the flag staunchly in his hands and marches up the aisle and then down the aisle, signifying—what? Ne'mind! But exactly! Don't explain it. *Do it!*

LIKE MOST CONFERENCES, THIS ONE HAD A CAREFULLY PREpared and printed schedule of meals, talks, seminars, group activities. The Pranksters made a good quick hash of that. They had no schedule and intimated nobody else should, either. The Sport Shirts would have a big seminar planned to capture the imagination of the Youth—something on the order of Student Rebellion in an Age of Mediocrity: Challenge and Responsibility—only at the appointed hour the Youth, the student rebels in an age of mediocrity, would be down by the beach, down around the damnable bus, where the Pranksters had their own program, and no schedule, friends and neighbors, everything happens at the hour of *Now* and all can join in the game of Power:::::

Somebody wins the Power and orders a game of football to be played on the beach, only with the Hermit as the football. Presently a whole group, Pranksters, ministers, conferees, are picking up the giggling Hermit and handing him off like a quarterback would and scrambling for him like a loose football, and so on. But soon the grief of it—*allegory!*—begins to sink in, this making of a human being a counter in the power game, always the weakest . . . Ahhh! One of the young ministers, one of the Young Turks, now has the power, and he orders that all go into the surf of the Pacific and wash one another's feet. Ritual of humility, allegory of life, but not a word of explanation need be spoken, and they all just sit down in the surf and wash one another's feet, and the Hermit's most meticulously, and the Pranksters really groove with this. They think this is great. And the kids now look at the Young Turk whose inspiration it was in a new light. He has made it. The Pranksters approve of him!

The Young Turks spent more and more time with the Pranksters, late into the night, while the music played on the bus, and the Pranksters brought huge strands of kelp out of the ocean and flailed it about and beat the sides of the bus with it, like a huge drum, and played the Power game and took the Now Trip and played the non-games of life, and kept rapping away, but more than rapping, *being,* being *alive*—the Young Turks were truly on the bus. From the lack of sleep and the pace and weird shaking of the foundations, they began to feel the *mysto* thing most profoundly.

Paul Sawyer was walking back to go to bed about 7 A.M. one morning after an all-night stand with the Pranksters when he was met by a delegation of conference officials. They wanted to have it out. They wanted to ask Kesey and the Pranksters to leave. Kesey might be sincere, they said, and he might not. But in any case he was disrupting the conference and causing a schism in the conferees, and setting an atrocious example for the Youth. It seemed that Dr. —, one of the Church's greatest liberals and a leader in the civil-rights movement, had already left the conference in protest and taken a couple of other ministers with him.

—Wait a minute, says Sawyer. We called this conference to shake the foundations. And, well, now they are beginning to shake, and it's time to see whether we have the courage of our convictions.

—Well, yes, Paul, but there are these *things* they are doing, and the park officials are quite upset. First of all, there is a very strong suspicion that they are indulging in marijuana. There is a very peculiar smell around that bus. But let us leave that aside. In any case, the bus is a very definite health nuisance, all those people living together on that bus by the side of the water. It isn't sanitary. But let us leave that aside, too. There is also the incident of the shower room. Park personnel caught two of these ... *Pranksters* taking a shower together, a man and a woman, in the men's shower room. Now *we* might overlook that sort of thing, but what kind of an example is that for the young people? And this one they call Mountain Girl. Every time she sees Dr. George Washington Henry, who is after all one of our most distinguished Negro ministers and thinkers, she yells out, *"Watermelon Henry!"*

—Watermelon Henry?

—Yes, it seems she saw him eating a watermelon the other day, and "enjoying it," as she insists on saying, and so now, every time she sees him, she sings out, "Watermelon Henry!" And you know the kind of voice she has. I suppose that's "bringing it all out front," or whatever they call it—but *really*—*Watermelon Henry*—

The upshot is, they want to throw the whole bunch out. But Sawyer holds his ground and says that if Kesey and the Pranksters are expelled, he is leaving too. This posed the possibility of a walkout of the Young Turks, which might create an even worse schism. So the elders agreed to ride it out.

—We think you're making a mistake, Paul, Kesey is *manipulating* this conference.

KESEY WAS, IN FACT, NOW TREMENDOUSLY INTERESTED IN THE whole phenomenon of ... Control. He had discovered that the Pranksters had been able to control the flow of the conference, not by any Machiavellian planning, but simply by drawing the conference into their movie. The conference was on a schedule, but the Pranksters always arrived ... *Now,* and in no time at all everyone had become a player in their movie. Kesey began to hold daily briefings for the Pranksters.

—From now on, he's saying, we've got to stick to the same costume every day. Every Prankster's got to have a clear identity to everybody here, so that everywhere you go and they see you, you're *on,* it turns them on to your thing, the thing you're doing.

Kesey has on the Yin-Yang jacket. Mountain Girl has on the purple robe. Babbs has on an incredible pair of pants of many-colored stripes, made by Gretch. And so forth.

Mountain Girl objects.

—I think we ought to forgit our own identity and the costumes and just do our thing and keep it open.

—That's right, but that won't do any good if they don't have a clear idea of what our thing is.

So they stuck to the costumes and it worked. Hour by hour it became clear that the Pranksters were on to a secret of . . . Control, in each and every situation.

Kesey's sense of timing was perfect. By Friday, Kesey had done a lot of talking, on stage, off stage, down by the bus, and things had gotten to the point where people might start saying, well, for a guy who says talking won't get the job done, he has done an awful lot of talking. Kesey emerged from the bus that afternoon with a huge swath of adhesive tape plastered across his mouth. He went around the whole day like that, silent, plastered over, as if to say, I'm through talking.

All the kids at Asilomar thought this was great, too. More and more of them were hanging around the bus, while the Pranksters flung kelp about and played like very children themselves. Nighttime and one girl really feels into the thing, and she wants nothing more in this world than to go on an acid trip with the Pranksters. She has never taken acid before. So they give her some and a group of them take acid, down by the bus, by the ocean, and christ, she starts freaking out. She starts wailing away. That's all they need. This one thing could wreck everything they've done. So Kesey quick says give her total Attention. So they gather around her, all the Pranksters, and bathe her in love and Attention and she breaks through the freakout, comes through the other side and starts grooving on it, and it's beautiful. It's like all the Pranksters' theories and professed beliefs have been put to a test in the outside world, away from La Honda, and they're working now, and they have . . . Control.

ON THE LAST DAY, SUNDAY, THE KIDS AT THE CONFERENCE PUT on a show, apparently a tradition at the conference. But this show is all about the Pranksters. They have a kid impersonating practically every Prankster. The best one they did was the Hermit, scuttling and sniggling and giggling around. But they also did Kesey and Babbs and some others. The grand finale of the show was a musical number, "Kelp I Need Somebody!", sung to the tune of the Beatles' song "Help!"

The Sports Shirts looked and endured. They had ridden it out and at least they had avoided a schism. Or had they? Hmmmmmmm. . . .

Paul Sawyer looked at Kesey . . . and he saw a prophetic figure. He had not *taught* or *preached*. Rather, he had created . . . an experience, an awareness that flashed deeper than cerebration. Somehow he was in the tradition of the great prophets. The modern world knows prophets only in the stiff, reverent language of the texts and scholarly limnings of various religions. Somehow Kesey had created the prophetic *aura* itself, and through the Pranksters many people at the conference had not observed but *experienced* mystic brotherhood, albeit ever so bizarre . . . a miracle in seven days.

THE FOLLOWING YEAR THERE WERE TWO CONFERENCES OF THE Unitarian Church. One, as always, was at Asilomar. And the Sport Shirts were there, as always. The other was in the High Sierras. The Young Turks held their own conference, in the High Sierras, up in the thin air. Somehow it wasn't quite what they expected, however. A certain psychic decibel level was lacking. Nevertheless, the age of bullshit was over. They were on the bus for good. The next year Sawyer spent a month living in

Haight-Ashbury, to explore the possibilities of a new kind of ministry for the young people; on the bus, as it were.

OH, THE VI-BRA-TIONS . . .

IT SO HAPPENED THAT ONE OF THE FEMALE DELEGATES TO THE Unitarian conference at Asilomar had her own little résumé of the conference printed up, and she mailed it out. The Pranksters read it out loud in the living room at Kesey's:

"So the Prophet Kesey came before us"—and did such and such.

"And the Prophet Kesey said"—this and that.

"And the Prophet Kesey made a sign"—signifying Christ knows what.

"And it was good, for as the Prophet Kesey says"—

—repeating this phrase, the Prophet Kesey, and adorning it with all the biblical rhetoric—only she was serious! straight! rapt! a true believer! and probably thought the Prophet Kesey would beam when he saw it.

So the Pranksters all look at Kesey. He has his head down and he says in a melancholy way:

"We're not on the Christ Trip. That's been done, and it doesn't work. You prove your point, and then you have 2,000 years of war. We know where that trip goes."

All the same, it was a sensitive moment. The old girl had tried to put it all into so many words—Kesey's role and the whole direction the Pranksters were taking. All the Pranksters—*we're on some kind of trip, Christ knows.* They all had religion, all right. It was . . . like the whole Prankster thing was now building up some kind of conclusion, some . . . ascension, and no one could give it a right name and still be called sane. A great burning column, reaching about the western horizon, perhaps . . .

Kesey himself was like someone possessed. The goddamn

scene here is enough to drive anybody off the freaking platter. It's getting like a circus, every freak in California now showing up, heads, bums, students, raggy little girls come looking for excitement, looking to get spaced out on LSD or for Christ knows what reason. Even spades turning up, like Heavy, who rises up in the woods in the middle of the night among the tents croaking like a bullfrog: *Have no worry, have no fear, hash-smokin' Heavy's here* . . .

It's even gotten to Babbs, this motley collection. "This is a zoo!" he's saying to Kesey. "This is where the love stuff gets you!"

But Kesey says, "When you've got something like we've got, you can't just sit on it. You've got to move off of it. You can't just sit on it and possess it, you've got to move off of it and give it to other people. It only works if you bring other people into it."

So everybody who wanted could stay, Prankster or not, and the more—who gives a shit. Kesey also had his court appearances to contend with and more lying, finking, framing, politicking by the constables than a body could believe—he looked like he had aged ten years in three months. He was now some indeterminate age between thirty and forty. He was taking a lot of speed and smoking a lot of grass. He looked haggard, and when he looked haggard, his face seemed lopsided. One day he came stumbling out of the backhouse and Sandy saw him and one eye seemed to be aimed one way and one the other, as if there had been a horrible wrench . . . although the grim shit was beginning to hit Sandy again, too . . .

No turning back, man! We're on the space ship now, fly by . . . Control . . . and Attention . . . going with the flow and we can't duck the weird shit, no matter how weird it is. Kesey was doing some acid rapping, taking 500, 1,000, 1,500 micrograms instead of the normal 100 to 250. He had always been against that. Acid rappers, freaks who made a competition out of who could take the most acid—they all seemed to end up loose in the head, that breed. But now it was as if no experiment could be left undone.

One night Kesey took about 1,500 micrograms and several other Pranksters took lesser doses and they got down on the floor and started the Humanoid Radio. They started babbling, going into echolalia, ululation, all manner of nonverbal expression, talking in Tongues, as it were. The idea was to try to hit that beam and that mode that would enable you to communicate with beings on other planets, other galaxies... They were all high as hell, of course, but one thought shot through the manic dendrite raps like a subliminal legend: *What if—and you'll never know until you do it if you have the*

POWER! THEY'RE SITTING AROUND A BIG ROUND TABLE IN KE-sey's living room. It is a big wooden table, now covered with the carved initials and inscriptions of Hell's Angels, "Ralph of Oakland," and so on, playing the game of Power. Page Browning wins and he orders: Now we all take DMT and hold hands, seated in a circle around the table.

And rrrrrrrrrrush those fantastic neon bubbles rushing up out of the heart square into the human squash and bursting into—*skull mirrors!* out of Nipponese kaleidoscope got it down Grant through a door of tesselated straw over the carvings of the Hell's Angels on the table here brought into *The Movie* because now, Hondo, on the space craft you can deal with *any*one just imagine them into The Movie, get so totally into the *moment* that whichever way you move the entire moment moves with you, not *causing,* bub, just *flowing—Go with the flow—Go*

OUTSIDE

Kesey hears a voice and it tells him to get up from the table, and he does, and there are Page and other Pranksters spaced out of their gourds and holding hands and ... keening, with their eyes closed because like with DMT *opening your eyes doesn't change a thing*—those eyelid movies just keep on pouring out into the living room and Kesey goes outside in the dark in the cool of the redwood dell and now it—

I AM THE ACE AND FAYE IS THE RED QUEEN

WHUMP?

in a flash the water heater out back of the house in the
dark—*meaning*—if he gestures it will

BLOW UP

and he gestures and it is blown up, the heater, demolished, a hell
of a blast—the voice says

GO OUT UPON THE MAIN ROAD

and he goes out over the wooden bridge, out onto Route 84 in
the dark with only the smallest blowwwwwwnnn glow from the
house to be seen, and a wind comes up. *Weird shit,* Major—the
wind never comes up in this gorge with all these hills and trees
around and strange the wind lifts under the thoracic box and
every convex leaf and the balloon canopy cathedral bowers and
now; he; is;

GOD

It is crazy and delirious and zonked out and real, with half of the
mesencephalon saying

YOU ARE HIGH

and the other half saying, Nevertheless

YOU ARE GOD

Car coming down the hill from La Honda around the last bend
on Route 84, the lights swooping over the redwoods

THE ENEMY

heading straight for him at 50 miles an hour as he balances tamping the earth with his feet on the very center line. No undue cause
for alarm and concern, however. He has but to

GESTURE

the car slows down and creeps around him, shuddering in the
weird wind, trying to hold itself together in the face of

THIS SURGE

and he knows with absolute certainty he has . . . all the Power in
the world can do what he wants with the Enemy in whatever
form—he flings out his arm

Gestures

the car stops. The enemy peers out. At this point he can do all

Destroy

Create

Galvanize

Call back

Send forth

—has only to decide, with power too great to use and too formidable to squander. He walks back over the bridge to the house as the wind dies down. The skull mirrors . . . *ring*—

Afterwards he knows it was the drug. And yet—Walker had been driving up near Skylonda in that selfsame moment and had suddenly felt a wind rise and said, How very strange! Too much!

Oh yes, Major, it was the drug, you understand—and yet—he was fully into the bare Halusion Gulp of the moment out there and there ::::: was the Power and the Call and this movie is big enough to include the world, a cast of millions, the castoff billions . . . Control Tower to Orbiter One

Control

chapter XV

Cloud

A HULKING GREAT SIGN ON THE GATE OUT FRONT
THE MERRY PRANKSTERS WELCOME THE BEATLES
The Beatles were going to be at the Cow Palace outside of
San Francisco on the evening of September 2. The papers, the radio, the TV could talk of nothing else. Kesey's idea, the current
fantasy, is that after the show the Beatles will come to La Honda
for a good freaking rout with the Merry Pranksters. Now as to
how this is to all come about . . .

But one has to admit the sign creates an effect.

THE MERRY PRANKSTERS WELCOME THE BEATLES

Out on Route 84, Mom&Dad&Buddy&Sis in their Ocelot Rabies
400 hardtop sedans, they slow down and stop and stare. The last
sign, the one reading THE MERRY PRANKSTERS WELCOME THE
HELL'S ANGELS, for that one they mainly just slowed down. After

all, it didn't say *when*. It might be 30 seconds from now—hundreds of the beasts, coming 'round the mountain in a shower of spirochetes and crab lice, spitting out bone marrow from the last cannibal rape job up the road.

Well, it worked with the Hell's Angels. They put up the sign THE MERRY PRANKSTERS WELCOME THE HELL'S ANGELS, and sure enough the Angels came, these unbelievable bogeymen for the middle class, in the flesh, and they became part of the Prankster movie, in the rich ripe cheesy Angel flesh. So they put up the sign THE MERRY PRANKSTERS WELCOME THE BEATLES and maybe the Beatles will come. There is this one small difference of course. Kesey *knew* the Hell's Angels. He invited them, face to face. Ah, but comes a time to put a few professed beliefs to the test. Control, Attention, Imagine the little freaks into the movie . . .

Kesey raps on to Mountain Girl out in the backhouse. They lie there on the mattresses, with Kesey rapping on and on and Mountain Girl trying to absorb it. Ever since Asilomar, Kesey has been deep into the religion thing. Miracles—Control—*Now*—The Movie—on and on he talks to Mountain Girl out in the backhouse and very deep and far-out stuff it is, too. Mountain Girl tries to concentrate, but the words swim like great waves of . . . The words swim by and she hears the sound but it is like her cerebral cortex is tuned out to the content of it. Her mind keeps rolling and spinning over another set of data, always the same. Like—the eternal desperate calculation. In short, Mountain Girl is pregnant.

And yet with all this desperation rolling and spinning going on, something he says will catch hold. They are that bizarre, but that plausible, Kesey's dreams are. It's a matter of imagining them into the movie. The Beatles. It is like an experiment in everything the Pranksters have learned up to now. We can't *make* the Beatles come out here to our place. We can't *cause* them to do it in the usual sense. But we can imagine them into the movie and work them into the great flow of acausal connection and then it will happen of its own accord. This sign starts the movie going, THE MERRY PRANKSTERS WELCOME THE BEATLES, and our movie becomes their movie, Mom's and Dad's and Buddy's and Sis's and all the Berkeley kids' and all the heads' and proto-heads' of the San Francisco peninsula, until our fantasy becomes the Beatles' fantasy . . . Wonder when they will first feel it . . . Despite the rolling and spinning and all, Mountain Girl can't hardly help but marvel at the current fantasy because there has already been so much . . . weird shit . . . that worked. Bringing the Angels in, like Kesey did, the most feared demons in America . . . and finding Good People like Buzzard and Sonny and Tiny and Frank and Terry the Tramp, who Done Well, and Beautiful People like Gut . . . And the poor tortured intellectual angels at Asilomar, from Watermelon Henry to freaking Rachel—for a week Kesey had mystified, like *mystified,* and taken over the whole Unitarian Church of California. They would never be the same again, which was just as well. A true Miracle, in fact, since they had been the same for so goddamn long. Control :::: and it was so plausible, the way it sounded in Kesey's certain Oregon drawl. So few humans have the *hubris* to exert their wills upon the flow, maybe not more than forty on the whole planet at any given time. The world *is* flat, it *is* supported by forty, or maybe four, men, one at each corner, like the cosmic turtles and elephants in the mythology books, because no one else dares. Mountain Girl is 18 and she is pregnant, but this is Kesey . . .

And *Miracles?* You haven't seen miracles yet, Job, until you see the Pranksters draw the Beatles into their movie.

SEPTEMBER 2. FAYE'S SEWING MACHINE IS THE FIRST THING everyone hears as they wake up. Faye and Gretch pull out the big costume chest, full of all sorts of ungainly theatrical shit, swash-buckle swords and plumed hats and Errol Flynn dueling shirts and Robin Hood boots and quivers and quail masks and Day-

Glo roadworker vests and sashes and medals and saris and sarongs and shades and beaks and bells and steelworker hard hats and World War I aviator helmets and Dr. Strange capes and cutlasses and codpieces and jumpsuits and football jerseys and aprons and ascots and wigs and warlock rattles and Jungle Jim jodhpurs and Captain Easy epaulets and Fearless Four tights—and Merry Prankster Page Browning special face paints. The Merry Pranksters are getting ready to head bombed out into the mightiest crazed throng in San Francisco history, come to see the Beatles at the Cow Palace.

One of the Pranksters' outer circle, so to speak, a fellow called C———, from Palo Alto—C——— had worked out some kind of a deal and gotten thirty tickets to the Beatles concert for the Pranksters, even though tickets were supposed to be impossible to get. C——— was one of the Pranksters' acid sources. Another was an old guy known as the Mad Chemist, an amateur chemistry genius who was also a gun freak. Anyway, this C——— worked out some kind of a deal and he also got enough acid for everybody for the trip. Just before the Pranksters, inner and outer circle, and kids, climbed on the bus, Kesey grinned and passed out the acid. It was in capsules, but it was such high concentration it just coated part of the inside of the capsules, so it looked like there was nothing in there. The Pranksters called it acid gas. So they all took acid gas and got on the bus. Cassady was off somewhere, so Babbs drove. Kesey was up on top of the bus, directing the movie. Well, it was colorful enough, this movie. The bus was super-rigged, all the sound equipment, two big speakers up top, records and tapes, plus the whole Prankster band up top of the bus, George Walker's drums, and basses and guitars and trombones and plumes spilling out the windows and flashes of Day-Glo and flapping epaulets, freaking flashing epaulets, and the Beatles album from the movie *Help!* screaming out the speakers, and up on top, Kesey and Sandy, Mountain Girl, Walker, Zonker, and a new Prankster, a little girl called Mary Microgram, and guitars and drums—*He-e-e-elp I ne-e-e-ed some-body*—the whole flapping yahooing carnival of a bus bouncing and jouncing and grinding up over Skylonda, Cahill Ridge, and down through Palo Alto and out onto the Harbor Freeway heading toward San Francisco, a goddamn rolling circus once again. Everybody was getting kind of high on acid, *wasted,* in fact, and starting, one by one, Mountain Girl and Sandy and Norman, who was inside the bus, to have that thing where the motion and the roar of the bus and the beat of the music and the sound of it are all one thing rolling together, and like Babbs is driving to the exact tempo and speed of the Beatles music, since they are all one thing together, growing high as baboons down through the freaking motels and electric signs and gull lights in Burlingame, near the airport, the Hyatt House super-America motel spires aloft—pitching and rolling and gunning along in *exact* time to the Beatles music, that being the soundtrack of this movie, you understand—and then off the expressway at the Cow Palace exit and down the swerving—*ne-e-e-ed some-body*—ramp, down an incline, down a hill, toward dusk, with the fever millions of cars streaming south on the freeway and the sun a low bomb over the hills, zonked, in fact. And grinding down to the stop light, thunk, and the brakes sound like a cast-iron flute A below high C—and at that very moment, that very moment of bus stop—the Beatles song *Help!* ends, in that very moment, and weird music starts, from the part of the movie *Help!* where the Arab is sneaking up behind Ringo, and in that weird moment the wind rises over the freeway and to the right there is an abandoned factory, all brick and glass, mostly glass, great 1920s factory glass panes and all of them bending weird in the wind and flashing sheets of that huge afternoon sun like a huge thousand-eyed thing pulsing explosions of sunlight in *exact* time to the weird Arab music—and in that very moment Kesey, Mountain Girl, Sandy, Zonker, all of them—no one even has to look at another because they not only *know* that everyone else is seeing it at once, they *feel,* they feel it flowing through one brain, Atman and Brahman, all one

on the bus and all one with the writhing mass sun reflector ripple sun bomb prisms, the bricks, the glass, the whole hulk of it,
Pranksters and Beatles and sun bombs flashing Arab music—
and then in *that* very moment, they all, the all in one, the one
brain flow, see the mouldering sign silhoutted against the sky
above the building:

CLOUD

Suddenly it seemed like the Pranksters could draw the whole
universe into . . . the movie . . .

AND THEN, CURIOUSLY, BEING AS IT IS, SO FREAKING HIGH OUT
here—Mountain Girl thinks what the fuck is this. It looks like a
slaughterhouse. In fact, it is the Cow Palace. She can't even focus
on the big hulking building itself for the miles and endless rings
of slaughterhouse fences around it, fences and barbed wire and a
million cars jamming in and being jammed in in the cold fag end
of the dusk. Curiously, it isn't terrifying to Mountain Girl, however. It is just a slaughterhouse, that's all.

But to other Pranksters—a concentration camp. We're going
to jail, for the rest of our lives only. Everybody scrambling down
off the bus, all still in motion with the ground and the
concentration-camp fences flailing in the gruesome gloaming
while billions of teeny freaks rush by them, screaming and freaking. They have their tickets in their hand like it is the last corner
of salvation extant but they can't even read the mothers. They are
wasted. The letters on the ticket curdle and freak off into the
teeny freak flow. Thirty Pranksters in full flapping epaulets and
plumes desperately staring at the minute disappearing tickets in
their hands in the barby ante-pens of the concentration camp.
They are going to arrest us and lock us away for the rest of our
lives. That seems very certain, almost like well, that's why we
came. Thirty acid heads, with innocent children in tow, in full

Prankster regalia, bombed out of their gourds on the dread LSD, veering, careening in delirium sun pulse. In public, stoned out of their skulls on LSD, not only in public but in this momentous heaving Beatles throng amid 2,000 red dog forensic cops, in full go-to-hell costume—*exterminate the monsters*—

... but ... no one lays a hand on them or says the first word, thousands of cops and not even one hassle ... because we're *too* obvious. Suddenly it couldn't be clearer to Norman. We're too obvious and we've blown their brains. They can't focus on us— or—we've sucked them into the movie and *dissolved* the bastids—

Inside the Cow Palace it is very roaring hell. Somehow Kesey and Babbs lead the Day-Glo crazies up to their seats. The Pranksters are sitting in a great clump, a wacky perch up high in precipitous pitch high up pitching down to the stage and millions of the screaming teeny freaks. The teeny freaks, tens of thousands of little girls, have gone raving mad already, even though the Beatles have not come on. Other groups, preliminaries, keep trooping on, *And now—Martha and the Vandellas* and the electrified throb and brang vibrates up your aorta and picks your bones like a sonic cleaner, and the teeny freaks scream—great sheets of scream like sheets of rain in a squall—and *kheew, kheew, pow, pow, pow*—how very marvelous, how very clever, figures Norman. From up out of the Cow Palace horde of sheet scream teeny freaks comes this very marvelous clever light display, hundreds of exploding lights throughout the high intensity lights, ricocheting off everything, what a marvelous clever thing they've rigged up here for our ...

—Mountain Girl smiles ... the incredible exploding lights explode out in front of her, a great sea of them, and then they explode on her retina in great sunburst retinal sulphur rockets, images and after-images that she will never forget as long as she lives, in truth—

... for our entertainment, and it is twenty or thirty minutes before Norman, stoned, realizes that they are flashbulbs, hundreds, thousands of teeny freaks with flashbulb cameras, aimed at the stage or just shot off in optic orgasm. Sheets of screams, rock 'n' roll, *blam blam,* a sea of flashbulbs—perfect madness, of course.

—Mountain Girl grins and takes it all in—

Other Pranksters, stoned, are slowly getting up tight, however, including Kesey and Babbs. The vibrations are very bad, a poison madness in the air—

Each group of musicians that goes off the stage—the horde thinks *now* the Beatles, but the Beatles don't come, some other group appears, and the sea of girls gets more and more intense and impatient and the screaming gets higher, and the thought slips into Norman's flailing flash-frayed brain stem ::: the human lung cannot go beyond this :::: and yet when the voice says *And now—the Beatles*—what else could he say?—and out they come on stage—*them*—John and George and Ringo and uh the other one—it might as well have been four imported vinyl dolls for all it was going to matter—that sound he thinks cannot get higher, it doubles, his eardrums ring like stamped metal with it and suddenly *Ghhhhhhwooooooooowwwwww,* it is like the whole thing has snapped, and the whole front section of the arena becomes a writhing, seething mass of little girls waving their arms in the air, this mass of pink arms, it is all you can see, it is like a single colonial animal with a thousand waving pink tentacles—it *is* a single colonial animal with a thousand waving pink tentacles,

—vibrating poison madness and filling the universe with the teeny agony torn out of them. It dawns on Kesey: it is *one being*. They have all been transformed into one being.

—Mountain Girl grins and urges them on—its scream does not subside for a moment, during after or between numbers, the Beatles could be miming it for all it matters. But something else . . . does . . . matter . . . and Kesey sees it. One of the Beatles, John, George, Paul, dips his long electric guitar handle in one direction and the whole teeny horde ripples precisely along the line of energy he set off—and then in the other direction, precisely along that line. It causes them to grin, John and Paul and George and Ringo, rippling the poor huge freaked teeny beast this way and that—

Control—it is perfectly obvious—they have brought this whole mass of human beings to the point where they are one, out of their skulls, one psyche, and they have utter control over them—but they don't know what in the hell to do with it, they haven't the first idea, and they will lose it. In Kesey the vibration is an awful anticipation of the snap—

Ghhhhhwoooooooooowwwww, thousands of teeny bodies hurtling toward the stage and a fence there and a solid line of cops, fighting to hurl the assault back, while the Beatles keep moving their chops and switching their hips around sunk like a dumb show under the universal scream. In that surge, just when you would have thought not another sound in the universe could break through, it starts—*thwaaaack*—*thwaaaack*—the sound of the folding chairs on the arena floor collapsing and smashing down on the floor, and the remains are down there amid the pink tentacles, crushed to a pulp, little bits and splinters that used to be folding chairs, debris being passed out from hand to hand traveling over the pink tentacles from one to the other like some hideously diseased lurching monster cockroaches. And then the girls start fainting, like suffocation, and getting tromped on, and they start handing out their bodies, cockroach chair debris and the bodies of little teeny freaks being shuttled out over the pitched sea like squashed lice picked off the beast, screaming and fainting and *Ghhhhhwoooooowwwwww* again up against the cop fence while the Beatles cheese and mince at them in the dumb show, utterly helpless to ripple them or anything else now, with no control left—

CANCER—Kesey has only to look and it is perfectly obvious—all of them, the teeny freaks and the Beatles, are one creature, caught in a state of sheer poison mad cancer. The Beatles are

the creature's head. The teeny freaks are the body. But the head
has lost control of the body and the body rebels and goes amok
and that is what cancer is. The vibrations of it hit the Pranksters,
in a clump, stoned out of their gourds, in sickening waves. Kesey—Babbs—they all feel it at once, and Norman.

—Mountain Girl looks very surprised. She wants to see the
rest of it. But Kesey and Babbs have decided they should all
leave—before the Monster Snap occurs, the big cancer wrap-up
of the whole process.

—Wait a minute, says Mountain Girl.

But the Pranksters get up in a clump and a rustle of plumes
and epaulets and Day-Glo, zonked out of their heads on acid,
and all sorts of people start getting up—but like, *concrete.* The
more headway they make toward the exits, the more it becomes
a claustrophobia of pens, an endless series of pens. They head
down long corridors, all concrete, and already hundreds are
jammed in the corridors, all looking kind of raggy—because—
They get the total vibration from them—everybody has the one
same feeling: suppose this thing snaps *now* and there is panic and
everybody makes a rush for it, the exit, but there is no exit, only
concrete walls and concrete ceilings weighing down like a thousand tons and ramps—toward nothing—leading down—then
up in a great clump of hump—and then down, outside, there is
the sky, but it is black, it is nighttime by now and sick ochre
floodlights, but they have merely made it to another pen, more
Cyclone fences and barbed wire with frantic raggy people—all
fleeing—milling around in it like rats, trying to get to the exit,
which is a turnstile, an upright turnstile with bars, like an iron
maiden, and you have to get inside of it, totally, one person at a
time, with a frantic crush on both sides, and even then you have
only made it to another pen, a parking lot, with more Cyclone
fence and barbed wire and now teeny freaks and cars crushed in
here, all trying to get out, seven and eight cars at a whack trying
to nose through an opening big enough for one. Cages, cages,
cages and no end to it. Even out there, beyond, where cars have

escaped and they are in a line with their lights on—trapped by
the hills, which are another great pen trapping the whole place
in . . . in . . . The Pranksters all silent and numb with the appre-
hension of the Great Cancer Snap to come—

—Except that Mountain Girl says Wait a minute—

—and Zonker, with his huge euphoric Zonker grin on, frater-
nizing madly with all teeny freaks as they stream out, saying to
all who listen: "The Beatles are going to Kesey's when they leave
here . . . the Beatles are going to Kesey's . . ." and the word
spreads among the crowd in the most delirious way—

Kesey plunges back in for survivors. See if there are any
Pranksters trapped inside. He tells the rest to go to the bus and
stay there, and he plunges in. The Pranksters touch the bus and
their morale revives a bit. They rev up the amplifiers and the
speakers and climb up on top in their crazy costumes and start
idling over the drums and the electric guitars. The thousands of
little raggy girls keep pouring out into the parking lot, still
wound up like a motorcycle and no release and of course they see
the bus and these strange Day-Glo people. One group of kids is
protesting that the music business is rigged and they're carrying
placards and screaming and they figure the Pranksters support
them—the Pranksters grin and wave back—everybody figures
the strange Day-Glo people are for whatever they're for. They
start piling around the bus, these little teeny freaks, and start
pelting it with jelly beans, the hard kind, the kind they brought
to throw at the Beatles. The Pranksters sit on top of the bus with
the jelly beans clattering off the side and the flaming little teeny
freaks pressed around screaming—So *this* is what the Beatles
feel, this mindless amok energy surging at them for—what?

At last Kesey returns with the last to be rescued, Mary Microgram, looking like a countryside after a long and fierce war, and
Kesey says let's haul ass out of here. Babbs starts the bus up and
they pull out, bulling their way slowly out toward freedom.

Cancer! We saw it. It was there. Bad vibrations, say all. Endless
cages. They all rock and sway, stoned on acid.

"Hell," thinks Mountain Girl. "I have to come here with a bunch of old men who never saw a rock 'n' roll show before."

ON THE WAY BACK THEY PUT THE BEATLES TAPE ON AGAIN, from *Help!* but it was no use. They were all too dispirited. Except for Mountain Girl and Zonker. Mountain Girl said she'd wanted to stay and see the rest of the show. Well—what the hell. Zonker was smiling about the Beatles coming. Well—that was what he had told the whole world anyway. And where the hell *else* would they go from there? In fact, the current fantasy—the imminent arrival of the Beatles—had hardly crossed anybody's mind for the last hour, not even Kesey's. Get the hell out of there, that was the main thing. Where were the Beatles? Who the hell knew. The little vinyl dolls had probably cheesed and minced off into a time warp. . . . In any case, it wasn't very hulking likely they were coming to La Honda.

Finally the bus comes grinding around the last curve round the mountain, up to Kesey's place, and the bus noses across the bridge and the headlights hit the yard—and the sight is gruesome and comical at the same time. It is like a super version of the nightmare of the man who just wants to go home and go to bed. The Pranksters have guests. In fact, they have three or four hundred guests. They are all jammed into the big yard between the main house and the backhouse, with big bitter lollipop eyes. It's like every head, freak, boho, and weirdo in the West has assembled in one spot, the first freakout, with a couple of hundred teeny freaks thrown in for good measure. Half of them are hunkered down with their big lollipop eyes turned up like somebody spit them up against the house and they slid down to the ground like slugs. Naturally they all came for the big beano with the Beatles. The party. Zonker did his work in the highest Prankster tradition. The sign still hangs on the gate:

THE MERRY PRANKSTERS WELCOME THE BEATLES

Kesey is not in the mood for a goddamned thing and heads into the house. The whole head-freak-boho-slug mob stares at him, all these lollipop eyes, as if he is going to produce the Beatles from out of a sleeve. Then they start grumbling, like a bunch of prisoners who haven't been fed but don't know whether this is the time for the slave revolt or not. It is a debacle, except that it is so damned comical. The look on their faces.

That, and the appearance of Owsley.

A COCKY LITTLE GUY, SHORT, WITH DARK HAIR, DRESSED LIKE an acid head, the usual boho gear, but with a strange wound-up nasal voice, like a head with the instincts of a roller-skating rink promoter—this little character materializes in front of Kesey from out of the boho-slub multitudes and announces:

"I'm Owsley."

Kesey doesn't say Hi, I'm Kesey. He just looks at him, as if to say, all right, you're Owsley and you're here—and then what?

Owsley looks stunned—*I'm Owsley*. In fact, Kesey never heard of him. It was like, if Owsley suddenly found himself in a place where nobody ever heard of him, he didn't know what to do. He and Kesey are just standing there trading eyeballs until finally Owsley produces a little bag he has and opens it and it is full of capsules of acid. He's Owsley, the greatest LSD manufacturer in the world, which turns out to be just about right, the Sandoz Chemical Corporation included.

Mountain Girl looks and just smiles. Everything gets funnier and funnier on the Beatles patrol! He's got his little bag of acid. Mountain Girl figures him for a wiseacre right away. Kesey looks at the bagful of acid. One thing the little wiseacre's got is acid.

The world's greatest acid manufacturer, bar none, standing out in the dark in the middle of nowhere amid the boho-slug multitudes under the shadowy redwoods.

By and by they had most of the boho-slubs off the place and sliding up the highway in the dark looking for christ knows

what, seeing as how the Beatles never made it. Kesey and Owsley
and the Pranksters sat down around a fire out by the big stump.
And who the hell shows up but the Mad Chemist. He and
Owsley start sniffing and eyeing each other. It's like the slick
sharp young neurological doctor genius from out of the Mayo
Clinic face to face with the old blowsy homey country doctor—on the most puzzling and difficult case in the history of
medicine. Owsley and the Mad Chemist start arguing over
drugs. It's like a debate. All of the Pranksters, even Kesey, keep
out of it and the two of them start hammering away. Let the little wiseacre have it, Mad Chemist, Mountain Girl keeps thinking
and most of the Pranksters feel the same way. But Owsley, the little wiseacre, is tearing him up. Owsley is young and sharp and
quick and the Mad Chemist—the Mad Chemist is an old man
and he has taken too much dope. He's loose in the head. He tries
to argue and his brains all run together like goo. Owsley, the
Pranksters figure—well, maybe he never even took acid himself.
Or maybe he took it once. It is just something they sense. And the
poor old Mad Chemist, he has taken so much dope—caressing
his guns and hooking down dope—he is loose in the head, and
Owsley just tears him up. The Mad Chemist is getting crushed.
The Mad Chemist never came around again but once or twice, it
was all so humiliating. So the Pranksters had this little wiseacre
Owsley on their hands whether they liked it or not. But he did
make righteous acid and he had money. Between the two of
them, Owsley and the Pranksters, they were about to put LSD all
over the face of the globe.

Little by little, Owsley's history seeped out. He was 30 years
old, although he looked younger, and he had a huge sonorous
name: Augustus Owsley Stanley III. His grandfather was a
United States Senator from Kentucky. Owsley apparently had
had a somewhat hungup time as a boy, going from prep school to
prep school and then to a public high school, dropping out of
that, but getting into the University of Virginia School of Engi-
neering, apparently because of his flair for sciences, then drop-

ping out of that. He finally wound up enrolling in the University of California, in Berkley, where he hooked up with a hip, good-looking chemistry major named Melissa. They dropped out of the University and Owsley set up his first acid factory at 1647 Virginia Street, Berkeley. He was doing a huge business when he got raided on February 21, 1965. He got off, however, because there was no law against making, taking, or having LSD in California until October 1966. He moved his operation to Los Angeles, 2205 Lafler Road, called himself the Baer Research Group, and paid out $20,000 in $100 bills to the Cycle Chemical Corporation for 500 grams of lysergic acid monohydrate, the basic material in LSD, which he could convert into 1.5 million doses of LSD at from $1 to $2 apiece wholesale. He bought another 300 grams from International Chemical and Nuclear Corporation. His first big shipment arrived March 30, 1965.

He had a flair, this Owsley. By and by he had turned out several million doses of LSD, in capsules and tablets. They had various whimsical emblems on them, to indicate the strength. The most famous, among the heads, were the "Owsley blues"—with a picture of Batman on them, 500 micrograms worth of Superhero inside your skull. The heads rapped over Owsley blues like old juice heads drawling over that famous onetime brand from Owsley's Virginia home territory, Fairfax County Bourbon, bottled in bond. Owsley makes righteous acid, said the heads. Personally he wasn't winning any popularity contests with the heads or the cops, either. He is, like, arrogant; he is a wiseacre; but the arrogant little wiseacre makes righteous acid.

In fact, Owsley's acid was famous internationally. When the acid scene spread to England in late 1966 and 1967, the hippest intelligence one could pass around was that one was in possession of "Owsley acid." In the acid world, this *was* bottled-in-bond; certified; guaranteed; and high status. It was in this head world that the . . . Beatles first took LSD. Now, just to get ahead of the story a bit—after Owsley hooked up with Kesey and the Pranksters, he began a musical group called the Grateful Dead.

Through the Dead's experience with the Pranksters was born the sound known as "acid rock." And it was that sound that the Beatles picked up on, after they started taking acid, to do a famous series of acid-rock record albums, *Revolver, Rubber Soul,* and *Sergeant Pepper's Lonely Hearts' Club Band*. Early in 1967 the Beatles got a fabulous idea. They got hold of a huge school bus and piled into it with thirty-nine friends and drove and wove across the British countryside, zonked out of their gourds. They were going to . . . make a movie. Not an ordinary movie, but a totally spontaneous movie, using hand-held cameras, shooting the experience as it happened—off the top of the head!—cavorting, rapping on, soaring in the moment, visionary chaos—a daydream! a black art! a chaos! They finished up with miles and miles of film, a monster, a veritable morass of it, all shaky and out of focus—blissful Zonk!—which they saw as a total breakthrough in terms of expression but also as a commercial display—shown on British TV it was—that might be appreciated even outside the esoteric world of the heads—

THE MOVIE

—called *Magical Mystery Tour*. And . . . the great banner rippled on the Prankster gate in the nighttime in ripples and intergalactic billows of great howling owsley electro-mad-chemical synchronicity . . .

THE MERRY PRANKSTERS
WELCOME THE BEATLES

XVI

The Frozen Jug Band

SYNCHRONICITY SPOKEN HERE!
—and the Pranksters sit around Kesey's living room at night, grooving on many strange events. Like the day of the great Blackout in New York City, the great power failure that knocked out subways, elevators, lights, air conditioners, TVs, clocks, buildings and the rest of the hulks in the great cancer capital of the East. The Pranksters grooved over the cataclysm and grokked it. Such consternation in the cancer capital! A huge *surge* of electricity had suddenly rolled through the wires and freaking *blown* everything. The utility companies didn't know what had *caused* this surge, but bygod they had experts working on it and they would figure it out and such a surge would never occur again.

A *surge,* Mahavira?—

Meanwhile, there was one story in the newspapers that the Pranksters grooved on most truly. It seems that some kid had been playing hooky from school in New York that day and had gone off to the movies finally and come out of the movie house about 5:15 P.M. and started walking home, feeling guilty already, and he picked up a stick out of the gutter and he started whacking parking meters with it. When he got to the corner, he whacked the big utility pole there and

IN THAT VERY MOMENT

all the lights in New York went out

NOW

and the kid ran home in the dark, crying, confessing all to his mother—*I did it, I did it, but I didn't mean to*—

And Kesey and the Pranksters did groove on that. The kid was right, that was the funny part. Or at least as right as the utility companies. For no doubt there was a *great surge,* friends, and it came through that kid just like it came through everything and every being that existed in that moment. Just as Severn Darden blew out the candles on his birthday cake *in that very moment*—and they poked through every Con Ed transformer in the system and they never did find the *cause.*

Cosmo!

—*and once you find out about Cosmo, you know he's running the show* . . . It's like we're strands of wire intertwined in a great cable that runs through a slot, the Pranksters, the Beatles, the Vietnam Day Committee—*the Vietnam Day Committee?*—running through a slot, and all the wires are vibrated by Cosmo. Most people lead two-dimensional lives. All they can see is the face of the slot, a cross section, so that the wires look like a mass of separate little circles looking bigger or smaller according to how close you are. They don't—they can't see that these "circles" are just cross sections of wires that run backward and forward infinitely and that there is a great surge through the whole cable and that anybody who is truly into the full bare essence of the thing . . .

There is food in the *thing*.
My comrades are envious.

> But they cannot harm me.
> Good fortune.
>
> —the *I Ching*

. . . tends to react against political disorder because he is concerned with the deep basic religious experience, the deepest sources of life; transient politics are insignificant to him.

—Joachim Wach

It was against this backdrop, namely, the ultimate and the infinite, that an organization known as the Vietnam Day Committee invited Kesey to come speak at a huge antiwar rally in Berkeley, on the University of California campus. I couldn't tell you what bright fellow thought of that, inviting Kesey. Afterwards, they didn't know, either. Or at least none of them would own up, despite a lot of interrogations and recriminations and general thrashing about. "Who the hell invited this bastard!" was the exact wording. A regular little rhubarb they had for themselves. The main trouble with the Vietnam Day Committee was that they couldn't see beyond the marvelous political whoopee they had cooked up. Why should they? From where they were looking in the fall of 1965, they were about to sweep the country. Berkeley, the New Left, the Free Speech Movement, Mario Savio, the Rebel Generation, the Student Revolution, in which students were going to take over the universities, like in Latin America, and drive some fire up the clammy rectum of American life—you could read about it in all the magazines. And if you don't believe it, come here and watch us, Mr. Jones—and so forth.

They never looked beyond that, as I say, but it might have been no use, in any case. Maybe there was no way in the world anybody could have made the Vietnam Day Committee realize how their whole beano looked to Kesey and the Pranksters. *Come rally against the war in Vietnam*—from the cosmic vantage point the Pranksters had reached, there were so many reasons why this little charade was pathetic, they didn't know where to begin . . .

Nevertheless, Kesey was invited, and that was how the fun started. Marchers were pouring into Berkeley from seventy-one cities and twenty-eight states, for whatever such sums are worth—at any rate, thousands of students and professors from all over. There were to be teach-ins all day and also an all-day rally starting in the morning, with thirty or forty speakers to whip things up, and then at 7:30 in the evening, when the fever pitch was reached, they would all rise up off the Berkeley campus and march over into Oakland, fifteen or twenty thousand souls in a massive line, marching on the Oakland Army Terminal. The Oakland Army Terminal was where men and supplies were shipped out to Vietnam. Just to spice things up a bit—a large supply of gelignite had been stolen, and everybody had visions of Oakland, Berkeley, San Francisco, the whole clump, blowing up in a gelignite earthquake of cops, peaceniks, Birchers, and probably spades and innocent women and children. Nobody had any idea which side had stolen the gelignite, but that only made it better.

The gelignite scare seemed to give Kesey the inspiration for this prank. Kesey's saving grace was that he never got serious where he could say it just as well with a cosmic joke. Kesey's fantasy for the occasion was to come upon the huge anti-war rally as a freaking military invasion. It was a true inspiration, this fantasy. They were going to rig up the bus as a rolling fortress with guns sticking out and all the Pranksters would dress military. Then they would get cars and rig them up the same way, and at the head of the whole convoy, there would be—the Hell's Angels, in running formation, absolutely adangle with swastikas. *Swastikas.* If would freaking blow their minds, or at least give their cool a test like it never had before.

First they painted the whole bus a dull red color, the color of dried blood, in fact. Right on over the greatest riot of Day-Glo design in history went this bloody muck. But who gave a damn.

Art is not eternal. Then they started painting military symbols on the dried blood, swastikas, American eagles, Iron Crosses, Viking crosses, Red Crosses, hammers & sickles, skulls & bones, anything as long as it looked rank. That very night, naturally, the seasonal rains started, and like the Chief said, art is not eternal. All the paint started running until it was the most dismal mess imaginable. Somehow that was appropriate. The next day, Gut and his girlfriend, Little People, showed up. Gut was in a kind of transition period, between the Angels and the Pranksters. He had his old Hell's Angels sleeveless denim jacket on, but he had taken the insignia off, the lettering and the emblem of a skull with a helmet on, but you could see where it had all been, because the denim was lighter underneath. It was what you might call a goodbye-but-not-forgotten Hell's Angels' jacket. Anyway, Gut amazed the Pranksters by painting a big beautiful American Eagle on the bus, a little primitive, but strong. The big hulking jesus angel had talent. The Pranksters were all pleased as hell. They felt they had brought it out of him, somehow. Gut got everybody revved up. They built a gun turret on the bus and rigged up two big gray cannons that you could maneuver. Norman made a machine gun out of wood and cardboard and painted it olive drab. Other people were knocking together wooden guns of various ridiculous descriptions. Faye's sewing machine was going. Pranksters, inner circle and outer circle, were driving in from all over. Lee Quarnstrom, of the outer circle, showed up with a huge supply of Army insignia, shoulder patches, arm patches, hashmarks, bars, stars, epaulets. Kesey was rigging up the bus with tapes and microphones and amplifiers and earphones and electric guitars. Hagen was rigging up his 16-millimeter camera and films. Bob Dylan and the Beatles and Joan Baez and Roland Kirk and Mississippi John Hunt were droning and clattering over the big speakers from over the way atop the dirt cliff. Then Allen Ginsberg turned up from Big Sur, with his companion Peter Orlovsky and an entourage of pale Chester A. Arthur High School hindus. Ginsberg sang mantras all night and jingled bells and finger cymbals. Cassady hooked down speed and worked himself up from a standing start, jerking, kicking, dancing—he seemed to be moving in time to the sewing machine on a long seam. Ginsberg seemed to be chanting in time to a Jainist's whisk broom. Cassady began fibrillating the vocal cords, going faster and faster until by dawn if he had gone any faster, he would have vibrated off, as old Charles Fort said, and gone instantly into the positive absolute. It was a nice weird party.

The next morning, October 16, the big day—the Pranksters blew the morning, naturally, all stroked out in various attitudes from the night before, and they were late getting off to Berkeley. Art is not eternal, friends. The plan was to meet the Hell's Angels in Palo Alto and go roaring down the freeway in formation. They put on Prankster tapes and Cassady got in the driver's seat. Everybody climbed on in their crazed military costumes, Hassler, Hagen, Babbs, Gretch, Zonker, June the Goon, Roy Seburn, Dale Kesey and all sorts of people, even the Mad Chemist—he showed up for this one—and Mary Microgram at the last minute. And then Kesey got on. Kesey was wearing a big orange coat of the sort highway workers wear so cars will see them. He had hashmarks on the sleeves and some kind of floppy epaulets flapping on the shoulders. He had a big orange Day-Glo World War I helmet on his head. It was so big and came down so far over his forehead his eyes were like two little flashlight bulbs under the lid. Kesey got up in the gun turret and they were off. Before they got to Palo Alto, in Woodside, in fact, the cops stopped them and hassled them and checked them over. The Pranksters did the usual, leaped out with cameras and shotgun mikes and tape recorders, filming and taping everything the cops said, and the cops left, but it ate up time.

"Aha," said the Mad Chemist, "the first skirmish."

"The Prankster Alert is out," said Babbs.

That was just about right. They kept getting stopped and hassled and checked over and losing time. They got to the rendezvous in Palo Alto—and no Hell's Angels. They waited and waited for the Angels, then gave up and took off down the expressway, to Berkeley.

They didn't get to the Berkeley campus until almost dusk, and their arrival didn't make any very momentous impression at first. Now, a full phalanx of Hell's Angels, looking like a cross between the Gestapo and the Tonton Macoute—that would have been a different story, no doubt. Good and noisy, too. But as it was, the bus just pulled into the parking lot by the Student Union building and the Pranksters cut up as best they could, ack-acking their wooden guns at birds and planes. The big rally had been going on all day. They were out on a big lawn, or plaza, on the campus, about fifteen thousand of them, the toggle-coat bohemians, while the P.A. loudspeakers boomed and rabbled and raked across them. There was a big platform set up for the speakers. There had been about forty of them, all roaring or fulminating or arguing cogently, which was always worse. The idea at these things is to keep building up momentum and tension and suspense until finally when it is time for action—in this case, the march—the signal launches them as one great welded body of believers and they are ready to march and take billy clubs upside the head and all the rest of it.

All the shock workers of the tongue were there, speakers like Paul Jacobs, and M. S. Arnoni, who wore a prison uniform to the podium because his family had been wiped out in a German concentration camp during World War II—and out before them was a great sea of students and other Youth, the toggle-coat bohemians—toggle coats, Desert Boots, civil rights, down with the war in Vietnam—". . . could call out to you from their graves or from the fields and rivers upon which their ashes were thrown, they would implore this generation of Americans not to be silent in the face of the genocidal atrocities committed on the people of Vietnam . . ." and the words rolled in full forensic boom over the P.A. systems.

·   ·   ·

THE FIRST PERSON IN THE VIETNAM DAY COMMITTEE CIRCLE
to notice Kesey approaching the speaker's platform was Paul
Krassner, the editor of *The Realist* magazine. Most of the
Pranksters were still on the bus, fooling around with the guns for
the befuddlement of the gawkers who happened by. Kesey,
Babbs, Gretchen Fetchin and George Walker came on over the
platform, Kesey in his orange Day-Glo coat and World War I
helmet. Krassner ran his magazine as pretty much a one-man operation and he knew Kesey subscribed to it. So he wasn't so surprised that Kesey knew him. What got him was that Kesey just
started talking to him, just like they had been having a conversation all along and something had interrupted them and now
they were resuming . . . It is a weird thing. You feel the guy's
charisma, to use that one, right away, busting out even through
the nutty Day-Glo, or maybe sucking one in, the way someone
once wrote of Gurdjieff: "You could not help being drawn, almost physically, towards him . . . like being sucked in by a vast,
spiritual vacuum cleaner." At the time, however, Krassner
thought of Flash Gordon.

"Look up there," Kesey says, motioning up toward the platform.

Up there is Paul Jacobs. Jacobs tends toward the forensic, anyway, and the microphone and loudspeakers do something to a
speaker. You can hear your voice rolling and thundering, powerful as Wotan, out over that ocean of big ears and eager faces, and
you are omnipotent and more forensic and orotund and thunder-
ous minute by minute—*It is written, but I say unto you . . . the jackals of history-ree-ree-ree-ree* . . . From where they are standing, off
to the side of the platform, they can hear very little of what Jacobs
is actually saying, but they can hear the sound barking and roaring and reverberating and they can hear the crowd roaring back
and baying on cue, and they can see Jacobs, hunched over squat
and thick into the microphone, with his hands stabbing out for
emphasis, and there, at sundown, silhouetted against the florid
sky, is his jaw, jutting out, like a cantaloupe . . .

Kesey says to Krassner: "Don't listen to the words, just the sound, and the gestures ... who do you see?"

And suddenly Krassner wants very badly to be right. It is the call of the old charisma. He wants to come up with the right answer.

"Mussolini ... ?"

Kesey starts nodding, Right, right, but keeping his eye on the prognathous jaw.

By this time more of the Pranksters have come up to the platform. They have found some electrical outlets and they have run long cords up to the platform, for the guitars and basses and horns. Kesey is the next to last speaker. He is to be followed by some final Real Barnburner of a speaker and then—the final surge and the march on Oakland.

From the moment Kesey gets up there, it is a freaking jar. His jacket glows at dusk, and his helmet. Lined up behind him are more Day-Glo crazies, wearing aviator helmets and goggles and flight suits and Army tunics, Babbs, Gretch, Walker, Zonker, Mary Microgram, and little Day-Glo kids, and half of them carrying electric guitars and horns, mugging and moving around in Day-Glo streaks. The next jar is Kesey's voice, it is so nonforensic. He comes on soft, in the Oregon drawl, like he's just having a conversation with 15,000 people:

You know, you're not gonna stop this war with this rally, by marching ... That's what they do ... They hold rallies and they march ... They've been having wars for ten thousand years and you're not gonna stop it this way ... Ten thousand years, and this is the game they play to do it ... holding rallies and having marches ... and that's the same game you're playing ... their game ...

Whereupon he reaches into his great glowing Day-Glo coat and produces a harmonica and starts playing it right into the microphone, *Home, home on the range,* hawonking away on the goddamn thing—*Home ... home ... on the ra-a-a-a-ange hawonkawonk ...*

The crowd stands there in a sudden tender clump, most of

them wondering if they heard right, cocking their heads and rolling their heads to one another. First of all, that conversational tone all of a sudden, and then random notes from the Day-Glo crazies behind him ripped out offen the electric guitars and the general babble of the place feeding into the microphone—did anybody hear right—

—all the while Kesey is still up there hawonking away on the freaking harmonica. *Home, home on the ra-a-a-a-a-a-ange*—

—ahhhh, that's it—they figure it's some calculated piece of stage business, playing *Home, home on the range*—building up to something like Yah! We know about that *home!* We know about that *range!* That rotten U.S. home and that rotten U.S. range!—

—but instead it is the same down-home drawling voice—

I was just looking at the speaker who was up here before me . . . and I couldn't hear what he was saying . . . but I could hear the sound of it . . . and I could hear your sound coming back at him . . . and I could see the gestures—

—and here Kesey starts parodying Paul Jacobs's stabbing little hands and his hunched-over stance and his—

—*and I could see his jaw sticking out like this . . . silhouetted against the sky . . . and you know who I saw . . . and who I heard? . . . Mussolini . . . I saw and I heard Mussolini here just a few minutes ago . . . Yep . . . you're playing their game . . .*

Then he starts hawonking away again, hawonking and ha-wonking *Home, home on the range* with that sad old setter harmonica-around-the-campfire pace—and the Pranksters back him up on their instruments, Babbs, Gretch, George, Zonker, weaving up there in a great Day-Glo freakout

—and what the hell—a few boos, but mainly confusion—what in the name of God are the ninnies—

—*We've all heard all this and seen all this before, but we keep on doing it . . . I went to see the Beatles last month . . . And I heard 20,000 girls screaming together at the Beatles . . . and I couldn't hear what they were screaming, either . . . But you don't have to . . . They're screaming Me! Me! Me! Me! . . . I'm Me! . . . That's the cry of the ego, and that's the cry of this rally! . . . Me! Me! Me! Me! . . . And that's why wars get fought . . . ego . . . because enough people want to scream Pay attention to Me . . . Yep, you're playing their game . . .*

—and then more *hawonkawonkawonkawonkawonka*—

—and the crowd starts going into a slump. It's as if the rally, the whole day, has been one long careful inflation of a helium balloon, preparing to take off—and suddenly somebody has pulled the plug. It's not what *he* is saying, either. It's the sound and the freaking sight and that goddamn mournful harmonica and that stupid Chinese music by the freaks standing up behind him. It's the only thing the martial spirit can't stand—a put-on, a prank, a shuck, a goose in the anus.

—Vietnam Day Committee seethe together at the edge of the platform: "Who the hell invited this bastard!" "*You* invited him!" "Well, hell, we figured he's a writer, so he'll be against the war!" "Didn't you have enough speakers?" says Krassner. "You need all the big names you can get, to get the crowd out." "Well, that's what you get for being celebrity fuckers," says Krassner. If they had had one of those big hooks like they had on amateur night in the vaudeville days, they would have pulled Kesey off the podium right then. Well, then, why doesn't somebody just go up there and edge him off! He's ruining the goddamn thing. But then they see all the Day-Glo crazies, men and women and children all weaving and electrified, clawing at guitars, blowing horns, all crazed aglow at sundown . . . And the picture of the greatest anti-war rally in the history of America ending in a Day-Glo brawl to the tune of Home, home on the range . . .

—suddenly the hawonking on the freaking harmonica stops. Kesey leans into the microphone—

There's only one thing to do . . . there's only one thing's gonna do any good at all . . . And that's everybody just look at it, look at the war, and turn your backs and say . . . Fuck it . . .

—*hawonkawonkawonkawonka*—

—They hear that all right. The sound of the phrase—*Fuck*

it—sounds so weird, so shocking, even here in Free Speech citadel, just coming out that way over a public loudspeaker, rolling over the heads of 15,000 souls—

—*Home, home on the range hawonkawonkawonka,* and the Pranksters beginning to build up most madly on their instruments now, behind the harmonica, sounding like an insane honky-tonk version of Juan Carrillo who devised 96 tones on the back seat of a Willys Jeep, saved pennies all through the war to buy it, you understand, zinc pennies until the blue pustules formed under his zither finger nether there, you understand . . .

—*Just look at it and turn away and say . . . Fuck it*

—*say . . . Fuck it . . .*

hawonkawonkawonka blam

—*Fuck it—*

Hawonkafuckit . . . friends . . .

THERE WAS NO WAY ONE COULD PROVE KESEY HAD DONE IT. Nevertheless, something was gone out of the anti-war rally. The Real Barnburner spoke, and the Vietnam Day Committee tried to put in one last massive infusion of the old spirit and then gave the signal and the great march on Oakland began, through the gloaming. Fifteen thousand souls . . . shoulder to shoulder like in the old strike posters. At the Oakland-Berkeley line there was an arrow-shaped phalanx of police and National Guard. The Vietnam Day Committee marched in frantic clump at the head, trying to decide whether to force the issue, have a *physical confrontation,* heads busted, bayonets—or turn back when they ordered them to. Nobody seemed to have any resolve. Somebody would say, We have no choice, we've got to turn back—and somebody else would call him a Martin Luther King. That was about the worst thing you could call anybody on the New Left at that time. Martin Luther King turned back at the critical moment on the bridge at Selma. We can't risk submitting the crania of our devoted people to fracturization and degradation by those who do not shrink from a cowardly show of weaponry, he had said, going on like Social Science Negro in his sepulchral voice—the big solemn preachery Uncle Tom. Yah! yuh Tuskegee-headed Uncle Tom, yuh, yuh Booker T. Washington peanut-butter lecture-podium Nobel Prize medal head, yuh—*Uncle Tom*—by the time it was all over, Martin Luther King was a stupid music-hall Handkerchief Head on the New Left—and here they were, calling each other Martin Luther Kings and other incredible things—but nobody had any good smashing iron zeal to carry the day—O where is our Zea-lot, who Day-glowed and fucked up our heads—and there was nothing to do but grouse at the National Guard and turn back, which they did. What the hell has happened to us? Who did this? Why, it was the Masked Man—

So the huge march turned around and headed for Civic Center Park in Berkeley and stood around there eating hamburgers and listening to music by a jug band—a group that later became known as Country Joe and the Fish—and wondering what the hell had happened. Then somebody started throwing tear gas from a rooftop and Bob Scheer was bravely telling everybody to lie down on the grass, because tear gas rises—but the jug band just stood there, petrified, with their hands and their instruments frozen in the same position as when the gas hit. It seems the jug band was high on something or other, and when the gas hit, the combination of the gas and whatever they were already up on—it *pet*rified them and they stood there *in* stark stiff *medias res* as if they were posing for an Iwo Jima sculpture for the biggest anti-war rally in the history of the American people. The whole rally now seemed like a big half ass, with the frozen jug band the picture of how far they had gotten.

chapter XVII

Departures

Prepare for Mexico

And then Kesey posted cryptic words on his log-house
  Prankster bulletin board:
Let every thought, our whole direction, prepare for Mexico.

Every morsel you eat, every book you read, every high, every
  low, every Day-Glo deed . . .
But he never said why or when they might expect to go.

Mountain Girl Returns to Poughkeepsie

Now, Mountain Girl groks fully of the Pranksters' psychic
  takeoff
And is the very radiometer of their superpsychic pace.
No one ever plunged more fully in the psychedelic risk-all
Or ever blazed more radiant through the splays of inner space.

Yet not even a very Isis is immune against the crisis
That stamps a woman's psyche when she is going to bear a
     child.
It could never be easy to be three thousand miles from Kesey
But she had to Stop!
     And try to grok
     more fully . . . and go back East awhile

SANDY RETURNS TO NEW YORK

The path was soft as velvet, but Sandy heard it coming—
Ahor! rising, materializing from the mists of his devotion.
The demon Speed starts wrenching, leaves Sandy flinching in a
     bummer,
Dazed again in a half-crazed demonic DMT implosion

Causing psychosomatic, psychocidic cortical syndromes,
Even synarthrotic paralysis down the side of his lean face.
He tries to cure himself, purify the psychic venom,
But they're no use—all the Prankster arts of this limelit magic
     place.

Even *I Ching* says brain scans, EEGs, the whole clinical bit,
Which costs money—Kesey! Let me pawn the Ampex,
Four-hundred-dollar tape machine, for after all I brought it

Here in the first place—and then—stuck in his synarthrotic
     cortex
This thought: Kesey refused him the Ampex, Prankster
     salvation machine.
He goes back East for the clinical bit, but that won't be the end
     of it, Dream Warrior . . .

chapter XVIII

Cosmo's Tasmanian Deviltry

"CAN
YOU
PASS THE
ACID TEST?—"

Comes the call
Chiseled on each Prankster eyeball
in Lincoln gothic
As we moan
In this graveyard among moonstone tombstones
with a philosophic
It's *your* ass—
Can *you* pass the Acid Test?

Babbs and Kesey swaying
In a California graveyard, baying
deep

In the synch
Zonked on LSD on the brink
freaking steep
Of a missionary quest:
Can *you* pass the Acid Test?

Tombstones!
Vaults, coffins and bald carbon-dated bones
A dream transfusion
From the Community Breast:
Can *you* pass the Acid Test?

The group mind
Flying high, Major, but not blind
in the moonshine
Was inspired
With the ceremony that would be required
in the moon shot
To extend
The Prankster message to the ends
Of the earth. A mindfest:
a moon ship
The Acid Test . . .

. . . and Kesey emerged from the weird night in the graveyard
with the vision of turning on the world, literally, and a weirdly
practical way of doing it, known as

THE ACID TEST

For, as it has been written: . . . *he develops a strong urge to extend
the message to all people . . . he develops a ritus, often involving music, dance, liturgy, sacrifice, to achieve an objectified and stereotyped
expression of the original spontaneous religious experience.*

Christ! how many movements before them had run into this
selfsame problem. Every vision, every insight of the . . . original . . . circle always came out of the *new experience* . . . the

kairos . . . and how to tell it! How to get it across to the multitudes who have never had this experience themselves? *You couldn't put it into words.* You had to create conditions in which they would feel an approximation of *that feeling,* the sublime *kairos.* You had to put them into ecstasy . . . Buddhist monks immersing themselves in cosmic love through fasting and contemplation, Hindus zonked out in Bhakti, which is fervent love in the possession of God, ecstatics flooding themselves with Krishna through sexual orgies or plunging into the dinners of the Bacchanalia, Christians off in Edge City through gnostic onanism or the Heart of Jesus or the Child Jesus with its running sore—or—

THE ACID TESTS

And suddenly Kesey sees that they, the Pranksers, already have the expertise and the machinery to create a mindblown state such as the world has never seen, totally wound up, lit up, amplified and . . . controlled—plus the most efficient key ever devised to open the doors in the mind of the world: namely, Owsley's LSD.

For months Kesey has been trying to work out . . . the fantasy . . . of the Dome. This was going to be a great geodesic dome on top of a cylindrical shaft. It would look like a great mushroom. Many levels. People would climb a stairway up the cylinder—*buy a ticket?*—*we-e-e-elllll*—and the dome would have a great foam-rubber floor they could lie down on. Sunk down in the foam rubber, below floor level, would be movie projectors, video-tape projectors, light projectors. All over the place, up in the dome, everywhere, would be speakers, microphones, tape machines, live, replay, variable lag. People could take LSD or speed or smoke grass and lie back and experience what they would, enclosed and submerged in a planet of lights and sounds such as the universe never knew. Lights, movies, video tapes, video tapes of themselves, flashing and swirling over the dome from the beams of searchlights rising from the floor from between their bodies. The sounds roiling around in the globe like a typhoon. Movies and tapes of the past, tapes and video tapes, broadcasts and pictures of the present, tapes and humanoid sounds of the future—but all brought together *now*—here and now—*Kairos*—into the dilated cerebral cortex . . .

The geodesic dome, of course, was Buckminster Fuller's inspiration. The light projections were chiefly Gerd Stern's, Gerd Stern of the USCO group, although Roy Seburn had already done a lot with them and Page Browning showed a talent that surprised everybody. But the magic dome, the new planet, was Kesey and the Pranksters. The idea went beyond what would later be known as mixed-media entertainment, now a standard practice in "psychedelic discotheques" and so forth. The Pranksters had the supra-medium, a fourth dimension—acid—Cosmo—All-one—Control—The Movie—

But why a dome? The answer to all the Prankster fantasies, public and private, the whole solution—they already found it; namely, the Hell's Angels party. That two-day rout hadn't been a party but a show. It had been more than a show even. It had been an incredible concentration of energy. Not only Pranksters, but people from all over, heads, non-heads, intellectuals, curiosity-seekers, even cops, had turned up and gotten swept up in the incredible energy of the thing. They had been in the Prankster movie. It was one show that hadn't been separated into entertainers and customers, with the customers buying a ticket and saying All right, now entertain me. At the Angels' party everybody got high together and everybody did his thing and entertained everybody else, Angels being Angels, Ginsberg being Ginsberg, Pranksters being Pranksters, and cops being cops. Even the cops did their thing, splashing those big lush evil revolving red turret lights off the dirt cliff and growling and baying and hassling cars.

CAN
YOU
PASS THE
ACID TEST?

Anybody who could take LSD for the first time and go through all that without freaking out...Leary and Alpert preached "set and setting." Everything in taking LSD, in having a fruitful, freakout-free LSD experience, depended on set and setting. You should take it in some serene and attractive setting, a house or apartment decorated with objects of the honest sort, Turkoman tapestries, Greek goatskin rugs, Cost Plus blue jugs, soft light—not Japanese paper globe light, however, but untasselated Chinese textile shades—in short, an Uptown Bohemian country retreat of the $60,000-a-year sort, ideally, with Mozart's *Requiem* issuing with liturgical solemnity from the hi-fi. The "set" was the set of your mind. You should prepare for the experience by meditating upon the state of your being and deciding what you hope to discover or achieve on this voyage into the self. You should also have a guide who has taken LSD himself and is familiar with the various stages of the experience and whom you know and trust...and Fuck that! That only clamped the constipation of the past, the eternal *lags,* on something that should happen *Now.* Let the setting be as unserene and lurid as the Prankster arts can make it and let your set be only what is on your...*brain,* man, and let your guide, your trusty hand-holding, head-swaddling guide, be a bunch of Day-Glo crazies who have as one of their mottoes: "Never trust a Prankster." The Acid Tests would be like the Angels' party plus all the ideas that had gone into the Dome fantasy. Everybody would take acid, any time they wanted, six hours before the Test began or the moment they got there, at whatever point in the trip they wanted to enter the new planet. In any event, they would be on a new planet.

The mysteries of the synch! Very strange...the Acid Tests turned out, in fact, to be an art form foreseen in that strange book, *Childhood's End,* a form called "total identification": "The history of the cinema gave the clue to their actions. First, sound, then color, then stereoscopy, then Cinerama, had made the old 'moving pictures' more and more like reality itself. Where was the end of the story? Surely, the final stage would be reached when the audience forgot it was an audience, and became part of the action. To achieve this would involve stimulation of all the senses, and perhaps hypnosis as well . . . When the goal was attained, there would be an enormous enrichment of human experience. A man could become—for a while, at least,—any other person, and could take part in any conceivable adventure, real or imaginary. . . . And when the 'program' was over, he would have acquired a memory as vivid as any experience in his actual life—indeed, indistinguishable from reality itself."

Too freaking true!

THE FIRST ACID TEST ENDED UP MORE LIKE ONE OF THE OLD acid parties at La Honda, which is to say, a private affair, and mostly formless. It was meant to be public, but the Pranksters were not the world's greatest at the mechanics of things, like hiring a hall. The first one was going to be in Santa Cruz. But they couldn't hire a hall in time. They had to hold it out at Babbs's house, a place known as the Spread, just outside of Santa Cruz in a community known as Soquel. The Spread was like a rundown chicken farm. The wild vetch and dodder vines were gaining ground every minute, at least where the ground wasn't burnt off or beaten down into a clay muck. There were fat brown dogs and broken vehicles and rusted machines and rotting troughs and recapped tires and a little old farmhouse with linoleum floors and the kind of old greasy easy chairs that upholstery flies hover over in nappy clouds and move off about three-quarters of an inch when you wave your hand at them. But there were also wild Day-Glo creations on the walls and ceilings, by Babbs, and the place was private and tucked off by itself. In any case, they were stuck with the Spread.

About all the advertising they could do was confined to the day of the Test itself. Norman Hartweg had painted a sign on some cardboard and tacked it onto some boards Babbs had used as cue signs in the movie, and put it up in the Hip Pocket Bookstore. CAN *YOU* PASS THE ACID TEST? The Hip Pocket Bookstore was a paperback bookstore that Hassler and Peter Demma, one of the Prankster outer circle, were running in Santa Cruz. They left word in the store that afternoon that it was going to be at Babbs's. A few local bohos saw it and came out, but mainly it was the Pranksters and their friends who showed up at the Spread that night, including a lot of the Berkeley crowd that had been coming to La Honda. Plus Allen Ginsberg and his entourage.

It started off as a party, with some of the movie flashed on the walls, and lights, and tapes, and the Pranksters providing the music themselves, not to mention the LSD. The Pranksters' strange atonal Chinese music broadcast on all frequencies, à la John Cage. It was mostly just another La Honda party—but then around 3 A.M. a thing happened . . . The non-involved people, the people just there for the beano, the people who hadn't seen the Management, like the Berkeley people, they had all left by 3 A.M. and the Test was down to some kind of core . . . It ended up with Kesey on one side of Babbs's living room and Ginsberg on the other, with everybody else arranged around these two poles like on a magnet, all the Kesey people over toward him and all the Ginsberg people toward him—The super-West and the super-East—and the subject got to be Vietnam. Kesey gives his theory of whole multitudes of people joining hands in a clump and walking away from the war. Ginsberg said all these things, these wars, were the result of misunderstandings. Nobody who was doing the fighting ever *wanted* to be doing it, and if everybody could only sit around in a friendly way and talk it out, they could get to the root of their misunderstanding and settle it—and then from the rear of the Kesey contingent came the voice of the only man in the room who had been within a thousand miles of the war, Babbs, saying, "Yes, it's all so *very obvious.*"

It's all so very obvious . . .

How magical that comment seemed at that moment! The magical eighth hour of acid—how clear it all now was—Ginsberg had said it, and Babbs, the warrior, had certified it, and it had all built to this, and suddenly everything was so . . . very . . . clear . . .

The Acid Test at the Spread was just a dry run, of course. It didn't really . . . reach out into the world . . . But! soon . . . the Rolling Stones, England's second hottest pop group, were coming to San Jose, 40 miles south of San Francisco, for a show in the Civic Auditorium on December 4. Kesey can see it all, having seen it before. He can see all the wound-up wired-up teeny freaks and assorted multitudes pouring out of the Cow Palace after the Beatles show that night, the fragmented pink-tentacled beast, pouring out still aquiver with ecstasy and jelly beans all cocked and aimless with no flow to go off in . . . It *is* so very obvious.

For three or four days the Pranksters searched for a hall in San Jose and couldn't come up with one—naturally—it really seemed natural and almost right that nothing should be definite until the last minute. All that was certain was that they *would* find one at the last minute. The Movie would create that much at least. And what if the multitudes didn't *know* where it was going to be until the last minute? Well, those who were meant to be there—those who were in the pudding—they would get there. You were either on the bus or off the bus, and that went for the whole world, even in San Jose, California. At the last minute Kesey talked a local boho figure known as Big Nig into letting them use his old hulk of a house.

Kesey had hooked up with a rock 'n' roll band, The Grateful Dead, led by Jerry Garcia, the same dead-end kid who used to live in the Chateau in Palo Alto with Page Browning and other seeming no-counts, lumpenbeatniks, and you had to throw them out when they came over and tried to crash the parties on Perry Lane. Garcia remembered—how they came down and used to get booted out "by Kesey and the wine drinkers." *The wine drinkers*—the middle-class bohemians of Perry Lane. They both, Kesey and Garcia, had been heading into the pudding, from different directions, all that time, and now Garcia was a, yes, beau-

tiful person, quiet, into the pudding, and a great guitar player.
Garcia had first named his group The Warlocks, meaning sorcerers or wizards, and they had been eking by playing for the
beer drinkers, at jazz joints and the like around Palo Alto. To the
Warlocks, the beer drinker music, even when called jazz, was
just square hip. They were on to that distinction, too. For
Kesey—they could just play, do their thing.

The Dead had an organist called Pig Pen, who had a Hammond electric organ, and they move the electric organ into Big
Nig's ancient house, plus all of the Grateful Dead's electrified
guitars and basses and the Pranksters' electrified guitars and
basses and flutes and horns and the light machines and the movie
projectors and the tapes and mikes and hi-fis, all of which pile up
in insane coils of wires and gleams of stainless steel and winking
amplifier dials before Big Nig's unbelieving eyes. His house is old
and has wiring that would hardly hold a toaster. The Pranksters
are primed in full Prankster regalia. Paul Foster has on his Importancy Coat and now has a huge head of curly hair, a great
curly mustache pulling back into great curly mutton chops roaring off his face. Page Browning is the king of face painters. He
becomes a full-fledged Devil with a bright orange face and his
eyes become the centers of two great silver stars painted over the
orange and his hair is silver with silver dust and he paints his lips
silver with silver lipstick. This very night the Pranksters all sit
down with oil pastel crayons and colored pens and at a wild rate
start printing handbills on 8½ × 11 paper saying CAN *YOU* PASS
THE ACID TEST? and giving Big Nig's address. As the jellybean-
cocked masses start pouring out of the Rolling Stones concert at
the Civic Auditorium, the Pranksters charge in among them. Orange & silver Devil, wild man in a coat of buttons—Pranksters.
Pranksters!—handing out the handbills with the challenge, like
some sort of demons, warlocks verily, come to channel the wild
pointless energy built up by the Rolling Stones inside.

They come piling into Big Nig's, and suddenly acid and the
worldcraze were everywhere, the electric organ vibrating

through every belly in the place, kids dancing not *rock* dances, not the frug and the—what?—*swim,* mother, but dancing *ecstasy,* leaping, dervishing, throwing their hands over their heads like Daddy Grace's own stroked-out inner courtiers—yes!—Roy Seburn's lights washing past every head, Cassady rapping, Paul Foster handing people weird little things out of his Eccentric Bag, old whistles, tin crickets, burnt keys, spectral plastic handles. Everybody's eyes turn on like lightbulbs, fuses blow, blackness—wowwww!—the things that shake and vibrate and funnel and freak out in this blackness—and then somebody slaps new fuses in and the old hulk of a house shudders back, the wiring writhing and fragmenting like molting snakes, the organs vibromassage the belly again, fuses blow, minds scream, heads explode, neighbors call the cops, 200, 300, 400 people from out there drawn into The Movie, into the edge of the pudding at least, a mass closer and higher than any mass in history, it seems most surely, and Kesey makes minute adjustment, small toggle switch here, lubricated with Vaseline No. 634–3 diluted with carbon tetrachloride, and they *ripple,* Major, *ripple,* but with meaning, 400 of the attuned multitude headed toward the pudding, the first mass acid experience, the dawn of the Psychedelic, the Flower Generation and all the rest of it, and Big Nig wants the rent.

"How you holding?"

How you holding—

"I mean, like, you know," says Big Nig to Garcia. "I didn't charge Kesey nothing to use this place, like *free,* you know? and the procedure now is that every cat here *contributes,* man, to help out with the rent."

With the rent—

"Yeah, I mean, like"—says Big Nig. Big Nig stares at Garcia with the deepest look of hip spade soul authority you can imagine, and nice and officious, too—

*Yeah, I mean, like—*Garcia, for his part, however, doesn't know which bursts out first, the music or the orange laugh. Out the edges of his eyes he can see his own black hair framing his face—it is so long, to the shoulders, and springs out like a Sudanese soldier's—and then big Nig's big earnest black face right in front of him flapping and washing comically out into the glistening acid-glee red sea of faces out beyond them both in the galactic red lakes on the walls—

"Yeah, I mean, like, for the *rent,* man," says Big Nig, "you already *blown* six fuses."

Blown! Six fuses! Garcia sticks his hand into his electric guitar and the notes come out like a huge orange laugh all blown fuses electric spark leaps in colors upon the glistening sea of faces. It's a freaking laugh and a half. A new star is being born, like a lightbulb in a womb, and Big Nig wants the rent—a new star being born, a new planet forming, Ahura Mazda blazing in the world womb, here before our very eyes—and Big Nig, the poor pathetic spade, wants his rent.

A freaking odd thought, that one. A big funky spade looking pathetic and square. For twenty years in the hip life, Negroes never even *looked* square. They were the archetypical soul figures. But what is Soul, or Funky, or Cool, or Baby—in the new world of the ecstasy, the All-one . . . the *kairos*. . . .

IF ONLY THERE WERE THE PERFECT PLACE, WHICH WOULD BE a place big enough for the multitudes and isolated enough to avoid the cops, with their curfews and eternal hassling. Shortly after that they found the perfect place, by acci—

By *acc*ident, Mahavira?

The third Acid Test was scheduled for Stinson Beach, 15 miles north of San Francisco. Stinson Beach was already a gathering place for local heads. You could live all winter in little beach cottages there for next to nothing. There was a nice solid brick recreation hall on the beach, all very nice—but at the last minute that whole deal fell through, and they shifted to Muir Beach, a few miles south. The handbills were already out, all over the head sections of San Francisco, CAN *YOU* PASS THE ACID TEST, advertising Cassady & Ann Murphy Vaudeville and celebrities who *might be* there, which included anybody who happened to be in town, or might make it to town, the Fugs, Ginsberg, Roland Kirk. There were always some nice chiffon subjunctives and the future conditionals in the Prankster handbill rhetoric, but who was to deny who *might be* drawn into the Movie . . .

Anyway, at the last minute they headed for Muir Beach instead. The fact that many people wouldn't know about the change and would go to Stinson Beach and merely freeze in the darkness and never find the right place—somehow that didn't even seem distressing. It was part of some strange analogical order of the universe. Norman Hartweg hooked down his LSD—it was in the acid gas capsules that night—and thought of Gurdjieff. Gurdjieff wouldn't announce a meeting until the last minute. We're gonna get together tonight. The people that got there, got there; and there was message in that alone. Which was, of course: *you're either on the bus or off the bus.*

Those who were on the bus, even if they weren't Pranksters, like Marshall Efron, the round Mercury of Hip California, or the Hell's Angels . . . all found it. The cops, however, never did. They were apparently thrown off by the Stinson Beach handbills.

Muir Beach had a big log-cabin-style lodge for dances, banquets, and the like. The lodge was stilted up out in a waste of frigid marsh grass. A big empty nighttime beach in winter. Some little log tourist cabins with blue doors on either side, all empty. The lodge had three big rooms and was about 100 feet long, all logs and rafters and exposed beams, a tight ship of dark wood and Roughing It. The Grateful Dead piled in with their equipment and the Pranksters with theirs, which now included a Hammond electric organ for Gretch and a great strobe light.

The strobe! The strobe, or stroboscope, was originally an instrument for studying motion, like the way a man's legs move when he is running. In a darkened chamber, for example, you aim a bright light, flashing on and off, at the runner's legs as he runs. The light flashes on and off very rapidly, maybe three times as fast as a normal heartbeat. Every time the light flashes on, you see a new stage in the movement of the runner's legs. The successive images tend to freeze in your mind, because the light flashes off before the usual optical blur of the motion can hit you. The strobe has certain magical properties in the world of the acid heads. At certain speeds stroboscopic lights are so synched in with the pattern of brain waves that they can throw epileptics into a seizure. Heads discovered that strobes could project them into many of the sensations of an LSD experience without taking LSD. *The strobe!*

To people standing under the mighty strobe everything seemed to fragment. Ecstatic dancers—their hands flew off their arms, frozen in the air—their glistening faces came apart—a gleaming ellipse of teeth here, a pair of buffered highlit cheekbones there—all flacking and fragmenting into images as in an old flicker movie—a man in slices!—all of history pinned up on a butterfly board; the *experience,* of course. The strobe, the projectors, the mikes, the tapes, the amplifiers, the variable lag Ampex—it was all set up in a coiling gleaming clump in the Lincoln Log lodge, the communal clump, Babbs working over the dials, talking into the microphones to test them. Heads beginning to pour in. Marshall Efron and Norman, Norman already fairly zonked . . . Then in comes Kesey, through the main door—

Everyone watches. His face is set, his head cocked slightly. He is going to *do* something; everyone watches, because this seems terribly important. Drawn in right away by the charismatic vacuum cleaner, they are. Kesey heads for the control center, saying nothing to anyone, reaches into the galaxy of dials, makes . . . a single minute adjustment . . . yes! one toggle switch, double-pole, single-throw, double-break, in the allegory of Control . . .

Babbs is there, bombed, but setting up the intricate glistening coils of the tapes and projectors and the rest of it. Each of the Pranksters, bombed, has some fairly exacting task to do. Norman is staring at the dials—and he can't even see the numbers, he is so bombed, the numbers are wriggling off like huge luminous parasites under a microscope—but—*function under acid*. Babbs says, "One reason we're doing this is to learn how to function on acid." Of course! Prepare for the Day—when multitudes, millions, civilizations are on acid, seeking satori, it is coming, the wave is spreading.

The heads are all sitting around on the floor, about 300 of them. Into the maelstrom! Yes. At Big Nig's in San Jose, a lot of the kids the Pranksters had corralled coming out of the Rolling Stones show did not take LSD that night, although there were enough heads at Big Nig's stoned on various things to create that sympathetic vibration known as the "contact high." But this is different. Practically everybody who has found the place, after the switch from Stinson Beach, is far enough into the thing to know what the "acid" in the Acid Test means. A high percentage took LSD about four hours ago, rode out the first rush and are ready . . . now to groove . . . The two projectors shine forth with The Movie. The bus and the Pranksters start rolling over the walls of the lodge, Babbs and Kesey rapping on about it, the Bus lumping huge and vibrating and bouncing in great swells of heads and color—Norman, zonked, sitting on the floor, is half frightened, half ecstatic, although something in the back of his mind recognizes this as his Acid Test pattern, to sit back and watch, holding on through the rush, until 3 or 4 A.M., in the magic hours, and then dance—but so much of a rush this time! The Movie and Roy Seburn's light machine pitching the intergalactic red science-fiction seas to all corners of the lodge, oil and water and food coloring pressed between plates of glass and projected in vast size so that the very ooze of cellular Creation seems to ectoplast into the ethers and then the Dead coming in with their immense submarine vibrato vibrating, *garanging,* from the Aleutian rocks to the baja griffin cliffs of the Gulf of California. The Dead's weird sound! agony-in-ecstasis! submarine somehow, turbid half the time, tremendously loud but like sitting under a waterfall, at the same time full of sort of ghoul-show vibrato sounds as if each string on their electric guitars is half a block long and twanging in a room full of natural gas, not to mention their great Hammond electric organ, which sounds like a movie house Wurlitzer, a diathermy machine, a Citizens' Band radio and an Auto-Grind garbage truck at 4 A.M., all coming over the same frequency . . . Then suddenly another movie

THE FROGMAN

Babbs and Gretch and Hagen made it down in Santa Cruz, the story of Babbs the Frogman, arising from the Pacific in black neopreme Frogman suit from flippers to insect goggles, the pranking monster, falling in love with the Princess, Gretch, with floods of frames from elsewhere—the Bus Movie?—brittering in stroboscopically Frogman woos her and wins her and loses her to the Pacific Chohans in submarinal projection

BABBS! GRETCH!

Norman has never seen a movie while under acid before and it deepens, deepens, deepens in perspective, this movie, the most 3-D movie ever made, until they are standing right before him, their very neopreme fairy tails and the Pacific is so far in the distance and black out beyond the marshes around the Muir Beach lodge until Babbs and Gretch are now in the room in the flesh in two separate spots, here before me on the beach and over here in this very room in this very lodge on the beach, Babbs at the microphone and Gretch nearby at the new Hammond organ—such *synch!* that they should narrate and orchestrate their own lives like this, in variable lag, layer upon layer of variable lags

HEEEEEEEE

into the whirlpool who should appear but Owsley. Owsley, done up in his $600 head costume, has emerged from his subterrain of espionage and paranoia to come to see the Prankster experiment for himself, and in the middle of the giddy contagion he takes LSD. They never saw him take it before. He takes the LSD and

RRRRRRRRRRRRRRRRRRRRRRRRROIL

the whirlpool picks him up and spins him down into the stroboscopic stereoptic prankster panopticon in full variable lag

SUCH CREATURES

Hell's Angels come reeling in, shrieking Day-Glo, then clumping together on the floor under the black light and then most gentle Buddha blissly passing around among themselves various glittering Angel esoterica, chains, Iron Crosses, knives, buttons, coins, keys, wrenches, spark plugs, grokking over these arcana winking in the Day-Glo. Orange & Silver devil gliding through the dancers grinning his Zea-lot grin in every face, and Kesey crouched amid the gleaming coils, at the

CONTROLS

Kesey looks out upon the stroboscopic whirlpool—the dancers! flung and flinging! *in ecstasis!* gyrating! levitating! men in slices! in ping-pong balls! in the creamy bare essence and it reaches a

SYNCH

he never saw before. Heads from all over the acid world out here and all whirling into the pudding. Now let a man see what

CONTROL

is. Kesey mans the strobe and a twist of the mercury lever

UP

and they all speed up

NOW

the whole whirlpool, so far into it, they are. Faster they dance, hands thrown up off their arms like confetti in the strobe flashing, blissful faces falling apart and being exchanged, for I am you and you are me in Cosmo's Tasmanian deviltry. Turn it

DOWN

and they slow down—or We turn down—It—Cosmo—turns down, still in perfect synch, one brain, one energy, a single flow of intersubjectivity. It is *possible,* this alchemy so dreamed of by all the heads. It is happening before them

CONTROL

CURIOUSLY, AFTER THE FIRST RUSH AT THE ACID TEST, THERE would be long intervals of the most exquisite boredom. Exquisite, because it was so unsuspected after the general frenzy. Nothing would happen, at least not in the usual sense. Those who were . . . not on the bus . . . would come to the realization that there was no schedule. The Grateful Dead did not play in *sets;* no eight numbers to a set, then a twenty-five-minute break, and so on, four or five sets and then the close-out. The Dead might play one number for five minutes or thirty minutes. Who kept time? Who *could* keep time, with history cut up in slices. The Dead could get just as stoned as anyone else. The . . . non-attuned would look about and here would be all manner of heads, including those running the show, the Pranksters, stroked out against the walls like slices of Jello. Waiting; with nobody looking very likely to start it back up. Those who didn't care to wait would tend to drift off, stoned or otherwise, and the Test would settle down to the pudding. The Prankster band started the strange Chinese cacophony of its own, with Gretch wailing on the new electric organ. Norman got up and danced, it being that time. He even fooled about a bit with a little light projection thing of his own, although he didn't think it was good enough, but the magic hours were coming on like electric velvet. Kesey spoke softly over the microphone. They were into the still of the hurricane, the pudding.

AT DAWN — A FREAKING COLD LIGHT ON THE MARSH GRASS AND the beach. A purple shadow all over the ocean like one huge stone-cold bruise. Suddenly the main door bursts open and it's Owsley.

Owsley is lurching and groping and screaming
"Survival!"

It comes out like a steam whistle forced out of a constricted little opening
"Survival!"

Owsley, the Acid King, in his $600 head outfit, groping through the blue bruise dawn with his eyes like disaster craters, hissing

"Survival!"

The sight of Kesey apparently hits him with a surge of adrenaline, however, because he recovers his voice and starts in on Kesey:

"Kesey!"

The gist of it is that Kesey can't do this again. This is the end. The Acid Tests are over. Kesey is a maniac and the Tests are maniacal and the roof is falling in. Taking LSD in a monster group like this gets too many forces going, too much amok energy, causing very freaky and destructive things to happen, and so on. It's his acid and he says this is the end. None of them can figure out precisely what he is saying. Just that he has flipped and Kesey did it.

Little by little, they piece it together. He has had quite a trip for himself on his own LSD, has Owsley. It seems that Owsley took the LSD, a good dose, apparently, and the strobe light and the incredible layers of variable lag began rocking and rippling him and it threw him into a time warp, or parallel time dimension. The heads were always talking about such things. They could cite some serious thinkers, scientists even, such as C. D. Broad and his theory of a *second temporal dimension*—"events which are separated by a temporal gap in one dimension may be adjoined without any gap in the other, just as two points in the earth's surface which differ in longitude may be identical in latitude"—or J. W. Dunne's theory of serialism, or infinite regress—or Maurice Maeterlinck. The heads were always talking about such things and Owsley was primed for it. Then he got high. Then he got caught in the whirlpool, spun out of his gourd by all the special effects of the Pranksters' variable lag devices—and the legend of the trip he took eventually was told as follows:

Back he went into the eighteenth century, Count Cagliostro! no longer plain Giuseppe Balsamo of Palermo, the Oakland of the Mediterranean, but the good Count, alchemist, seer, magician, master of precognition, forecaster of lotteries, alchemical

creator, from out of base elements of... *this diamond,* greatest
and most dazzling in history—*here,* Cardinal Louis de Rohan—*but!*—persecuted as a thaumaturge—thrust into this spinning black donjon, the Bastille, seeping with lurid water and
carbonated moss and twitching dismembered rats, anatomized in
the flashing light of the diamond they wouldn't believe, a rat
shank here, a rat metacarpal there, rat teeth, rat eyes, rat tails
leaping and frozen in the air like city lights—that noise—a mob
in the streets—either salvation—or—the Bastille begins to disintegrate into absorbent felt cubes—

—and so on. The world began fragmenting on him. It began
coming totally to pieces, breaking up into component parts, and
he wasn't even back in the twentieth century yet, he was
trapped—where?—Paris in 1786? ... The whole world was
coming to pieces molecule by molecule now and swimming like
grease bubbles in a cup of coffee, disappearing into the intergalactic ooze and gasses all around—including his own body. He
lost his skin, his skeleton, his pulmonary veins—sneaking out
into the ooze like eels, they are, reeking phosphorus, his neural
ganglia—unraveling like hot worms and wiggling down the
galactic drain, his whole substance dissolving into gaseous noth-
ingness until finally he was down to one cell. *One human cell:* his;
that was all that was left of the entire known world, and if he lost
control of that one cell, there would be nothing left. The world
would be, like, *over.* He has to rebuild himself and the entire
world from that one cell with a gigantic act of will—too overwhelming. Where does a man start? With California Route 1 so
he can get out of here in his car? or will it turn out to be merely
the filthy Rue Ventru with the Bastille mobs waiting? or start
with the car? the differential? how do they make the bastards? or
the beach? all those freaking grains of sand? the marsh grass? the
tourist cabins? got to put *every* blue door back? or the ocean? or
leave it dry? save making all those filthy blind bathosphere black
animals down there ... or the sky? how far does it go? the Big
Dipper? the Ursa Minor? the Delphinium? suppose it is really

infinite concentric spheres of crystal making infinite gelatinous submarinal vibrations? the Dead? the Pranksters? Kesey, Kesey's *out* for good, Kesey and the bathosphere brutes—but with a superheroic effort he begins. But by the time he gets himself remade, it is too much. It is overwhelming. He makes his car. He makes the parking lot and the beginning of the road out. He'll make the rest of it as he goes along. *Freak it! Split!* Leave the rest of the known world to its own devices, out in the gasses. He jumped into the car and gunned off; and smashed it into a tree. A tree he hadn't even put *back* yet. But the crash somehow pops the whole world back. There it is; back from the fat-bubbling ooze. The car is smashed, but he has survived. Survived!

SURVIVAL!

and he plunges into the lodge to seek out the maniac Kesey. *That* sombitch has prolly popped back, too.

chapter XIX

The Trips Festival

OWSLEY'S FREAKOUT! OWSLEY BECAME OBSESSED WITH IT himself. Whenever the subject was the LSD experience—which it was most of the time around Owsley—he would recount his experience at Muir Beach. It seemed to horrify and intrigue him at the same time—such morbid but wonderful details. Everyone listens . . . can such things be? In any case, it sounded like Owsley thought Kesey was a demon and he was going to cut off their LSD supply.

Richard Alpert was also unhappy with the Acid Tests. Alpert, like Timothy Leary, had sacrificed his academic career as a psychologist for the sake of the psychedelic movement. It was hard enough to keep the straight multitudes from going hysterical over the subject of LSD even in the best of circumstances—let alone when it was used for manic screaming orgies in public places. Among the heads who leaned toward Leary and Alpert, it was hard to even freaking believe that the Pranksters were pulling a freaking prank like this. Any moment they were expecting them to explode into some sort of debacle, some sort of mass freakout, that the press could seize on and bury the psyche-delic movement forever. The police watched them closely, but there was very little they could do about it, except for an occa-sional marijuana bust, since there was no law against LSD at the time. The Pranksters went on to hold Tests in Palo Alto, Port-land, Oregon, two in San Francisco, four in and around Los Angeles—and three in Mexico—and no laws broken here, Lieu-tenant—*only every law of God and man*—In short, a goddamn outrage, and we're *powerless*—

The Acid Tests were one of those outrages, one of those *scan-dals,* that create a new style or a new world view. Everyone clucks, fumes, grinds their teeth over the bad taste, the bad morals, the insolence, the vulgarity, the childishness, the lunacy, the cruelty, the irresponsibility, the fraudulence and, in fact, gets worked up into such a state of excitement, such an epitasis, such a slaver, they can't turn it loose. It becomes a perfect obsession. And now they'll show you how it *should* have been done.

The Acid Tests were the *epoch* of the psychedelic style and practically everything that has gone into it. I don't mean merely that the Pranksters did it first but, rather, that it all came straight out of the Acid Tests in a direct line leading to the Trips Festival of January 1966. That brought the whole thing full out in the open. "Mixed media" entertainment—this came straight out of the Acid Tests' combination of light and movie projections, strobes, tapes, rock 'n' roll, black light. "Acid rock"—the sound of the Beatles' *Sergeant Pepper* album and the high-vibrato elec-tronic sounds of the Jefferson Airplane, the Mothers of Invention and many other groups—the mothers of it all were the Grateful Dead at the Acid Tests. The Dead were the *audio* counterpart of Roy Seburn's light projections. Owsley was responsible for some of this, indirectly. Owsley had snapped back from his great Freakout and started pouring money into the Grateful Dead and, thereby, the Tests. Maybe he figured the Tests were the wave of the future, whether he had freaked out or not. Maybe he thought "acid rock" was the sound of the future and he would become a kind of Brian Epstein for the Grateful Dead. I don't know. In any case, he started buying the Dead equipment such as no rock 'n' roll band ever had before, the Beatles included, all manner of tuners, amplifiers, receivers, loudspeakers, microphones, cartridges, tapes, theater horns, booms, lights, turntables, instruments, mixers, muters, servile mesochroics, whatever was on the market. The sound went down so many microphones and hooked through so many mixers and variable lags and blew up in so many amplifiers and roiled around in so many speakers and fed back down so many microphones, it came on like a chemical refinery. There was something wholly new and deliriously weird in the Dead's sound, and practically everything new in rock 'n' roll, rock jazz I have heard it called, came out of it.

Even details like psychedelic poster art, the quasi-*art nouveau* swirls of lettering, design and vibrating colors, electro-pastels and spectral Day-Glo, came out of the Acid Tests. Later other impresarios and performers would recreate the Prankster styles with a sophistication the Pranksters never dreamed of. *Art is not eternal, boys.* The posters became works of art in the accepted cultural tradition. Others would even play the Dead's sound more successfully, commercially, anyway, than the Dead. Others would do the mixed-media thing until it was pure ambrosial candy for the brain with creamy filling every time. To which Kesey would say: "They know *where* it is, but they don't know *what* it is."

IT WAS ACTUALLY STEWART BRAND WHO THOUGHT UP THE great Trips Festival of January 1966. Brand and a San Francisco artist, Ramon Sender. Brand was 27 and an ex-biologist who had run across the Indian peyote cults in Arizona and New Mexico. Brand founded an organization called America Needs Indians. And then one day he took some LSD, right after an Explorer satellite went up to photograph the earth, and as the old synapses began rapping around inside his skull at 5,000 thoughts per second, he was struck with one of those questions that inflame men's brains: *Why Haven't We Seen a Photograph of the Whole Earth Yet?*—and he drove across America from Berkeley, California, to 116th Street, New York City, selling buttons with that legend on them to Leftists, Rightists, Fundamentalists, Theosophists, malcontents, anyone with the health or stealth of paranoia or the put-on in their souls . . .

He and his friend Sender got the idea of pulling together all the new forms of expression that were kicking around in the hip world at that moment and having a Super Acid Test out in the open. Hire a hall and call in the multitudes. They found an impresario for the thing, Bill Graham, a New Yorker who had a lot of cachet in the hip world of San Francisco as a member of the San Francisco Mime Troupe, which used to get busted for putting on political dumb shows in the park, that kind of thing. The Trips Festival was set for Friday, Saturday, and Sunday nights, January 21–23, at the Longshoremen's Hall in San Francisco. The Trips Festival was billed as a big celebration that was going to simulate an LSD experience, minus the LSD, using light effects and music, mainly. The big night, Saturday night, was going to be called The Acid Test, featuring Ken Kesey and the Merry Pranksters.

Kesey and the Pranksters were primed for the Festival. Even Mountain Girl was on hand. She had wrestled the thing out in her mind and was back on the bus. The Pranksters had just held an Acid Test at the Fillmore Auditorium, a big ballroom in the middle of one of San Francisco's big Negro slums, the Fillmore district. It was a wild night. Hundreds of heads and bohos from all over the Bay area turned out, zonked to the eyeballs. Paul Krassner was back in town, and he heard the word that was out on . . . The Scene. Everybody would be "dropping acid" about 5 or 6 P.M. to get ready for the Acid Test to begin that night at nine o'clock at the Fillmore Auditorium. Krassner arrives and—shit!—he sees:

. . . a ballroom surrealistically seething with a couple of thousand bodies stoned out of their everlovin' bruces in crazy costumes and ob- scene makeup with a raucous rock 'n' roll band and stroboscopic lights and a thunder machine and balloons and heads and streamers and electronic equipment and the back of a guy's coat proclaiming Please don't believe in magic *to a girl dancing with 4-inch eyelashes so that even the goddamn Pinkerton Guards were contact high.*

Kesey asks him to take the microphone and contribute to a running commentary on the scene. "All I know," he announces into the din, "is that if I were a cop and I came in here, I wouldn't know where to begin."

Well, the cops came in, and they didn't know where to begin. They came in to close the Test down at 2 A.M. in keeping with a local ordinance and the whole thing was at its maddest height. Mountain Girl had hold of a microphone and was shrieking en- couragement to the flailing dancers. Babbs was beaming spot- lights at heads who were veering around bombed and asking them spectral questions over another microphone—Say there, what's your trouble—have you *l-o-s-t y-o-u-r mi-i-i-i-i-i-nd!* Page Browning was grinning Zea-lot. The cops started shouting for them to close down but couldn't make themselves heard and started pulling plugs out, microphone plugs, loudspeaker plugs, strobe plugs, amplifier plugs—but there were so many goddamn plugs, the most monumental snake pit of wires and plugs in his- tory, and as fast as they would pull eight plugs out, Mountain Girl would put ten plugs back in, and finally Mountain Girl had a microphone up on the balcony somewhere and was screaming instructions to the dancers and the cops—*louder music, more wine*—and they couldn't find her. Finally they ordered the Pranksters to start clearing the place out, which they did, except for Babbs, who sat down in a chair and wouldn't budge. We said get busy, said the cops.

"I don't have to," said Babbs. "I'm the boss here. *They're* work- ing for *me.*"

Yeah?—and one of the cops grabs Babbs by a luminous vest he has on, succeeding only in separating Babbs from the vest. Babbs grinning maniacally but suddenly looming most large and fierce.

"You're under arrest!"

"For what?"

"Resistin'."

"Resistin' what?"

"You gonna come quietly or do we have to take you?"

"Either way you want it," says Babbs, grinning in the most frightening manner now, like the next step is eight karate chops to the gizzards and giblets. Suddenly it is a Mexican stand-off—with both sides glaring but nobody swinging a punch yet. It is a grand hassle, of course. At the last minute a couple of Kesey's lawyers arrive on the scene and cool everything down and talk the cops out of it and Babbs out of it and it all rumbles away in the valley as part of the *Welthassle.*

THE LAWYERS—YES. KESEY'S ORIGINAL MARIJUANA CHARGE, on the big arrest at La Honda, had been ricocheting around in the San Mateo County court system for nine months. Kesey's lawyers were attacking the warrant that enabled the various constables to make the raid. The case had started with a Grand Jury hearing, which is of course a secret procedure. The County claimed it had all sorts of evidence to the effect that Kesey and the Pranksters had been giving dope to minors. Kesey's lawyers were trying to get the whole case thrown out on the grounds that the original warrant for the raid was fraudulent. This didn't work, and Kesey now had the choice of facing trial and a lot of lurid testimony or waiving open trial and letting a judge decide the case on the basis of the transcript of the Grand Jury proceedings. It was finally arranged that Kesey would let the judge do it. He would most likely be getting a light sentence. Even after that he could still appeal the case on the grounds that the warrant had been trumped up. This whole thing with the judge was the equivalent, in a roundabout way, of pleading no contest. On January 17, 1966, four days before the Trips Festival, the judge duly found Kesey guilty and sentenced him to six months on a work farm and three years on probation. This was about what his lawyers expected. It wasn't so bad. The work farm was right near La Honda, ironically enough, and the prisoners did a lot of their work clearing out a stretch of forest back of Kesey's place. There was something very funny about that. Lime-light bowers for the straight multitudes. There was more irony. McMurphy, in *One Flew Over the Cuckoo's Nest,* started his adventures with a six-month stretch on a work farm. Kesey had been a McMurphy on the outside for four years. Now maybe he would be a McMurphy on the inside, for real. Maybe . . . anyway it was far from the goddamn end of the world. Then an uncool thing happened.

THE NIGHT OF JANUARY 19, TWO NIGHTS BEFORE THE TRIPS Festival, Kesey, Mountain Girl, and some of the Pranksters went over to Stewart Brand's apartment, in North Beach, San Francisco, to make plans for the Trips Festival. Sometime after midnight Kesey and Mountain Girl went up on the roof on top of the building and spread out an old blue pad that had been in the back of somebody's station wagon on the gravel up there and stretched out on the pad, grooving on the peaceful debris of North Beach. It's nice and homey boho quaint, North Beach. Slums with a view. Out there the lights of the bay and the fishing boats and the honky-tonks and more lights climbing up the hills of San Francisco and nearer, all the asphalt squares of the other rooftops, squares and levels and ladders—grooving on the design, which is nice and peaceful and a little arty-looking, but that is North Beach. Mountain Girl all dark brown hair and big brown eyes, coming on ornery and fun-loving—it occurs to Kesey—*rather like the eyes of an Irish setter pup just turning from awkward carefree frolic to the task of devotion.*

Mountain Girl is being enthusiastic about the Trips Festival.

"With that big new speaker," she says, "we'll be able to wire that place so you can hear a *flea* fart!"

Awkward carefree frolic to the task of—Kesey is feeling old. *Once a stud so gorged with muscle tone*—his face feels lopsided with the strain, of . . . the eternal hassling, the lawyering, the legally sanctioned lying on all sides, politicking, sucking up, getting lectured at, cranking on the old lopsided diplomatic smile . . .

"—hear a flea fart!"

"Hasn't happened yet," says Kesey.

"With this many days to set it up? Always before we were in the hall that night and maybe set up before we finished in the morning."

And so forth and so on—Kesey and Mountain Girl lie on their stomachs with their chins in their hands, gazing down four stories to the alley below and occasionally scraping gravel off the rooftop and tossing it down . . .

. . . yes . . . ummm . . . at 1:53 A.M. the cops of the 19th Precinct got a call from a woman at 18 Margrave Place saying some drunken tormentors or something were throwing rocks at her window. Shortly after 2 A.M. a police car pulls into the alley. So Kesey and Mountain Girl groove on that. Yup, a police car right down below, police car come here. A red light on a hillside drive about 50 yards away blinks. A red light blinks and a police car tools in the alley. Ah, always the *synch,* friends. The cops are coming in this building. Wonder on earth what for. *Do I learn anything? Or once again lie loaded and disbelieving as two cops climb five stories to drag me to the cooler.* . . . Oh, the logic of the groove and the synch. Kesey and Mountain Girl see it all at once, now, so clearly. It is so very obvious that it fascinates. They see it all, grok it all—*Scram, split, run, flee, hide, vanish, disintegrate*—the red alert is so very clear, it blinks and blinks, red, nothing, red, nothing, red, nothing, red, nothing, and yet *move?* and *miss it all?* turning so slow in the interferrometric synch? It is like a weird time he was in Olympic wrestling eliminations, in 1960, in the

San Francisco Olympic Club, first round against a hulking stud, and he took a couple of vitamins before the fray, revved up, revved up, not *doped,* oh mom&dad&buddy&sis&dear-but-square-ones, all Olympian athletes are doped, force-fed pill-heads, see them lead them, all gorged with glistening muscle veins and crewcut and led to the training table and by every plate a lineup of capsules like the wineglasses at the gourmet dinner, capsules for iron, capsules for calcium, capsules to make you squeeze your colon and flex your heart, capsules of B_{12} mighty as pure amphetamine turn your blood vessels into black snakes, capsules to make you long and brute in the teeth, make you clean & jerk in the arms, mad ape in the neck, sharp in the tusk, panther in the solar plexus lineup of crewcut stud bulls concocted out of chemicals force-fed every day at every plate—revved up, revved up, revved up waiting for the referee to snap his hand up in mid-air to start the match, *snap* . . . and it is so very fascinating . . . he is like a motor running at top speed with the clutch in . . . it is intriguing, not intimidating, the way this great stud grabs him above the knee with his huge hand and starts pulling down—Kesey is two people, revved up here on the mat and revved up here in the ethers like an astral body, watching—interesting!—no man could be as strong as this guy here and execute a takedown by pulling downward on the knee—no danger, friends, just fascination—and so the guy won a trophy for the fastest pin of the tourney, while the motor revved in *synch* with a different bummer—

—*fascinating!*—so—

—out the scroffy arty rooftop door come two cops, Officers Fred Pardella and Thomas L. O'Donnell of the 19th Precinct, by designation—

What happened next became the subject of two trials in San Francisco, later, many fugitive months later, both ending in hung juries, the second one 11 to 1 against Kesey. According to Officers Pardella and O'Donnell, they found the suspects Kesey and the Adams girl and a plastic bag containing a quantity of brownish vegetation. Whereupon Officer O'Donnell sought to collect the evidence, and Kesey wrestled him for it, throwing the bag onto an adjoining arty rectangle rooftop and very nearly Pardella along with it, whereupon Officer O'Donnell drew his gun and brought both Kesey and the girl into custody. The plastic bag, retrieved, contained 3.54 grams of marijuana.

THIS WAS A BEAUTIFUL MESS AND NO TWO WAYS ABOUT IT. A second offense for possession of marijuana carried an automatic five-year sentence with no possibility of parole. At the very least he stood to get the full three-year sentence in San Mateo County now, as one of the judge's conditions had been that he no longer associate with the Pranksters. Mountain Girl was ready to take the whole rap herself. "We were just tying it off," she told the press. "He wasn't supposed to hang around with any of us wild, giddy people any more. This was the last time we were gonna see him." Well . . . she tried. Kesey's probation officer in San Mateo County advised him for godsake stay away from the Trips Festival or he was in for it, but the whole thing was miles beyond in-for-it, out towards old Edge City, in fact.

Kesey left Municipal Court in San Francisco on January 20 with Mountain Girl and Stewart Brand and onto the whole bus full of Pranksters to roll through San Francisco advertising the Trips Festival. They got out at Union Square. Kesey wore a pair of white Levi's with the backsides emblazoned with HOT on the left side and COLD on the right and TIBET in the middle.— and a pair of sky-blue boots. They all played Ron Boisie's Thunder Machine for loon vibrations in Union Square in the fibrillating heart of San Francisco.

If nothing else, Kesey's second arrest was great publicity for the Trips Festival. It was all over San Francisco newspapers. In the hip, intellectual, and even social worlds of San Francisco, the Trips Festival notion was spreading like a fever. *The dread drug LSD.* Acid heads. An LSD experience without the LSD, it was being billed as—moreover, people actually believed it. But mainly the idea of a new life style was making itself felt. Do you suppose this is the—*new wave* . . . ?

And you buy y'r ticket, f'r chrissake—an absurd thought to Norman Hartweg—*and we've got a promoter*—all absurd, but the thousands pour into the Longshoremen's Hall for the Trips Festival, thousands even the first night, which was mostly Indian night, a weird thing put on by Brand's America Needs Indians, but now on Saturday evening the huge crush hits for the Acid Test. Norman is absolutely zonked on acid—and look at the freaks running in here. Norman is not the only one. "An LSD experience without LSD"—that was a laugh. In fact, the heads are pouring in by the hundreds, bombed out of their gourds, hundreds of heads coming out into the absolute open for the first time. It is like the time the Pranksters went to the Beatles concert in full costume, looking so bizarre and so totally *smashed* that no one could believe they were. Nobody would *risk* it in public like this. Well, the kids are just having an LSD experience without LSD, that's all, and this is what it looks like. A hulking crazed whirlpool. That's nice. Lights and movies sweeping around the hall; five movie projectors going and God knows how many light machines, interferrometrics, the intergalactic science-fiction seas all over the walls, loudspeakers studding the hall all the way around like flaming chandeliers, strobes exploding, black lights with Day-Glo objects under them and Day-Glo paint to play with, street lights at every entrance flashing red and yellow, two bands, the Grateful Dead and Big Brother and the Holding Company and a troop of weird girls in leotards leaping around the edges blowing dog whistles—and the Pranksters. Paul Foster has wrapped black friction tape all around his shoes and up over his ankles and swaddled his legs and hips and torso in it up to his rib cage, where begins a white shirt and then white bandaging all over his face and skull and just a slit for his eyes, over which he wears dark glasses. He also wears a crutch and a sign saying, "You're in the Pepsi Generation and I'm a pimply freak!" Rotor!

Also heads from all over, in serapes and mandala beads and Indian headbands and Indian beads, the great era for all that, and one in a leather jerkin with "Under Ass Wizard Mojo Indian Fighter" stenciled on the back. Mojo! Oh the freaking strobes turning every brain stem into a cauliflower erupting into corrugated ping-pong balls—*can't stand it*—and a girl rips off her shirt and dances bare-breasted with her great mihs breaking up into an endless stream of ruby-red erect nipples streaming out of the great milk-and-honey under the strobe lights. The dancing is ecstatic, a nice macaroni of braless breasts jiggling and cupcake bottoms wiggling and multiple arms writhing and leaping about. Thousands of straight intellectuals and culturati and square hippies, North Beach style, gawking and learning. Dr. Francis Rigney, Psychiatrist to the Beat Generation, looking on, and all the Big Daddies left over from the Beat period, Eric "Big Daddy" Nord and Tom "Big Daddy" Donahue, and the press, vibrating under Ron Boise's thunder machine. A great rout in progress, you understand.

And in the center of the hall—the Pranksters' tower of Control. It had come to that, and it was perfect. Babbs had supervised the building of a great scaffolding of pipes and platforms in the center of the hall. It rose and rose, this tower, as the Pranksters added equipment, all the mikes and amplifiers and spots and projectors and all the rest of it, the very architecture of Control, finally. Babbs at the controls, Hagen up there taking movies; the Movie goes on. Kesey, meanwhile, was up on an even higher plateau of control, up on a balcony in a silver space suit complete with a big bubble space helmet. He conceived of it first as a disguise, so he could be there without the various courts being raggy and outraged, but everyone recognized the Space Man immediately, of course, and he perched up above the maelstrom with a projection machine with which you could write messages on acetate and project them in mammoth size on the walls.

Zonker dancing in a spin of pure unadulterated bliss, higher than he had ever been in his life, which for Zonker was getting

up there. Norman, smashed, but with a mission. Norman to cir-
culate among the multitudes with movie camera. Only he has no
power pack, so he has to plug the camera in a wall socket and go
out with a great long cord. His eye pressed against the sighting
lens and gradually the whole whirlpool coming into his one eye,
unity, *I,* the vessel, receiving all, Atman and Brahman, letting it
all flow in until—*satori*—the perfect state is reached and he realizes he is God. He has traveled miles through this writhing macaroni ecstasy mass and could the camera still possibly be plugged
in?—or could that possibly matter? *deus ex machina,* with the
world flowing into one eye. Becomes essential that he reach the
Central Node, the Tower of Control, the great electric boom of
the directional mike picking up the band sticking out from atop
the scaffolding tower—*and there it is*—it is all there in this moment. Starts clambering up the scaffolding with the huge camera
still over his shoulder and up to his eye, all funneling in, and the
wire and plug snaking behind him, through the multitudes. And
who might *these* irate forms be?—in truth, Babbs and Hagen,
Babbs gesturing for Norman to get off the platform, he's in the
way, *there's no room, get the hell off of here*—a cosmic laugh, since
obviously they don't know who he is, viz., God. Norman, the
meek, the mild, the retiring, the sideliner, laughs a cosmic laugh
at them and keeps on coming. At any moment, he fully realizes,
he can make them disappear down . . . his eye, just two curds in
the world flow, Babbs and Hagen.

"Norman, if you don't get the hell off of here, I'm going to
throw you off!"—Babbs looking huge and untamable in the same
stance he gave the San Francisco cops at the Fillmore, and Norman's mind split just slightly along the chiasma, like a San An-
dreas fault, one part some durable hard-core fear of getting
thrown off and breaking his ass, him, Norman, but the other, the
Cosmic laugh of God at how useless Babbs's stance is now, vibrating slightly between God and not-God, but then the laugh
comes in a wave, just the cosmic fact that he, Norman, now dares
do this, *defiance,* the new *I* and there is not one thing, really, they

can do about it—Babbs staring at this grinning, zonked figure with the huge camera clambering up the scaffolding. Babbs just throws his hands up, gives up, Norman ascends. *God!* in the very Tower of Control. *Well, if I'm God, I can control this thing.* Gazing down into the whirlpool. He gestures—and it comes to pass!—there is a ripple in the crowd *there* and again and there is a ripple in the crowd *here*—also so clear what is *going* to happen, he can predict it, a great eruption of ecstatic dancing in *that* clump, under the strobes, it will *break out now,* and it does, of course—a vibration along the crack, the fault, *synchronicity* spoken here, and we are at play, but they *do* it—*start the music!*—and it starts—satori, in the Central Node, as it was written—but I say unto you—and at that very moment, a huge message in red is written on the wall:

ANYBODY WHO KNOWS HE IS GOD GO UP ON STAGE

*Any*body?—The chiasmic halves vibrate, the God and the not-God, and then he realizes: Kesey wrote that. Kesey up on the balcony in his space suit wrote that with his projection machine and flashed it on the wall, in that very moment. What to do, Archangel of mine, Norman stares unbelieving—unbelieving in what?—up on stage climbs a spade with a wild head of natural spade hair with a headband wrapped around the hairline so the hair puffs up like a great gray dandelion, a huge shirt swimming under the lights, and it is Gaylord, one of the few spades in the whole thing, gleaming the glistening grin of acid zonk and going into a lovely godly little dance, this Gaylord God . . . What the hell. Norman gestures toward the crowd, and it does not ripple. Not here and not there. He predicts *that* clump will rise up in ecstatic levitation, and it does not rise up. In fact, it just sinks to the floor like it was spat there, sad moon eyes glomming up in the acid stare. Sayonara, God. And yet . . . And yet . . .

. . .   .   .

THREE NIGHTS THE HUGE WILD CARNIVAL WENT ON. IT WAS A big thing on every level. For one thing, the Trips Festival grossed $12,500 in three days, with almost no overhead, and a new night-club and dance-hall genre was born. Two weeks later Bill Graham was in business at the Fillmore auditorium with a Trips Festival going every weekend and packing them in. For the acid heads themselves, the Trips Festival was like the first national convention of an underground movement that had existed on a hush-hush cell-by-cell basis. The heads were amazed at how big their own ranks had become—and euphoric over the fact that they could come out in the open, high as baboons, and the sky, and the law, wouldn't fall down on them. The press went along with the notion that this had been an LSD experience without the LSD. Nobody in the hip world of San Francisco had any such delusion, and the Haight-Ashbury era began that weekend.

The Trips Festival changed many things. But as soon as the whirlpool died down, Kesey was right back where he started, so far as the grinning lopsided frowning world of the San Mateo and San Francisco County courts were concerned. The bastids were digging in for prisoner's base. They had already dug him out of the place in La Honda. Part of the fiat of Judge de Matteis was that Kesey get out of La Honda and sell his place to some-body who had nothing to do with him or his works and stay out of San Mateo County except to see his probation officer or travel through on the Harbor Freeway or over the territorial bound-aries of San Mateo County by airplane and remove himself and all his influences from said County. So Kesey and Faye and the kids moved into the Spread, Babbs's place, in Santa Cruz. Wind-ing his way down there on January 23—there was a warrant waiting for his arrest on the grounds of violating probation.

Well, that's their Movie, Tonto, and we all know how that one ends. Three years in the San Mateo donjon, plus the five or eight or twenty they come up with in San Francisco to teach a lesson while the iron and the spittle are hot to all the Trips Festival dope fiends. Kesey called an immediate briefing, and remember that

little abjuration a couple months ago about prepare for Mexico . . . ?

So they gathered at the Spread.

"If society wants me to be an outlaw," said Kesey, "then I'll be
an outlaw, and a damned good one. That's something people
need. People at all times need outlaws."

The Pranksters comprehended it all at once.

So here is the current fantasy: tonight he is going to split for
Mexico. He'll go across the border in the back of Ron Boise's
truck. Boise was down at Babbs's at the time, and he had a truck
that served as a kind of mobile studio. It had all his welding
equipment and acetylene torches and the like and he would work
back there on the mud flats out back, shaping old car fenders into
the erotic poses of the Kama Sutra. Finally Roy Seburn's psychedelic car, his miniature bus, had been fed to the torches back
there, too, as it was broken down for good. Nothing lasts. Art is
not eternal. They would head for Puerto Vallarta. He would use
another Prankster's driver's license as I.D. in case he needed it
down there. Meanwhile, as a cover story, one last grand prank.
The Suicide Trip.

Kesey would write a suicide note. Then D——, who looked un-
commonly like him—Dee would dress up like him and get in an
old panel truck that was around there and drive up the coast, toward Oregon, and pick out a likely cliff and smash the truck into
a tree trunk and get out and leave the suicide note on the seat of
the truck and throw his sky-blue boots down by the shore so it
would look like he had dived in the water and gone out to sea,
never to come back to his swamp of troubles. The idea was that
Dee would look enough like Kesey, especially in a Prankster costume, so that if anybody did happen to see him driving along the
way, they would remember him as someone answering Kesey's
description. Let 'em unravel that one. Even if they don't fall for
it, at least it might take the heat off. Why should we go to all this
trouble—the ninny *might* be lying on the bottom of the ocean,
them damn dope fiends . . .

"I hope Dee doesn't do a Dee-out," Mountain Girl said. But she was optimistic. The whole thing had a lot of *élan du Prank*.

That night Kesey and Mountain Girl got stoned on grass and started composing the great suicide note:

"Last words. A vote for Barry is a vote for fun. I, Ken Kesey, being of (ahem) sound mind and body, do hereby leave the whole scene to Faye, Corporation, cash and the works (and it occurs to me here that nobody is going to buy this prank and now it occurs to me that I like that even better) . . ."

Shee-ut, this was fun. Put-on after put-on bubbled up in their brains, and all the bullshit metaphors of destiny, all the bullshit lines a good bullshit poet would come up with upon looking the Grim Creeper in the arsehole:

"Wind, wind send me not this place, though, onward . . ."

More! More! Louder music, more wine!

". . . Ocean, ocean, ocean, I'll beat you in the end, I'll break you this time. I'll go through with my heels your hungry ribs . . ."

On and on it went, like a running account of the mad-drive-to-be up the coast, looking for his favorite cliff, to jump off of, presumably, the whole scene bubbling up in his brain and Mountain Girl's on the ratty rug in Babbs's living room. Hell, let's throw in some acid—they'll *believe* the damn ninny dope fiend would take the dread LSD and break his ass for good—and hell, slam the freaking vehicle into a tree, bleed verisimilitude all over the California littoral:

". . . I've lost the ocean again. Beautiful. I drive hundreds of miles looking for my particular cliff, get so trapped behind acid I can't find the ocean, end up slamming into a redwood . . ."

Beautiful. Ready, Ron? He gets into Boise's truck and they head off south for San Diego, the Mexican border, Tijuana and the land of all competent Outlaws.

The Electric Kool-Aid
Acid Test

WHAT HAPPENED TO THE PRANKSTERS AFTER KESEY'S flight to Mexico was so much like what happened to the League after Leo fled in Hermann Hesse's book *The Journey to the East*—well, it was freaking weird, this particular *synch* . . . exactly . . . the Pranksters! and the great bus trip of 1964! their whole movie. No; it went on. Hesse's fantasy coincided with theirs all the way. It went *on*—all the way to this weird divide—

The leader of the League in *The Journey to the East* was named Leo. He was never openly known as the leader: like Kesey, he was the "non-navigator" of the brotherhood. And Leo suddenly left "in the middle of the dangerous gorge of Morbio Inferiore," just when the League was deepest into its Journey to the East, in the critical phase of a trip that was being alternately denounced and wondered at. "From that time, certainty and unity no longer existed in our community, although the great idea still kept us together. How well I remember those first disputes! They were something so new and unheard-of in our hitherto perfectly united League. They were conducted with respect and politeness—at least in the beginning. At first they led neither to fierce conflicts nor personal reproaches or insults—at first we were still an inseparable, united brotherhood throughout the world..." Things got more and more bitter, and the narrator, "H.," left after the Morbio Inferiore. And the narrator, Hartweg, left after...

Very weird, the *synch!*

With Kesey gone, Babbs became the leader. There was no meeting, no vote, not even a parting word from Kesey. Babbs becomes the leader—the ... group mind knew that at once, without a second thought. They packed up everything at La Honda and took it up to Oregon, to Kesey's parents' home. The Archives they stashed at the Spread and, later, up at Chuck's house in Oregon. This and that they bequeathed to other heads, like the great round table with the Hell's Angels' carvings all over it. They gave that to a new psychedelic group, the Anonymous Artists of America, at a place called Rancho Diablo up at Skylonda. Whatever they could use for the Acid Tests they took along.

Babbs moved the Acid Test scene to Los Angeles and the bus lumbered on down there. They had hardly gotten there before the soft rumblings started—"certainty and unity no longer existed in our community, although the great idea still kept us together. How well I remember those first disputes!" *Babbs gives too many orders*—Kesey, the non-navigator, merely expressed a will and merely waited for it to move forward in the Group Mind. *Babbs runs this like the Army ... like the Boy Scouts ...* Babbs's put-ons suddenly seemed pure sarcasm. His cryptic comments, his candor, seemed cruel. Some of the Pranksters even took to sympathizing with poor wretches like Pancho Pillow; the universally put-down acid-rapping fool, Pancho.

Pancho, ever in the throes of self-laceration, was still desperate to be *on the bus.* The poor bastard spent his last earthly dime and traveled from San Francisco to Los Angeles and caught up with the bus in Lemon Grove one day. Pancho came ambling up with a huge grin of brotherhood and started to climb up the steps and Babbs met him at the door of the bus.

"I don't think anybody wants you here," said Babbs.

"What do you mean?" says Pancho. "Can't I come on the bus?"

"There's nobody on the bus who wants you on the bus."

Pancho's grin is wiped off, of course, and his eyes start batting around like pinballs, trying to make out who is inside the bus—*you all know me, I'm Pancho!*

"Well . . . I know I get on some people's nerves," says Pancho, "but I came all the way here to be with you guys, and I spent all my money getting here—"

"We don't care," says somebody else's voice, *on the bus.*

"Look," says Pancho, "I'll shut up, I'll do whatever you want. I just want to help with the Tests. I'll do anything—"

"We don't care." Somebody *else's* voice, *on the bus.*

"—odd jobs, run errands, there must be a thousand things—"

"We don't care."

Pancho stands there, speechless, his face bursts with red.

"See," says Babbs, "it's like I said. I don't think there's anybody who wants you on here."

Numb Pancho backs down off the steps and trudges off in Lemon Grove.

Well, they had a good laugh over that. The freaking Pancho Pillow! A bad-trip freak if there ever was one! A breaker of balls extraordinaire! The human bummer: ::::: but it was a laugh with a metallic aftertaste, this joke on Pancho :::::

Babbs had gotten hold of an old mansion in L.A., called the Sans Souci, a great incredible moldering old place with a dome and a stone balustrade, all crumbling and moldering, but with style. When the owner found a bunch of *beatniks* in there, he freaked, but that was later. Anyway, one day they were all in there and one Prankster said a very unPrankster thing. He spoke up and said:

"I want to voice this idea: I can't stand Margie and I don't want her around."

Unfreakingbelievable. He was talking about Marge the Barge. So then all eyes went to Babbs, who was now thrust into the Kesey role of resolving all. Babbs turns to Marge the Barge and says:

"What do you think about that?"

Marge says: "I think that's ridiculous," and with such quiet flat conviction that nobody else says anything.

A small moment—but one more moment in the gathering schism, the Babbs loyalists versus the had-enough-of-Babbs. Later they would realize they were in many cases merely blaming Babbs for the mysterious sense of loss in their venture. They were casting about for an explanation, and Babbs was It. What they had lost of course, was the magical cement of Kesey's charisma. "It seemed that the more certain his loss became, the more indispensable he seemed; without Leo, his handsome face, his good humor and his songs, without his enthusiasm for our great undertaking, the undertaking itself seemed in some mysterious way to lose meaning."

IN FACT, BABBS CARRIED THE ACID TESTS INTO LOS ANGELES with an amazing determination. The Pranksters were now out of their home territory, the San Francisco area, but they performed with an efficiency they never knew they had before. It was as if they were all picking up on Babbs's exhortation of months ago: "We've got to learn how to function on acid." They were soaring out of their gourds themselves, but they were pulling off Acid Tests that seemed like they were orchestrated.

Babbs was in great form, as I say, and he had also hooked up with a remarkable head named Hugh Romney, a poet, actor, and comedian who had gone the whole route, starting back in the Beat Generation days and was now into the LSD thing and had "discovered the Management," as he put it, "and when you discover the Management there's nothing to do but go to work for it." So Romney and his friend Bonnie Jean were now on the bus, and they all set out to—nothing more, nothing less—*turn on Los Angeles to the Management* . . . Yesss . . . The first Test was at Paul Sawyer's church in Northridge, just out from Los Angeles in the San Fernando Valley . . . Sawyer has never lost his willingness to experiment and is on the bus himself. And if the Sport Shirts could see these . . . *new experimental rites . . . including music, dance, and sacrifice*—the sacrifice?—well . . . it was not strictly an Acid Test, but a "happening," which had become a harmless and un-loaded word in Cultural circles, even in Sawyer's Valley Unitarian-Universalist Church. A marvelous modern building shaped like a huge Bermuda onion, it was, forming one great towering . . . Dome, with fantastic acoustics like it had been created for the current fantasy itself. So the Pranksters moved in and wired and wound up the place, and hundreds arrived for the "happening," partaking of Prankster magic and pineapple chili, which was a concoction the Pranksters served, on the vile side in taste, but *pineapple chili* nonetheless, a wacky thought in itself. And Cassady had a microphone and started rapping, and Romney had a microphone and started rapping, and he was great, and Babbs and Paul Foster, flying with the God Rotor and not stuttering at all . . . People dancing in the most ecstatic way and getting so far into the thing, the straight multitudes even, that even *they* took microphones, and suddenly there was no longer any separation between the entertainers and the entertained at all, none of that well-look-at-you-startled-squares condescension of the ordinary happening. Hundreds were swept up in *an experience,* which built up like a dream typhoon, peace on the smooth liquid centrifugal whirling edge. In short, everybody in The Movie, on the bus, and it was beautiful . . . They were like . . . *on!* the Pranksters—now primed to draw the hundreds, the thousands, the millions into *the new experience,* and in the days ahead they came rushing in ::::::

:::::: Clair Brush, for one. Yes. She was a girl in her twenties, a

pretty redhead, who worked for Art Kunkin, the editor of the hip circuit weekly, the Los Angeles *Free Press*. Her old friend Doc Stanley had called her up before the Test at Sawyer's church and said, Clair, there is going to be a happening in a Unitarian church in the Valley that you really ought to pick up on, and so forth ... But one of the things Clair did at the *Free Press* was compile a calendar of events for the hip circuit and this was the big season of "happenings" and she had been through all that a dozen times, and each one was always billed as the wave of the future, and was inevitably a drag. So she didn't go. Ummmm :::::
However :::::

::::: In hearing about it from people who did attend, though, she decided to go to the next one :::::

::::: which was set for Watts, on Lincoln's Birthday, February 12, 1966. *Watts!* the very Watts where hardly five months before the freaking revolution of the blacks had broken out, the symbol of all that was catastrophic and hopeless in American life, and *what is this strange space ship now approaching Watts, the very Youth Opportunities center itself—Youth Opportunities!—for the trip beyond catastrophe* :::::

::::: "I think what decided me"—Clair is recalling it for me—"was someone's description of Art Kunkin's spontaneous participation and enjoyment of the evening in the church. Most of the people there were given to improvisation as required, but Arthur and I share a reserve in crowds.

"Anyway. The Watts site—it was actually Compton, an incorporated city on the fringe of Watts—was chosen for reasons unknown to me. The best guesses I've heard have to do with the politics of taking such a party into the recently stricken neighborhood, as a friendship-thing; also a humorous—ironical?—site for such carryings-on.

"The building was a warehouse, part of a Youth Opportunities center, but still vacant. They—the Center people—were using or were going to use the building as a workshop for manual trades, possibly automotive? Job-retraining, etc. It was legally leased for 24 or 48 hours by Kesey's group, with money, and the caretaker of the center was present at all times during the Acid Test.

"Announcements were made in the usual way, Free Press and KPFK calendar, etc., and around 200 people were in attendance. When I arrived, nothing had started . . . people were clustered in small groups, sitting on mats and blankets around the walls. The room, the main room, was huge . . . my conception of feet, in yards and such, is bad, but I'd guess maybe 50 by 25. There was a smaller room to the east and bathroom to the west, and the large room had a corridor running along the south wall which had open windows waist-high without glass . . . through which the scene inside could be observed.

"I had driven my car down, giving two people a ride, but I left them immediately . . . went to join some friends who had some rosé wine and were sitting on a pad on the floor. As I said, none of the effects had started . . . but shortly there was an announcement (I think by Neal Cassady, but I didn't know him then) that the evening would begin. Films were projected on the south wall, with a commentary . . . films of Furthur, the bus, the people in the bus . . . the commentary was a rather dull travelogue and the film seemed fairly uninspired and confused.

"Remember now, I'm a novice. I'd never even been 'high' on 'pot' or any kind of pill or anything . . . my strongest experience had been with alcohol. I knew a few 'heads' but didn't think much of the whole thing . . . had tried pot a few times and nothing impressed me, except for the unpleasant taste.

"This may explain why a lot of people were digging the film, laughing, and also why a lot of people were there . . . I'm sure that I was one of a minority who had no idea what to expect. The word must have been passed, but didn't get to me. Also I think a lot of those in attendance had heard of Kesey's things and were very aware of what was being done. Not old unworldly Clair. Story of my life.

"The film continued, some slides were shown of flowers and

patterns, this and that . . . then a large trash can, plastic, was carried to the middle of the room, and all were invited to help themselves to the Kool-Aid it contained. There was no big rush to the refreshment stand . . . people wandered up, it was being served in paper cups, and since Kool-Aid is a staple in the homes of Del Close and Hugh Romney and other friends of mine, I thought it quite a natural thing to serve . . . had a cup, had another, wandered and talked for a while, had another . . ."

. . . Ironically, for Clair, anyway, it was Romney's inspiration to serve Electric Kool-Aid, as he called it. They had all . . . yes . . . laced it good and heavy with LSD. It was a prank, partly, but mainly it was the natural culmination of the Acid Tests. It was a gesture, it was sheer generosity giving all this acid away, it was truly turning on the world, inviting all in to share the Pranksters' ecstasy of the All-one . . . all become divine vessels in unison, and it is all there in Kool-Aid and a paper cup. Cassady immediately drank about a gallon of it. Actually there were two cans. Romney took the microphone and said, "This one over here is for the little folk and this one over here is for the big folk. This one over here is for the kittens and this one over here is for the tigers," and so forth and so on. As far as he was concerned, he was doing everything but putting a sign on the loaded batch saying LSD. Romney was so thoroughly into the pudding himself it never occurred to him that a few simpler souls might have wandered into this unlikely way station in Watts and simply not know . . . or think that all his veiled instructions probably referred to gin, like the two crystal bowls of punch at either end of the long white table at a wedding reception . . . or just not hear, like Clair Brush—

"Severn Darden was there, and Del Close, of course, and I knew them from the Second City in Chicago. Severn and I were standing under a strobe light (first time I'd seen one, and they are kicky) doing an improvisation . . . he was a jealous husband, I an unfaithful wife, something simple and funny. He was choking me and throwing me around (gently, of course) and suddenly I began to laugh ... and laugh ... and the laugh was more primitive, more gut-tearing, than anything I had ever known. It came from somewhere so deep inside that I had never felt it before ... and it continued ... and it was uncontrollable ... and wonderful. Something snapped me back and I realized that there was nothing funny ... nothing to laugh about ... what had I been laughing at?

"I looked around and people's faces were distorted ... lights were flashing everywhere ... the screen (sheets) at the end of the room had three or four different films on it at once, and the strobe light was flashing faster than it had been ... the band, the Grateful Dead, was playing but I couldn't hear the music ... people were dancing ... someone came up to me and I shut my eyes and with a machine he projected images on the back of my eyelids (I really think this happened ... I asked and there was such a machine) ... and nothing was in perspective, nothing had any touch of normalcy or reality ... I was afraid, because I honestly thought that it was all in my mind, and that I had finally flipped out.

"I sought a person I trusted, stopping and asking people what was happening ... mostly they laughed, not believing that I didn't know. I found a man I knew not very well but with whom I felt simpatico from the first time we met. I asked him what was happening, and if it was all me, and he laughed and held me very close and told me that the Kool-Aid had been 'spiked' and that I was just beginning my first LSD experience ... and not to be afraid, but to neither accept nor reject ... to always keep open, not to struggle or try to make it stop. He held me for a long time and we grew closer than two people can be ... our bones merged, our skin was one skin, there was no place where we could separate, where he stopped and I began. This closeness is impossible to describe in any but melodramatic terms ... still, I did feel that we had merged and become one in the true sense, that there was nothing that could separate us, and that it had meaning beyond anything that had ever been. (Note, a year and two months later . . . three months . . . I later read about 'imprint' and that it was possible that we would continue to be meaningful to each other no matter what circumstances . . . I think this is true . . . the person in question remains very special in my life, and I in his, though we have no contact and see each other infrequently . . . we share something that will last. Oh hell! There's no way to talk about that without sounding goopy.)

"I wasn't afraid any more and started to look around. The setting for the above scene had been the smaller room which was illuminated only by black light, which turns people into beautiful color and texture. I saw about ten people sitting directly under the black light, which was back-draped by a white (luminescent lavender, then) sheet, painting on disembodied mannequins with fluorescent paint . . . and on each other, their clothes, etc. I stood under the light and drops of paint fell on my foot and sandal, and it was exquisite. I returned to this light frequently . . . it was peaceful and beautiful beyond description. My skin had depth and texture under the light . . . a velvety purple. I remember wishing it could be that color always. (I still do.)

"There was much activity in the large room. People were dancing and the band was playing—but I couldn't hear them. I can't remember a note of the music, because the vibrations were so intense. I am music-oriented—sing, play instruments, etc.—which is why this seems unusual to me. I stood close to the band and let the vibrations engulf me. They started in my toes and every inch of me was quivering with them . . . they made a journey through my nervous system (I remember picturing myself as one of the charts we had studied in biology which shows the nerve network), traveling each tiny path, finally reaching the top of my head, where they exploded in glorious patterns of color and line . . . perhaps like a Steinberg cartoon? . . . I remember intense colors, but always with black lines . . . not exactly patterns, but with some outlines and definitions.

"The strobe light broke midway . . . I think they blew something in it . . . but that was a relief, because I had been drawn to it but it disturbed the part of me that was trying to hang onto reality . . . playing with time-sense was something I'd never done . . . and I found it irresistible but frightening.

"The Kool-Aid had been served at ten or so. Almost from the first the doorway was crowded with people walking in and out, and policemen. There were, throughout the evening, at least six different groups of police . . . starting with the Compton City police, then the Highway Patrol, sheriff's deputies, L.A.P.D. and the vice/narco squad. I seem to remember them in groups of five or six, standing just inside the doorway, watching, sometimes talking to passers-by, but making no hostile gestures or threatening statements. It seems now that they must have realized that whatever was going on was more than could be coped with . . . and a jail full of 150 people on acid was infinitely undesirable . . . so they'd look, comment, go away, and others would come . . . this continued through the night.

"Dignitaries from the neighborhood attended . . . I'd guess around midnight, but I've no sense of the time of any of this, until 6 A.M. or so, when I finally sat down (I had walked, danced or stood from 10 P.M. on, not wanting to sit down . . . for what reason I can't imagine). There were two or three women, about seven men. One of the men was dressed in a white suit and had a Shriner's cap on—I thought he was Elijah Muhammed. They smiled, watched, talked with some of the people . . . stayed for about half an hour, and left, wishing us a happy evening. No Kool-Aid was in evidence at that time, of course . . . it had been removed quickly. The neighborhood people were Negro, naturally. They seemed to have no idea of the party as being anything but a gathering of young people, and appeared to be pleased to welcome us to the neighborhood. I remember one of the women was carrying a child and many people stooped to play with him . . . probably a two-year-old boy.

"The caretaker of the building was present for the whole time. It seems he'd go back to the office part and sleep for a while, or maybe just get away from the noise and the chaos . . . but periodically would check to see that everything was all right. He was friendly, happy, but very, very confused at the strange activities.

"Mostly I'd call the Acid Test a master production. Everything was very carefully meshed and calculated to produce the LSD effect, so that I have no idea where the production stopped and my own head took over. The films being shown were so vivid, with patterns and details of flowers and trees and often just color surrounded by black lines and fast-moving scenery and details of hands and such . . . again, I avoided getting hung up watching them . . .

"People were standing outside . . . it was a cold, clear night . . . someone panicked, got in his car and drove away, burning rubber . . . I wanted to go back to my house, but knew that driving would be insane. Bonnie (who was Hugh Romney's lady) was standing alone . . . we touched hands and smiled, knowing, caring . . . Furthur was parked in the street. I went alone and sat in the bus, and heard and felt the spirits of the people who lived in it . . . we (the bus and I) went on a journey through time, and I knew them so well . . . I went back inside and found the man whose face was painted half gold and half silver, with a bushy head of curly hair, who had seemed earlier to be frightening and strange"—

—this was Paul Foster—"and looked at him and understood. The costumes of the Merry Pranksters had seemed bizarre, and now they were beautiful and right. I recalled a poster which we'd had on the ceiling of the Free Press when our offices were under the Fifth Estate . . . it's a poster for a production of 'The Beard' and has 'Grah roor ograrh . . . lion lioness . . . oh grahr . . .' (like that) printed on it . . . and for that moment I understood exactly what was being said.

"A great flash of insight came to me. I've forgotten it now, but there was one instant when everything fell into place and made sense, and I said aloud, 'Oh, of course!' . . . why didn't I see all this before, why couldn't I have realized all these things and not resisted them so much. That didn't last, and hasn't recurred.

"There was a witch who was very kind and sent out the best warm and lovely vibrations. She was wearing red velvet and she's an older lady, really a witch in the best possible way. I was glad she was there, and she was smiling and understanding and enjoying, mothering those few who were not reacting well.

"There was one girl who was wrestling with God. She was with friends, and I think she was all right after a few hours. There was one man who became completely withdrawn . . . I want to say catatonic, because we tried to bring him out of it, and could not make contact at all . . . he was sort of a friend of mine, and I had some responsibility for getting him back to town . . . he had a previous history of mental hospitals, lack of contact with reality, etc., and when I realized what had happened, I begged him not to drink the Kool-Aid, but he did . . . and it was very bad. These are the only two people I know of who did have bad experiences, but I'm sure I wasn't in contact with everyone.

"I told you about the tape recording ('Who CARES? . . . I don't care . . .') and how it was used again at the next one. Show biz."

—Show biz—*yesssss*—and nooooo—Clair was soaring on LSD, wondering what was happening to herself and whether she was going mad, and so forth, and the most crazed scream rang out:

"Who cares!"

And then: "Ray! . . . Ra-a-a-a-ay! . . . Who cares!"

Not even such a manic scream could have been heard over the general roar and rush of the Test ordinarily, over the Grateful Dead wailing, or certainly not with such clarity, except for the fact that it was being picked up by a microphone and amplified out of huge theater horns—

"Who cares!"

That was just the thing for somebody like Clair to hear, Clair who thought *she* was going mad—the sound of a woman freaking out, blowing her mind, all of it amplified as if it were tearing out of every gut in the place and up through every brain. So Clair's protector and impromptu guide put his arms around her again and told her, "It's a tape they made. It's just a put-on. Hugh Romney made it." Well, that seemed plausible. Hugh was an actor and a great satirist and put-on artist and prankster . . . In fact, between screams, there was Hugh's voice sure enough, coming over the microphone:

"Ladies and gentlemen, there's a cop who's come apart in the next room! Will somebody go in there and put that cop back together again!"

"Ray! Ra-a-a-a-ay! . . . It's too perfect!"

Then Romney's voice coming back in: "Does anybody have any tranquilizers? There's somebody having a little trouble in the next room."

The next room was the anteroom off the big hall that Clair had started out in. There was a girl in there sitting on the floor and freaking out in the most complete way. Just the thing for acid veterans. These things happen, what you need is—and Pranksters and other hierophants of the acid world heard about the girl sitting in there and screaming. *Who cares!* and freaking out. Norman Hartweg and Romney came in there, and here was a fairly pretty girl, if only her face wasn't so contorted, with one crippled leg, shrieking *Who cares!* and *Ra-a-a-a-ay.* Ray, the very Ray himself, and Romney looks at Ray and sees the picture at once. Ray is a big guy with a crewcut and a T-shirt and a sleeveless jacket or vest or something on, which shows his muscles very well. He looks like some sailor who fell in with a bunch of hippies and *now* he wonders what in the fock has happened—

"Ray!"

The worst possible guy in the world to deal with the Who Cares Girl. This is a job for experts, and we have them here, some of the greatest acid experts in the world, Romney, Norman, the Hassler—he comes in—and here comes Babbs—and they're all gathered around her in a bunch—*Attention!*—remember Rachel Rightbred!—and it came to pass!—and they give her the freakout expertise:

"... don't fight it ..."

"... go with it ..."

"... neither accept nor deny ..."

"... go with the flow ..."

"... we're with you ..."

"... you're in the hands of experts ..."

—*experts*—and the Pranksters are there rapping over her, riff after riff of words—and then Romney got hold of some Thorazine, a tranquilizer that is good at aborting bad LSD trips and he says, "Here, take this—"

—*take this*—the Who Cares Girl and Ray look at this costumed freak amid a group of costumed freaks, all zonked, trying to hand her a capsule of God knows what—*diabolism*—and Ray throws the Thorazine away and the Who Cares Girl throws it away, the capsules go skidding across the floor, and the Who Cares Girl goes:

harruummmppparummmparrrrumppparruuuuuuumparum pauharuharummmpa mumbling along, drifting in and out of the freakout, giggling for a stretch and they say ah she's coming out of it and then:

"Who cares! ... Ray! ... Ra-a-a-a-ay! ... Oh, what's the use! ... Sex! ... Ray! Sex! ... Who cares!"

That phrase!—it sticks in Romney's head. He can't get it out. Her scream shrieks over the hall, because now Babbs has brought up the microphone and holds it near her, right in front of Ray, solicitously, like *this* will do it. Ray's head sprockets around inanely. Babbs is getting it all over the microphone to make it *part of the test*—not an isolated event—but All-one, anachoretic freakout—*Who cares!* Romney looks at Babbs and Who cares!—well, Babbs cares, with one part of him, but with another his devotion is to the Test, to the Archives, a freakout for the Archives, freaked out on tape in the Archives, Who Cares in the Prankster Archives, and the cry wails over the hall, into every brain, including Clair's—

Romney can't get this insane cry out of his head, *Who cares,* and it becomes the Who Cares Test for him, and he is back at the microphone, with his mission now, his voice furrowing into the microphone:

"Listen, this girl's brains are coming out! and who cares? This girl's coming apart! and who cares? This girl's breaking up into crispy chips! and who cares? This girl's caked in the dust, nylon wall-to-wall on her eyeballs! and who cares?"

—and it was very clear. Everybody who cared would do something, pour on the Energy if nothing else, bleed Dimensional Kreemo for her, if they truly cared. It became a test for Romney, he could feel it, to find the depths of how much he cared—

Who cares! she shrieks

He cares! he feels it, and feels himself growing—

—while the tapes reel it all in.

FINALLY, EVEN AT THE WATTS TEST THEY WEAR DOWN, AND those who are not into the pudding begin to drift off, and the Prankster diehards and a few discoverers like Clair Brush are still there, and Norman can tell it is coming, the magic hour, and Hassler gets up in a blue pageboy costume and does a funny beautiful slow dance to the music that is just perfect . . . and Page is working behind him with the projectors, the film projectors and the slide projectors, and he sets up a really kind of gorgeous collage, moving projections on top of still projections . . . and the Pranksters sit amazed and delighted and he makes slow changes, abstract patterns and projections from the slides and . . . *it all fits together* . . . everything . . .

About 6 A.M., more cops, narcos now, six in plainclothes—and one of the diehard three-o'clock discoverers walks up to them and announces with a look of total acid-stoned glistening sincerity:

"Listen, I've got more Awareness, more . . . Awareness, in my little fingernail . . . My Awareness is so superior to yours that . . . uh . . ."—obviously from the glistening strain on his face, there is no metaphor, no conceit, that can be concocted in the English language that is enormous enough to express just *how* superior, and so his face falls back into a sweet sincere look, slightly played out, and he says: "How about getting us some cigarettes? We're all out."

Strangely, one of them did and returned very quickly with a carton of Kools, which he passed around. Around 9 A.M. only the Pranksters, Clair and a few others are still around—and more cops—and finally they say to Babbs that he ought to get everybody out now, the L.A. sun is up, the good spades of Watts are going to work . . . and the Pranksters troop out into the L.A. sunlight, the Devil with an orange face with silver stars, a tall wildhaired guy with half his face silver and half gold, Day-Glo crazies trooping out into the sunlight at 9 A.M. out of the chilled Pandemonium hatchery . . .

And Clair Brush: "It seems that's about it . . . I've rambled incredibly . . . Did it last? Am I different? I can't remember. It seems so, but I am not sure. When I get under black light, or a strobe, it comes back vividly . . .

"Del Close told me later I was wandering around looking 'wonderful . . . in the sense of full of wonder.' That's the best description I can imagine.

"I've taken LSD twice since then. Each time was different and much less dramatic, more personal, milder. The only strong similarity is the physical effect, which, for me, consists of contractions quite like labor pains and a quivering of the nerve-endings . . . anticipatory . . . for prolonged periods, the feelings of being on the verge of orgasm without any contact at all . . . these things occurred all three times. Otherwise, all have been different.

"Take it again? Oh, probably someday . . . but no urgency, no desire to run to my friendly corner pusher. I think the best way is to take it with a lover, but someone you're willing to have live in your head for a long, long time. Not too many of those around. It's a closeness not easily dismissed.

"All, all. Enough, I hope."

. . .

ABOUT 1 P.M. THE PHONE STARTS RINGING IN ROMNEY'S apartment, waking him up: "Romney, you guys ought to be shot! . . ." "Seven people committed!" . . . "Freaked out!" . . . "Atrocity!" And finally one from the L.A. police:

"Are you Romney? Listen, we got some *two-tone dude* down here—"

Oh, the Di-men-sion-al Kree-mo . . . That would be Paul Foster. Four, five, six hundred people had been in that madhouse all night long having a goddamned orgy for themselves—and the cops couldn't lay a hand on them. So—in the sour-milk L.A. sunlight of 9 A.M. they had seen this gangling character rocking away from the building like a Druid, half his face gold, the other half silver, so they *busted* the mother, for being . . . well . . . drunk in public, or something equally likely. But by 1 P.M. they wish to hell somebody would come pick up this two-tone dude . . .

Christ, man! It's too much for us even! We wash our hands of this ::::: Atrocity :::::

::::: what . . . exactly have we done? and :::::

::::: even to some Pranksters, the anti-Babbs faction, the Test was a debacle. They doubted the ethics of springing the acid in the Kool-Aid, on the one hand, and thought the treatment of the Who Cares Girl, piping her freakout over the speakers, was cruel. Shortly after they got back to L.A. from La Jolla, the Schism broke out true and rife, out front. This was a great little Morbio Inferiore all its own, the *Life* Magazine Divide.

The Watts Test in L.A., coming on top of the Trips Festival in San Francisco, had caused the fast-rising psychedelic thing to explode right out of the underground in a way nobody had dreamed of. Leary and Alpert and their experiments had had plenty of publicity, but that seemed like a fairly isolated thing with a couple of Harvard docs at the helm and being pretty solemn-faced and esoteric about it, all in all. This new San Francisco–L.A. LSD thing, with wacked-out kids and delirious rock 'n' roll, made it seem like the dread LSD had caught on like an infection among the youth—which, in fact, it had. Very few realized that it had all emanated from one electric source: Kesey and the Merry Pranksters.

A team from *Life* magazine turned up, led by a photographer, Larry Schiller, who was on to the LSD world and had taken the pictures at the Hollywood Test. They interviewed the Pranksters and took pictures and said they were going to do a big spread on the acid scene and, they hoped, put the Pranksters on the cover. So they hailed the bus on over to a big photo studio and Schiller convened them all. Then—Babbs refused to go in. But the rest of them, Norman, Hagen, Cassady, a whole flock of them, went on in, and Schiller took a lot of pictures. To Norman it seemed square. For one thing, the guy was working in black and white, and the most obvious thing about the Pranksters was color, Day-Glo, the brighter the better, the more vibrations the better. Then Schiller had them all sit down in a group, against a black background, and in the middle they had Cassady stand up and wave his arms up and down like a crow. He took the pictures in strobe, and this would make Cassady look like he had multi-arms, like the great god Shiva. This strobe thing was at the time new in psychedelic photography, and the mass media would never tire of it. Recreates the acid experience, etc. Then Schiller told certain people to stay around for individual shots, colorful characters like Cassady, and Paul Foster with his wild mutton chops and Importancy Coat, and Norman, maybe because he had a beard. The usual . . . The others went on outside where Babbs was. Finally they all left, the ones who had stayed for the individual shots, and when they got outside, the bus was gone. Clean gone. Babbs, Mountain Girl, Zonker, Walker, and the others—split.

Hagen couldn't believe it. "Why—we've been *pranked!*" he said.

Pranksters—and the Pranked.

Things being like they were to begin with, the prank took on fundamental meaning. Those who got pranked finally made their way back to the moldering Sans Souci, and Babbs & Co. had cleared out of there, too, taking all the money and the food. Babbs left word that they, the inner nucleus, were going off to hold a Test of their own and would rejoin the Satellites for the UCLA Acid Test, scheduled for March 19. "The great idea still kept us together"—and Norman, Cassady, Hagen, Paul Foster, Roy Seburn, Marge and a couple others made a stab at preparing for the UCLA Test. But UCLA backed out of the deal because of the notoriety after the Watts Test, and that did it. All began drifting off. It was a strange time and a strange feeling. Nobody could figure why Babbs had pranked Cassady; the others maybe—— although that Hagen would get pranked was pretty strange, too—but Cassady—that was unbelievable.

Cassady said fuck it and headed for San Francisco. Norman and Paul Foster went to stay at Hugh Romney's. Then by and by Norman got a chance to go to New York with Marge the Barge and Evan Engber, so they headed east by car.

"HARDLY HAD LEO LEFT US, WHEN FAITH AND CONCORD amongst us was at an end; it was as if the life-blood of our group flowed away from an invisible wound."

One day Paul Foster cranked up the great God Rotor and sat down and worked on a very intricate illuminated billhead. When he got through, there was an ornate black border, and in the middle the words

IN MEMORIAM

in florid Old English lettering, and at the bottom: January 23, 1966, the day Kesey disappeared. Nothing else, just *In Memoriam* and the date. He hung it up on the wall.

chapter XXI

The Fugitive

HAUL ASS, KESEY. MOVE. *SCRAM. SPLIT FLEE HIDE VANISH DISINTE-grate.* Like *run.*

Rrrrrrrrrrrrrrrrrrrrrrrrrevrevrevrevrevrevrevrevrevrev or are we gonna have just a late Mexican re-run of the scene on the rooftop in San Francisco and sit here with the motor spinning and watch with fascination while the cops they climb up once again to *come git you—*

THEY JUST OPENED THE DOOR DOWN BELOW, ROTOR ROOTER, SO YOU HAVE MAYBE 45 SECONDS ASSUMING THEY BE SLOW AND SNEAKY AND SURE ABOUT IT

Kesey sits in a little upper room in the last house down the beach, $80 a month, on paradise-blue Bandarias Bay, in Puerto Vallarta, on the west coast of Mexico, state of Jalisco, one step from the floppy green fronds of the jungle, wherein flourish lush steamy baboon lusts of paranoia—Kesey sits in this little rickety upper room with his elbow on a table and his forearm standing up perpendicular and in the palm of his hand a little mirror, so

that his forearm and the mirror are like a big rear-view mirror
stanchion on the side of a truck and thus he can look out the window and see them but they can't see him—

COME ON, MAN, DO YOU NEED A COPY OF THE SCRIPT TO SEE HOW
THIS MOVIE GOES? YOU HAVE MAYBE 40 SECONDS LEFT BEFORE
THEY COME GET YOU

—a Volkswagen has been cruising up and down the street for no
earthly reason at all, except that they are obviously working with
the fake telephone linesmen outside the window who whistle—

THERE THEY GO AGAIN

—whistle in the slow-brain brown Mexican huarache day-
laborer way, for no earthly reason except that they are obviously
synched in, finked in, with the Volkswagen. Now a tan sedan
comes along the street, minus a license plate but plus a stenciled
white number—*exactly like a prison stencil*—police and two coat-
less guys inside, both in white shirts so they're *not* prisoners—

ONE TURNED LOOKED BACK!

IF YOU WERE WATCHING ALL THIS ON A MOVIE SCREEN YOU KNOW
WHAT YOUR REACTION WOULD BE THROUGH A MOUTHFUL OF POP-
CORN FROM THE THIRD ROW: "WHAT MORE DO YOU NEED, YOU
DOLT! SCREAM OUTTA THERE . . ."

—But he has just hooked down five dexedrines and the old motor is spinning and rushing most nice and euphorically in fascination and a man can't depart this nice $80-a-month snug harbor
on paradise-blue Bandarias Bay just yet with a cool creek of
speed rush in his veins. It is such a tiny little fink scene as he sees
it in the hand mirror. He can tilt it and see his own face entropied
with the strain and then tilt it—a sign!—a sparrow, fat and sleek,
dives through the dwindling sun into a hole in one of the lamp-
posts; home.

MORE TELEFONO TRUCKS! TWO LOUD WHISTLES THIS TIME—FOR
NO EARTHLY REASON EXCEPT TO COME GIT YOU. YOU HAVE MAYBE
35 SECONDS LEFT

—Kesey has Cornel Wilde Running Jacket ready hanging on the
wall, a jungle-jim corduroy jacket stashed with fishing line, a

knife, money, DDT, tablet, ball-points, flashlight, and grass. Has it timed by test runs that he can be out the window, down through a hole in the roof below, down a drain pipe, over a wall and into thickest jungle in 45 seconds—well, only 35 seconds left, but head start is all that's needed, with the element of surprise. Besides, it's so fascinating to be here in subastral projection with the cool rushing dex, synched into *their* minds and his own, in all its surges and tributaries and convolutions, turning it this way and that and rationalizing the situation for the 100th time in split seconds, such as: If they have that many men already here, the phony telephone men, the cops in the tan car, the cops in the Volkswagen, what are they waiting for? why haven't they crashed right in through the rotten doors of this Rat building— But he gets the signal even before he finishes the question:

WAITING! THEY KNOW THEY'VE GOT YOU, FOOL, HAVE KNOWN FOR WEEKS. BUT THEY'RE CERTAIN YOU'RE CONNECTED WITH ALL THE LSD BEING SMUGGLED UP FROM MEXICO AND THEY WANT TO TAKE IN AS BIG A HAUL AS POSSIBLE WHEN THEY FINALLY SLAM IT. LIKE LEARY; THEY MUST HAVE BEEN WATCHING A DREADFUL LONG TIME BEFORE THEY WERE CONTENT THEY HAD SOMETHING WORTH HIS SIZE. THIRTY YEARS. FOR A HARVARD DOCTOR WITH GRASS. THAT'S HOW BAD THEY WANTED THE WHOLE BUSINESS LOCKED AWAY. THAT'S HOW DANGEROUS THEY CONSIDER THE WHOLE BUSINESS. AND THEY WERE COMPLETELY CORRECT—IF NOT IN THEIR FANTASY, THEN AT LEAST IN THEIR EVALUATION OF THE PRESENT AND EVER-GROWING PSYCHEDELIC THREAT

A NOISE DOWN BELOW.

THEM?

30 SEGUNDOS LEFT?

—maybe it's Black Maria, come back with good things for eating and stuff for the new disguise, Steve Lamb, mild-mannered reporter and all-around creep—

RUN, FOOL!

—Shhhhhhhhhhhhhhhhhh. Such a quiet secret muffled smile will be on Black Maria's face.

Rrrrrrrrrrrrrrrrrrrevrevrevrevrevrevrevrevrevrev It could have been all so quiet, just him and Zonker and the smoldering Black Maria in this $80-a-month paradise-blue Bandarias Bay in Puerto Vallarta. If the suicide ruse and the rest of the main Fugitive fantasy had but worked.

The trip into Mexico was easy, because everything with Boise was easy. Boise always *knew*. They picked up Zonker in L.A., and then Jim Fish, and they coasted on over the line at Tijuana. No hassle to cross over into Mexico. The border at Tijuana is like a huge superhighway toll station, a huge concrete apron and ten or fifteen customs booths in a row for all the cars pouring over into Tijuana from San Diego and points north, all plastic green and concrete like part of suburban superhighway America. So they rolled on over the line with Kesey hidden in the back of Boise's old panel truck and heart don't even thump too bad. Spirits up, a little of the Prankster élan back in the cosmos. In true Prankster fashion they spent one third their money stash on a Madman Muntz autostereo rig to go along with all the other valuables, like tape recorders and many tapes.

The next likely hassle is visas, because this shapes up as a long stay. Might be hot to try to get Kesey one in Tijuana, because Tijuana is just a California annex, really, the slums of San Diego, and they just might very well know about the case.

"We'll do it in Sonoita, man," says Boise. "They don't give a shit there. Put down a couple of bucks and they can't see anything else."

Sonoita is almost due east of Tijuana, just south of the Arizona border. Kesey uses his good shuck ID there and all is jake in Sonoita. Fugitive!—real-life and for sure now.

Then south down so-called Route 2 and so-called Route 15, bouncing and grinding along through the brown dust and scrawny chickens and animal dung brown dust fumes of western Mexico, towns of Coyote, Caborca, Santa Ana, Querobabi, Cornelio, El Oasis, hee, Hermosillo, hah, Pocitos Casas, Cieneguito, Guaymas, Camaxtli, Mixcoatl, Tlazolteotl, Quetzalcoatl, Huitzilopochtli, Tezcatlipoca haunting the Dairy Queen Rat Queen crossroads in the guise of a Rat, a Popoluactli-screeing rat, Tetzcotl, Yaotl, Titlacahuan he whose slaves we are, Ochpaniiztl priesty Angel-freaked out in a motorcycle made from the vaseline skin of Gang Bang Girl Meets White Trash . . . A confetti of skulls and death in western Mexico, the Rat lands. Not one inch of it is picturesque burros and shawls or nova Zapata hats or color-TV pink chunks of watermelon or water lilies or gold feathers or long eyelashes or high combs or tortillas and tacos and chili powder or fluty camote vendors or muletas or toreros or olés or mariachi bands or water lilies or blood of the dahlia or tinny cantinas or serapes or movie black marias with shiny black hair and steaming little high round pubescent bottoms. None of the old Mexico we know and love on the 21-day excursion fare. Just the boogering brown dust and bloated rat corpses by the road, goats, cows, chickens with all four feet up in the air at the Tezcatlipocan skull rot crossroads of Mexico.

To Kesey it was a hopeless flea-bitten desert he was fleeing into. But Boise made it bearable. Boise always *knew.* Boise was wizened and thin-faced and he had the awfulest New England high flat whine, and he didn't belong anywhere near here, but he was *here, now,* and he *knew.* The truck breaks down for the fourteenth time—

"No hassle, man. We just back it up on a rock, man . . . Then we just take the tire off and fix it."

More flat, Rat country, mosquito and flea, into total nothing, like the lines of perspective in a surrealist painting, but Boise makes you realize it is all the same, here as anywhere. Boise lecherously scanning the streets as they bounce through the dead chicken towns just like it was only Saturday night on Broadway in North Beach, spotting a good looking gringa muchacha padding along the side of the road with honest calves,

25 SECONDS LEFT, FOOL!

and he says, "Shall we get her over and *ball* her, man?" all in the same New England whine, as if he were saying, Wanna Coke, or not? Kesey looks at Boise's lined face and his thin lips, looks ancient, only a glitter comes out of the eyes, nice and lecherous, dead certain and crazy alive at the same time. And Boise in that moment is in the tiny knot of Perfect Pranksters, the inner circle, ascending into the *sangha* for good.

In Guaymas, on the gulf, Jim Fish wants out. *An early attack of paranoia, Jim Fish?* and catches a bus back to the U.S., leaving Kesey, Boise and Zonker and the equipment. But was it not ever so? You're either on the bus or off the bus. Kesey's spirits were picking up. Boise was pulling everything together ::: this crazy New Englander is *here* in these Rat lands.

"Hey, man . . ." Boise points at a construction scene they're going by. "*. . . see that?*" as if to say, There's the whole thing, right there.

A whole gang of workmen are trying to put the stucco on the ceiling of a building they're finishing up. One fat man is mixing up the stucco in a washtub. One skinny one is scooping the stucco up out of the tub with a little trowel and pitching it up underhanded at the ceiling. A little of it sticks—and three or four guys stand on a plank scaffolding taking stabs at smoothing it out—but most of it falls down on the floor and three or four more are hunkered down there scraping it up off the floor and shoveling it back in the tub and the skinny guy skinnies up another little gob with his skinny trowel and they all stare again to see what happens. They are all hunkering around in huaraches, worthless flat Rat woven sandals, up on the scaffolding, down on the floor, waiting to see what happens, how fate brings it off with this little gob of nothing pitched up at the Rat expanse . . .

And it's all there—the whole Mexico Trip—

"They have a saying, 'Hay tiemp—' " Boise hooks the steering wheel to get around an ice-cream vendor in the middle of the road " '—o,' 'There is time.' "

20 SECONDS, IDIOT!

Huaraches, which are *the* Rat shoe. It all synches. Mexico is the
Rat paradise. But of course! It is not worthless—it is perfection.
It is as if the Rat things of all the Rat lands of America, all the
drive-ins, mobile-home parks, Dairy Queens, superettes, Sunset Strips, auto-accessory stores, septic-tank developments, souvenir shops, snack bars, lay-away furniture stores, Daveniter
living rooms, hot-plate hotels, bus-station paperback racks,
luncheonette in-the-booth jukebox slots, raw-concrete service-
station toilets with a head of urine in the bowl, Greyhound bus
toilettes with paper towels and vomit hanging over the hockey-
puckblack rim, Army-Navy stores with Bikini Kodpiece Briefs
for men, Super Giant racks with matching green twill shirts and
balloon-bottom pants for honest toilers, $8,000 bungalows with
plastic accordion-folding partitions and the baby asleep in there
in a foldaway crib of plastic net, picnic tables with the benches
built onto them used in the dining room, Jonni-Trot Bar-B-Q
sandwiches with a carbonated fruit drink, aluminum slat
awnings, aluminum sidings, lukewarm coffee-"with" in a china
mug with a pale brown pool in the saucer and a few ashes, a
spade counter chef scraping a short-order grill with a chalky
Kitchy-Brik and he won't take your order till he's through, a
first-come-first-serve doctor's waiting room with modest char-
women with their dresses stuck on the seats of shiny vinyl chairs
and they won't move to get loose for fear you'll look up their
dress, plaid car coats from Sears and a canvas cap with a bill, syn-
thetic dresses for waitresses looking like milky cellophane, Rat
cones, Rat sodas, Rat meat-salad sandwiches, Rat cheezis, Rat-
burgers—it is as if the Rat things of all the Rat lands of America
had been looking for their country, their Canaan, their Is-ra-el,
and they found it in Mexico. It has its own Rat aesthetic. It's
hulking beautiful . . .

Then they reached Mazatlan, the first full-fledged resort you
reach on the west coast of Mexico, coming down from the States.
Everybody's trip was fishing in Mazatlan. Along the old Avenida

del Mar and the Paseo Claussen, white walls with nice artistic Rat fishing scenes and hotel archways with great shiny blue marlins hanging inside the arches and gringos with duckbill caps here to catch some marlin. Mariachi music at last, with the trumpets always breaking and dropping off the note and then struggling up again. Zonker has the bright idea of going to O'Brien's Bar, on the beach front, place he got beat up out back of once by thirteen Mexican fags. Zonker enjoys revisiting scenes of previous debacles. *Like also spends hours on the beach telling them how his true and fiercest fear is of being attacked by a shark while swimming . . . as he picks flea-bite scabs until his legs stream blood to the luscious world . . . then goes swimming.*

O'Brien's brings on the paranoia right away. It is a break in the Rat movie. It is dark and a Mexican band plays—signaling to the Rat sensibility that it will cost too much. Rat souls everywhere fear dark, picturesque restaurant, knowing instinctively they will pay dearly for the bullshit ambiance, dollar a drink probably. O'Brien's was crowded, and then through the cocktail gloom: *heads.* A bunch of kids with the jesuschrist hair, the temple bells and donkey beads, serape vests, mandalas; in short, American heads. Zonker recognizes them immediately. They're not only American heads, but from San Jose, and some had been to the Acid Tests. *Just what the Fugitive needs to blow the whole suicide ruse.* "Guess who I saw in Mexico . . ." Naturally, Zonk, with his zest for debacle, hails them over. Kesey is introduced as "Joe," and nobody pays him much mind except for one dark little girl, Mexican-looking, with long black hair.

"When were you born?" she says to Kesey. She doesn't sound Mexican. *She sounds like Lauren Bacall speaking through a tube.*

"I'm a Virgo." *No sense hitting a ball three bits you can see coming if you can cut across the fourth.*

"I thought so. I'm a Scorpio."

"Beautiful."

The black Scorpio obviously knows Zonk best. She knows

him when. But Zonk belongs to the ages and it comes to pass that
Zonk or no Zonk, she and Kesey relax out in the open air on the
pier one night down by a Mazatlan Rat beach, all dirt and scrabble, but the waves and the wind and the harbor lights do it up
right and the moon hits some kind of concrete shaft there,
putting her in the dark, in the shadow, and him in the light, lit
up by the moon, as if some designer drew a line precisely between
their bodies. *Black Maria,* he decides.

So Black Maria joins the Fugitive band and they go off to
Puerto Vallarta. Puerto Vallarta is out of the Rat lands. All pic-
ture-book Mexico. Paradise-blue Bandarias Bay and a pure white
beach and white latino cottages right up against the jungle,
which is a deep raw green, and clean. Fat green fronds lapping
up against the back of the houses on the beach. Macaw sounds, or
very near it. Secret poisonous orchid and orange pops and petals
winking out when the foliage moves. A nice romantic Gothic
jungle. Zonker hassles with an oily little real-estate man and gets
the last house on the edge of town for $80 a month. The rent is
low because the jungle is too close for the tourists, the jungle and
too many Mexican kids and chickens and the rural dung dust.
Boise heads back to the U.S. and Kesey, Zonker and Black Maria
move in. They have the upper half of the house, one floor and a
spiral staircase up to the roof. Up on the roof is a kind of thatched
hut, the highest perch around, a perfect lookout post and a snug
harbor. Kesey decides to risk a phone call to the States to let Faye
and everybody know he's O.K. He goes into town and calls Peter
Demma in the Hip Pocket Book Store in Santa Cruz. A little
metallic clanking about by the telefonista señoritas down at central. And then,

"Peter?"

From many Rat miles away: "Ken!" Very surprised, naturally . . .

So Kesey whiled the time sitting in the snug hacienda on the
edge of Puerto Vallarta sipping beer and smoking many joints

and writing in a notebook occasionally. He wanted to get a little of all this down and send it to Larry McMurtry.

"Larry:

"Phone calls to the states eight bucks apiece besides was ever a good board to bound my favorite ball of bullshit prose offen, it was you . . ."

Like all about Black Maria. In many ways she was so great. She is quiet and has a kind of broody beauty. She cooks. She looks Mex and speaks Mex. She can even hassle Mex. She sounds out the Mayor of Puerto Vallarta as to how safe Kesey will be here in town. Hay tiempo, he says. The extradition takes forever. Very nice to know . . .

And yet Black Maria is not completely a Prankster. She wants to be a part of all this, she wants to do this thing, but *she does it without belief.* It is like the Mexican part of her Black Maria thing. She has all the trappings of Mexican—she looks it, she speaks it, her grandfather was even Mexican—but she is not Mexican. She is Carolyn Hannah of San Jose, California, under everything else, even the blood. He wrote in the notebook::*Moving the dark Indian*

10 SECONDS LEFT, YOU FREAKING EE-JOT!!!!

body out of the Indian land weakened the Indian blood with chicken soup and matzoh balls. So much of the fire concealed by the dark and broody beauty lies just that deep. Because she does it without belief. And yet is is very nice up here in this thatched perch atop the last house. A car heads up the street—Zonker and Black Maria coming back to the house. He peers over the edge at the car kicking up the dust, then writes in the notebook, it is a perfect lookout, *allowing me to see them, without them seeing me.* Many things . . . synch.

.   .   .

ZONKER AND BLACK MARIA DROVE DOWN THE ROAD, SCATTER-
ing up the kids and the chickens and the dust, and Black Maria
pointed up to the top of the house and said to Zonker:

"Look, there's Kesey." Then she looked out the window and
stared at the jungle. "I bet he thinks we can't see him."

THE JIG IS UP. ZONKER BRINGS A TELEGRAM FROM PAUL
Robertson back in San Jose and it is a bear. It is not even a warn-
ing, it

    5 SECONDS—5 SECONDS LEFT—YOU REALLY JES GON' SIT THERE
    FOR THE SQUASH?

is final. THE JIG IS UP, is says. Meaning, it turned out, that the suicide ruse had been exposed and the cops knew he was in Puerto
Vallarta. Exposed?—hell, the suicide prank had turned into a
goddamn comic opera. For a start, Dee had pulled a sort of Dee-
out, as Mountain Girl feared. Dee had driven up looking for a
cliff near Humboldt Bay, about 250 miles north of San Francisco,
up near Eureka, California, not far from the Oregon border in
redwoods country. He got up to the last hill going up there and
the panel truck wouldn't pull the hill. So he called into town for
a tow truck and the garage man and the tow truck pulled the suicide vehicle up the last mile. Hired and paid for and thanks a lot.
Always nice to hire some help to commit suicide. Next Dee
dropped Kesey's distinctive sky-blue boots down to the shore below—but they hit the water instead and sank without a bubble.
Next, the goddamned romantic suicide desolate foaming cliff
was so goddamned desolate, nobody noticed the truck for about
two weeks, despite the Ira Sandperl for President sign on the rear
bumper. Apparently people figured the old heap had been abandoned. The Humboldt county police finally checked it out on
February 11. Next, the suicide note, which seemed so ineluctably
convincing as Kesey and Mountain Girl smoked a few joints and

soared into passages of Shelleyan *Weltschmerz*—it gave off a giddy scent of put-on, even to the straight cops of the Humboldt. There were certain inconsistencies. Like the part about the truck smashing into a redwood. Well—even in a Dee-out, Dee couldn't exactly ask the tow-truck man, Well, now that you've towed it up here, how about jamming it into a tree for me. Demma had really been bowled over to hear from Kesey. A lot of people, a lot of people who liked him, had really been worried that he was dead. And now here was Kesey calling him—*alive*—with a message for Faye and the whole thing. That was Saturday. The next night, Sunday, February 13, Demma dropped into Manuel's Mexican Restaurant in Santa Cruz, and there was his old friend Bob Levy. By way of making conversation, Levy says,

"What have you heard from Ken?"

"I just got a *call* from him!" says Demma. "From Puerto Vallarta!"

That's interesting.

Levy happened to be a reporter for the Watsonville *Register-Pajaronian,* Watsonville being a town near Santa Cruz. The next afternoon, Monday, the lead story in the Watsonville *Register-Pajaronian* carried a five-column headline reading:

MISSING NOVELIST TURNS UP IN MEXICO

The next day, Tuesday, the San Jose *Mercury* picked up the story and put a little more spin on it with a story headlined:

KESEY'S CORPSE HAVING A BALL IN PUERTO VALLARTA

2 SECONDS, OH CORPSE OF MINE!
THAT'S NO BLACK MARIA SHHHHHHHHUFFLING UP THE STAIRS OUTSIDE
    THE DOOR, DOLT, IT'S A COP CLUMP UP THE STAIRS NO EARTHLY
    SOUND LIKE IT
    SHARP WHISTLE FROM THE TELEFONISTAS

VW BACKING DOWN THE STREET

THIS IS TRULY IT, TRULY IT

GRAB THE CORNEL WILDE RUNNING JACKET, FOOL! MAKE THE
BRAIN CATCH HOLD! RRRRRRRRRRRRRRREVREVREVREV SPINNING
AND IN THE GIANT PYRAMIDAL CELLS OF BETZ OF PRE-CENTRAL
CEREBRAL CORTEX RISE AND HEAVE AND SLIP GANGLIONIC LAYER
SHUDDERS AND GIGGLES SYNAPSES LIGHT LIKE RANDOM BEATLE
FLASHBULBS KHEEWWW BLASTING OUT SILLY FROM MOTOR HO-
MUNCULUS YOU MISSED YR FLASH OH MIGHTY MASTICATOR,
SALIVATOR, VOCALIZER, SWALLOWER, LICKER, BITER SUCKER BROW-
KNITTER LOOKER BLINKER RUBBERNECKER THUMBER PRODDER UP-
YOURS FINGERER RINGWEARER NOSEPICKER WAVER DRINKER
ARMLIFTER BODYBENDER HIPSWIVELER KNEER SPRINGER RUNNER
ZERO::::::::OOOOOOOOO::::::::: RUN!

Sonbitch! The gears catch at last, he springs up, grabs Cornel
Wilde jacket, leaps through the back window, down through the
hole, down the drainpipe—now vault the wall, you mother, into
the jungle floppy—

AWWRRRRRAMMMMANNNNNNN

WHAZZAT?

His head is down but he can see it

WHAZZAT!

Up there in the window he just jumped out of

BROWN!

He can feel it. There is a vibration on the parasympathetic effer-
ent fibres behind the eyeballs and it hums

HRRRRRRRRRMANNNNNNNNNNNN

Two of them one brown dumpy Mex with gold-handle butt gun
one crewcut American FBI body-snatcher watching him flying
like a monkey over the wall into the jungle the brown Mex holds
gold gun but the brain behind that face too brown moldering
Mex earth to worry about couldn't hit a peeing dog

PLUNGE

into the lapping P.V. fronds bursting orchid and orange the motor homunculus working perfect now powerful gallop into the picturebook jungles of Mexico—

A MOMENT LATER BLACK MARIA WALKED INTO THE APART-ment. She found Kesey gone and the Cornel Wilde jungle running jacket gone. That trip again. Well, he'll come back when he's ready to, worn out, and things will be cool for a while. Kesey had gotten paranoid as hell, but that wasn't the only thing. He *liked* this Fugitive game. Man, he'd scram out in the jungle and hide out there for two or three days and smoke a lot of grass and finally straggle in. That started before the telegram even. There was a whole signal they worked out. Or he worked out. When the coast was clear, she was supposed to hang up a yellow shirt of Zonk's on the line outside the back window, facing the jungle. It was a yellow shirt with a black and brown print on it, on the *faggy* side, if you asked Black Maria. The flag would go up and finally Kesey would straggle back home beat, having run himself about to death in the jungle or along the beach.

And yet it was nice. It was crazy but nice. Kesey was the most magnetic person she had ever met. He radiated something, a kind of power. His thoughts, the things he talked about, were very complex and metaphysical and cryptic but his manner was back-home, almost back-country. Even while he was reeking with paranoia, he seemed to have total confidence. That was very strange. He could make you feel like part of something very . . . He had even given her a new name, Black Maria. She was . . . Black Maria.

As a girl in San Jose, California, she had felt like everything she really was had been smothered under layers and layers of games she couldn't control. Externally there was nothing wrong. Her father and mother were both teachers and life in San Jose was comfortable and serene in the California suburban manner. But half the time nobody ever understands about growing up in this country. Little Penguin Islands full of kids playing Lord of the Flies, a world of pygmy tribes, invisible to the Isfahan adult eye, these little devils, tribes of studs, tribes of rakes, tribes of IntelFinks even, tribes of greasers, and an amorphous mass of hopeless cases left over. Until—psychedelics started around there, mainly grass and acid. The new scene started and suddenly all sorts of . . . well, *beautiful people* blossomed forth from out of the polyglot, people who really had a lot to them, only it had been smothered by all the eternal social games that had been set up. Suddenly they found each other.

One night she was high and experienced the unity, the All-one. A light was behind her in the room and hit her body from behind and broke up into beams and shone out before her, hitting the floor and the walls in spokes of light with shadows in between. The room broke up before her eyes and separated in just that pattern with bars of light vibrating. Suddenly it became very clear, the way the room was put together, the way the parts fit, the way the parts of *every*thing fit, as if someone had taken an Indian puzzle ring apart for her. It was clear how *every*thing fit together and it wasn't really a world split up into pointless games and cliques. That was merely the way it looked before you knew the key. And now there were beautiful people who knew the key and this experience could be shared.

Her mother gave her money for the second semester at San Jose State, and although it would hurt her mother at first, she knew what she had to do. She took the money and headed off to Mexico with some beautiful kids. It was a little more complicated than that. She knew Zonk at San Jose State and she knew he was heading for Mexico, for Mazatlan, although she didn't know about the Kesey prank, and so she was following Zonk, for if there were beautiful people, Zonk was one of them.

Mazatlan was just beginning to be the acid heads' favorite spot on the Mexican west coast. It wasn't a place the real hard-core tourists were onto yet. They went on down the coast to Acapulco, generally. At the same time Mazatlan wasn't so unbearably Mexicali . . . *sad* . . . like the true Acid Central of Mexico, Ajijic, on Lake Chapala. Those poor sad Lake Chapala villages, Ajijic, Chapala, Jocotepec, with the lake drying up and the old suck-smack lily-pad scum mud showing and failed American aesthetes padding around earnestly in sandals, 48-year-old bohos sucking up to young heads of the new generation of Hip. Very sad. It is truly a sad thing when an American boho says fuck this and picks up and leaves this fucking tailfin and shopping plaza and war-crazy civilization and goes to live among real people, the honest folk-type folk, in the land of Earth feelings, Mexico, and the hell with tile baths—and then he *sits* there, in Mexico, amid the hunkering hardcheese mestizos, and, man, it is honest and real here . . . and just as miserable as hell, and he is a miserable aging fuckup with no place else to go.

But Mazatlan—the head scene there was a happy thing and a groove. So she sat down in Mazatlan and wrote her mother a Beautiful People letter . . .

And she found Zonk and, unexpectedly, the famous Ken Kesey and beautiful people. But one thing about the beautiful people themselves. . . . Namely, the Merry Pranksters. She had heard of the fabulous Merry Pranksters even in San Jose. Kesey and Zonk talked about them all the time, of course. The fabulous Babbs, the fabulous Mountain Girl, the fabulous Cassady, Hermit, Hassler and the rest. She had a Prankster name, Black Maria, but she was not yet a Prankster. She was sensitive even to the contours of Kesey's world, too. Sooner or later Kesey would reunite with the Pranksters . . .

Well . . . put out Zonker's shirt when the coast is clear. Zonker's billowy faggy-looking shirt. Let him stay out on his jungle run for a while. If he enjoys the Fugitive game, why spoil it.

Shhhhhhhhhhhwaaaaaaaaap

flopping lush P.V. fronds Kesey thrashes out of the jungle and across the road—

CARS? ONE MEX ONE AMERICAN COMING IN PALE TAN VW?
no, no cars, man, and then down across the road to rocky scrabble down by the ocean on the rocks, his heart rattling away, he
sinks down in his Cornel Wilde running jacket listening

WHOP!
surf hits the rocks, just a little holiday in picturesque P.V. with the
sea kicking up at twilight. He concentrates on the surf—analogy
spoken here?—but the surf is too aimless this way. His heart rattles tachycardiac at this speed, and the surf is synched in to another thing WHOPping against the rocks

BRANNGGGH
a tin-door sound up on the road like the ominous tin-car-door
sounds in *Hud* always bring on the bad action—like brown Mex
and crewcut drip-dry American up on the road eyes rocketing
around, Brown Mex puffing *I'm-supposed-to-be-off-duty-now-
señor.* Kesey faces out to sea, pulls a tablet out of the jacket. Makes
the pink cover visible as if to prove just an aimless surf artist
drawing water swells furl by furl like Leonardo who *must* have
been a head, all the minute instincts, to sit by the water drawing
the little furls as the water laps up on beach then starts rolling
back toward the sea and minute little churning furls in the lead
edge of the water, he drew it all, furl by furl, like a very meth
head plugged into the great God Rotor. More surf, then

KABOOM!
first—they're FIRING on him. They don't give a shit.

HOT PURSUIT!
we got the guns and the rights, signed on this piece of paper here,
one move blow yr fucking head off and you have *already moved,*
Kesey—

HOT PURSUIT!

KABOOM!
but nothing happens. Silence except for the surf.

THAT IS VERY PARANOID, HONDO
why would they try to blast you out of the tub with elephant guns
anyway. It must be workmen using dynamite. So he edges up

to the road and it is workmen all right, sweating and heaving while the green fronds flap up the hill. He'll just sit here and watch them dynamite

SURE

just watch them dynamite while every gringo car comes spinning off the shore drive out here Baskin-Robbins tourist matron look-out and say *"Hey, Honey, that's Ken Kee-zee..."*

Back into the jungle, Cornel Wilde. Heart still banging up to the edge of fibrillation, through the lush shadowy danks of the jungle. Well, yessir, lookee here a minute, what's this. A three-sided hut in the jungle, some kind of woodsman's hut, with a cot in it and a little hoard of mango papaya, some kind of pallid little fruit. He sinks back on the cot, unzips his fly to air out his sweating nuts and dips into his jacket and pulls out three roaches and wraps a leaf around them like a cone and lights up. He cuts open a fruit and it bleeds meek white and he puts it aside.

A TRAP FOR JUNGLE RUNNERS

this perfect little snug harbor to suck you in, a hut, a cot, meek milk white fruit to eat, a joint of sorts, oh to be back in Baskin-Robbins country just one time facing endless beige tubs of ice cream 31 flavor decisions to make, pointed cone or cup-style

¡PARANOIA!

but this is the real-life jungle, Major. Two-winged flies, dapple-wing Anapholes, Culex tarsalis, verruga-crazed Phlebotomus biting 8-day fever and Oriental sores, greenhead rabbit-fever horseflies, tularemic Loa loa, tsetse mites, Mexican fleas, chinches, chiggers, velvet ants, crab lice crawling up your balls up your belly under your arms right up to your eyelashes for a nice fix of Mexican murine typhus, puss caterpillars, cantharidae beetles, Indian bedbugs, ticks, itch mites nice for scabies and rickety pox, Pacific Coast female tick hiding in the hairs at the base of the head sucking in the death bloat with blood, paralysis coming up from the toes will it reach the lungs before the big blood sausage mother drops off, a blood bag with tiny feet wriggling like worm hairs

DDT!

he gets down and pulls the DDT can out of the jacket and starts
dusting all around the ground there around the cot, setting up a
mighty defense perimeter against the mites of the jungle—which
is very funny, come to think of it—down on all fours in deadly
battle with the microscopic mites while

THEY

close in to slam you away for five, eight, twenty years . . . driven
at last out onto the edge of your professed beliefs. You believed
that a man should move off his sure center out onto the outer
edges, that the outlaw, even more than the artist, is he who tests
the limits of life and that—The Movie :::: by getting totally into
Now and paying total Attention until it all flows together in the
synch and imagining them all into the Movie, your will will de-
termine the flow and control all jungles great and small

NEXT TO LAST JOINT IN ALL OF MEXICO

he pulls it out of his pocket and lights up. *Maybe I'll knock off the
grass for a while.* Su-u-u-ure.

AND THEN BELIEVE ALL THAT CRAP YOU'VE BEEN CLAIMING ABOUT
ALTERING BY ACCEPTING. BELIEVE IT! OR YOU ARE A GONER, AND
BOY, A WALKING DEAD MAN FOREVERMORE FADING FINALLY IN-
AUDIBLE LIKE THE VOICES MUMBLING BITONES IN THE CATHE-
DRAL!

And now that I've got your attention—if he sits very still, the
rush lowers in his ears, he can concentrate, pay total attention, an
even, even, even world, flowing into *now,* no past terrors, no anticipation of the future horror, only *now, this* movie, the vibrating
parallel rods, and he can *feel* them drawn into the flow, his, every
verruga fly, velvet ant, murine fleas and crabs, every chinch and
tick, every lizard, cat, palm, the very power of the most ancient
palm, held in his will, and he is immune—

chapter XXII

¡Diablo!

MOUNTAIN GIRL STUCK IT OUT WITH BABBS, GRETCH,
Walker—for the sake of the great idea—and she meant
it—but any way she thought it out, it came out Kesey.
Mountain Girl was almost eight months pregnant now. The bus,
The Movie, was at a total standstill now, sinking into the
swamper bogs. One day a package came in by mail, from Mexico,
a tape, from Kesey, to Mountain Girl. And there was his voice.
She could hardly make out a word he said, the quality of the tape
was so bad—all she could make out was, he was in the jungle
somewhere and paranoid as hell and smoking a lot of grass.

O DEAR DEAD ONE!

Then Babbs made the decision to take the bus to Mexico. They
were a little paranoid themselves, about the heat put on the Acid
Tests. Two days after the story broke about Kesey being in Puerto
Vallarta, the good fink California press ran another big one: KE-
SEY'S PALS IN LSD PARTY IN L.A.—a barnburner about the Watts

Test. But mainly they couldn't hack it any more; not even Babbs. Get the goddamn bus moving, that was the main thing.

Mountain Girl had one more ordeal to go through. She had to stand trial in San Francisco for possession of marijuana, result of the bust on the rooftop. All the shit in society that the Pranksters had liberated themselves from through years of arduous initiation—the shit rolled in, in lava gulps. She had to sit there, great with child, like a prisoner of war in a bamboo cage, while the straight world put her on prize exhibit and clucked and remonstrated and scolded and then shook its head and blubbered a little over her. Doped, seduced and abandoned, the poor miscreant teenager. She got a little Prankster mileage out of it even then, although she had to play it fairly straight, just to let them play out their game so she could get on with it. Their fantasy for her was a new dawn for this unfortunate girl, not a beeline for Mexico, but that was their fantasy.

Mountain Girl showed up in court on March 20 in a red dress, four inches above the knees, and this was long before minidresses were on every eyeball, and pregnant as hell. She came to court on the arm of the Cavalier Hassler. Hassler was great throughout the whole thing. He was her sanity. Hassler came to court with her, wearing a green velveteen shirt, yellow bouclé stretch pants and red boots, and when the reporters came up slavering for sob stuff, he put them on so righteously, it was beautiful.

"We must do everything possible," he would say, peering out as sincere as the Student Council president from under his Prince Valiant locks, "to get Carolyn on her feet and out of this life of crime"—Carolyn Adams, naturally, being the fantasy that the Court knew her by. "I'm going to be the strong stabilizing force in her life"—vibrating yellow and green. "She's had a lot of misjudgment."

"My misjudgment may extend to you," said Mountain Girl. Great fun had by all.

The sob-story angle was the fantasy they all came up with for her in court, her lawyer included. It was like they had all looked at her and thought it over and hmmmmmmmm this poor misguided runaway girl 20 years old, lately a teenager, you understand, and more than seven months in the family way seduction by the demon Kesey who left her to take the whole blame for the dope charge *as well as* abandoning her with an unborn child. Urgggggggggghhhhhh the prosecutor agreed on it, her lawyer agreed on it, the Judge agreed on it. So went the Justice game. And where was the demon Kesey who left so fast breathing dope from every nostril—it was as if everybody was going to be nice to her by way of pointing out the lesson of Kesey's evil.

Her lawyer, Steven Dedina, said: "Carolyn is no dope fiend, no dope addict. Her one addiction is a perennial overdose of solicitude for persons who are far away. Were it not for that particular addiction, this defendant would not be standing in this particular place at this particular time."

So on March 22 Mountain Girl was let off with a fine of $250 for possession of marijuana. Yet if Kesey had left her in a lurch, it was a lurch that they would never understand in a million years.

THE TRIP DOWN INTO MEXICO WAS THE BUS AT ITS MOST AWful. Mountain Girl, so pregnant, just held on and forced back the bilious as the thing bounced and pitched and rolled through the desert. She felt like a 200-pound egg. But moving again! that was the main thing. Anything was better than what she had been going through. And this was truly something. Every 20 miles it seemed like the bus broke down and Babbs sweated over it. All the vibrations outside were bad. Corpses, chiefly. Scrub cactus, brown dung dust and bloated corpses, dogs, coyotes, armadillos, a cow, all gas-bellied and dead, swollen and dead, Babbs, Gretch, Faye and the kids, Walker and Mountain Girl.

The fantasy this time had been dreamed up by Zonker. Zonker had gotten in touch with them, and Hagen had already

driven down in an old car. Now the bus was going to keep a secret rendezvous with them in Mazatlan. Kesey had lit out for
Mazatlan after the big scare in Puerto Vallarta.

In Puerto Vallarta, Kesey had sure enough had something to
worry about after all. Chief Arturo Martínez Garza of the Mexican Federales had ordered a search of Puerto Vallarta on February 16, two days after the story broke in the California papers.
They had hassled all strange bohemian-looking Americans on
the streets and so on. But Kesey had already made a run for it,
back to Mazatlan. Zonker had arranged the rendezvous for the
beach at Mazatlan, such-and-such a day, such-and-such an hour.

Babbs flogged the bus through the corpse horizon day and
night, desperate to make it on time, with the bus breaking down
over and over again, everybody ill, not just Mountain Girl, but
flogging on like it was life or death. And finally, Mazatlan, the
sea, the big curve of the malecón—they *made* it. This was the
flow, and it was a sickening horrible flow, but they had *made* it,
and they tooled up to the rendezvous point—no Kesey. No
Zonker and no Hagen.

It was too much, this particular predictable fuckup, after all
that. It wasn't a cool thing for them to just sit there by the beach
in this lurid freak of a bus, such as Mexico had never seen, but
this was too much, and they sat there, beat, and let the hours tool
by. They were a hell of a hit with the Mexicans, however. They
never saw anything like it. "¡Diablo!" they kept saying. Women
hid their children with their skirts. A whole bunch of locals gathered around the bus and grinned their hideous magenta-
gummed native grins and stared at the crazies.

Heeeee!—an old car with no windows in the mother comes
by, slowing down. The face at the driver's window, with the in-
credulous look—Hagen. And that old gray head peeking over
the window's edge in the back, just peeking over ever so gingerly—could it *possibly* be . . . Hagen stops and gets out. Then the
back door opens ever so gingerly and out steps a gray-haired soul

with his head cocked to one side, radiating surprise and appall and not at all happy about the Diablo multitudes.

He has on a hincty washed-out faded tourist sport shirt and balloon-seat pants. He walks like a repertory theater shambles. He looks ten or fifteen years older, like an old workadaddy on the 21-day plan to Mexico. *Ecce* Fugitive.

Shee-ut, it's all too freaking absurd, this secret rendezvous. The bus glowing Day-Glo on the beach at Mazatlan, the Diablo multitudes whooping it up like a cock fight, Mountain Girl beautiful and fulsome with her hair down to her waist and dyed yellow from the last Test—they could have sold tickets.

You're looking at the New Super Fugitive, Mountain Girl: Steve Lamb—45-year-old gray-haired ninny. Certified I.D.; Zonker's driver's license with the Steve Lambrecht doctored to read Steve Lamb and the birth date altered to make him 45 instead of 25. Mild-mannered lamb among men, Steve Lamb, 45-year-old reporter, creep and amateur ornithologist, broadcaster for KSRO, Mighty 590 on your dial. Got his tape recorder right here, yessir, for collecting bird calls. Also you never know when the spot news will break and the diligent reporter is always ready, even on holiday. Old mild-mannered Steve Lamb has learned the secret of invisibility, which is to crawl into the rut, the bottomest awfulest part of the sunken way society has dug for all those who properly fear her might, O Mighty 590.

But hardly seem worth it, somehow, with the bus beginning to glow in the Mexican dusk. ¡Fuck it! ¡Diablo! ¡Cosmo! Let's bull it through, here in the Rat lands! Glittering Prankster glances all around. Paint it big enough and bright enough and they won't even be able to see it! Kesey and Mountain Girl and Babbs and Gretch and Faye and the kids standing here in the Rat vistas . . . and along the edge of the circle a little Mexican-looking girl with long black hair just emerged from the old car . . . Black Maria stares out to sea.

XXIII

chapter

The Red Tide

FOCKING RED TIDE, MAN, AND EVERYBODY IN MANZANILLO is up tight. Tropic of Cancer, heat 110 degrees, no wind, many mosquitoes, and the red tide killing the fish. Thousands, tens of thousands focking dead fish floating belly up in the red tide. The stench you would not believe, and there is something in the air spewed up from the ocean that makes your eyes smart. Some people they feel like they have it in the lungs, like the flu. There is no greater calamity than the red tide, because we live on the fishing here in Manzanillo. Unless it is the American crazies. On top of the red tide, appearing like they rose up out of the red tide itself, we have the American crazies. Focking plague themselves, riding about in a devilish criminal bus. They ride into the plaza, near the great jaracanda tree, in a devilish bus covered in crazed fluorescent cholera flowers, gaudier than the red blossoms of Manzanillo's great jaracanda tree

RED TIDE!

and old women and children say, "¡Diablo!", and cross themselves, which the American crazies think is very funny. We do not, however.

The biggest of them, with a great mocking grin and American lightbulb eyeballs and pants of many colors, comes into our marketplace with a blond woman whom he calls Gretch and a trail of blond children behind him, rolling his grinning head around until he sees that all the world is watching, and then he throws his great arms of an ape up into the air and turns his eyeballs up and shouts:

"¡Eat alley! ¡Eat alley! ¡Take me to eat alley!"

"You mean the *market,* señor?"

Then he grins and stares with an intensity at the poor mestizo as if he has just uttered the most penetrating remark in the history of all Mexico and says:

"Yeah! Yeah! Right! Right! Right!"

And all the world gives way, wondering, as this strange train goes escombering into the marketplace.

There is much talk here about the crazies. Many think that these people are Germans, refugees from a cabala that failed. They mistake their strange talk for German. Some people think that they are American gangsters, in hiding. But I think that they came up out of the red tide.

¡Aguaje!

In truth! Out in the ocean, where the water was once deepest blue-green, or, at worst, yellow-green near the beach, there are now vast streaks of reddish water, as if there were a channel cutting through the ocean itself, stretching for miles, hot and turbid, thick as mucus. The fish die almost at once when they enter it. I have watched a mullet come upon it. She swam from the blue-green water into the red tide and suddenly she is keeling over, as if paralyzed, then struggling to come upright again, then thrashing about crazily as if dizzy, then heading for the surface, where she whirls, flashing in the sunlight, then collapses, keeling over on her side again, paralyzed, then sinks, and then, by and by, without doubt, floats back up, dead, to join the great stinking school of dead fish, dead crabs, dead sea bass, mullets, thread herring, mackerel, shrimp, even barnacles, coquinas, sailfish, marlin, porpoises, turtles, huge gobs of reeking gluey tissue floating in a grisly death school on the red tide. Struck dead—

—by what? By the plankton. All the world knows that the plankton cause the red tide—as if that could be called a cause. For the plankton are always there, millions of invisible animiculae, thousands to a cupful of seawater. It is they who reflect blue-green and give our ocean its color, although elsewhere they reflect red and make the Red Sea red, without harm to any animal, and the Vermillion Sea vermillion and the Lake of Blood a rose-red milk of sulphur. But here, off the placid Bay of Manzanillo in the Pacific Ocean, this little invisible ... um ... dinoflagellate, *Gymnodinium brevis,* just one cell to him and two whips, whipping and darting about, begins to multiply. And suddenly he appears to *explode,* should one look at him under a microscope, as Charles Darwin once did, and he divides into two dinoflagellates, and they divide into four, and so on, in a progression of utmost rapidity until there are in truth ten million of them in a cup of water, and the water turns red from their red pigment, which reflects light, until finally, from the focking millions of explosions, a poison as powerful as aconitine gives off into the water—but *why?*—*why* has it started *now,* this malignant explosion of the plankton into—

—one vast immortal Group Animicula, fifteen miles long and three miles wide, immortal, in truth. The first little *Gymnodinium brevis* still lives just as surely as the 128-billionth as the red tide spreads. For they increase simply by cell division. The great marlins die, the porpoises, all the creatures of the sea die, and the fishermen die, but the *Gymnodinium* is immortal, the instant brother of every *Gymnodinium brevis* who ever lived, no past, no future, only Now, and immortal, the little fockers. No *cause,* señor, no *starting point* in time, just the point at which your game intersected the 256-octillionth *Gymnodinium* and all his ancestors and successors in old Manzanillo and brought you up tight. We

know only that yesterday there were fish, and today the fish are
dead and the poison plankton and the American crazies are alive,
and tomorrow we must find out the cause and the cure—or
could it *possibly* be that yesterday and tomorrow are merely more
of Now stretching fifteen miles and three miles wide immortal—

THEN, NOW, ESAU, JUDITH, BASHEMATH, REUEL, SUSPENDED
in the mucus; what a bummer. Mountain Girl lies on the bed in
her room; staring at the ceiling; a pisspoor job of plastering it is,
too; and all of them suspended in 110-degree mucus. She; Kesey;
Faye; their children; George Walker; the new chick, Black
Maria; have a house by the beach; new; raw certified Rat construction; cinderblock and plaster; she could scrabble through it
with her hands. Fifty yards away, across the beach road, The Rat
Shack; this being a Purina Chow factory; *yep;* inhabited by Babbs,
Gretchen Fetchin and Babbs's children; a curious little building
empty of Purina Chow and glistening with tiles inside. All of
them gittin stuck and stranded like flies in this 110-degree mucus
of Manzanillo with the red tide stinking the place up for good
measure; Hagen, with his leg in a cast; Julius Karpin, the Hardest Head in the West, from Berkeley, of the Prankster outer circle, here with *his* leg in a cast. They picked out Manzanillo for
these very reasons, however; isolated, few Americans in the summer, off the tourist trail; secure desert island. Stranded in an up-
tight town; no roads leading north and no roads leading south;
nine or ten hours of hell by bus to Guadalajara the only way to
git back to the rest of the world; can't git out in the daytime and
do anything because of the heat; can't git out at night because of
the mosquitoes; the jungle beyond the Rat Shack filthy with cocoa palms and all sortsa jungle shit; itching crawling alive like a
chigger-ridden groin; all manner exotic vermin; sting inflame
chigger-blister mosquito heaven, with scorpions for good measure coming up outta the dung dust like lobsters as the crab louse
is to the crab. Standing dead still in this shit; jes waiting; for

what; for bread, mainly; every day in supplication at the altar of
the Telégrafo, for money from Stateside; Kesey's lawyers supposed to be hassling up money; and everyday some soul, like the
chick Kesey picked up, Black Maria, down to the Telégrafo using an alias waiting for telégrafo coming from some lawyer in
San Francisco; or from the Mexico City lawyer Kesey's stateside
lawyers had gotten hold of to straighten things out with the Mexican police; he was called Estrella; for Star Lawyer? who the fuck
knows; here on Devil's Island, us fugitives; no sense of time at all;
unbelievable bad news is all that filters from the U.S.; Ron Boise,
who had a rheumatic heart, has died of a heart attack at the age
of thirty-two; Norman Hartweg in an accident on the drive east
with Marge the Barge and Evan Engber, and he is in a hospital
in Ann Arbor, almost completely paralyzed; unbelievable things
out of the time-death Karma; and here *no time;* jes a dead still
now stretching back eternally and forward eternally.

So Mountain Girl lies on the bed and stares up through the
heat waves rising in the 110-degree mucus of Manzanillo; and
she is not high on anything; maybe slightly out of her head, but
not high; no, not even out of her head; but it's like that acid time-
warp thing; like they're all thrust back permanently into a primitive time; this *is* permanent; Kesey can't go back ever; they will
slam him away for good; meaning she can't go back ever, either;
how? back to the bamboo cage to be clucked and lectured and
blubbered over until she drowned?; none of them can go back;
'cause there is nothing to go back to; it is all here now; Mexico,
even as Kesey foresaw that day in La Honda and she started
learning Spanish; which none of them really know, however, except Black Maria; always in a cocoon shut off from the worthy
up-tight nativos; only the Pranksters are the primitives; thrown
back on their own resources; reliving the primitive life of man
with only the dwindling hope of a bountiful miracle from the sa-
cred Telégrafo to possibly break the spell . . . of 3,000 years ago.

Three thousand years ago Mountain Girl walks down to the
water, the backwater, every day to wash clothes, diapers and

sundry other shit; every day walking through the heat waves under the salty sun through the scrub grass and dung sand, to wash clothes, by the waters of the . . . Nile and the daughter of Pharaoh came down to wash herself at the river; and her maidens walked along by the river's side; and when she saw the ark among the flags, she sent her maid to fetch it . . . it is as if she is walking down to the river and she is watching herself, a maiden, 3,000 years ago, walking down to the river, at the same time, in . . . the Middle East; it is always the Middle East somehow, out of an old illustrated Bible; 110 degrees, bulrushes and the eternal laundry bummer; nothing to read here but *The Nova Express* by William Burroughs; the Nietzsche and Dostoevsky that Kesey has; and in the Bible; everybody goes through *Nova Express* in a couple of hours; but the Bible they can *linger* over . . . and gradually without anybody hardly saying anything about it, without getting high even, they are in another time dimension; biblical tribe, biblical tribeswoman washing in the water; living like the children of Isaac and Rebecca in the First Book; even taking biblical identities; they each choose, become a character in the Bible; *in truth;* it *is* 3,000 years ago, now stretching back infinitely to . . . the very Genesis; to Esau; Kesey is Esau; the hairy one; and Esau was a cunning hunter; a man of the field; and Jacob was a plain man, dwelling in tents; 13. Did they grow up alike? Describe them.—Esau was a skillful hunter, and Jacob was a quiet man, fond of home; 14. Which was the first born?—Esau; 15. Did he value his birthright? The proof?—He sold it, when hungry, and faint, to Jacob for a dish of potted beans or other food. So thousands, for present pleasure, will risk or lose their souls; 16. To whom did he sell it, and for what?—See No. 15; 23. Whom did Esau choose as his wives?—Judith and Bashemath, Hittites. Gen. 26:34.; 24. Did his parents approve his choice?—No; they were grieved by it; and Bashemath bore Reuel . . . 3,000 years ago; for there is no time in this place; only an eternal now stretching on infinitely over the entire world and all the history thereof; for the world seeketh its own level; which is the sea; and all living creatures of the sea shall die; but the *Gymnodinium brevis,* which knoweth no time, except now, shall live forever; ye have heard that it was said by them of old time, The earth is round; but I say unto you . . .

KESEY WOULD LIE OUTSIDE THE CASA GRANDE IN A HAMMOCK. Black Maria, in tight black slacks, would keep brooding, staring out to sea with her back to them, which annoyed everyone. They would occasionally snigger slightly, which made her more up tight, of course. Julius and Mike Hagen both had their casts painted most lurid and glorious Day-Glo in bus designs. Kesey lay in the hammock reading Nietzsche :::: who would have thought the old whiskered Valkyrie was such a head, into the pudding . . .

And little cycles within cycles. Hagen kept repeating trau-matic injuries. In Barcelona he had a motorcycle accident and kept riding and ended up with a permanently injured shoulder. In Canada the same thing all over again. And now in Mexico with his broken leg in a Day-Glo cast he felt something . . . grisly . . . under there, and spied a tick, and cut open the cast and found two more and pus oozing under the cast. He closed the whole thing up by wrapping adhesive around the cast.

"Why'd you put that tape over your pretty cast, Mike?"

"Looking for ticks."

Couple of days later he couldn't even walk as far as the Rat Shack. Nothing to do but deliver himself up to the Rat ministry of the Hospital Civil.

"Give me some speed, Julius, so I can deal with the bastards."

Kesey tries to cheer him up by telling him he can film the forthcoming wedding between Mountain Girl and George Walker.

"Hey!" says Hagen. "Maybe we can get the guy, the *mayor jefe,* to do the ceremony out here."

Hagen begins to jack-leg around on the cast, snapping his fingers. *The dexedrine is beginning to stir and tickle at the boy inside the cast.*

"Fuck that," says Mountain Girl.

"And a lot of flowers!"

"Fuck that."

Mountain Girl looks like a great gorgeous Amazon—and very down-in-the-mouth, with her lurid Acid Test yellow hair hanging down to her waist but a little circle of black on top, like a cap where it is coming in natural at the roots. *Like Mike, she'll put off the mundane bullshit she loathes just so long as possible. We've known for three weeks that she'd love to be legally married, for her child to have legal Mexican rights and she's known for nine months when that marriage deadline would have to be met.*

George, Faye and Zonk come back from the market with food, George wearing Zonker's blue velour pants, a shirt with broad orange and white vertical stripes, by Gretchen Fetchin, and knee-high boots he has painted in diagonal orange and white stripes, and his hair with orange tips from the Acid Test lurid bleach. All is arranged at city hall for the marriage, Miss Carolyn Adams and Mr. George Walker, and at the Hospital Civil for the baby.

"—and we'll buy a cot of white—"

"Fuck that."

"—and we'll film it on the beach at sunset with microphones. Babbs can run a cable out and a speaker—and *music*—we can have Gretch on the organ with *The Wedding March!*"

"Fuck that," says Mountain Girl.

SO MOUNTAIN GIRL AND GEORGE WERE MARRIED, QUIETLY, IN town. And Mountain Girl had the baby in the Hospital Civil, a healthy blond girl, whom she named Sunshine. At sea level . . .

Kesey in la casa grande—*there's always a taffy triangle being pulled at the house, what with four private rooms laced with endless variations on the Faye—me—George—Mountain Girl theme.*

Mountain Girl is grimming on: "Look at this wall. It's awful. No, I'm serious, look at it. I could scrabble through this wall in five minutes."

"Whyn't you go roll us a joint?"

"Can we smoke it in my room so I don't have to keep jumping every time Faye bangs the door?"

"Hmmmm . . ."

"Never mind. That's a tricky question. Besides it keeps me on my toes in here."

SPIRITS PICKING UP SLIGHTLY IN THE RED TIDE TORPOR. Pranksters beginning to do small Prankster things. Hagen back from the Hospital Civil hobbling but hassling with the old sweet Vesper boy charm. No stereo rigs, projectors, video tapes to be hassled hereabouts on Devil's Island, but he finds the biggest rig there is and hassles some poor local out of it—a turtle. A huge sea turtle, weighs about 50 pounds. Much jubilation over the monster, but nobody knows what to do with it, not even Faye, the pioneer wife and master cook, dietician, technician and mechanic. No caldron they are ever likely to get can deal with it. So they put a huge skull and crossbones in Day-Glo on its shell and put it back in the sea, thinking happily of another 200 years of life they have assured it. Nobody in Zecotopetl death-god Mexico will seek this one for *his* stewpot . . .

Babbs, after many days of glumming in his Purina Chow redoubt, strolls over, lewding out, *"Hi, Je-e-e-ed!"* to Kesey's three-year-old son. Only Babbs in his Be-elzebabbs best could greet a three-year-old with such lewd lubricious loonacy.

Page Browning has pulled in, ready to go, enchanted with Huaraches and the Rat thing. Huaraches on every foot in Mexico! Zea-lot himself could not have devised a more devilish troublesome contrivance.

"They keep 'em strung out on huaraches! You can't run in 'em, you can't walk in 'em, they never fit, they hurt your feet. All you can do is sit tight. That's how they keep this country straight. They keep 'em strung out on this bummer!" and so on.

Suddenly—Sandy Lehmann-Haupt turns up, back from way over the edge, on a motorcycle. He drove all the way from New York City on this motorcycle, halfway across the U.S.A. and all the way through the Rat lands to this southwesternmost edge of Mexico, no mean stint even for a Neal Cassady. Kesey looks at him and can't believe it. He looks stronger, healthier, calmer, more confident than he has ever seen him. It gives him a foreboding that he can't put a name on . . .

Even Bob Stone sails in, Bob Stone from way back from old Perry Lane days. He pulls in in a Hertz car. He flew into Mexico City, got a Hertz car. He has an assignment from *Esquire* to do a story on Kesey in Exile. Ah; so the old world still waits. Stone, still hypersensitive, seeing the FBI and Federales behind every cocoa palm—or else scorpions—and in that very moment, however, plunging head first, as always, into whatever chaos debacle any Prankster cares to dream up, crying lissen this is dangerous as he swandives off every handy cliff.

Hooking down dexedrine. Stone and Babbs go off in Stone's car, high on pills, heading up Tepic way, in Rat country. Come back giggling and carrying on over weird experience with the Road Animal. They had driven through the dung dust, days without sleep and soaring on dex, scrub country and burros, and night fell and it got really weird. Stone sees little Mex bridges and they become gila monsters, and Babbs sees them, too. The road becomes the veriest little tightrope between the no-man's land of the monsters, and then all at once the monsters take command of the road!—up ahead, the biggest road monster any man has ever seen, so huge it straddles the road, like a tarantula with legs 10 feet high, on the edges of the road, and its huge filthy body and jaws over the middle waiting for *food* and their car is bearing down toward it, don't dare stop and don't dare go on—

"No! Don't go near it!" shouts Stone.

"No," says Babbs, "we've got to. We've got to go through it."

"Through it!!"

"We've *got* to," says Babbs. "If we don't, we'll never make *any progress.*"

Suddenly it seems the most crucial thing in the history of the world that they *make progress.*

"I know! But it's too—"

"Got to go through it!" says Babbs. They steel for the debacle, Armageddon, the end of all—

—and sail *through* it!—

—it's a focking great road-building machine of some sort, tooling down the highway at Mex huarache speed, the mestizos up top look down bewildered at this car that just shot *under* them at 60 or 70 . . .

Stone and Kesey tooling up toward Sonora, nice and high on speed. Stone thinks he's behind tinted glass in a cab, although he is doing the driving. So like a taxi! They pick up a kid, an American, hitchhiking back to California. They can take him as far as Sonora. We're going to California, says Stone, and they gun off.

"Californee!" says Kesey, in the stupidest country way possible.

"Yeah," says Stone. "I'm driving this fella here"—Kesey—"up to California to see the sun come up. He's never seen the sun come up."

"Awww," says Kesey, "yer pullin my leg. Ain't no *sun* come up."

"I wouldn't put you on," says Stone. "The sun comes up and you're going to see it." Passing strange somehow to be riding in a taxi cab through the Mexican nowhere with Kesey, behind a tinted glass.

"Awwwww," says Kesey. The kid, meanwhile, is deathly quiet.

"I'm not lying!" says Stone. "Look up there. There it is, the *sun!*"

"Uhhh, uhhhh, *God,* you was right, there it is, the *sun!* Why . . . it fi-i-i-i-lls the sky! It li-i-i-i-i-ights up the valley! It shi-i-i-i-ines upon the ocean!"

After a few miles the kid speaks up in a casual way, best he can, "Say, fellows, I think I'll get out in Tepic instead of Sonora. I just remembered, I got to see somebody there."

So he gets out.

Never trust a Prankster!

And Cassady—Cassady barreling onto the Rat strand in yet another Cassady vehicle, revved up revved up revved up at the eternal Cassady speed, with a new typical Cassady Excalibur. He has a four-pound sledge hammer with the handle wrapped in Day-Glo tape, which he throws about from noon to doom like an Indian club, flipping it up in the air and catching it, flipping it up in double spins, triples, quadruples, true spins, eccentric spins, sprocketing his shoulders his elbows his knees his feet about in the jerky beat. The Prank and the Schism are apparently long forgotten. If there's any soul can break up this focking red tide and clear the mucus air sailing speedily on all channels, it is Cassady. So they smoke some grass and climb up on top of la casa grande and sit up there while Cassady circuses and sprockets with his sledge hammer off on his speedy trip just the barest 1/30th second from Now at dusk. Cassady does his wild American sledge hammer ballet by the side of a pool of backwater and they can see Cassady's reflection in the pool and their own reflection looking down at Cassady, but looking *up* in the pool in perfect asymmetric playback, winking Day-Glo and dusk, invoking apparitions from the past, a moon door, for the world in the immense act of contemplating itself, Domnu, *sattva* and *rajas* all at once, *fons et origo,* instant Movie—Now

Wet-handle Harry!

And the Halusion Gulp begins to shake its wings again like leather paddle flaps on the wheel o' fortune carnival game, a Rat bird, but it knows the one hole in the sky. Kesey in la casa grande with the wind up and the sky cloudy, and the Gulp flapping, and the Rat plaster paneled with pages from out of Marvel comics, whole scenes of Dr. Strange, Sub Mariner, the Incredible Hulk, the Fantastic Four, the Human Torch—Superheroes, in short. All heads believe them to be drawn by meth freaks, because of

the minute phosphorescent dedication of their hands. Superheroes! Übermenschen! It was passing strange that Nietzsche,
that curious little Peter Lorre misanthrope with whiskers and a
sour black Tübingen professorial frock coat on, should be into
the essence of the thing—

—and Kesey can hear Bob Stone telling him, "Nietzsche is up
in Heaven now, Ken, saying 'I dig what you're doing—but don't
read my books' "—

—yet the old Valkyrie was into the thing. The world not a line
of cause and effect heading forward forever, but finite and ever-
repeating, so that all that ever was and ever will be is caught up
in *now,* in endless Recurrence, only waiting for the Superheroes
to resurface; after which, a total revaluation. And combining
Nietzsche's inspiration with his own of *at-present-best*—of man
forever watching his own movie and never being able to get to
the paradise beyond the screen: as Nietzsche glimmered, life is a
circle and so it is the going, not the getting there, that counts. *Live
in the moment. Lots of good heads said it. I tried. I devoted much
time and much energy. To find that those good heads had been
tricked—that simple trick of I was right about living in the moment
but we can never get in the moment! Orggggggg!*

Yet, as Pranksters and many close and near believe, he knows
he has somehow caught sight of the great flapping beast and is
somewhere beyond this side of the screen and into the true old
full bare essence of the thing—he is onto what is popularly
thought of as enlightenment . . . thinking back:

Nighttime and he had gone out to the water, high on grass,
and sat down and the light from the electric signs—Coca-
Cola?—in the town came across the bay, and every line of light
came off straight, the primitive line, Stone Age, the line of grass

CUT TO

nighttime, same spot, high on acid, and the lines come off not
straight but in perfect half circles, the acid line, the line of the

present, the perfect circle, like the spiders they injected with acid, and they wove perfect little round webs

Cut to

nighttime, same spot, high on opium, only time he ever took hard dope, and the lines came off starting into circles and instead finished with a little hook, like the little hook in the water of a Japanese print, like the little hook even in the lines of that strange comic strip, *The Spirit,* and this was the line of the future, completing the circle without having to go all the way every time, getting there by knowing the beginning of the trip

Cut to

Nighttime and an electrical storm in the Mexican heat flashes, high on acid, the lightning breaking out—*there!*—*there!*—and the electricity flows through him and out of him, a second skin, a suit of electricity, and if the time was ever now it is—*Now!*—and he hurls his hand toward the sky to make the lightning break out where he points—*Now!*—we've got to close it, the gap between the flash and the eye, and *make* it, the reentry into *Now* . . . as Su-perheroes . . . open . . . until he falls to the beach and Mountain Girl finds him holding his throat and choking as if he is gagging on sand . . .

Beyond acid. They have made the trip now, closed the circle, all of them, and they either emerge as Superheroes, closing the door behind them and soaring through the hole in the sapling sky, or just lollygag in the loop-the-loop of the lag. Almost clear! *Presque vu!*—many good heads have seen it—Paul telling the early Christians: hooking down wine for the Holy Spirit—sooner or later the Blood has got to flood into you *for good*—Zoroaster telling his followers: you can't keep taking haoma water to *see* the flames of Vohu Mano—you've got to be*come* the flames, man—And Dr. Strange and Sub Mariner and the Incredible

Hulk and the Fantastic Four and the Human Torch prank about on the Rat walls of la casa grande like stroboscopic sledgehammer Cassadys, *fons et origo* ::::: and it is either make this thing permanent inside of you or forever just climb draggled up into the conning tower every time for one short glimpse of the horizon :::::

XXIV

The Mexican Bust

HAGEN, MEANWHILE, WAS MORE AND MORE . . . HAGEN. The irresistible charmer . . . and it seems some beautiful deb from California had insisted on following him to Mexico. *Dear Dad. Don't worry about me. I am in Mexico with some beautiful people* . . . Her father sensed *beatnik* and *dope* right away, of course, and pulled all manner of strings to find out where she was and get her back. At least the Pranksters figured later that was what explained the mysterious debacle that came next, on the road to Guadalajara.

Hagen, Kesey and Ram Rod were driving up toward Guadalajara in a panel truck one night when they came upon a roadblock manned by Mexican Federales. What to do? Turn around? bust through? fake it? At the time, everything had been so cool with the local legals, they were feeling strong and confident, and so Kesey decided to stop and just do the old thing of draw them into the movie. God knows the Pranksters had coped with many cops before.

But—of course, they couldn't speak Mexican, so they couldn't even get the Movie going with these Federales. The Federales grabbed all three of them and searched the truck immediately for grass, which they found, and that wrapped that up. Out in the rain and the dark in the Rat lands. The Mexicans don't hassle people over grass as much as the American cops, but they have the same kind of laws, and they are not delighted to have American heads guests of their country, and Kesey was "hot," as they say. A certified debacle, in a word.

This Route 15 ran along the railroad tracks that come up from the Guatemalan border. Between the road and the tracks were the spiky dark clumps of a lot of high foliage, scrub and shit, thorns, razor leaves. Kesey smiles sadly and goes through a big well-you-got us, fellas, fair-and-square pantomine, that's the way it goes. The Federales take his turista card, which is a fake. Yup-you-win-fellas, and say, Lemme just go over in them bushes a second before you haul us off. Fella has to take a leak; all men equal, gringos and Mex and whatever, when the piss call comes, right-fellas? So the Federales say O.K. and Kesey goes off in the scrub—

—out the corner of his eye he sees a train easing over the siding on the tracks, coming around the bend slow—

—Haul ass! Rotor Rooter! Kesey plunges into the brush toward the tracks, thorns and razor leaves raking his legs, the light from the train shaking that weird sick ochre cast over the spiky brush clumps, thrashing through this shit, up against the side of the train jumps up on top of a coupling, grabs a ladder to the top of the boxcar. Rain comes in a sudden sheet, lightning breaks out, lighting up the whole scene and his body—Federales huffing and galomping through the scrub like comic-movie Mexicans popping buttons off their guts and screaming ¡hoy! ¡pronto! and then

HRHAAAAAAAAAAAMMMNNNNNNNNNN

The bastards are *shooting* at him! Mama don't 'low no grass-smokin' in hyar! Testy out here on edges of professed belief—

blackness—then Cosmo let him in on it for an instant with a flash of lightning—more huffing harroomping

Hrhaaaaaaaaammmnnnnnnnnnn

comic latino cops—until the train picks up speed and he lies battened down to the top of the car heading off to somebody's Edge City somewhere.

Which turns out to be Guadalajara. He has no money on him, no grass, no nothing. He heads for the inevitable mariachi square, hunkers down in the dark, wet and shivering. Wonder do they tolerate gringo bums in this town? Daylight a Mexican comes through the park and strikes up a conversation, speaks English. He is a slender guy in his twenties, very handsome like a Valentino, almost feminine

¡Queer!

offers to let Kesey rest up in his hotel room

¡Queer!

so beat and shivering he takes him on it. The hotel is one step above a flophouse, but clean. He has a neat little room, this Mario, a snug harbor. "Go ahead, get some sleep." Kesey tries to fight off the sleep fantasy

¡Queer assault!

but he falls asleep anyway, wakes up a long time later, all intact. Mario is broke himself, but gets off a collect telegram to Manzanillo under Kesey's new alias, Sol Almande. *Salamander,* you understand—the beast that lives in fire. Wait around all day and the next, Mario being nothing but a totally sweet person.

What's his game?

Down to the holy telégrafo to pray. All the huarache telégrafo workers sitting around under fluttering leaves of telegrams piling up. *Hay tiempo.* You have to know how to approach them, says Mario. Goes upstairs in the telégrafo. Presently the Huarache Chief rummages through the whole heap for a message for the burning Almande. But—nothing.

Next morning Kesey decides to risk it, goes down to the

American consulate as a poor broke grizzled balding American fisherman stranded and got to get back to Manzanillo. A girl there, a Miss Hitchcock, gives him 27 pesos for third-class bus fare to Manzanillo, and he gets on, with Mario waving a sweet valedictory goodbye. That was your bummer, Kesey, not to understand that the pure humble Mexican strain of sweetness—that was all that Mario was about, just a muy simpático human being. The bus ride was horrible, eighteen hours of bouncing through the Rat lands, half road and half no road, the Rat lands and yet so many open faces. They look at you just like a head, totally open, wanting to find something rather than hide something. Many piss stops, and Kesey can only struggle around grizzled, waiting for the driver to get on with it. Kesey is hungry and burnt out like a husk. About ten hours out, they're stopped and the driver walks back and stares at Kesey with the wide-open simpático look and gives him six pesos, just like that, without a word, worth about 17 cents but good for a taco or suchlike, and walks on back to the front of the bus. A strange land, this Rat land! Sometimes they *know.* There is hope!—not just for the Superaware elected few, but for the unsuspected multitudes who open up and look. They are waiting, here in this Rat land.

Back in Manzanillo, and the adrenaline was flowing again. Hagen and Ram Rod were salted away in jail. Like everything in Mexico, the jail scene was tough and soft at the same time. It was filthy, crawling with ticks, lice, scorpions, the whole scene. The food was filthy, too. But you could have anything you wanted to put down your gullet sent in, if you could pay for it, from luscious enchilada meals to grass, speed and acid. Hagen and Ram Rod stayed delightfully high and miserable.

In any case, Kesey began to feel like it was only a matter of time before they closed in. It wasn't so much the Mexicans he was worried about. The Mexicans were always ready to make a deal. It was the Stateside zealots. The FBI bodysnatchers worried him. He knew about Morton Sobell, the atom spy, who suddenly turned up one day at a border town in the custody of an FBI agent, walking across the border with the Feds. If the FBI can grab you in Mexico, physically, the Mexicans will play along with that, too. And the zealous head-buff San Mateo County cops. Word was that San Mateo cops were taking their vacations in Mexico for no other reason than to go Kesey-hunting and make more fat headlines. La casa grande and the Rat Shack becoming steadily more uncool as first one head and then another showed up, with big comradely grins on, kids from California, even from New York, who had somehow learned *where Kesey is*. They always came on like naturally the Pranksters would be shining with joy to see them—*we holy few, we initiates of the acid scene*—with the grins spilling out over the edge of their lower teeth. Obviously it was a big thing on the acid scene in the States to *know where Kesey is*. That was being very inside the thing. *Yeah—I saw Kesey down there*. Then—various Pranksters brought friends over. Including girls, of course. And Page struck up with a tall blond girl, kind of a Danish maiden sort, whom they all called Doris Delay. It was getting like La Honda, the tropical annex, La Honda in the Tropic of Cancer. People were bunked in and straggled all over the place, in the house, in the Rat Shack, on the bus. A girl named Jeannie got bit by a scorpion one night. Everybody woke up and what to do. They pondered awhile and decided to go with the flow and they all went back to sleep. She survived.

Kesey remained very permissive about the whole thing. Nobody got shunted off. *Put my professed beliefs to the Test*. In any case, it was no longer possible to believe there was any semblance of secrecy about the whole Fugitive movie now. It was just a matter of time or lackadaisicalityityityityityityityity ... The whole scene would get Kesey up tight and he would get in a car and drive up on a bluff overlooking the ocean and smoke grass and watch the ocean ... like Black Maria, come to think of it.

Black Maria was going through a private hell. Namely, she was lonely as hell. *Lonely?* One means, how could a truly outfront person feel lonely amid so many truly out-front people doing so many things together and getting high together all the time. Would *Mountain Girl* ever feel lonely? Would *Mountain Girl* ever feel desperate? It was unthinkable; Mountain Girl was synched into this whole thing. She, Black Maria, was probably the only person in the history of this whole thing to get lonely . . . in the Prankster hierarchy.

Prankster hierarchy? There wasn't supposed to *be* any Prankster hierarchy. Even Kesey was supposed to be the non-navigator and non-teacher. Certainly everybody else was an equal in the brotherhood, for there was no competition, there were no games. They had left all that behind in the straight world . . . but . . . call it a game or what you will. Right now, among the women, Mountain Girl was first, closest to Kesey, and Faye was second, or was it really vice versa, and Black Maria was maybe third, but actually so remote it didn't matter. Among the men, there was Babbs, always the favorite . . . and *no games* . . . but sometimes it seemed like the old *personality* game . . . looks, and all the old *aggressive, outgoing* charm, even athletic ability—it won out here, like everywhere else . . .

Yet by and by Black Maria was a Prankster. It was just there, in the air, the fact that she was now a Prankster. She had altered the flow, and not by accepting it, either.

Page's girl, Doris Delay, was going through the same thing. There was something she wanted to ask somebody, but how could she ask it. Finally she came up to Sandy Lehmann-Haupt and said, "What do they mean—*Never trust a Prankster?*"

chapter XXV

Secret Agent
Number One

AFTERNOON—PAGE COMES BUSTING IN LA CASA GRANDE
saying,
   "Hey! There's a guy across the road taking pictures of us!"
Sure enough. There is a guy peeking over the edge of a window in an unfinished cottage across the beach road, another cinderblock Rat wonder. The sun highlights off his camera lens. Kesey gets the adrenaline pumping for a run, but Page charges across the road to the cottage like he owns the place, followed shortly by Babbs.

Inside the cottage he finds a Mexican, dressed like a businessman, metallic suit, white shirt and tie, looks like he's in his thirties.

"What the hell do you think you're doing?" says Page.

"Hello, amigo!" the guy says, looking fairly cool. He speaks English. "I theenk maybe I buy thees house. You like the beach here?"

"Yeah! Yeah! Right! Right! Right!" says Babbs. Babbs has his friendly put-on grin turned up to such maximum intensity the guy flinches his cool momentarily, but he gets it back.

"Yes?"

"Yeah! Yeah! Right! Right! Right!"

"Yes. I am glad. I like another person's opeenion in thees theengs. Well—so long, amigos!"—and he steps outside like he's going.

"Send us some pictures if they turn out good," says Babbs.

"Some pictures?"

"Yeah! Yeah! Right! Right! Right!"

"What pictures?"

"Of us. We like pictures. We have a whole scrapbook. We like *candid* pictures, you know? I bet you took some good ones."

"Yes." The Mexican looks very thoughtful. "I tell you, fren, maybe you can help me."

"Yeah! Yeah! Right! Right! Right!"

"I am weeth the Mexican Naval Intelligence, and maybe you can help . . . us. We have reports of Russian submarines operating in these waters."

"Sub-ma-rines!" says Babbs in total put-on wonderment.

Several Pranksters have gathered in front of la casa grande to watch Babbs and Page and the Mexican outside the Rat cottage.

"Yes," says the Mexican. "We have reports that thees submarines are coming een to shore at night, in thees waters. Have you notice eeny such acteevity?"

"*No*-tice!" says Babbs. "Well I reckon by Christ we *have!* You oughta come out here some night! Some nights there's so goddamn many of them, you can't go to sleep for the signal lights. Shine right in the windows, blinking something fierce, and it's a *tough code*. A *tough* code. But we'll break it yet. We got a lotta good heads working on it. Why, this fella right here"—pointing to Page, and rattling on about the incredible brazen activity of the Russian submarines in these waters—while Cassady comes across the road, flipping his sledge hammer, singles, doubles, triples, way up in the air looping it, catching it behind his back,

and so on, but not looking at them for a second. Cassady sets a
brick up on a fence about fifteen feet from the Mexican, but
doesn't say a word or even look, ratcheting his arms and legs this
way and that to his private Joe Cuba. Then he heads back across
the road.

"Yes," says the Mexican. "Please may I ask you thees. We have
a report on one of thees Russian who maybe was landing here
from a submarine. He ees about five feet eleven, he ees a . . . muscular man . . . he looks about thirty years old . . . he has . . . blond
hair, hees hair ees curly and he ees a leetle bald on the top . . .
Have you seen eeny such person?"

"*One* of these Russians!" says Babbs. "Have you been to Eat
Alley?"

"Eat Alley?"

"Yeah! Yeah! Right! Right! Right! The marketplace. All you
hear in the marketplace is Russian. They're all over the place.
This thing is wide open *already,* man!"

The guy cocks his head and stares at Babbs through his shades
as if maybe this will bring him into focus—

—just then—

Feeoofeeoofeeoofeeoofeeoofeeoofeeoofeeoo

¡Whop!

—Cassady—twenty feet away across the beach road has suddenly wheeled and fired the four-pound sledge hammer end-
over-end like a bolo and smashed the brick on top of the fence
into obliteration, fifteen feet from the Mexican.

"Yes," says the Mexican. "Thank you, fren." And he wheels
and walks off at a good clip, down the road, and gets into a sedan
and hauls out of there.

THE NEXT DAY, HOWEVER, THE LITTLE DUDE IS BACK, WALKING
along the beach road with a bounce, so Babbs goes out to meet
him.

"Amigo!" the guy says. "Have you seen any Russians today!"—this with a big sparkling grin, as if to say it's all been a grand joke among us fellows who are in on it.

So Babbs thinks it over and says, Let's go up to the Polynesian palace and have a talk about the whole thing. Man to man.

So the Mexican says O.K. and they head up toward town toward a Polynesian restaurant up the way. Well, that gets the guy away from la casa grande, at least. Kesey has been primed for this, ready to make a run for it in one of the cars. He could head for the jungle, but the jungle is such a total bummer. On the other hand the road out is no bargain, either. If they are really closing in, they could have Route 15 bottled up so fast he'd never make it. Well, get out of la casa grande, in any case. So he and Stone get into Stone's car and drive up to the bluff overlooking the ocean and have a couple of tokes to assess the situation.

They park up on the bluff and look down at the festering red tide. The focking festering red tide. They turn the situation this way and that, and then Kesey decides: it is no use running either into the jungle or up the road. That's *their* game, the cops-and-robbers game. That's *their* movie, and they know their movie backward and forward, and *they* know how that one comes out, and *we* know how it comes out. Justice triumphs after a merry chase and the Fugitive eats dung dust in the last reel to show the horror of his dope-fiend ways. The only way out is to make it the Prankster movie and imagine this metallic little dude into the Prankster movie. There's no one to run to to say, Mommy, this movie is no fun any more, it's too *real,* Mommy. Up tight against the professed beliefs, Major, and you better believe! or else draggle your ass inaudible . . . They get to talk about Fugitive movies they have seen in which the Fugitive wins out, and they hit upon *Casablanca,* the Humphrey Bogart picture. Bogart was a fugitive in Casablanca, in the Moroccan desert, operating a restaurant during World War II, aiding and abetting Resistance fighters from Europe, and the Nazi-type or Vichy France–type FBI man, the cop heavy, in any case, comes in to question him.

"Why did you come to Casablanca?" he says.

"For the waters," says Bogart.

"There is no water here," says the cop heavy. "We are in the middle of the desert."

"Oh?" says Bogart. "I was misinformed."

There it is! The Movie! So Stone and Kesey drive back and join Babbs and the Mexican dude in the Polynesian bar.

The Mexican dude and Babbs have been having quite a time. Six or eight beer bottles are on the table, and the Mexican dude is waxing very high and expansive, gesturing grandly, urging them to sit down and carrying on. He wants to know Kesey's name and Kesey says Sol Almande. Babbs has given him a shuck name of his own, and Stone says he is from *Esquire* magazine. He studies an expense voucher from *Esquire* that Stone has as if it is a highly suspicious document. Then he whips out his billfold from inside his coat and flips it open, displaying a big badge with the number 1 on it.

"What's that?" says Babbs.

"*That!* I am Agent *número uno!*"

"Se-cret A-gent Num-ber One!" says Babbs.

"Yeah! Yeah! Right! Right! Right!" says Agent Number One, drawing his head back and taking an angle on Babbs. It is like a cross between Zorro and Nero.

Then he goes into a history of his famous cases.

"Eleezabeth Taylor ees coming to Mexico City? Sí. That ees my case. I know her very well. Sí. I am going around to her hotel, and she has all thees people—Uhhh"—he turns his hands up and pulls his chin down under his collarbone as if to say it is doubtful they could even comprehend how many people she has—"all thees functionaries doing thees and doing that, een the corridor outside even, and one of theem, thees beeg mari-cón"—meaning queer—"he tells me, 'No one can go een! No one.'"

" 'No one, ay,' I tell heem. He ees a beeg maricón. I can tell.

There ees a look they have, thees maricóns. They have cojinas the size of habichuelas, one can see it een the face, een the voice ... they are soft like sheet, thees maricóns ...

" 'Maricón!' I say to heem.

"Hees voice, eet jes *'oops!'*—you know?—like a leetle theeng of water.

" 'Out of my way, maricón!' "—Agent Number One half leaps out of his chair with the reenactment, his eyes bouncing off his shades, shooting up like he is galvanized with a thousand volts.

Then he sinks back.

"We-e-e-ellll," he says very softly, and smiles like someone getting ready to drop off to sleep. The way he says it, you can see the maricón collapsing, dissolving, turning into little driblets of jelly and opening the door to Miss Taylor's suite.

There is no stopping Agent Number One now. Exploit after exploit bubbles up in his brain. Cornered like a rat, he faces them down. About to be cut down in fusillades, he whips his revolver and fires one shot, *one shot,* amigo, and that takes care of that. The sonsabeetches theenk they have him outsmarted, ready to make their move, and he has already made his move and is waiting for them, like a bucket under a faucet, and so on.

The strange thing, however, is that none of these fabulous cases has anything to do with celebrities. They're all marijuana cases, usually involving Americans. Yes.

Finally he takes out his camera and takes a picture of each of them.

Kesey says, "Why don't you come to our party tomorrow night? A *lot* of people will be there."

"Your party?"

"Yeah, we're having a farewell party tomorrow night."

"Farewell?"

"Yeah. We're leaving Mexico and going back up to California, so we're giving a farewell party."

"Well, thank you, amigo. I weel be there."

So began the first Mexican Acid Test.

AGENT NUMBER ONE WASN'T THE MOST BRILLIANT COP IN THE Americas, but time was obviously running out in old Mexico. It was time to get the Movie going on all projectors. And the bus. The new fantasy was to get on the bus and keep moving; roam through Mexico and give Acid Tests and be *on the bus,* keeping the Pranksters movie going at top speed at all times.

They held the Manzanillo Test in the courtyard of Babbs's Rat Shack, under the aegis of the Purina Chow. It was a small one, with all random heads in the area welcome. No Grateful Dead, of course, so they gave the Polynesian restaurant latino combo ten bucks to come down the road and play during their intermissions. Between times the Pranksters themselves furnished the music, rolling all the fantastic coils of wire out, with Gretch on the organ, and the movies and lights and all the rest. The night was full of heat lightning, which was nice, and the Prankster musicians screeled their weird Chinese tones, wailing electronically in the Rat netherlands. But no Secret Agent Número Uno.

Kesey actually hoped the guy would turn up. He was just crazy enough to be adaptable for the Movie. He was a creature of fantasy himself. In any case, better him there gathering more data for his fabulous career than lurking in the cocoa palms working himself up to spring his ultimate cop fantasy on them. Well, if so, they would go out freaking and wailing on the shores of the red tide.

The Polynesian players came down the road again and played. It was nice to get freaked to latino syncopation. Then a lull, and then the shit—

¡Hoy! ¡Pronto!

—this piping shout from the other side of the Rat Shack. And where have I heard that cry before, Cosmo?

¡Hoy! ¡Pronto!

And all veer stroked out waiting for the pounce. More pounce to the ounce in a Mexican bust. Well, let's have it—let's see the Federales do their fantasy to mariachis, breaking on the high notes and struggling up again and huffing and galomphing with gold butts and stars in their teeth

¡Hoy! ¡Pronto!

Come on in, fellas, it's strictly Dutch freak here inside—

—and around the corner comes only the owner of the Polynesian palace, pissed off because his combo is hung up on the crazies here long past intermission and he has enough problems in the red-tide doldrums without them malingering with the crazies.

"¡Hoy! ¡Pronto!" he keeps shouting. ¡Hurry up! Get your asses back to the store! prodding and herding them out of the Purina Chow palace delirium.

¡Hoy! ¡Pronto!

The heat freak lightning flashes crazy enough and it is a good sign. The Movie is going.

THE PRANKSTERS PULLED OUT OF MANZANILLO THE NEXT DAY without a word or a move from Agent Number One, big as life on the bus, plus a small caravan of cars. They headed to Guadalajara and gave an Acid Test in a restaurant there. The Test went on two nights and each night a well-dressed Mexicano with the gleaming nighttime Mexico white shirt over his staunch midriff turned up with a go-go girl and stayed right through, although they didn't take acid. Smiled and danced and seemed to enjoy themselves. Turned out he was the local jefe of detectives. We are not alone.

The bus tooled into Aguascalientes, 364 miles northwest of Mexico City, loaded for Acid Tests. Aguascalientes is 6,000 feet up in tierras frescas with a paradise climate in late summer, a nicely weird city, built above a vast system of tunnels by . . . an unknown race . . . Pranksters in the time warp of many millennia ago. Suddenly Sandy was immensely enthusiastic. Sandy had packed his motorcycle onto the bus. He was getting more and more robust day by day, all for this Mexican adventure.

The mineral springs! said Sandy. You got to try them! A warm soothing mineral spring bath soaking late-summer paradise into every bone—*Cleanliness is Next*. Aguascalientes was what all these tierras del fuego were piled up rock by rock for, this little bit of Heaven in the upper altitudes.

Mountain Girl listened to all this and she knew, well, that would be that. They would hang around Aguascalientes the rest of the day. If there was one thing Kesey couldn't resist, it was the prospect of a long warm soak. He would stay in a warm tub one hour any time, and the paradisiacal Aguascalientes were good for four or five hours, easy.

So Kesey and many Pranksters went off and immersed up to their chops in the warm springs. Hagen was delegated to stay behind and watch the bus and all the Acid Test equipment inside. Sandy went off to take a spin on his motorcycle.

Presently Sandy turned back up at the bus. He looked most big and bright. He had on an orange jacket gleaming Day-Glo and much orange Day-Glo on his bike and was looking strong. Sandy climbed up in the bus and went back in there and presently he emerged carrying the big Ampex.

"What are you doing with that?" says Hagen.

"I need something heavy to put on the back of my bike for a test run," says Sandy. "I'm going to be carrying a lot of stuff back to New York and I want to find out how much I can maneuver with on this thing."

"Well—I don't know," says Hagen. Man, there's something wrong with this. "Prankster equipment isn't supposed to leave the bus. You know what the Chief says."

"It's not *leaving* the bus," says Sandy. "I just want to take it down a few blocks to see how the bike handles with a weight on it."

All the time Sandy is tying the huge clump of equipment down on the back rider's seat of the bike. It's so heavy and bulky it doesn't look like he could make ten miles with it.

"I don't think you should," says Hagen.

"I'll be right back," says Sandy—and he guns off, with the bike drooping in the back.

An hour goes by, two hours, and he isn't back. Hagen is worried. Then Kesey shows up, back from the baths. *Let's go!* says Kesey. He sees the whole thing right away. The fateful Ampex that Sandy had hassled over a year ago. The sombitch has *split*.

They jump in a car and take off up the highway north, toward Zacatecas. He has a big start but he won't be getting very far with that back end loaded down like it is. They go barreling through the Coca-Cola and Carta Blanca crossroads of old Mexico, up past Chicalote and Rincón de Romos and San Francisco, everywhere stopping and shouting at the Mex drugstore cowboys on the corner.

"Hey! Have you seen a crazy gringo on a motorcycle—all dressed in orange?"

"No." "No." "No."—the bastards, they're too battened down in their huaraches to say so anyway—and they barrel on up through the dung dust but finally give up and trail on back to the bus.

"Shit," says Mountain Girl, "that Ampex is the guts of the Acid Test."

The whole complicated thing of the instruments, the variable lag, the synchronicity, the taping for the Archives—they can't do it without the Ampex. Sandy has taken the Prankster Ampex—to the Pranksters there was not the slightest doubt in the world that the equipment was the Pranksters'. Not Prankster Sandy Lehmann-Haupt's but the Pranksters'. The Prankster family, the Prankster order, superseded all straight-world ties, contracts and chattel laws and who is my mother or my brethren? And he looked round about on them which sat about

him, and said, Behold my mother and my brethren! For whoso-
ever shall do the will of God, the same is my brother, and my sis-
ter, and my mother.

And there was nothing left but the vision of the sombitch tooling up the Mexican National Highway, struggling on his Suzuki
to haul . . . *possessions* back to New York. New York. So this was
what he had built up the strength for. Six thousand freaking
miles on a 250-pound motorcycle to seek out his electronic chattel and draggle it back, freaking Day-Glo in the sundown toward
the border.

ABOUT 4,500 FEET AWAY, SANDY RESTED IN THE SHADOW BE-
hind a big corrugated tin shed. Out in the open sun there—the
runway of the Aguascalientes airport with brown Mexicans in
coveralls lollygagging around. Sandy had been a man of his
word, up to a given point, so to speak. He had gone a couple of
blocks, like he said. Then he took a right and rode on over to the
city airport and parked behind the shed . . . and waited . . . and
was Kesey really so far into Now, such a master precognition,
that he would shoot the Zen arrow . . . or let him *draw* it, rather,
and come straight there and hassle him upside the bus again and
in that moment let him know irrevocably who has the Power, the
control over his mind forever . . .

Strangely, the paranoia lasted only for a twinge as he caught
his breath in the shade. In fact, he was strangely calm, as if the
chase were now over, rather than begun. He had *done* it. It had
been *his* movie. He had drawn them into *his* scenario. Mike Hagen. "We-e-e-e-ll," he had said. "I don't kno-o-o-ow. You know
what the Chief says." He knew. He had been on the bus for three
years. The trip had been liberation and captivity all at the same
time, liberation, power, will, the greatest in the world—and
whose will? The group mind's? Well, he had never had a dream
war with the group mind, he had never been held in thrall by the

group mind, he had never been subject to absolute judgment by the group mind, waiting for the one cryptic word that will say, It's O.K., Sandy.

Naturally he could never haul the big Ampex 3,000 miles on a motorcycle. It would be a little pile of gleaming whimsy, like one of Paul Foster's acid-bag transistor radios, by the time he reached the border, from the interminable bouncing. But he had that figured out. There was a Railway Express Agency in Aguascalientes. He would take the Ampex over there and ship it to New York collect and ride back on the motorcycle free as a bird. Which he did.

A YEAR LATER I TALKED TO SANDY IN CENTRAL PARK, DOWN BY the edge of the lake near Central Park South. He looked good, strong, calm. He was going with a good-looking blonde whom I had met. He had a job as a sound engineer with one of the recording companies. We got to talking for a long time about his adventures with the Pranksters, and dusk came on, and we related what we had each heard of Kesey recently, and it started getting dark, so we got up and left the park. And in all of it Sandy spoke with warmth, about Kesey, about the whole experience, with no traces of rancor. It started getting dark and we got up and walked out of the park. Just before we parted, Sandy turned to me and said, "You know . . . I'll always be on the bus."

"LEO! LEO! YOU ARE LEO, AREN'T YOU? DO YOU NOT KNOW ME any more? We were League brothers together and should still be so. We were both travelers on the journey to the East."

THE PRANKSTERS MOVED ON TO MEXICO CITY AND ENVIRONS, giving a couple of Acid Tests, but without any astounding gusto.

American heads from the Ajijic–San Miguel de Allende–Mexico City Circuit gathered proudly—*Yeah*—*I ran into Kesey and the Pranksters in Mexico and we all got stoned.* A few Indians came and got taciturnly freaked.

Meanwhile, Kesey's lawyers were hassling with Mexico City immigration legals in Mexico City to see about getting him a proper visa for a long haul, and they blew hot and cool. And then cooler and cooler. They seemed to be followed, the Pranksters and the bus, by carloads of well-dressed Mexican dudes here and there. Stone saw more than anyone else but kept driving. Cassady hauling the bus over the Mexico tierras frías with his new goal up against now of going the length and breadth of Mexico without using the brakes and without stopping for anything, hauling off onto crumbling scrubroot shoulders rather than stop for carts or cars or animals, smoothing out his stroke, from the Joe Cuba spastokinetic jerk, the sudden straight lines, into a new line—*the new line*—Kesey can see it happening even in the eternal Cassady—but of course!—in him first of all—from Fire to Water, from the Stone Age into the Acid Age and in a moment—*now*—Furthur—

HAUL ASS, KESEY! IT WAS NOW TIME TO BRING THE FUTURE back to the U.S.A., back to San Francisco, and brazen it out with the cops and whatever else there. The Mexican legals were hinting at booting him out, maybe in a month, on the technicality of no visa. But the Rat lands were spent anyway. They had junked it through on the fabulous junk of Mexico. They had gorged it up. They had . . . in truth, Major, there were no more spas to water at in the Rat lands.

The current fantasy was to take the Outlaw prank to its ultimate, be a Prankster Fugitive Extraordinaire in the Baskin-Robbins bosom of the U.S.A. You have never seen a Prankster Fugitive? Now watch that movie; draws you right in . . .

Kesey had a good melodrama for going back in. Paint it big enough and bright enough, and they will never see you. He figured to sneak back in on the purloined-letter principle. If you are gross enough about the whole thing, they will never know it's you.

Kesey picked Brownsville, Texas, for the reentry. It was the easternmost entry point on the Mexican border, practically on the Gulf of Mexico, and the least likely spot for heads to pick to go back in at. Most of the heads used the western end, the Tijuana end, because they were going back to California.

So he put on a cowboy hat and just before the U.S. Customs and Immigration Station at Brownsville raunched into view, he rented a Mexican's swayback white horse and got on with his cowboy hat cocked on crazily, playing a guitar and lolling his head around like he was drunk. He came cross the border lurching along on an old white horse as "Singing Jimmy Anglund."

"How long you been in Mexico?"

"Too damn long."

"May I see your visa?"

"I don't have it."

"Where is it?"

Visa—how the hell did he know. Came down to play a country & western show in that fuckin Matamoros, and be damned if they didn't get him drunk, them fuckin Mexes, their fuckin women and their margaritas, and they rolled his ass in the streets of Matamoros, took his money and his papers, cleaned him out, and he got drunker and he stayed drunker in this godderned Mexico, bricked up his bowels with terra cotta, and him just a good old boy from Boise, Idaho, and that's where he's going back, no more Mexico, no more Las Vegas—

"Have you got any identification?"

"All I got's this here—"

—and he shows the browntrooper a credit card, Bank of America, reading James C. Anglund, Las Vegas, Nevada.

So they let him across and he headed down the road clawing

on the guitar and lolling around on the back of the horse, although they retrieved the horse from him—can't let any *disease* sneak across the border from the Rat lands, you understand—

Singing Jimmy Anglund started thumbing out in the dust with his Rat-tar under the other arm . . .

XXVI

The Cops and Robbers
Game

Singing Jimmy,
Hocking hoarse and phlegmy,
Sticks his grizzle
In the dust-muck Brownsville drizzle,
Starts to thumbing
Up the Texas belly bumming,
Heeee! the cops and robbers game.

Lone superhero,
Superhighway Cosmo hero,
Never lies.
Honesty's the best disguise
In the cops and robbers game.

See, cop fellas?
Freaked-out head-buff Cercosporellas
Here's my Rat-tar

And my buckskin cowboy suit.
Prankster red boots
From Guadalajara.
My cowboy hat
Shows you where I'm at
In the cops and robbers game.

I ain't Clark Kent.
I ain't Steve Lamb.
Popeye the Sailor I am what I am
In the cops and robbers game.
Came a car
Didn't take him very far
In the cops and robbers game.

At the wheel
In this fuckedup dust-muck hitchhike deal
Was a Mississippi kite
With a smile of ebonite.
Inchy road
Heavy duty, heavy load
In the cops and robbers game.

Shit.
The Cosmos Kid, he
Split
At the coffee-light eggs-lookin-atcha bus depot.
On the bus!
In the cops and robbers game.

Greyhound humid
Most mightily piss-fumid
All the way to Salt Lake City
On the bus
In the cops and robbers game.

Oh
Riding second class
With shock absorbers up my ass
Reminds me
Of the F.B. Eyes left behind me
Out front! superhero
Of the cops and robbers game.

Took a flight
To San Francisco late at night.
Cop alert?
For hero in a buckskin shirt?
Cocked to shoot?
At superdude in red dude boots?
Not hardly.
Official mind destroyer,
This prankster suit of flaming Orlon paranoia
Hardly visible,
This risible cowboy
Cardiac drummer
Marching to a different bummer
In the cops and robbers game.

From the airport
With creamy Prankster pudding escorts
Neal and Hugh
Day-Glo Marvel Comic crew
Commence the movie:
Freak the cops!
Shuck the narcos
Shuck the Feds
Shuck the San Mateo Sheriff
Shuck the San Francisco Chief
Shuck the Judges in their chambers
We shall not flag or fail

We shall go on to the end
We shall shuck you on the beaches
We shall shuck you on the landing grounds
We shall shuck you in the fields, in the streets, on the hills
And in the trees.
Groovy plot
Hot movie
In these trees.
See the very hunted coons
Salt J. Edgar Hoover's wounds!

Yah! the cops and robbers game.

Kesey holes up at his old friend ————'s house in Palo Alto. He is in a strange state of mind. He is in the cops' movie now, the Cops and Robbers Game, and eventually they will win, because it is their movie—*Gotcha!* Unless he makes it his movie, which will take the utmost risk and daring. Here I am, boys . . . In the cops and robbers game you creep and skulk about in a state of tachycardia, and they like to think of you in your reptile misery—so—

Break skulk!

In short, the fantasy is now to become a kind of Day-Glo Pimpernel, popping up here and there, right out in public, then vanishing, reeking legend in the wake. He will be like one of those movie criminals who send florid coded notes to the police about *au pair* girls he intends to garrote—and then does it—while all the world pants for next week's broken hyoid bone. Only he hasn't been strangling, merely smoking grass. You would never know that, however, from the excitement in San Francisco . . .

A strange sort of guest to have in the house— and ————hardly knows what to make of the performance, Kesey veering wildly from paranoia and hyper-security to extraordinary disregard for his own safety, one state giving way to the other in no fixed order. Kesey gets up about noon or 1 P.M., eats,

then goes out in the garden out back and sits there in his buckskin shirt playing a Prankster flute. If one plays anything much
more bizarre than a transistor radio out back in the garden in
Palo Alto, it amounts to freaking insurrection; let alone a big
muscular Mountain Man in a buckskin shirt playing a flute.
Then at night—a few tokes here, a few tokes there, it adds up,
Major, Kesey and a Prankster or two start to rapping, gently

Rapping
Cortex tapping
Rat-tat-tatting
Tatter-ratting
Fooling, puling, ululation
Skeel goose screeling glossolalia
Crested screamers! Megascops!
Bust the eardrums! FREAK THE COPS!

until 2 A.M. the house would be reeling with enough Rat-tars,
loon cries, tapes and howling grass euphoria to wake up all of
sweet dream tunnel Palo Alto for the next fifteen years—but
then suddenly at 4 A.M., or 5, after outlasting everyone in the mad
howl, Kesey would suddenly decide it was time for maximum security precautions and would disappear into the cellar to a snug
nest behind the packing cases, in the cobwebs. Well, at least the
bastards won't get him with Gestapo tap on the shoulder—*All
right, Kesey . . .*

That movie—but then awakening and starting his movie almost at once. Neal, Hugh Romney, Kesey and a small detachment of Hell's Angels head for a three-day "trips festival" in
progress at San Francisco State College, Saturday night, October
1. The seeds one has sown . . . The Acid Tests have already
caught hold in the college world. San Francisco State has become
the acid heads' true *universitas,* sort of the way Ohio State is for
football freaks. They are trying the whole thing, the Acid Test,
with the utmost faithful eclecticism.

Alpha,
Beta,

Delta Handa Poker.
Movies at the smoker.
Collegiate!
Donkey beads,
Temple bells,
Sandles and
Mandalas
Psychedelic!

The Hell's Angels are riding shotgun for the Fugitive. They like this. They can freak out any approaching cops, in cruiser or battalion. For some suitable weird reason all the lights are left on in the campus buildings. The festival is in the gymnasium—full of scaffolding and people sweeping the ceilings with movies and light projections—Control towers—and the Grateful Dead on the bandstand, all careful homage to the original Acid Tests, and then suddenly

KESEY

will be there, broadcasting into the gymnasium from a campus radio station . . . a very tight ship, this fantasy, even up to Hell's Angels standing guard outside the studio. Except that by the time they get all the wiring hooked up, and start rapping, Cassady with a microphone inside the hall—introducing

KEN KEEEEE-ZEEEEEE

it is about 4 A.M. Kesey is hidden in the studio, talking over the hugest Prankster hookup of wires, running long over the college campus to the gymnasium. Freewheeling Frank, the Hell's Angel, zonked on acid, barges into the studio, and sees Kesey there sitting on a stool with an electric guitar and wires running all around his legs and his neck, branging on the guitar, rapping poetry into the microphone with fluorescent light and ON THE AIR sign filling up the room—The *god of LSD—He's so wired up it scares me—This god reminds me of a satellite that flies around in the skies*—whereupon Frank hugs him and feels an immediate surge of electricity and sits down on the floor and starts playing a harmonica and Kesey raps on for the benefit of the hundreds watch-

ing the swirling light shows in the gymnasium: "You who stand
sit and crawl around and about the floor about you and above you
on the ceiling that madness that's running in color is your
brain!"—and then he stalks out of the room—

He's mad because he has not captured my mind—thinks
Frank—*he has so many million minds that he has captured that not
even a smile is left on his face.*

But there were no millions or even hundreds left in the gymnasium because it was so late it was down to a group of hard-core
heads, many of whom were so high they were used to all sorts of
time and geography warps. *Everything* was real, Mani, Madame
Blavatsky's Chohan maya, Ken Kesey broadcasting over the p.a.
system . . . Kesey finally comes out and walks through the
residue, but they are all wacked out and he is hardly visible . . . in
his Prankster suit of flaming Orlon paranoia . . .

Nevertheless! the word is now out among the heads of
Haight-Ashbury. Kesey is back, the *Man,* the Castro who won
them what they have today in the first place. The seeds we . . .

. . . *HAVE SOWN* . . . DOWN IN RAT LAND RED TIDE MANZANILLO,
Kesey and the Pranksters had been so cut off they got almost no
news from San Francisco. It was all perfect Devil's Island down
there. They had only a dim idea of what was going on among the
heads in Haight-Ashbury. But now, like, you don't even have to
look for it. It hits you in the face. It's a whole carnival . . . All you
have to do is walk up into the Haight-Ashbury—and Kesey
chances a run through . . . Hell, in Haight-Ashbury a muscular
guy in cowboy boots and a cowboy hat—he . . . looks *healthy*. The
cops are busy trying to figure out these new *longhairs,* these *beatniks*—these crazies are somehow weirder than the North Beach
beatniks ever were. They glow blue like a TV tube. The hippie-
dippies . . . their Jesus hair, men with hair falling down to the
shoulders and beards to their chests, all lank and thin and limp
like . . . *lungers!* Sergeant, they're lollygagging up against the

storefronts on Haight Street up near that Psychedelic Shop like somebody hocked a bunch of T.B. lungers up against windows and they've oozed down to the sidewalks, staring at you with these huge zombie eyes, just staring. And a lot of weird American Indian and Indian from India shit, beaded headbands and donkey beads and temple bells—and the *live* ones, promenading up and down Haight Street in costumes, or half-costumes, like some kind of a doorman's coat with piping and crap but with blue jeans for pants and Mod boots... *The cops!*—oh, how it messed up their minds.

The cops knew drunks and junkies by heart, and they knew *about* LSD, but this *thing* that was going on... The heads could con the cops blind and it was wild. Haight-Ashbury had always been a brave little tenement district up the hill from the Panhandle entrance to Golden Gate Park, with whites and Negroes living next door in peace. Rents had been going up in North Beach. A lot of young couples with bohemian enthusiasms had been moving to Haight-Ashbury. Some of the old beats had moved in. They hung around a place called the Blue Unicorn. But the Trips Festival of eight months before was what really kicked the whole thing off. Eight months!—and all of a sudden it was like the Acid Tests had taken root and sprung up into people living the Tests like a whole life style.

The Grateful Dead had moved into a house in Haight-Ashbury, and it wasn't just the old communal living where everybody piled into some place. They lived in Prankster-style, as a group with a name and a mission, which was music and the psychedelic vision... Yes... A thin, almost caved-in guy with *incredible* freaking light-brown Jesus hair and beard flowing all over him and round wire-rim spectacles, named Chet Helms, had a group called the Family Dog. They also lived in Prankster-style, in a garage at 1090 Page, holding rock 'n' roll dances amid a lot of Indian symbols. They had taken part in the Trips Festival. Helms was a head but a very practical head. He saw it coming, with the Trips Festival, the whole wave. He started an ongoing Trips Festival, every week, selling tickets, at a ballroom, the Avalon, at Van Ness and Sutter. Bill Graham, the impresario for the Trips Festival, was into the thing too and had a Trips Festival scene going in the Fillmore Auditorium, a dancehall at Fillmore and Geary. Graham and Kesey had had a falling out at the Trips Festival itself over things like who was going to handle the gate and it ended in a badass moment when Graham put out his hand to shake and make up and Kesey just looked at it and walked away. But Graham picked up on the Acid Test format exactly. Both the Fillmore and the Avalon did the Pranksters Acid Test with all the mixed media stuff, the rock 'n' roll and movie projections and the weird intergalactic amoeba light shows. The Avalon even had it down to details like the strobes and sections of the floor where you could play with Day-Glo paint under black light. Everything but the ... fourth dimension ... Cosmo ... the three o'clock thing ... the experience, the *kairos* ... *They know* where *it is, but they don't know* what *it is* ... Still, the ballrooms were like a big announcement and a front door ... into The Life.

The new communal groups themselves were into the pudding. Like the Diggers, led by a guy named Emmett Grogan, whose hero was Kesey. They went in for pranks. They had a Frame of Reference, a huge frame nine feet tall that they set up in the street and asked people to walk through ... "so we'll all be in the same frame of reference." Then they started handing out free food to all comers, heads, winos, anybody, at 4 P.M. in the Panhandle part of the park. The food they cadged from wholesalers, and boosted, and so on. It was a goddamn sketch, seeing them ladle out the stew every day out of big milk cans ... Up at Fulton and Scott is a great shambling old Gothic house, a freaking decayed giant, known as The Russian Embassy. A new group called the Calliope Company lives in there, led by Bill Tara, an actor. Many colorful characters like Paul Hawken, and Michael Laton, who always wears a Russian astrakhan hat, and Jack the Fluke, who is a laughing grizzly Irishman with a beard like an Airedale and a cab driver's cap and flapping tweeds bought from the Slightly Soiled Shop . . . all of them sitting around the great parlor, bare but a glory of old carved wood, fourteen-foot ceilings . . . Jack the Fluke tells about his girlfriend Sandra, a teenage girl who just pulled in from Bucks County, Pa.:

"I come in"—and he motions with his head up toward his room on the top floor—"and, dig: she has a joint rolled *this big,* like a *cigar,* man!—and she's goofing off the radio and puffing on this, I mean, *Corona corona* joint and goofing and puffing—it was *beautiful!* It really takes me back."

But of course! the esoteric nostalgia of those first days of *discovery,* the first little easing open of the doors of the mind with marijuana and *that thing you do* at that stage!—that goofing off the radio thing—*You know?* And it's beautiful, the kids beginning to pour in to Haight-Ashbury . . . for The Life . . . It's a carnival! the Garden of Eden! one big urban La Honda scene! right out in the open! with all things available. Money is floating around in the air. That's no hassle. Hell, in three hours you can pick up nine or ten bucks panhandling. Christ, when the straight citizens see a kid in a beard and beads and flowers with a sign around his neck saying *My Heart is Prouder than my Stomach,* it fucking blows their minds, and they lay quarters on you, dollar bills. It's too much. And if worse comes to worse, there is always . . .

"Anybody want a straight job?" says a girl named Jeannie, who lives here at The Embassy. Michael Laton says yeah, and it turns out Jeannie is working three or four hours a night as a Topless Shoe Shine girl in a little shoeshine shack on Broadway in North Beach, and they need a barker outside on the sidewalk to spiel in customers. Michael Laton takes this, yes, straight job, and stands out there at night in a tuxedo and a tall hat hawking in the dentists who are crawling all over North Beach panting over the Topless. They come inside the shack and climb up on the shoeshine stand and put their feet on the shoeshine stirrups and watch Jeannie's tits dangle and jiggle for ninety seconds while she

shines their shoes for two dollars and a big lugubrious spade
stands by with his hand near a lead beer bottle to smash wiseguys
and sex fiends with and they all come out saying the exact same
thing: "And the funny part is, it's a damned good shoeshine!"

". . . so I dropped a little acid, like just for the flash, you know,"
says Michael Laton, "and these two Marines come up, this big
sergeant and another one, with hashmarks on their sleeves, like
up to here. I'm eight feet tall by this time, and they're like *ants,*
I'm so stoned, and I yell right in their faces: 'If they stop the
war, you guys will be out of a job!' And the sergeant says
Yeahhh?—and man! like it *reverses*—now *they're* eight feet tall all
of a sudden and *I'm* an ant! and . . ."

A very carnival! and it wasn't politics, what he said, just a
prank, because the political thing, the whole New Left, is all of a
sudden like *over* on the hip circuit around San Francisco, even at
Berkeley, the very citadel of the Student Revolution and all.
Some kid who could always be counted on to demonstrate for the
grape workers or even do dangerous things like work for CORE
in Mississippi turns up one day—and immediately everybody
knows he has become a head. His hair has the long jesuschrist
look. He is wearing the costume clothes. But most of all, he now
has a very tolerant and therefore withering attitude toward all
those who are still struggling in the old activist political ways for
civil rights, against Vietnam, against poverty, for the free peoples.
He sees them as still trapped in the old "political games," unwit-
tingly supporting the oppressors by playing their kind of game
and using their kind of tactics, while he, with the help of psychedelic chemicals, is exploring the infinite regions of human consciousness . . . Paul Hawken here in The Embassy—in 1965 he
was an outstanding activist, sweat shirts and blue jeans and toggle coats, went on the March from Selma, worked as a photographer for CORE in Mississippi, risked his life to take pictures of
Negro working conditions, and so on. Now he's got on a great
Hussar's coat with gold frogging. His hair is all over his forehead
and coming around his neck in terrific black Mykonos curls.

"I take it you aren't too tight with CORE any more."

He just laughs.

"What about all the things you were involved in last year?"

"All that's changed. You should have seen them leaving for Sacramento"—Cal students leaving Berkeley for Sacramento and a demonstration.

"Yeah," says Tara.

"It was all fraternity men with sports shirts and crew cuts and their own cars and painted signs, you know, like you get from a commercial artist. There was a lot of bread out there."

"Yeah," says Tara, "and they're all talking about *channels.* They're going to do this and that through *existing channels,* or they can't do this or that through existing channels, they're all talking about channels."

"Yeah," says Paul, "and shaking their fists"—he raises his fist and shakes it in a big shuck way—"and saying, 'We're off to Sacramento to protest, with our dates!' It's all changed. It's all a bunch of fraternity men in their Mustangs."

A bunch of fraternity men in their Mustangs! In the intellectual-hip world of California, there is no more scathing epithet imaginable. *A bunch of fraternity men in their Mustangs.* Just *sa*vor it. Oh Mario, and Dylan, and Joan Baez, oh Free Speech and Anti-Vietnam—who in his right mind would have ever dreamed it could come to this in twelve months—abandoned to the super-market and the breezeway scions—*a bunch of fraternity men in Mustangs*—and it is, unbelievably, all as the *provocateur* Kesey has prophesied it, droning on his goddamned harmonica and saying *Just walk away and say fuck it . . .*

Square hip! Boy Scout bohemians! and the great rallies at Berkeley that used to pull 10,000 are now lucky to get a thousand. All changed! Even the thing with the spades. All of a sudden the Negroes are out of the hip scene, except for a couple of pushers like Superspade and a couple of characters like Gaylord and Heavy. The explanation around Haight-Ashbury is that Negroes don't take to LSD. The big thing with spades on the hip scene has always been the quality known as *cool*. And LSD freaking well blows that whole lead shield known as *cool,* like it brings you right out front, hang-ups and all. Also the spades don't get much of a kick out of the *nostalgia for the mud* that all the white middle-class kids who are coming to Haight-Ashbury like, piling into pads and living freaking *basic,* you understand, on greasy mattresses on the floor that the filthiest spade walkup in Fillmore wouldn't have, and slopping up soda pop and shit out of the same bottle, just passing it around from mouth to mouth, not being hung up on that old American plumbing&hygiene thing, you understand, even grokking the weird medieval vermin diseases that are flashing through every groin—*crab lice!* you know that thing, man, where you first look down at your lower belly and see these little *scars,* they look like, little *scabs* or something, tiny little mothers, and like you pick one, root it out, and it starts *craw*ling! Oh shit! and then they're all crawling and you start exploring your mons pubis and your balls and they're *alive*. It's like a jungle you never saw before, in your own crotch, your own shag, and it's alive, a freaking bestiary, in fact, the little bastids, like softshell crabs that could dance on the head of a pin, and you keeping picking them off but every time you look you see *eight* more creeping over the veld and the savannas and you practically go *blind* staring at the little Africa down there between your legs and it's A-200 Time, man—A-200! Pyrinate Liquid—the only solution—that *little green bottle,* man! do you *remem*ber! and so on . . . *Nostalgia for the mud!* . . . The . . .

. . . Life . . . Even down in a place like La Jolla, in north San Diego, the poshest resort on the Pacific beaches, T———, one of the great young surfers, turns up one day with a three-wheel trunk motorcycle, the kind drugstore delivery boys use, and he pulls up into one driveway after another and the kids come out and—*help yourself!*—and he's got every pill and capsule you ever imagined, plus lids of grass, and . . . The Life is on. Even devoted surfing cliques like the Pump House Gang—the mysterioso sea and all that!—are easing into The Life, and some move up the beach from the Pump House, away from the everlasting *sets* of goodsurfing waves they used to wait for like Phrygian sacristans, up from the Pump House to the Parking Lot, where they sit in cars with special amethyst-tinted windows and grok in fullness the Pacific sun as it comes through the weird glass and the cops wonder what in hell they're doing in cars all day instead of being on the beach, and they roust them and search the cars and find nothing, but warn—*We know you kids are drinking beer out here*... Beer!... One of the Pump House Gang leaders, Artie, pulls into Haight-Ashbury, because this is the underground word in The Life in all the high schools in California already, even though Haight-Ashbury has never been mentioned in the newspapers... Haight-Ashbury! they know the whole new legend, right down to Owsley, now known as The White Rabbit, the paranoid acid genius... Artie pulls into Haight-Ashbury, walking along amid those endless staggers of bay windows, slums with a view, and who is sitting out on a curbing on Haight Street but J——— of Pump House days gone by, just sitting there with an Emporium shopping bag beside him.

"Hi, J———!"

J——— just barely glances at him and says, "Oh, hi, Artie," as if naturally they're both in Haight-Ashbury and have been for years, and then he says, "Here, have a lid," and he reaches in the shopping bag and just offers him a whole lid of grass, free, out in the open... Artie looks up Anchovy's communal pad. Anchovy, who was little known in La Jolla in the old surfing days, he wasn't a surfer, is now a beautiful person and the good shepherd in Haight-Ashbury for all the La Jolla kids up here. Artie makes the rounds in Haight-Ashbury and it's... a carnival!—everybody working for the Management in wondrous ways, popping Owsley LSD up from out of Pez candy dispensers, smoking grass, taking methedrine and fucking and carrying on wherever and whenever they feel like it, on the streets practically... Later Anchovy has love-ins called Trans-Love Airways going on the San Diego campus of the University, and everybody is freaking

out on the grass to the loudest rock 'n' roll in history and smoking grass in a goddamned *green cloud,* f'r chrissake, and taking
movies of it all for . . . the *archives,* and they're allied now with
real people, Good People, a motorcycle band known as the Pall-
bearers, the local version . . . of the Hell's Angels . . . ah umm-
mmm . . . and Artie leans up against a tree smoking a fake joint
rolled of plain Bull Durham tobacco, because you got to *look* like
you're into the thing at all times . . . but, in fact, it is getting to be
too much . . . About nine different constabularies stage a mass
raid to wipe out the dope plague from the San Diego County
high schools and they pounce on La Colonia Tijuana, which
means the Tijuana Slums, name here in La Jolla underground
for the apartments a lot of people in The Life share this summer
near the beach, and some good Pump House souls are busted, but
that is The Life, the world divided into surfer *heads* and surfer
lames . . . Besides, it was a laugh and a half, the look on the cops'
faces when they saw the ceilings of La Colonia Tijuana, canopied
in huge laceworks of interlocked pop-top rings off beer cans billowing in such groovy silvery ripples of grokkable reflections . . .

The Probation Generation! Not the Lost Generation or the
Beat Generation or the Silent Generation or even the Flower
Generation, but the Probation Generation, with kids busted
right and left up and down the coast for grass, and all get off the
first time, on probation—*What's probation!*—with this millennium at hand, and it *is,* because there's no earthly stopping this
thing. It's like a boulder rolling down a hill—you can watch it
and talk about it and scream and say Shit! but you can't stop it.
It's just a question of where it's going to go. Right now there are
two ways it can go in Haight-Ashbury. One is the Buddhist direction, the Leary thing. There are good heads like Michael
Bowen and Gary Goldhill who want to start the League for Spiritual Discovery here and pull the whole movement together into
one church and give it a focus and even legal respectability. And
they have given up much for this dream. Goldhill is a beautiful
head! He is an Englishman who was writing this experimental

stuff for TV in England and the BBC sent him to the U.S. to apply for a big grant, a Guggenheim or something, and he took a vacation in Mexico and ran into some American heads in San Miguel de Allende who said, Man, you got to come back here when the rainy seasons start and take some magic mushrooms, and damned if they didn't send him a telegram in Guadalajara or wherever—RAINS CAME MUSHROOMS UP—and he returned out of curiosity and took the mushrooms, just as Leary had, and discovered the Management and gave up all, all the TV BBC game and dedicated himself to The Life . . . And Bowen has an apartment with India-print spreads lining the walls and couches on the floor and hand-made Indian teapots and cups and three small crystals suspended from the ceiling by almost invisible threads and picking up lights like jewels in the air, a place devoid of all the shit and gadgetry of the modern American plastic life, for, as Leary has said, a home should be a place of purity that the Gautama Buddha himself could walk into from 485 B.C. and feel at home. For some day grass must grow again in the streets, in pastoral purity, for life is shit, a duress of bad karmas, endless fight against catastrophe, which is to be warded off finally only by utter purification of the soul, utter passivity in which one becomes *nothing* . . . but a vessel of the *All* . . . the All-one . . .

. . . as against the Kesey direction, which has become the prevailing life style of Haight-Ashbury . . . *beyond catastrophe* . . . like, picking up on anything that works and moves, every hot wire, every tube, ray, volt, decibel, beam, floodlight and combustion of American flag-flying neon Day-Glo America and winding it up to some mystical extreme carrying to the western-most edge of experience—

The Day . . . was coming, but the movement lacked a single great charismatic leader, a visionary who could pull the whole thing together. Leary was too old, heading toward fifty years old, and too remote somehow, holed up in Millbrook, N.Y. As for Kesey—he is swamp-bound in exile in some alligator-infested Mexican hideaway, it was presumed . . . Yet here come the Merry

Pranksters pulling back into San Francisco from Mexico via their own route . . . The Calliope Company gives them their Warehouse on Harriet Street to live in for a month, a place Tara wants to turn into a theater, an old garage in an abandoned hotel in the Tenderloin where Jack Dempsey used to train in a special amphitheater with a sloping wooden floor now all fully claimed by the vermin and the winos—but *Colored Power!* and the Day-Glo bus and the Pranksters come rolling in, and good heads start gathering around in the Day-Glo gloom of the place, like the Telepathic Kid who gets unspoken messages—*we need beds*—and he climbs a ladder and starts rigging the platforms on the theater scaffolding in here . . . as the Pranksters assemble from all over, Hermit—back from dark adventures in Napa Valley; Stewart Brand and Lois Jennings—back from the Southwest; Paul Foster—back from India . . . all joining the veteran Mexican band, Cassady, Babbs, Gretch, Mountain Girl, Faye and the children, Ram Rod, Hagen, Page, Doris Delay, Zonker, Black Maria . . .

. . . and all at once it dawns, the main truth, spreading over the jungle drums all over the Haight-Ashbury: *Kesey himself is back, too* ::::: *The Man* ::::

SUCH WAS THE BACKGROUND OF THE UNDERGROUND SUMMIT meeting between Kesey and Owsley. It was as crazy a scene as anybody ever dreamed up. For a start, it was in the apartment of Margot St. James, which looks like she once read a historical novel about a Roman banquet. The meeting began to shape up as a debate. Owsley, the White Rabbit, was sitting over here—and Kesey, the Fugitive, was sitting over there. Owsley was dressed like an uptown head—long hair, a dueling shirt with billowing sleeves, a sleeveless jacket, and beads, amulets, mandalas hanging down over his chest, tight pants and high boots. Kesey had on his buckskin shirt and tight ginger-corduroy pants and the Guadalajara red Prankster boots—and he was in a chuckling, giggling mood. Standing around, along with Margot, were various Pranksters, Haight-Ashbury heads, San Francisco State heads, Berkeley heads, and two or three Hell's Angels, including Terry the Tramp.

Kesey presents his theory of going "beyond acid." You find what you came to find when you're on acid and we've got to start doing it without acid; there's no use opening the door and going through it and then always going back out again. We've got to move on to the next step...This notion has Owsley slightly freaked, naturally. He has his voice wound all the way up:

"Bullshit, Kesey! It's the *drugs* that do it. It's all the drugs, man. None of it would have happened without the drugs"—and so forth.

Kesey keeps cocking his head to one side and giggling in the upcountry manner and saying: "No, it's not the drugs. In fact"—chuckle, giggle—"I'm going to tell everyone to start doing it without the drugs"—and so forth.

People in the room start following this exchange like a tennis match, the heads batting this way and that. One unfortunate kid from San Francisco State happens to get into this state of obsession about one foot in front of Terry the Tramp. He keeps edging closer and batting his head around, and edging in closer, until he is standing in front of Terry the Tramp and cutting off his line of vision, which is bad enough, but then he has to take out a cigarette and light it, all of this practically in Terry the Tramp's face, or within a couple of feet of it, which is all the same to Terry.

One billow comes up from the kid's cigarette and Terry the Tramp says, "Hey, man, how about a cigarette?"

He says it with a tone you have to hear to fully comprehend. It is the patented Hell's Angels tone of soft grinning menace, kind of like the tone the second-story man uses on the watchdog, "Come here, fel-la...(SO I CAN SQUASH YOUR HEAD WITH THIS BRICK)." He says it soft, but it stops the whole room like High Noon.

"Hey, man, how about a cigarette?"

The kid smells debacle in the air. It registers from his solar plexus to his earthworm lips. But he hasn't quite figured out what it's all about. He just hurries into his shirt pocket and takes out the cigarettes and shakes one free and offers it to Terry the Tramp, who takes it and puts it in his pocket. Then he says, with the soft grin menace smile snaking up out of his beard:

"How about another one?"

The kid mumbles O.K. and fishes into his pocket and shakes loose another cigarette and Terry the Tramp takes it and puts it into his pocket. The kid, meantime, is frozen, like a rabbit frozen by the eyebeams of a cougar. He knows it is time to split, but he can't move. He is stricken and fascinated by his own impending destruction. It's like there is nothing to do but play out the sequence. He puts the cigarettes back in his pocket— and precisely *then,* naturally, comes again the milky atropine:

"How about another one?"

O.K.—and Terry the Tramp takes another one and the kid puts them back in his pocket and Terry the Tramp says,

"How about another one?"

O.K.—and Terry the Tramp takes another one, and now every eye in the room watches the rabbit and the snake, panting for the next broken hyoid bone—how many cigarettes does the kid have left, fans? Eight—ten?—and what then, after all the cigarettes are gone?

How about your shirt?

O.K.—uhhh—

How about your boots?

O.K.—uhh—

How about your pants?

O.K.—uhhh—

And now your HIDE, *mother!*

My . . . hide!

Your very HIDE, *mother! Your very* ASS! *The last vestige of your pride and honor!* AAARRRRRRRCHHHHHHHHH!!!! . . . and his bones crunched like baked baby ortolans . . .

Everyone in the room can see the entire movie in an instant, like some crucible of the prison brutes, Terry the Tramp slowly picking meat off the turkey—fascinating!—stay tuned in for next week's broken hyoid bone!—

—until a couple of Pranksters intervene, with overtones of He's just a baby, Terry, don't snuff him. So the Kesey-Owsley debate resumed.

It was a small moment. No heads were broken. Certainly, the Angels have done worse. The kid even got away that night with a whole half a pack of cigarettes. Yet it stuck in the throat. One way or another, the Hell's Angels came to symbolize the side of the Kesey adventure that panicked the hip world. The Angels were too freaking real. *Outlaws?* they were outlaws by choice, from the word go, all the way out in Edge City. Furthur! The hip world, the vast majority of the acid heads, were still playing the eternal charade of the middle-class intellectuals—Behold my wings! Freedom! Flight!—but you don't actually expect me to jump off that cliff, do you? It is the eternal game in which Clement Attlee, bald as Lenin, lively as a toy tank, yodels blood to the dockworkers of Liverpool—and dies buried in striped pants with a magenta sash across his chest and a coin with the Queen's likeness upon each eyelid. In their heart of hearts, the heads of Haight-Ashbury could never stretch their fantasy as far out as the Hell's Angels. Overtly, publicly, they included them in—suddenly, they were the Raw Vital Proles of this thing, the favorite minority, replacing the spades. Privately, the heads remained true to their class, and to its visceral panics . . . One trouble with this Kesey was, he really meant it.

BUT! STEP UP THE MOVIE. HE SUDDENLY TURNED UP ONE AF-ternoon at Ed McClanahan's creative-writing class at Stanford. He sticks his head in the door and smiles from underneath a cowboy hat and says, "Happy birthday, Ed . . ." In truth, it is his birthday. Then he comes on in, the Fugitive in buckskin shirt

and red Guadalajara boots; tells the students why he wants to
move beyond writing to more . . . electric forms . . . then vanishes, that damned Pimpernel.

Then the Haight-Ashbury heads held the first big "be-in," the
Love Festival on October 7, on the occasion of the California law
against LSD going into effect. Thousands of heads piled in, in
high costume, ringing bells, chanting, dancing ecstatically, blowing their minds one way and another and making their favorite
satiric gesture to the cops, handing them flowers, burying the
bastids in tender fruity petals of love. Oh christ, Tom, the thing
was fantastic, a freaking mindblower, thousands of high-loving
heads out there messing up the minds of the cops and everybody
else in a fiesta of love and euphoria. And who pops up in the middle of it all, down in the panhandle strip of the Golden Gate
Park, but the Pimpernel, in Guadalajara boots and cowboy suit,
and just as the word gets to ricocheting through the crowd real
good—*Kesey's here! Kesey's here*—he vanishes, accursed Pimpernel.

Just in case there was anybody left who didn't get the Gestalt
here, Kesey made his big move in the press. He met with Donovan Bess, a reporter for the San Francisco *Chronicle,* and gave
him the story of his flight to Mexico and his plans, as The Fugitive. The story was a real barn burner, Secret Interview with
Fugitive Wanted by FBI, with all the trimmings, awash in
screamers all across the San Francisco *Chronicle.* The line that
captured all imaginations was where Kesey said:

"I intend to stay in this country as a fugitive, and as salt in J.
Edgar Hoover's wounds."

Then—this next prank was beautiful. A TV interview. The
Fugitive on TV, while all, F. B. Eyes and everyone, watch helpless as the full face of the Fugitive, Kesey, beams forth into every
home and bar and hospital and detective bureau in the Bay Area.
It was beautiful to even think about, this prank. It was set up,
much sly planning, with Roger Grimsby, a San Francisco television personality, on Station KGO, the local ABC outlet. The fan-

tasy was that Grimsby would tape an interview with Kesey in a
hideaway in the Portrero section of San Francisco, which was far
away from both Haight-Ashbury and North Beach, and then put
it on the air a couple of days later, October 20, a Friday. This fantasy came off like a dream. Grimsby taped the interview, and all
was cool, and on Friday afternoon Kesey's face beamed into every
home, bar, hospital and detective bureau, saying it all again, in
person:

"I intend to stay in this country as a fugitive, and as salt in J.
Edgar Hoover's wounds . . ."

See the very hunted coons
Salt J. Edgar Hoover's wounds!
Yah! the cops and robbers game.

All that remains to be done is the grand finale. Fugitive Extraordinaire! In this fantasy Kesey will present himself in person,
in the flesh—*Kesey!*—only *inches* away from the greatest collection of cops in the history of the drug scene and then

Vanish

like Mandrake. The Pranksters will hold a monster trips festival,
the Acid Test of all times, the ultimate, on Halloween, in San
Francisco's largest hall, Winterland, for all the heads on the West
Coast or coast to coast and galaxy to galaxy. Naturally, the cops
will converge on this hideous bacchanal to watch for Kesey and
other felons and bad actors. But of course! An integral part of the
fantasy! It will be a masked ball, this Test. Nobody will know
which freak is who. At the midnight hour, Kesey, masked and
disguised in a Superhero costume, on the order of Captain America of the Marvel Comics pantheon, will come up on stage and
deliver his vision of the future, of the way "beyond acid." *Who is
this apocalyptic*— Then he will rip off his mask—*Why*—*it's Ken
Kee-zee!*—and as the law rushes for him, he will leap up on a
rope hanging down from the roof at center stage and climb, hand
over hand, without even using his legs, with his cape flying,

straight up, up, up, up through a trap door in the roof, to where Babbs will be waiting with a helicopter, Captain Midnight of the U.S. Marines, and they will ascend into the California ozone looking down one last time into the upturned moon faces of all the put-on, nonplused, outwitted, befuddled befreaked *shucked!* constables and sleuths Yeah! Yeah! Right! Right! Right!

right right right right an even even even even even world twenty-five minutes after the Grimsby TV show Friday afternoon, October 20, Kesey and Hassler driving out of San Francisco on the Bayshore freeway, toward Palo Alto, in an old red panel truck. The current fantasy . . . this movie is too *real,* Mommy—but they have actually pulled it off. They have just been in town in the hideaway watching Kesey the Fugitive on TV, and this prank was too beautiful. The FBI and all cops everywhere *shucked* in the most public galling way. The sun slants down on the Bayshore freeway in the afternoon and all the shiny black-shoe multitudes are out in their 300-horsepower fantasy cars heading into the rush hour, out the freeway, toward the waiting breezeway slots. It's actually peaceful, this rush hour

We pulled it off

thousands of cars sailing up the swooping expressway like so many Salt Flat Futur-o-matics with taillight bands like hard red candy . . . It's relaxing, the rush hour is, and hypnotic, it drones, and it winks like red hard candy with the sun shining through it, and the sun shines in Kesey's side of the panel truck, very relaxing, and he takes off his disguise, the cowboy hat and dark glasses

See the very hunted coons

Salt J. edgar hoover's wounds

Hassler, driving, vaguely aware of the cars floating by in the rush hour, shiny hulls with so many shaved globes sticking up inside . . .

Kesey!

Suddenly coming up on his left Hassler sees a car full of shiny haircut faces, jammed full of them, all staring at them—Hassler and Kesey—and now gray Alumicron arms flapping out the window, stabbing and motioning Pull Over, much grimacing and shouting soundlessly into the slipstream of the rush hour, and one with his wallet dangling out the window, flapping his badge at them

Run! Split! Vanish!

But there is no place to vanish to. It is all clear in a flash—trapped in the rush hour for a start—and the panel truck can't outrun their sedan anyway. Opposite side pickoff!—Hassler tries to squeeze between cars and lose them that way, like a basketball play, but it's no use. The cops keep floating abreast, grimacing and flapping, and drifting back and pulling even again

There!

Kesey motions to the shoulder of the expressway, by an embankment and Hassler cuts over there, skids to a stop

Thrash!

Kesey out the door and plunges over the guardrail and down the embankment, with the dust flying ...

Hassler just sits there as the sedan skids to a stop in front of him, cutting him off. Seems like twenty doors fly open, haircut faces and gray-Alumicron bodies popping out in every direction, leaping over the guardrail—

All in shiny black shoes

One orders Hassler out of the panel truck and Hassler gets out and sits down on the edge of the freeway. Very strange. The great swarm of cars with hard-candy tails keeps sailing past, hypnotically. Hassler gets into the lotus position, sitting cross-legged on the asphalt, looking straight ahead. Three sets of

Shiny black FBI shoes

standing around him now. *They all have these shiny black shoes on.* Then one of them goes back to the sedan and comes back with a flare gun and stands over him with that. Hassler wonders if he intends to shoot him with a flare. A very Day-Glo death. Thread-soul, the causal body, ablation, Upanishads, Krishnamurti, the karmic vestiture of the soul, the nirvanic consciousness—it all runs together right here, like a tinned stew, and Hassler isn't even high. On the other side of the expressway, on the edge of the bay, great fat seagulls are wheeling in the air in a great weird O pattern, coasting down below the level of the highway, then struggling up, dripping garbage out of their gullets, but a nice pattern, all in all—

THE VISITACION DRAIN

It's the Visitacion Drain they've picked to work out their karma in . . . ah, we're synched up this afternoon . . . and the gulls wax fat gulping garbage at the drain and grease a slippery fat O in the sky and it occurs to Hassler that today is his twenty-seventh birthday.

Skidding down the embankment chocking up dust like in a Western the blur of the Drain flats out beyond Kesey vaults over an erosion fence at the bottom of the embankment

RI-I-I-I-I-IP

a picket catches his pants in the crotch rips out the in-seams of both pants legs most neatly flapping on his legs like Low Rent cowboy chaps running and flapping through the Visitacion flats poor petered-out suckmuck marginal housing development last blasted edge of land you can build houses on before they just sink into the ooze and the compost poor Visitacion Drain kids playing ball in the last street before the ooze runs flapping through their ballgame stare at him

AND AT THE GHOST ON MY HEELS?

like the whole world turns into an endless kids' ballgame on the edge of the ooze thousands of Drain kids furling toward the horizon like an urchin funnel

AND THAT ALUMICRON BLUR BEHIND ME?

shiny black shoes tusking up behind him stops stock still in the Visitacion Drain and

GOTCHA!

in the cops and robbers game.

chapter XXVII

The Graduation

THEY HAVE KESEY ON THREE FELONIES: THE ORIGINAL CON-
viction in San Mateo County for possession of marijuana,
which he never served time on; the arrest for possession in
San Francisco, after which he fled to Mexico; and a Federal
charge of unlawful flight to avoid prosecution. A felon and a
fugitive . . . who; yes; was going to rub the FBI's nose in it for
good measure . . . and all about dope, at that . . . and throw away
the key . . . For three days they shuttle Kesey back and forth between County and Federal courthouses and jails in Redwood
City and San Francisco. It will take a miracle to even get him out
on bail, an inspiration, a vision ::::: ummm, a vision ::::: we can
work it out ::::: Kesey's lawyers, Pat Hallinan, Brian Rohan and
Paul Robertson, have a vision. The next morning they're in the
courtroom in Redwood City at a bail hearing. The new style of
Courtroom Modern, this courtroom, all great lineless slabs of
blonde wood, and lowslung like . . . the *friendly banks* of the suburbs. All very sunny under the fluorescent tubes. Kesey sits at the

defense table wearing a blue workshirt. Robertson is on his feet telling the judge about a certain vision Mr. Kesey has had, of "beyond acid," an inspiration, a miracle, a light he has seen, although never mind the details of the beach in Manzanillo, not . . . those lights . . . In any case . . . Mr. Kesey has a very public-spirited plan . . . He has returned voluntarily from exile in his safe harbor, to risk certain arrest and imprisonment, in order to call a mass meeting of all LSD takers, past, present and potential, for the purpose of telling them to move beyond this pestilent habit of taking LSD . . . Robertson's talking a streak. It's a grand speech. Kesey is sitting up straight at the table staring blue bolts at the judge. But Robertson's words are like a fog. Kesey disappears in the soup, he reappears in a mist, undergoing metamorphosis before your very eyes. He's found religion, contrition, redemption, the error of his ways, and now he's going to tell The Youth his sad lesson . . . Faye and the kids are in the audience. Also many of their old Perry Lane friends, Jim and Dorothea Fadiman, Ed McClanahan, Jim Woltman, and some others . . . Several will stake their homes as bail security, $35,000 worth . . . Repentance and redemption are sailing around the courtroom like cherubim. All us reporters are scribbling away . . . Now Kesey is standing up facing the judge with his arms folded and the judge is giving him a lecture . . . He may be a great literary lion and a romantic figure to some misguided youth but to this court he is a childish ass, an egotist who never grew up, a . . . The judge is pouring it on, pouring it down his throat like cod-liver oil, but it's obvious it's just a buildup to saying he's going to grant bail anyway under the circumstances . . . Nevertheless Kesey is burning . . . You can see him setting his jaw and getting ready to move his lips . . . God knows Hallinan and Robertson can see it. They're crouched beside him like bandits. The first peep out of him they're going to grab him around the throat . . . *Keep your mouth shut, damn it. Don't blow it now. It's only cod-liver oil* . . . But the judge has finished and it's over. He's out on bail in San Mateo County.

The whole dam breaks after that. The FBI drops the Federal charge of unlawful flight to avoid prosecution. All of a sudden they don't seem very interested in the case, despite the salt in J. Edgar Hoover's wounds and the rest of it. Then back in San Francisco, and Kesey is standing in front of the judge in a faded sport shirt, work pants and boots. The judge has a terrific speech ready, saying this case has been blown up out of proportions in the press and it is only a common dope case as far as he is concerned, and Kesey is no dragon, just an ordinary jackass . . . and Kesey is starting to say something and Hallinan and Rohan are crouched for the garrote, but again it's over and Kesey is out on bail in San Francisco, too. It's unbelievable. He's out after only five days.

In the San Francisco jail
Before he got out on bail
Kesey met a kid with magic fingernails.
"Take a lick," said the kid
And everybody did.
They all licked his nails and blew their lids.
Twenty-seven psyches
Going off like Nike
Missiles through the lye-scoured
Concrete skyways of the San Francisco jail.
The kid had LSD on his magic fingernails.

Now—
Kesey told this story
To the local news reporters
Who pressed around him in the courtroom,
After the hearing on his bail,
Just to prove how hopeless
Was the drive to stamp out dope
With things like cops and jails.

Try and stop a kid with magic fingernails!
The headlines said
LSD ORGY IN THE SAN FRANCISCO JAIL!

Ah . . .
Certain local heads cried Judas.
Finked on a stash, this Judas!
While he himself so shrewdly
Copped out of jail, on bail.
A finking fingernail stash betrayal!

If the truth be known—
These good hearts flapped in fibrillation.
They feared the rogue vibrations
From the freaking Acid Graduation
Kesey and the Pranksters planned;
Their freaking Day-Glo last round-up in Winterland.

Like, I mean,
You know,
Can't you *see it coming:*
Ten thousand children of the flowers and grass and acid, speed
and poppers, yellow jackets, amyl nitrate,
Ten thousand heads, freaks, beats, hippy-dippies, teeny-boppers
descending from the crest of Haight Street
Tinkling, temple bells, rattling, donkey beads, reeking, grass,
shuffling, elf boots, swarming prostrate
Before the returning Prophet in the bowels of Winterland.
All of psychedelphia moaning to the polyphonic droning of the
Merry Prankster band!

It's too easy for this headline-blazing superhero
This amazing Cagliostro Elmer Gantry Day-Glo Nero—

.   .   .

ON THE TOP FLOOR OF THE RUSSIAN EMBASSY, IN AN EX-
tremely crummy brown room ... It looks inflammable, or spon-
taneous-combustible, the next cough, maybe, and it's all up in
here. Jack the Fluke sits up in bed, namely, a mattress on the
floor, with his back against the wall ... wearing nothing except
his cabbie's cap and the grizzle on his face and the grizzle on his
Camembert chest ... a brown blanket pulled up to his waist ...
Take a look at that! if you want to know about Kesey. A large
message tacked up on the wall on a sheet of drawing paper:

> DEAR KEN,
> THE BOYS IN THE
> TANK SAY HELLO.
> THEY WANT TO KNOW
> ABOUT THEIR MONEY. SHOULD
> THEY ASK YOU OR THE
> JUDGE OR WHO?

Sandra, the girl from Bucks County, sits in a clump at the foot of
the mattress. She is a very pale, tender little teenage clump. A single morsel, gone at one gulp, sitting under the room's one article
of furniture, a bridge lamp, no longer goofing off the radio, just
sitting in a teenage clump and listening to Jack tell me about the
letter:

"Oh man, there were a lot of good heads hassled and busted after Kesey told about that."

"You mean the cops—"

"The very ones. It was a bad scene. Like there's a lot of cats up
here who are not enchanted with Ken Kesey. They sent him this
letter."

Well, obviously they haven't, because there it is, up on the wall.
But the thought is there ...

Creaks on the inflammable stairs, and into the room sidles a
dark little guy in a T-shirt and jeans carrying a round plastic box
of cheese spread and a knife in a scabbard—

"Jack!" he says in this weird whisper

—one of those long knives with a lot of fancy mother-of-pearl on the handle that you see in a Chinatown souvenir shop.

"It was a bad scene," Jack the Fluke tells me. He ignores the guy.

"Jack . . . look at this," says the kid.

"That's nice, Frenchy," says Jack.

"Jack . . . it's *beautiful,*" says Frenchy.

"Like there's a lot of cats up here," Jack says to me again—

"It's beautiful," says Frenchy. "Jack—you know where there's any morphine?"

"No," says Jack, then resumes: "Like there's a lot of cats up here—"

"It's a beautiful thing," says Frenchy.

"—who are not enchanted with Ken Kesey and they sent him this letter."

"Jack—"

And Frenchy hunkers down on the floor and opens the cheese spread and pulls the knife out of the scabbard and sinks the blade into it. Quite a blade! a foot long and engraved with Chinese demons. He wipes gobs of cheese spread onto his tongue with the blade. Sandra sits silent in a clump, grooving on the full life. Jack raps on about perfidy in high places . . .

I don't know what the reference to money is—"they want to know about their money." But the gist of it is clear enough. Kesey has sold out to keep from getting a five-year sentence or worse. Next he'll nail it down by calling all the kids to Winterland and telling them to stop taking LSD . . . Freaking cop-out . . .

It's quite a mess for Kesey, of course. If he had lectured back at the judges like a Superhero, that would have been the end of everything, probably, with him salted away for many years. On the other hand, if he just stares back Orientally as the current fantasy of "beyond acid" is put forth, he looks like a cop-out in Haight-Ashbury . . .

All those good-loving heads . . . they've been having quite a time for themselves . . . a summer of euphoria, the millennium, in fact, LSD and hundreds of beautiful people already on the scene, and no more little games. They would just spread out like a wave over the world and end all the bull-shit, drown it in love and awareness, and nothing could stop them. I'll have to hand it to the heads. They really want to end the little games. Their hearts are pure. I never found more than one or two cynics or hustlers among them. But now that the moment is at hand, everyone is wondering . . . Hmmmmmmm . . . who is going to lead the way and hold the light? Then just one little game starts, known as politics . . . Hmmmmm . . . As I say, their hearts are pure! Nevertheless, Chet Helms and the Family Dog have their thing, Bill Graham has his thing, the Grateful Dead have theirs, the Diggers have theirs, the Calliope Company have theirs, Bowen has his, even Gary Goldhill . . . It's a little like the social-ist movement in New York after World War I—the Revolution is imminent, as all know and agree, and yet, Christ, everybody and his brother has a manifesto, the Lovestonites, the Dubinsky Socialists, the CPUSA (Bolshevik), the Wobblies, everybody has his own typewriters and mimeograph machines and they're all cranking away like mad and fuming over each other's mistrans-lations of the Message . . . Not that the heads in Haight-Ashbury are wrangling with each other yet, but what do they do about Ke-sey? Just sit back and let him and the Pranksters do their thing? Let them try to turn a lot of impressionable kids off LSD, the way the newspapers say he intends? Or let him suddenly make a big power play at Winterland and take over the whole move-ment? Politics, in a word . . .

And the Pranksters . . . by and by . . . I find them in the Cal-liope garage on Harriet Street, the old garage, the ex-pie factory in the bottom of the old hotel. I kept peeking around in the crazy gloom of the place, amid all the scabid wood and sour corners and ratty blankets and scaffoldings and beat-up theater seats and the luminous bus hulking in its own grease and the rotting mattresses where people stretched out and slept and the Shell station up the corner where everyone copped urinations, and I couldn't figure out what they had to be so exultant about. It beat me. As I look back on it, they were all trying to tell me . . . Hassler with his discourse on the world full of games and futile oppositioning and how the Pranksters meant to show the world how to live . . . with his toothbrush case shimmering . . . He was a kind man! He was trying to give me the whole picture at once. It wasn't about cops and robbers in Mexico, it was about . . .

Pranksters arriving from far and wide . . . The old Schism forgotten . . . Paul Foster back from India, looking emaciated, his mustache and mutton chops gone, his head shaved, but with the great God Rotor roaring and digging away . . . Page telling me about huaraches . . . Mountain Girl, Doris Delay, The Hermit, Freewheeling Frank the Hell's Angel, Cassady flipping his sledgehammer, Babbs, Gretch, George Walker . . . Zonker coming in with an Arab headdress as Torrence of Arabia . . . Finally Kesey pulling in, Faye and the kids coming out . . . The Flag People, the bus glowing, the mystic fog rising . . .

IN THE STUDIO OF JOHN BARTHOLOMEW TUCKER'S TELEVISION show, station KPIX, on Van Ness Avenue, I'm sitting in the studio audience up in the gloom behind the black backsides of the spotlights, the cameras, the dollies, the coils of wire . . . Well, this is going to be fun—

THE DANGER OF LSD

—coming on in big letters on the screen of the monitor sets in the studio, with a drawing of three sugar cubes under it . . . the symbol of LSD, of course, like four X's XXXX, for whiskey, . . . and the voice-over saying

". . . and author Ken Kesey . . ."

Out in the clearing, beyond the jungle of light stands and wires and the rest of it, in a big pool of light, there's Kesey in his buckskin shirt and red Guadalajara boots sitting in one of those milky-white fiberglass-coated Saarinen swivel chairs that TV interview shows go for . . . and Tucker, whose show it is, looking California Ivy League . . . and his other guest, Frankie Randall, looking sort of Las Vegas Yachtsman, as if any moment he is going to tell a long story about something very frustrating that happened to his El Dorado convertible in a parking lot in L.A. You can see this show has *balance,* as they say . . . It fills up your head like a daydream . . . brain candy . . . a little talk with Randall about the Persian Room and dining at Sardi's and lying on the sands at Malibu—"Well, where do you go from here, Frankie!" "Well, I'll be at Lake Tahoe next week, John!"—and then, gravely, he'll bring on the elder statesman of psychedelphia, talking about the dangers of LSD and telling the kids to turn off, as if Kesey were an ex-Communist, reformed and returned from the class wars, with a few sizzling stories and then a moral. Just the ticket! a whiff of the dope dens and then a cold shower.

"Well, tell me, Ken, could you give some idea of what an LSD trip is like?"

"Yeah, it blows you out of your gourd."

Tucker stares at him—

"Well—now, you're—going to tell all the people not to take it any more, is that correct?"

"I'm going to tell them to move on to the next step."

"The next step?"

"It's time to move on to the next step in the psychedelic revolution. I don't know what this is going to be in any way I could just spell out, but I know we've reached a certain point but we're not moving any more, we're not creating any more, and that's why we've got to move on to the next step—"

The next step? . . . it keeps going that way . . . They can't figure out what in the name of Christ this big cowboy is saying . . . What about the *danger,* man, those *sugar cubes* we had up there . . . and down in front of me, amid the wires and lights, a technician and a production assistant are frantically scrawling away on a big cue board with a marking pencil and they thrust it close to Tucker and Kesey, just out of camera range—

Don't forget about danger of LSD! Say about LSD being dangerous—especially for kids!

—and Kesey just looks at them and gives them the biggest, most inscrutable upcountry smile, which on the screen looks as though he has suddenly gazed off toward an old buddy who is saying, What a shuck, Kee-zee . . .

Later in the day, rolling across the TV screens of San Francisco again, Kesey and the Pranksters and the bus pull up to Winterland to look it over for the Acid Test Graduation . . . TV microphones . . . Kesey in Flag People coveralls and a ten-gallon straw hat . . .

"Ken! Ken!" A TV announcer heaves into position. "Ken, could you tell us something about the message you're going to have for the kids at this Acid Test Graduation?"

Kesey says, "I'm going to tell them, 'Never trust a—' "

Braaaaaaaaaaaang

A huge glob of feedback screels into the microphone—

"Could you repeat that, Ken?"

"Braaaaaaaaaaaang," says Kesey.

"Ha-ha. No, what you were saying."

"Never trust a Prankster," says Kesey. The scene breaks up in a covey of Flag People bobbing off the bus . . .

Never trust a Prankster! . . . Shit! . . . That shakes them up all over again in Haight-Ashbury, there's no getting around that. A whole new inflammation of paranoia. The lunger heads are slithering up and down the store fronts on Haight Street. They're hunkered down gabbling in the India-print living rooms. The whole thing takes a Stakhanovite left turn. Kesey is not a right deviationist but a left deviationist. He's not going to cop out by telling the kids to stop taking LSD, that's just the cover story. Instead he's going to pull a monster prank that will wreck the psychedelic movement once and for all ... Well, the acid heads in Haight-Ashbury are like a tribe in one respect, anyway, I can see that. It's all jungle drums and gossip with them, they love it, they swim in it, like fish in a stream in a cave ... A terrific thought bubbles up in the universal brain ... The Acid Test Graduation is scheduled for Winterland on Monday, October 31, Halloween. The next night the California Democratic Party is holding a big rally in Winterland for Governor Brown, who is running against Ronald Reagan. Kesey and the Pranksters hold their Winterland blast on Halloween. Right? Far from being an "acid graduation," it will be an Acid Test of unbelievable proportions. Electric Kool-Aid will rain in the air like a typhoon, swizzle up every vein, 6,000 heads smashed out of their nuts, ricocheting off the walls like electric golf balls ... The sky falls ... But that's not all. They won't stop there! these maniacs ... The Pranksters will smear all the doors, railings, walls, chairs, the heating system, the water fountains, with DMSO ... laced with LSD ... Dig? ... DMSO is close to being an old alchemical ideal, the universal solvent. Put a drop of DMSO on your fingertip and thirty seconds later you can taste it in your mouth. It goes right through your skin and through your system that fast. DMSO with LSD ... What a vision! The following night the entire Democratic Party of California will get turned on, zonked out of their apples. Eight thousand emphysematous fatbacked Senators, Assemblymen, National Committeemen, National Committeewomen, Congressmen, the Governor himself, wailing like banshees, flopping around and gurgling and spitting and frying like a pile of insane pancakes, whereupon the Deaf Policemen descend on the whole psychedelic movement with knouts flailing ...

Christ! what a stew ... Now the heads don't know whether Kesey is selling them out or shoving a big Roman candle up the universal arse. They're fascinated. They come around the Warehouse and peep into the gloom. Their eyes shine at the doorway with a hepatic fever ... They come into the Warehouse, they stare at the bus, they stare at Kesey, Mountain Girl, Cassady, Babbs ... A whole platoon of them comes in, beads rattling, teetering around like gauchos, staring at the bus and going "Wowwwww! Wowwwwwww!" and smiling at each other, like, it's so groooovy, and suddenly all the Pranksters fall silent. "Cops," says Mountain Girl in total disgust. "How do you know?" "Look at their shoes." They have on lace-up boots like telephone linesmen. "You could never git heads to wear heavy shoes like that," she says. Only a momentary downer, however. The fact is, the Pranksters are sailing. They've got the whole town into their movie by now, cops and all. Kesey is all over TV, radio, and newspapers. He's a celebrity, the perfect celebrity, the Good-Bad Guy, reeking all the secret Zea-lot delights of sin but promising to do good. They were all over town on the bus, befuddling the communal brain ... Even into Fillmore, the big Negro section, with the loudspeakers playing rock 'n' roll and American flags flying and a big sign on the bus reading

Colored Power

moving through the ghetto in a blur of Day-Glo swirls. The spades in Fillmore didn't know what the hell to make of that. Were these white freaks *serious,* only they got the term wrong? Or was it a shuuuuuuuuuuuck—by the time they figured it out, the bus was long gone, wailing off somewhere else. Then the big sign

Acid Test Graduation

went up on the bus, and the bus went wheeling through Haight-Ashbury and downtown San Francisco and North Beach and Berkeley advertising the world's biggest convocation of all the heads. Pranksters flapping from every portal. George Walker up on top on the drums, Page on the electric guitar. Mountain Girl

hanging out the back of the bus exploding sunballs and screaming at the nonplused multitudes on the subject of the race for
governor and Kesey's various busts

"Kesey for Governor!"

"A man of convictions!"

"He stands on his record!"

"The idiot's choice!"

"A joint in every stash!"

"No hope without dope!"

They were *immune* again. The whole freaking town was into the
movie. And after . . .

. . . WINTERLAND; YES . . . THE HARDEST PART OF THE WHOLE
fantasy, as usual, has been finding the right place. Winterland is
perfect, the biggest indoor arena in the city limits, and a tight
ship, used for ice shows and so on. The Winterland management
didn't want to deal directly with Kesey and the Pranksters. Maniacs! jailbirds . . . That was where Bill Graham came in. There
was no love lost between Graham and Kesey, but Graham agrees
to serve as producer, impresario, the sane hand on the controls,
and sign the contract. Graham's job is to stay up on top of the new
wave. But it's an aesthetic and moral thing with him, too. He's a
believer, underneath it all . . . Hmmmm . . . There's Kesey . . .
Well . . . Anyway, Hallinan and Rohan draw up a contract between Graham and Intrepid Trips, Inc. It's signed and a deposit
is down, all legal and locked up.

Then there's the Grateful Dead. Kesey wants them for the
Acid Test Graduation. They're essential, he says. But the Dead
have a contract to play at an annual Halloween costume ball at
California Hall. Ironically, the Pranksters' benefactors, the Calliope Company, were sponsoring it, and they had an impresario
named Bob McKendrick running it. Kesey and McKendrick and
a couple of the Calliope Company, Paul Hawken, Michael Laton
and Bill Tara, are up in an apartment on the top floors of a rick-

ety building on Pine Street, all wood slats and bay windows. There are no furnishings, just a mattress in the living room. The sun makes a huge glare in here. Kesey sits on the mattress and everybody else is hunkered down on the floor. Except McKendrick. He is standing up in the middle of the floor like someone dancing on a hot plate. He has on tight black pants, black shark toe slip-on shoes, a soft black sweater and open-neck shirt . . . dressed Main Stem hipster, in short. He's broken up in the glare, twenty-seven parts, all fidgeting.

"Look, Ken," he's saying, "you're a leader, a prophet, you might say, and you have an important message, and I dig that, you know? I respect that . . . But I have to think of this in other terms. I'm responsible to a lot of people, and there's a lot of money involved."

Twenty-seven parts!—all moving, doesn't anyone see that this is a main chance, this dance at California Hall, in the impresario game. Kesey just sits there and keeps working on him like how long is it before he will see how it's going to be—Hell, man! join forces with the Pranksters. Move your scene to Winterland, cosponsor it. If he doesn't, everybody on . . . The Scene will go to Winterland anyway, and he and his whole California Hall scene will be wiped out anyway. McKendrick is beside himself. His black pants shimmy in the glare. He smells disaster either way. Put me back together again! Everyone stares. It's all glare and myopia in here! He comes to a stop. He agrees. He pulls out of California Hall, freeing the Dead, thrash, crumble—

—bits and freaking pieces, grumbling. The heads start grumbling about Kesey's power play. *Kesey's power play.* The Grateful Dead . . . They've been doing all right! Since the Acid Tests they have become a *thing,* the pioneers of the new sound, acid rock, with the record companies beginning to sniff around :::: hmm-mmm :::: *the very next thing?* Freak that. All and everyone in one bag now, Winterland.

Friday night and the Pranksters decide to drop in on the Fillmore. Like, well, it's Friday night. Kesey, Cassady, Babbs, Page, about a dozen of them, all in the Flag People coveralls, Cassady flipping his sledgehammer. The scene around the Fillmore is a freak show for sure. The dance hall is set down right in the middle of the Negro slums, at Fillmore and Geary, and it's Friday night with a lot of young spades with Stingy-Brim hats on out on the street having the usual Friday night on the streets and old Negro women doing the groceries for the weekend, liquor stores, drugstores, cars inching along, black faces all over the streets. Right in the middle of them, the white freaks. Kids in psychedelic dress burbling and gaggling up to the Fillmore—Colored Power! the kids have that, all right. Kesey and the Pranksters walk up the stairs to the dance hall, which is on the second floor. Kesey talks to the ticket seller and the ticket taker. There's a big conference. The ticket taker goes upstairs. He comes back . . . like, very bad vibrations . . . They can't come in unless they buy tickets . . . Graham . . . bad vibrations, a freaking insult, in fact. The Pranksters go back out on the street to mull that one over. There's a Cyclone fence at the rear entrance of the Fillmore with a freaked-out chomping police dog behind it . . . Graham . . . Cassady goes off . . . A few minutes later he's back.

"I ran into Bill Graham," he says. "He was out on the street checking tire treads to see if they'd picked up any nickels. I says, 'Bill . . .' and he says, 'Look, Neal, we're in two different worlds. You're a hippie and I'm a square. *Square.*' He did it like this"—and Cassady makes a square in the air with his forefingers to show how he did it—" 'You're a hippie and I'm a square.' Says, 'I got off the subway in 1955, but you're still on it. We're in two different worlds. You're a hippie and I'm a square.' I'm telling you, Chief," he says to Kesey, "I had some very negative feelings. I remembered what you said about negative feelings, but I had some very negative feelings." Kesey laughs, but—

All day Saturday the Pranksters are working like mad. They're hassling up all sorts of equipment, mikes, spots, amplifiers, speakers, strobes, even an electronic music machine, all the stuff they had at the Acid Tests and more. They can't get into

Winterland until Sunday to start rigging it up because there's
some show in there Saturday night. Anyway, they're working *en
charrette* Saturday and into Saturday night . . . At five o'clock in
the morning, Sunday, it hits the fan. Kesey's lawyer, Rohan, gets
wakened up at 5 a.m., at home . . . Graham is on the phone, very
excited, explaining a million things a mile a minute.

   They are having quite a little session up in Graham's office at
the Fillmore. All night it's been going on. Graham has been
wrestling with many negative feelings. He knows that term, too.
By heart—also Chet Helms knows it, and the Grateful Dead,
and the Quicksilver Messenger Service, and more and more :::::
three fourths of The Scene is here, says Graham, the're all over
the place, hanging on the walls . . . Everyone is in a terrific sweat.
Are we actually going to let Kesey do this thing? pull off this debacle? Go :::: *beyond acid,* whatever that may be, which, whatever
it is, is no good for anyone here . . . They've hauled out all the
versions, the cop-out, the power play, the way Kesey twisted
McKendrick's arm, the DMSO . . . the DMSO! . . . That's it!
Christ, Bill, can't you see . . . They're putting pressure on Graham to pull out of the deal . . . They've got me by each limb, wild
tow trucks heading to the four points of the compass . . . The
more they talk, the more urgent it is to *do* something, else, Christ,
why have we been here all night . . . Hope incubates in the warm
loam of every armpit . . . Helms has it figured out. Kesey's men-
tality is military. He thinks in terms of power differentials. He's
playing the desert fox—lure the enemy into your own battle-
ground by doing a turn-face claiming you came back to stop kids
from taking acid, and when you have thousands of these straight
people together, turn them on to acid. Kesey's playing the tactical
deceit and façade game—and so on . . . And the Dead . . . Why
should we blow our hard-earned scenes for Kesey? As Ralph
Gleason the columnist says . . . Kesey's going to blow the whole
new San Francisco scene for us. And Graham . . . I ran into Cassady on the street. He's waving this sledgehammer at me like he's
going to knock my head off if I don't play ball . . . Many negative

feelings. Kesey's an Elmer Gantry, says Graham ... That's it! Elmer Gantry, the evangelical demagogue ... Freaking debacle either way ... If he blows it, he blows it for us all. If he succeeds, he takes over the whole psychedelic movement and leads it into the Elmer Gantry thing, Father Divine, Daddy Grace, Cagliostro, charlatan limbo, sledgehammer theocracy, a phosphorescent fascist fandango, King Herod spavining the Flower Children, O Fuck & Corruption, G-narl, G-nash, Elmer Gantry Cagliostro Day-Glo Nero ... Stop Kesey ...

In short, Graham is pulling out of the deal and there will be no Acid Test Graduation at Winterland.

LATE IN THE AFTERNOON IN THE WAREHOUSE — CHRIST, IT'S dismal in here! The place is always a shambles, of course, but now the funk of the day's debacle is settling in like a sludge. The vermin are regaining the upper hand ... The lice! The pigeon fleas! The roaches! rats! scabies! impetigo! clap! piles! herpes! all rising up out of the debris like boils ... Faye, Mountain Girl, Babbs, Gretch, Black Maria, Page, Doris Delay, Stewart Brand, Lois, the Hermit, Roy Seburn, Gut the ex–Hell's Angel, Kesey's brother Chuck, Zonker—they're all rumbling around in the gloom, but they're not Flag People any more, the costumes are off like the war is over ... They're gathering around in a circle in folding chairs and old theater seats on one side of the bus ... Acid Test Graduation ... The sign is still stretched across the whole side of the bus ... Well, shit ... Kesey, in his buckskin shirt again, comes around in the midst of them carrying a huge easy chair—stuffed with tiny wings!—over his head—and sets it down with the back to the bus and sits down in it—a molting chair—and the Prankster circle rings out from him. Kesey stares at a spiral notebook he has and then starts talking in a voice so soft I can hardly hear him at first ... about what has just happened ... about Danny Rifkin and some others who came by to tell him they were pulling out of the Winterland fantasy.

"It didn't take long to know they wouldn't change their minds," he says. "They won't change because they have too much money involved . . . As soon as they left, I lay down and I thought about it and then I knew we have everything we want right here . . ."

RIGHT HERE?

". . . in this warehouse, and this is where we're going to do it. We're going to have the Graduation here and it's going to be our scene. We have a certain number of people we want to get close to us, and they're going to be here and it's going to be better than anything we could have done at Winterland . . ."

WHISTLING

". . . Here we're on our own grounds, and we can do what we want, for our own scene, and we don't have to do any more politicking or compromising. We'll do it our own way and we'll be the Bay Area's Superheroes . . ."

LAST HOLE IN THE SAPLING SKY

". . . One reason it didn't come off was that it was too big and too hot and they all got frightened. They all want to be eagles, but they don't want to act like eagles, so we're going to have to do it ourselves. We tried to do it the other way, but they weren't interested . . . So we're going to keep it down to those people who are going to make it as tight a scene as we can get. They are the kind of people who, if they've got anything to say, it will spread out from them, and they can say it straight, and it will spread out from them and there will be no stopping it. And that's the essential fantasy. We're moving it all in here, into the Rat Shack."

INTO THE RAT SHACK

Then Kesey's voice picks up and he starts assigning tasks: Page in charge of setting up a stage and chairs. Roy Seburn to decorate the place with a lot of cloth hangings. Faye and Gretch to get food and drink. Hermit to seal up all the holes in the walls. Zonk to draw up and post the guest list . . .

THE FEW!

The fantasy is to compile an invitation list and contact them all, far and wide, now, this afternoon and tonight, by telephone, messenger, whatever it takes, and everybody starts thinking of those people close in enough to

THE WHOLE FREAKING ADVENTURE

to invite to this last roundup . . . What a thought! . . .

DO YOU REMEMBER

all the Pranksters who have wandered far and wide, like June the Goon, Marge the Barge, Sensuous X, Anonymous, Norman Hartweg—

"Hire an ambulance to bring him from Ann Arbor!" Christ, all the memories . . . the Perry Lane people . . . Sandy Lehmann-Haupt—

BECAUSE, NEVERTHELESS, HE WAS THERE WHEN

the pudding whipped up creamy—

"Hugh Romney!"

"Bonnie Jean!"

And Paul Sawyer and Rachel Rightbred . . . and all the wild screwy people who got on the bus on the golden track wherever and whither—

"Mary Microgram!"

"That little guy who wrote the pot poem!"—and they write that down—

"That guy with the ears, that *weirdo!*" says Babbs—and they write that down—

"That couple in Portland!"—and they write that down—

"That pretty Indian boy on Haight Street!"—and they write that down—

"The Mad Chemist!"

YEAH! OH SHIT, DO YOU REMEMBER

"Big Nig!"

GIMME THE RENT

"Culley!"

"Owsley!"

SURVIVAL

"That guy in jail!"

"The Who Cares Girl!"

Ra-a-a-a-ay

"Ray!"

"Pancho Pillow!"

"J. Edgar Hoover!"—and they write that down—

See the very hunted coons

"Gaylord!"

"Jim Fish!"

"Agent Number One!"

¡Maricones!

"Cosmo!"

Cos-mo

Oh shit what a flow from eons ago in La Honda across the length and the breadth and the sleek and the Rat and it all comes flooding and bubbling back like a crest if they can just sit up on it and ride and ride and ride and ride here in the gloom and beat back those little crab lice in frogmen's suits six little neoprene rubber armlets for each little crab louse leg creeping about camouflaged like tiny scars in the brain the focking debacle infestation, the morose thought clumped somewhere in every brain until out through the starveling self-shuck fiesta euphoria Page brings it out front and out loud in the scabid sinkhole of the Warehouse, the ancient Shellube voice of please-don't-shit-me:

"It's great to be a part of the greatest jackoff in history."

NEVERTHEFREAKINGLESS! THE NEXT NIGHT, HALLOWEEN, the magic long-awaited hour ... I can hardly believe it, the Pranksters have transformed the place. You have to hand it to them, they must have worked like Turks. It's still a pestilence among buildings, you understand, this Warehouse, but there's verve in the air, Rat splendor. The most splendid thing is a huge orange-and-white parachute, an enormous thing, just the silk, not the strings and all, hooked to the ceiling at the apex, and billowed out to the far corners of the ceiling like some majestic canopy out of a Louis XV lawn revel in the Orangerie at Versailles. It glistens! *Grand luxe!* The very same parachute, it turns out, that Astronauts use on reentry for the splashdown . . . Hmmmmm . . . Yes . . . Quite a sight! The Pranksters have turned into the Flag People again, in their American Flag coveralls. Mountain Girl sits at the Sixth Street side in Flag coveralls checking guests against the invitation list which is posted up on the door in Paul Foster God Rotor script. Mountain Girl opens the Can't Bust 'Em coveralls and suckles Sunshine as the few, the faithful . . . the many! . . . come flapping by . . . Their faces are painted in Art Nouveau swirls, their Napoleon hats are painted, masks painted, hair dyed weird, embroidered Chinese pajamas, dresses made out of American flags, Flash Gordon diaphanous polyethylene, supermarket Saran Wrap, India-print coverlets shawls Cossack coats sleeveless fur coats piping frogging Bourbon hash embroidery serapes sarongs saris headbands bows batons vests frock coats clerical magisterial scholar's robes stripes strips flaps thongs Hookah boots harem boots Mexicali boots Durango boots elf boots Knight boots Mod boots Day-Glo Wellingtons Flagellation boots beads medallions amulets totems polished bones pigeon skulls bat skeletons frog thoraxes dog femurs lemur tibia kneecap of a coyote . . . A hell of a circus, in short, a whole carnival banner, a panopticon. Hell's Angels pulling in, in their colors, the death's-head jackets, full dress, beards combed and trimmed, Terry the Tramp, Pete the Drag Racer, Ralph of Oakland, plus their girls . . . miniskirts and raspberry stockings . . . Chocolate George . . . Chaos! Shitfire! Chocolate George doesn't see his name on the list and his girl keeps saying, "What's the matter, George, can't we get in?" until Mountain Girl gives a bullshit laugh and waves them in. A kid about ten pops out of the door onto Sixth Street and yells, "Who's smoking grass around here?"—in the most demanding voice you ever heard . . . aggressive little devil. There's even a nursery set up inside the door and they keep making the Hermit stay the hell out of there. Kesey is off to one side in a Flag People coverall, looking around, not saying much, listening to a big Angel from Oakland who has on a polka-dot shirt and a polka-dot tie under his Angels' jacket—"I wore a shirt and tie, Ken, on account of it's Halloween"—rock 'n' roll playing over the loudspeakers, which are all over the place, on the sides, on the ceiling, right up in the summit of the parachute canopy even . . . microphones, cameras, TV cameras . . . Yes . . . The Few and the Faithful!—all the same, the word of the hoopla in the scabid old Warehouse is around town like a chic piece of information. Irresistible, of course . . . Three TV stations have cameramen there, four radio stations with microphones and tape machines. Herbert Gold the novelist with an aftershave smile on. Ingrid Bergman's daughter, Pia Lindstrom . . . Oh, sweet adrenal edge! This is where it's at! what—could this be . . . *the new wave?* . . . Where? in comes the *Women's Wear Daily* correspondent in San Francisco, Albert Morch, a brassy little character with a Rolleiflex around his neck . . . Caterine Milinaire of *Vogue* with a miniature camera in a chain-mail evening purse, standing amid Angels, heads, and the Probation Generation like a Bulfinch princess . . . Larry Dietz the magazine writer from Los Angeles . . . And me . . . Kesey looking around and saying nothing and . . . wondering . . . Hmmmmm . . . The Few and the Faithful and the whole hulking world. It's a regular beano, all right. But, Mother! These costumes aren't for a Halloween party but for the liberation of dead souls . . . churchly vestiture, in truth . . .

Are   we   blind? . . . Oblation . . . Consecration . . . Communion . . . Well . . . The Anonymous Artists of America climbing up onto the stage . . . They're like freaking faëries out of *A Midsummer Night's Dream,* dueling shirts and long gowns of phosphorescent pastels like the world never saw before, Day-Glo death masks beaming out in front of the instruments. The music suddenly submerges the room from a million speakers . . . a soprano tornado of it . . . all-electric, plus the Buchla electronic music machine screaming like a logical lunatic . . .

Out into the middle, under the great parachute canopy and the

spotlights, sailing across the mungery carpet . . . Doris Delay of
the Pranksters in Flag People coveralls and Terry the Tramp of
Hell's Angels in an Ozark razorback stovepipe hat dark glasses
Angel beard, a huge brown-and-black striped sweater like a rac-
coon, the Angels' sleeveless jacket and the death's head, blue
jeans, motorcycle boots . . . Christ, here's a coming-out party for
you, Doris Delay and Terry the Tramp . . . stomping and flailing
about in a regular hoedown . . . but formal in a wacky way. They
dance for about a minute and then the others rush out, a storm of
them, couples in acid-head fancy dress, dancing to the rock 'n'
roll, only they're dancing clean out of their gourds, they leap,
they flail their arms up in the air, they throw their heads back,
they gyrate and levitate . . . they're in a state . . . they're ecstatic . . . Gary Goldhill looks on from the side. He has on a huge
lake-red Chinese pajama top with a gold dragon embroidered on
it. He's spooked about the Warehouse . . . Musty! . . . Insane! . . .
Friends or spirits? Well—Earth can be Heaven & Hell and he
takes the plunge . . . and reaches into his pants pocket and swal-
lows a potion . . .

Already a few enraptured grins breaking out in the crowd . . .
Rapt wet-lipped bliss . . . They glisten, their eyes are wide open
like plastic nodules. The Telepathic Kid is so high, grinning so
wet and glistening, he looks like one great psychic orgasm getting ready to unfold exfoliate into . . . a calla lily . . . and a blond
kid with a white Nehru coat on and a big silver pendant hanging
down over his chest kneeling before the rock 'n' roll band with
his hands brought up like in prayer and a grin of such pure acid
bliss on his face that his teeth sizzle . . . a pot full of boiling
pearls . . . The Pranksters, Babbs and Gretch and Page and others, take to the bandstand, all electrified, and they start beaming
out the most weird loud Chinese science-fiction music and
cranking up the Buchla electronic music machine until it ma-
neuvers itself into the most incalculable sonic corner, the last turn
in the soldered circuit maze, and lets out a pure topologically
measured scream. Ultima-time, with heavy-duty wiring, the

works. Kesey stands off to one side still, in the shadows, at ...
Control Central, only now he has the Flag People coveralls off
and is bare chested, wearing only white leotards, a white satin
cape tied at the neck, and a red, white, and blue sash running di-
agonally across his chest. It's ... Captain America! The Flash!
Captain Marvel! the Superhero, in a word ...

At the height of the frenzy suddenly the lights go out, the
sound goes out, all replaced by a single spotlight hitting the center of the floor. Kesey's brother Chuck is up in the rafters working the lights. You can hear Babbs's and Hassler's voices over
microphones in the dark, rapping back and forth in a shuck
manner: "Do you think they'd clear out of the center if we asked
them, Hassler?" ... "Sure, they're gonna clear out the center
faster than you can say clear out the center" ... But everyone just
mills around, caught in the blackout. Babbs says: "If they don't
clear out the center, then they're a bunch of assholes" ... Well,
let's try the direct approach! They clear out of the ellipse where
the spot beams down, and Kesey comes in out of the darkness.
He's taken the cape and the sash off, however. Too freaking
much, I guess. He's just wearing the white ballet tights and his
wrestler's build. A pair of jockey shorts show faintly under the
leotards—just the right touch ... here in the Rat Shack ... He
has a hand microphone up to his mouth. ... Kesey in the leotards
with the pool of light in front of him and the heads all packed in
around the loop of light in the darkness. ... It's good and theatrical ... in a weird weird way ... Some of the heads get the
point immediately. Without a sound, they start tossing things
into the pool of light, sugar cubes, capsules, cigarette papers, a
couple of joints, beads, amulets, headbands, all the charms and
totems of psychedelphia into the pool of light. It's ... an altar ...
Kesey starts talking over the microphone in the upcountry
drawl ...

"When we were down in Mexico, we learned a lot about
waves. We spent six months down there learning about waves.
Even in the dark you can feel the waves ..."

It's a wrench, that voice, what is it? up to now—a party, a frenzy. All of a sudden it's on a whole other level . . . of some sort . . . we can't figure it out. The TV crews are trying to edge up close and jockey for position. Is this where he tells the kids to turn off LSD? . . . Which is what—we came for . . . *Waves?*

"I believe that man is changing . . . in a radical basic way . . . The waves are building, and every time they build, they're stronger. Our concept of reality is changing. It's been happening here in San Francisco . . . I believe there's a whole new generation of kids. They walk different . . . I can hear it in the music . . . It used to go . . . life—*death,* life—*death* . . . but now it's . . . death—*life* . . . death—*life* . . ."

The TV crewmen are trying to hand their microphones to heads near Kesey. They want them to hold them near him to pick up the words better. They implore the heads, they half order them in stage whispers. The heads are disgusted. They just stare at them. Kesey shoots a few whammies their way . . . These bastards and their . . . *positioning* . . . they only want to use you for a little while . . . They're punctures in the dirigible, flatulent murmurs in the heart, they're—the TV crews are pissed, too. Snotty dope-head kids! . . . Coverage is a pain in the ass here in Edge City. Can't do with it, can't do without it—a grand hassle in the making—

" . . . For a year we've been in the Garden of Eden. Acid opened the door to it. It was the Garden of Eden and Innocence and a ball. Acid opens that door and you enter and you stay awhile . . ."

At which precise point—mysteries of the synch! yes—four policemen great dark-blue figures come walking in through the door on the Sixth Street side. The word starts firing around the crowd in the dark: Cops! Cops! . . . One last monster raid to finish off the debacle! There is a hell of a scurrying in the darkness, bodies hitting the walls of the garage, like gigantic fancy-dress rats looking for holes . . . Get the hell out of here! . . . It's the Probation Generation, of course, all the kids who are out on probation under firm admonition not to associate with known dope users . . . they're practically digging through the concrete floor . . . The four policemen keep walking in at a slow gait, looking this way and that. Cassady is on a microphone way behind Kesey now, up on the stage, in fact, beginning to rap about the cops coming in: "Four custom-tailored constables, you understand, looking for pearl heads among the swineherds . . ."

"The cops are here?" says Kesey. He sounds startled.

"The constabulary cops . . ."

"They come in waves, too," says Kesey, "they're a pattern that repeats" . . . Yah! . . .

By now the cops have just stopped on the edge of the crowd in the darkness, just looking around.

"There's cops and there's policemen," Kesey says. "The cop says, 'Don't do that. That's forbidden and that's all there is to that.' The policeman says, 'You can do that, but if you go too far, you're going to hurt yourself.' The policeman is the double line in the middle of the road. I'm talking about inside of us."

A spot suddenly comes on, hitting Cassady in a little cone of light. "It's like Ken once said," says Cassady. "If you ignore a cop for twenty years, then he's not there any more . . ."

"Haw!—Haw!—Haw!"—Hell's Angels in the corner—the four cops just survey the camp meeting, then start turning around to leave. Cassady keeps on rapping:

"Yes! Violence, you understand . . . There's not going to be any violence here. If we wanted some violence we have some fellows here who could furnish it . . ."

"Haw!—Haw!—Yah!—Yagggggh!—*A good cop is a dead cop!*"

"*A good cop is a dead cop!*"

But the cops just walk on out, rocking at the same slow gait, brushing through a clump of Hell's Angels like they weren't there. The cops are gone, but they punctured the atmosphere again. Kesey tries to build it up, in the same soft tones, but it's tough going. He plunges in with the vision, the vision of Beyond

Acid, how he saw the lines of light across the bay in Manzanillo, the line of grass . . .

". . . and I'd smoked some grass, some Acapulco Gold, as a matter of fact . . ."

Cheers go up in the dark, Acapulco Gold! Oh shit we're esoteric heads and we know the creamiest of all the marijuana. But it's a freaking puncture. Kesey plunges through the whole vision: the line of acid, the circle demanding completion, the little lights across the bay . . . It's metaphorical, allegorical, brains are getting messed up left and right . . . The rock 'n' roll, the frenzy, the TV cameras, the darkness, the cops, and now . . . *this* . . . It keeps ricocheting from level to level. Shit! what is Kesey . . . *doing* . . . Finally the line with the hook on it—completing the circle without going all the way. He's telling them the whole thing, but—what is . . .

"We've been going through that door and staying awhile and then going back out through that same door. But until we start going that far . . . and then going beyond . . . we're not going to get anywhere, we're not going to experience anything new . . ."

They're uncomfortable, they're stuffing their shirts in and pulling them out, too many rips in the balloon, and brains messed up . . . and the freaking TV jackals stabbing microphones around like tape-recording the hanging of Lenny Bruce—

"Let's find out where we are. Let's move it around. Let's dance on it."

The lights come back on, the music starts back up, the color is back, everything starts spinning like a top again. Goldhill is zonked by now. The music flows through his neural ganglia like a flood of relief . . . Love! Bless, bless! bright lights! The Hell's Angels are stomping around again, everybody dancing. But that doesn't last long. Kesey is out in the middle of the crowd. People close in around him. The music stops. Kesey looks slightly glazed over but plunging on, like he is determined to seize the whole debacle by the shoulders and shake it into place. He has a chunk of ice. He kisses it, he puts a big chunk in his mouth, he breaks off a chunk and gives it to Cassady. Cassady kisses a chunk and then rubs it all over his bare chest. An ice thing . . . The TV cameramen and radio reporters are trying to edge in. They're buffeted back. Everything is pitching and rolling. Kesey and Cassady are sitting on the floor communing over the ice. Pranksters and some other heads are getting into a circle on the floor with Kesey and Cassady . . . the lotus position . . . Gary Goldhill sits down with them. He's ready. The kid with the sizzling teeth sits down among them, zonked . . . the lotus position . . . His back is arched back stiff in the Nehru coat. He's rapt. The pot of pearls boils and boils. They all join hands and close their eyes—a communal circle . . . They close their eyes tighter and tighter, waiting for . . . *the energy.* It's coming! It's coming! A high-pitched keening noise rises up from the circle . . . Do you hear it! . . . It's weird . . . Half the people looking on are nonplused, they're *embarrassed.* What is this a Halloween party or a seance and the Holy Rollers? Christ . . . Albert Morch of *Women's Wear Daily* says to Caterine Millinaire: "Say! when I met you last night—I didn't know you were the Duke of Bedford's daughter!" . . . Got religion! The Angels are restless. They're standing around the edge of the circle. "Hey! Start the music!" . . . In the circle, Kesey, Cassady, and the rest—they're starting to rap back and forth. The kid with the boiling teeth hears the voice. His eyes are still tight shut. He grins and glistens. "A dead towhee," he says, "a rumpled road and a dead towhee." His voice is on the edge of delirium and tears . . . or else any moment he is going to break into an insane cackling laugh . . . "A dead towhee and a rumpled road and lying in the dust, a *mistake* . . . a *mistake,* but it's not *important* . . . Making a mistake is not *important* . . . it's the context in which the mistake is made . . . A rumpled road and a dead towhee and four gasoline stations, white and sterile, refueling tailfins in mid-air for fat men in sunglasses who do not see the rumpled road and the dead towhee . . ."

Goldhill sits rapt . . . Energy waves emanating from everywhere . . . Like . . . black spirits! . . . Kesey & Cassady—what are they trying to do with his mind . . . *Got* me, trapped me into the Big Wait—for what? an idea? a revelation? love? feeling? break-through—into what? or

PUT-ON

They're putting him on! Sucking him in! But—the *idea* we're waiting for—he can *feel* it, physically, it's surging through . . . He looks deep down inside, to describe it.

PRESQUE VU!

Mass daemonic hallucination it is! He looks around . . . All pitches and rolls . . .

A CIRCUS OR HELL

The tortured and the damned are all around him, the dead-for-good souls . . . He gets up radiating Chinese firecrackers from his dragon pajamas and heads for the Sixth Street door but . . . the Dead and the Damned! Faces!

HELL'S ANGELS

Hell's Angels are packed into the corridor leading to the door ready for

MASSACRE

He turns back into the crowd, sinks into a time warp . . . Like his life is an endless tape loop . . . Black spirits keep bubbling up out of the most ancient pits of licorice detergent

TRAP

That! Hare Krishna Hare Krishna Krishna Krishna Hare Hare Hare Rama Hare Rama Rama Rama Hare Hare and as he chants he becomes . . . Krishna! . . . Christ! . . . God . . . And he pops out of the time warp into the silver haze of . . . The Universal Mind . . .

"We almost had it," says Kesey, opening his eyes for the first time. "We would have had it. There's too much noise . . ." But it's like the cloud has passed.

People are milling around, starting to leave. They're befud-dled and embarrassed. What the hell kind of party . . . The An-gels are beginning to leave, the TV crews, Herbert Gold has had enough . . . Albert Morch . . . It's getting toward three o'clock . . .

People stare at the stage, but there's no sign of music. Is it over? Are you on the bus? . . . in the pudding?

Kesey plunges on. The lights go out again. The wrench is total now. It's a whole other . . . thing . . . Kesey moves to the other side of the floor and sits down. The spot hits him. The Pranksters start gathering from all over the garage: Mountain Girl, The Hermit, Babbs, Gretch, Doris Delay, Page, The Hassler, Cassady, Black Maria, Zonker, Gut, George Walker, Ram Rod, Stewart Brand, Lois Jennings, all heading toward Kesey. Hassler has a hand mike and he starts saying in the dark:

"Everybody who's with us, everybody who's with us in this thing, move in close. If you're not part of this thing, if you're not with us, then it's time to leave. You can move in close and get into this thing or you can leave, because . . . that's what time it is . . ."

Shitfire! that's it—those who were a little spooked by the turn the night is taking are now totally spooked. People heading for the Sixth Street door, flapping and burbling. The Pranksters, meantime, draw in close to Kesey, stepping by people, over people, then settling down, nestling in a circle around Kesey. Others pulling in, through the darkness, toward the cone of light lighting up Kesey's head and back. Kesey looks distraught. He looks up into the light. He has a hand mike. He makes a gesture as if to say, Let them through—

"I know these people," he says. "I've been with these people!"

The whole Allegory . . . A tableau of the Plains of . . . The tightest inner circle is packed in around him, then the Prankster outer circle. Then a few of the old Perry Lane crowd. Then various heads who are deep into the pudding, like Goldhill and the Kid with the Boiling Teeth, then rings and rings, the grades of faith . . . plus a few clumps up against the wall, of people with no faith at all, just too stroked out or curious to leave. Finally Cassady stepping over the hunkered-down, lotused, sitting bodies, heading toward the inner circle . . . Kesey looks up at him, then he seems to grow dizzy and sink . . . His head rolls . . .

"Goodbye, Neal!" he says. He looks like he might pass out. Cassady pulls closer. Kesey hunches over the microphone.

"They're saying, 'Look at him—the promising novelist . . . once surrounded by thousands . . . and now only these few' . . . But I can—"

—he drops the thought, however. The whole place is quiet and dark, just one small spotlight on Kesey . . .

"Get Faye and the kids." Silence. Then a rustle of Faye coming through the clump of people, leading the little girl, Shannon, and the oldest boy, Zane, and carrying the youngest, Jed. They've all been in the nursery section up by the Sixth Street door. One of them is crying, only it is like a scream. That's all you hear in here, it's eerie . . . Faye and the kids and Mountain Girl and Sunshine and all the Pranksters in a tight circle with Kesey. They all hold hands and close their eyes. Silence. Then the scream again

ARCHETYPICAL! MIND POWER!

Then a voice from one of the clumps of people by the wall, some girl, with a spondee voice like a Ouija medium:

"The—child—is—cry-ing—Do—some-thing—for—the—child—first—"

Kesey says nothing. His eyes are shut tight. The high keening sound rises from the circle with the kid's scream weaving through it. *Fantastic mind power crackle*—Goldhill registers the energy

THEY'RE ALMOST

But the girl on the other side doesn't let up: "See—a-bout—the—child—A—Child—is—cry-ing—That's—all—that's—hap-pening—A—child—is—cry-ing—and—no—one—is—do-ing—any-thing—a-bout— it—"

ALMOST HAVE IT—PRESQUE VU!

"—Why—is—the—child—cry-ing—Doesn't—an-y-bo-dy—care?—"

FEEL IT! THE VIBRATION LEVEL!

Kesey looks up. The spot hits him in the face. The Pranksters release hands. The music starts up. The Anonymous Artists of America play a rock 'n' roll version of Pomp and Circumstance with drum flourishes . . .

THE ACID TEST GRADUATION

By now the crowd is down to about fifty. The lights come up a little around the stage, but the rest of the garage is dark. Cassady is up on the stage in front of a microphone. He has on nothing but a pair of khakis hung down on his hips and a mortarboard hat on his head, the kind you graduate in. In one hand he has a whole stack of diplomas. He's wound up like a motorcycle, kicking and twitching and ticking and jerking at the knees, the elbows, the head . . . He's off on a dazzling run of words. The Anonymous Artists of America keep rolling away behind him. Every time the little blond girl on the drums gives the drums a good swat, Cassady stiffens, a spasmodic jerk, as if somebody just kicked him in the small of the back. He's rapping away, he's handing out the diplomas for the Acid Test Graduation. It's coming off after all . . . now . . . when? what the hell time is it? Five o'clock in the morning or . . . who the hell knows . . . Kesey is in the dimness sunk into the great easy chair. Some of the . . . *graduates* are here, Pranksters mainly. They put on black caps and gowns and come bouncing up to the stage and get a diploma from Cassady . . . scrolly convoluted things done by Paul Foster and the God Rotor. . . .

Gut the Hell's Angel lets out a whoop and does a little dance as his name is called. Many of the graduates aren't there. The Who Cares Girl . . .

"The Who Cares Girl," says Cassady. "Now, the Who Cares Girl couldn't be with us this evening, you understand, had to check in for choir practice in the oat bin two hundred fine voices tuned to a split hair screaming the name of the cowboy known as Ray, you understand, couldn't be with us either—ahem—lost in a Band-Aid factory swabbing the jake seats with A-200 . . ."

. . . and the drums roll and Cassady stiffens and jerks and

twitches and the Pranksters hasten forward, Hassler, Babbs, Zonker, The Hermit, Mountain Girl, Gretch, Paul Foster, Black Maria, Page, Walker, Hagen, Doris Delay, Roy Seburn, flying up and back in black robes... *graduate*—into what on the horizon... as the light of dawn breaks through the crack in the garage door behind the bandstand. Those cold goddamn silver slivers... and the light rises in the garage, a cockroach orange dimness, and there is perfect silence, the world stroked out this way and that as in... Lucite... And the heat of the day creeps in, and rising out of the funk and the musk and the Rat grease smears—now come the cinches, mites, crab lice, fleas, fruit flies, grubs, weevils, all the microbes and larval ooze—and start writhing and crawling and festering and frying and wriggling and sizzling. The straight world breathes in, coughs, gags, spaghetti trapped in every glottis and flapping in panic...

Back among the acid heads of San Francisco there were two or three days of post mortems after the collapse of the Prankster Winterland fantasy and the strange night in the garage. A little breast-beating here and there... Oh, did we give in to Fear and Doubts, which a good head cannot afford, and thereby stop a brave cat from doing his thing... But just as many said, Kesey was out to freak us out or cop out on us, and it was just as well. And then the communal mind, not willing to be anti-freak-out, settled on the cop-out theory of it. Kesey had been just copping out all along, to keep from going to jail. That settled something else, too, the troublesome... *souped-up* thing the Pranksters were always into, this 400-horsepower takeoff game, this American flag-flying game, this Day-Glo game, this yea-saying game, this dread neon game, this... *superhero* game, all wired-up and wound up and amplified in the electropastel chrome game gleam. It wasn't the Buddha, not for a moment. Life is shit, said the Buddha, a duress of bad karmas, and satori is passive, just lying back and grooving and grokking on the Overmind and leave Teddy Roosevelt out of it. Grace is in a far country, India by

name ... Oh, the art of living in India, brothers ... And so what
if there is no plumbing and the streets are dirty, they have mastered the art of living ...

The Pranksters had cleared all their debris out of the garage
before the Calliope Company had moved back in, and they had
piled it up in the vacant lot next door and then they headed off to
Babbs's old place, the spread, in Santa Cruz. The Prankster debris lay there in the lot, a vast weird junkhead of bits and pieces
of costumes and masks and pieces of wood with Day-Glo paint
all over them and weird signs painted in Day-Glo on swaths of
butcher paper and it lay there writhing like a maniac all day, and
at night ... it glowed ... A blot on the escutcheon of Harriet
Street. The neighbors there, industrious Japanese and others,
were disadvantaged souls, but they had their pride and they
formed a delegation to City Hall to insist on keeping their neighborhood clean. The Mayor's Office saw it as an example of the
kind of neighborhood pride that regenerates the City, for if they
could instill the good burgher spirit in even so lowly a neighborhood as the Tenderloin ... So the Mayor announced utmost co-
operation and it became a regular ceremony, with officials
showing up along with the Sanitmen, and the TV crews. And the
City pitched in, joining forces with the good neighbors of Harriet
Street, in the ceremonial destruction of the weird junk
heap—*Christ only knew what insane degenerate wino generations*
had combined to nearly take over this poor forgotten street like
jungle rot. The Day-Glo paint sputtered and sizzled to the
end ...

The Calliope Company held an Acid Test in the garage, and
Cassady, wheeling around San Francisco in his latest car, heard
about it somehow and showed up that night. He came in the
doorway on the Harriet Street side, now marked 69 Harriet
Street, after the humor of the times, and he was jerking and kicking at top speed to the unseen Joe Cuba ... He was sailing on
speed, as the thirty or forty heads there could tell by the way his
eyes jumped around, going tic tac tok tok tok tak toc tac tok tik

tik tik tik tik tac tok tac tok tik tik tik tik tik toc tac toc tac toc tac—either that or he was amazed at this Acid Test through and through. There were no lights except the slowest and most fluid light projections, no noise except the most mellifluous hi-fi playing... *what the fock*... sitar? sitar? sitar?... The garage was scrubbed and chaste and pure with wall hangings of the most meticulous sort, India-print coverlets, delicate and intricate of pure vegetable macrobiotic dyes. A few crystals in the air picked up rays of light one by one like... jewels... And all the good heads were stroked out most silently, propped up sitting against the walls or stretched out, each grooving on his own private inward thing, receptacles of the Buddha, the All-one invited guest, and the Buddha could have walked in at any moment and felt right at home, 485 B.C. or right now, the...

...dead-ass little gook... Cassady can't believe it... He is rapping a mile a minute, but nobody picks him up on it. They just stare at him through great amethyst eyes, full of tolerance and pity as his own eyes sprocket and his shoulders bob and weave...

"Hey! Don't you want to *do* anything—get it started, you understand—slide it around—"

They just stare at him, peaceful luminescent violet jewel children, smiling like a bunch of freaking nuns, full of peace and tolerance and pity... as he turns around shaking his head and his shoulders and kicking and flailing disappearing out onto Harriet Street again.

OH CHRIST ANOTHER LITTLE BUD IN THE HEAVES AND GASSES of the discovery pangs. Her eyes are opened up like morningglories, her lips are wet and glistening, she smiles like an entranced nun, her teeth are beginning to sizzle... hold on to the thoracic box. She has her face right up in yours, everybody's, and she is saying, ecstatic with the discovery—

"I'm—I'm—I'm—I'm—*getting the picture!* We're—all *here*—

right? We're all *here!* We're—*he-e-e-e-e-ere!*" and her hand
pans around to take in the Fantasia in-the-beginning cosmos . . .
which is, in fact, only a place known as The Barn, in Scotts Valley, ten miles from Santa Cruz. The Barn is Scotts Valley's first
psychedelic nightspot, a great barn, truly, once converted into a
theater and now into a psychedelic nightspot run by Leon
Taboory, Scotts Valley's first, and last, to hear the grousing from
the church down the way and the local constables and townfolk
and the local paper, but ne'mind all that. To the little girl it's her
first glimpse of Heaven itself, zonked as she is on LSD, her first
capsule—

"I'm—getting the picture! We're all he-e-e-e-e-ere and we can
do anything we want!"

—revealing all this to Doris Delay and Zonker, Doris, like a
good old helpful hand, says, "That's right. We're all here and
everything's all right and you're fine."

The little bud sinks into a folding chair beside Doris's and
gives her a look. "I should be suspicious of you . . ."

"The paranoia stage," Doris says to Zonker. I love to tell the
story—

". . . because I'm stoned."

"I know," says Doris. To tell the old, old story—love and glory
now playing in your neighborhood for the first run, in Scotts Valley . . .

About eighty of the local heads and hipfolk and jazz buffs,
etc., in here listening to a jazz trio called The New Dimensions,
Dave Molinari, Andrew Shushkoff, and a stocky little guy playing the bass. The little guy has on a sporty-type hat, wears it
while he plays, his signature, you understand, and a pair of
Cuban wrap-around sunglasses, although it is dark and appro-
priately nightclubby, except for some light projections, which
makes it . . . psychedelic . . . ah ummmmmm . . . and he is knead-
ing and slapping and flummoxing the bass like the creamy days
of Slam Stewart. *The New Dimensions*—now that's very funny,
you know. Ken Kesey and the Merry Pranksters have to smile

over that. Kesey and the Pranksters are off to one side of the Barn waiting for their turn to go on, setting up their instruments, the electric guitars and basses, Gretch's Hammond organ, Walker's drums, and the goddamnedest gleaming heap of wires, dials, amplifiers, speakers, headsets, mikes—testing, testing—The New Dimensions . . . Yeah. The trio is like a throwback to the late 1940s and the early 1950s when jazz was, like, the *final form,* funky and so fine. Molinari—or is it Shushkoff?—goes into a hell of a *riff*—Oh Christ, remember?—on the piano, with his head dug down deep into the profound soul funky depths of this thing. It's so . . . well, nostalgic . . . Scotts Valley troops into post–World War II hip America . . .

The Pranksters have their own speakers set up all over the barn and Babbs is trying to test the microphones, watching for the needle to jump over the dials . . . Babbs has on his Day-Glo spirit mask and it glows in the dark, also a Shazam shirt and pants of many stripes and colors and he blows into the microphones, then hums a bit and watches the needles, then keens a bit, then croons a bit, and that's nice, so he tries a little ululation, and that's nicer, and pretty soon he is keening and gooning along with the New Dimensions and his voice sails through their sound like a stoned ghost on the airwaves. Kesey sits on a folding chair in the Control Center testing the headsets. Cassady has the Rattar, now painted an infinite number of colors and totally without strings. Doris Delay plays kindly aunt with the zonked-out little girl who's getting the picture . . .

The New Dimensions finish their set and they're mad as hell, of course. What . . . *cube* was doing that screaming bit, f'r chrissake . . . The three of them come stomping up to the likely suspects, the Pranksters, led by the stocky guy with the hat and sunglasses. He walks up to Babbs and says,

"Like, I mean, who's doing all that—"

"Doing what?" says Babbs.

"Like, *later,* man, don't give me the doing-what bit. You know doing-what, man. I mean like—"

"Was somebody doing something?"

"Like, I mean, that's . . . *later!* You know! I mean, it . . . *grates!*"

"Oh, you mean that *funny noise!* I'd say feedback."

"Sure! Feedback!"

"Yeah! Yeah! Right! Right! Right!" Just a parlor sport, this is . . . fella could do it with his left hand. The little guy is furious. He tries to find the words to express his utter loathing.

"Like, man, this fuck-up bit on somebody else's set—it's SO—SQUARE!"

There! he said it! the worst insult he knows! Next, the fire next time—Kesey steps in as the peacemaker: "He wasn't working *against* you—he was trying to play *with* you."

The little guy stares at Kesey but doesn't say anything. He just screams it again into the void: "Like, it's so—SQUARE!"

"Yeah! Yeah! Right! Right! Right!" says Babbs. "And there's the guy who did it!" and he points at Cool Breeze, who is sitting at a little table with a candle on it, hunched over a piece of paper, doing some kind of intense meth-like drawing. "There he goes!" says Cassady, picking up on the thing. "Takes a phantom heart to catch a Cool Breeze, you understand—" and so forth and so on, a shuck, in a word, never trust a Prankster . . . And the New Dimensions walk off, disgusted . . .

They refuse to play any more and start packing up their instruments, which leaves Taboory, The Barn's manager, in a bind. He can't figure out who the hell to alienate. Kesey is a giant . . . on the other hand, the New Dimensions can play . . . But too late for all that. The New Dimensions stomp out, thumbing their noses at the whole scene. The Pranksters wind up for their set. They clamp on their headsets. The headsets are wired up to a variable-lag system. So the Pranksters don't hear what they are playing right now but what they were playing a second ago. They harmonize off themselves, break up all learned progressions, and only they can hear the full . . . orchestration, a symphony in their cortices, the music of the Prankster . . . ah ummmm . . . Only the kids in The Barn, can't figure out what's going on . . . It's like, *weird* . . . The Pranksters put on their headsets and pick up their instruments, Kesey on an electric guitar, Page on an electric guitar, also Hassler, Babbs on an electric bass, Gretch on the electric organ, George Walker on the drums. They look all ready to go, but nothing happens. They're waiting . . . for the . . . *energy* . . . to build up, to come crackling over the headsets . . . the spontaneous burst . . . but nothing works. Somebody starts and nobody else can pick it up and soon it's obvious that none of these crazy-looking people is going to play the instruments, except for the drummer . . . and they're not playing *songs,* they make it up as they go along . . . the leader, the muscular guy, Kesey, singing:

"It's a . . . road map! . . . that ought to have been issued, about how to reach the edge of time . . . on a horse who flies in tungsten red . . ."

And the guy in the mask on the bass singing: ". . . floods of screams on the beach in bomby raids of bloody rainbows . . . It's dark and I lose my vision . . ."

Well . . . the kids start leaving . . . what the hell . . .

Babbs belches over a microphone. That gets a laugh. But is it art? Kesey barks like a dog. George Walker says over his microphone: "Where'd that dog go? I heard a . . . *dog!* . . . under my very feet!"

They slough to a halt. Hassler starts chanting into his microphone, which is wired in only to the headsets . . . Only Pranksters can hear:

"Begin it like we began . . . at the beginning . . . Do it like we *did* . . . at the beginning . . . In the beginning . . . in the beginning . . ." Chanting over the inner space network.

But the slump and the slough are total . . . The kids all going in droves now . . . Just the Pranksters left . . . An atmosphere of total tedium . . . It's . . . all . . . too . . . much . . . for mortal—

Even Pranksters drifting off . . . leaving the main floor, going downstairs . . . Hagen shakes his head. "It's like a wake . . ." It's that burnt-out husk of the dark hours of the morning . . . Black Maria finds a mattress in a utility room and lies down . . . Cas-

sady, not high at all—low, in fact—offers to drive a girl home . . .
Now it's just Kesey on the electric guitar and Babbs on the electric bass, them and their head-sets picking up the sound of their
instruments and their song in variable lag . . . Taboory himself,
the manager, can't take it any more . . . "Just shut the door tight
when you leave," he tells Kesey, and he takes off . . . All the lights
are out now, just a little glow from the dials of Prankster Control
Center . . . Kesey and Babbs have their eyes closed, strumming
slowly . . . alone in the center of the vast gloom of the barn . . .
The whole world contracts, draws closer and deeper and crawls
inside the headsets, ricocheting in variable lag in the small hours,
and Kesey sings over his guitar, which twangs and wobbles:

". . . and every now and then you can hear her blowing smoke
rings around a cloud and trying to lace up her shoe . . ."

And Babbs: ". . . and the message goes out and it breaks out
just a little bit but—stops—"

And Kesey: "It's kind of hard, playing cello on a hypodermic
needle and using a petrified bat as a bow . . ."

And Babbs: "Yes, it's hard working with these materials, without the grins falling off your knees . . ."

And Kesey: ". . . and the soldiers think of the lowly fleas . . ."

And— ". . . the latrines wade back up around my knees . . ."

"So let's set here in this dilapidated people hutch and think
about the things we've done . . ."

". . . Yes . . . down in Mississippi, that bitch girl we diddled in
the cotton fields . . ."

"Still . . . you want to catch the first subway to Heaven . . ."

"If I can get myself a new set of scales, I'll get my ass off this
third rail . . . and so saying, he stood up and retched and looked
down on the rail on sparks and long and hairy slavers of various
flavors of dark intestinal brown . . ."

". . . and his teeth fell out by the dozen and Hitler and his in-
fested cousins began to grow in the cellar like a new hybrid corn
and the crows wouldn't touch him . . ."

"... and up the rail, old True Blue wiped his nose on his uncle's clothes ..."

"I took some pseulobin and one long diddle ..."

"WE BLEW IT!"

"... Ten thousand times or more ..."

"WE BLEW IT!"

"... so much we can't keep score ..."

"WE BLEW IT!"

"... just when you're beginning to think, 'I'm going to score' ..."

"WE BLEW IT!"

"... but there's more in store ..."

"WE BLEW IT!"

"... if we can get rid of these trading stamps that get in the way of the merchandise ..."

"WE BLEW IT!"

"... Ten million times or more! ..."

"WE BLEW IT!"

"... it was perfect, so what do you do? ..."

"WE BLEW IT!"

"... perfect! ..."

"WE BLEW IT!"

Epilogue

THREE WEEKS LATER, NOVEMBER 30, KESEY WENT ON TRIAL IN San Francisco for possession of marijuana—the bust on the rooftop. It ended with a hung jury, split 8 to 4 against him. Kesey's retrial, in April, ended with another hung jury, 11 to 1 against him this time. Rather than try him again, however, the state let him plead *nolo contendere* to a lesser charge, "knowingly being in a place where marijuana was kept." He got 90 days. In May he lost in his appeal of the original San Mateo County conviction for possession of marijuana—the La Honda bust. The sentence was six months on a county work farm, a $1,500 fine and three years' probation. He was allowed to serve the other sentence, the 90 days, concurrently.

Before he started serving time, Kesey took the bus and headed for his home town, Springfield, Oregon, with just Faye and the kids and Ram Rod on board. The Pranksters pretty much scattered. George Walker and Cassady were off in Mexico. Mountain Girl, with her baby, Sunshine, had already joined the Grateful

Dead's group. Black Maria and Paul Foster went to the Hog Farm, Hugh Romney's commune near Los Angeles. Babbs and Gretch went to San Francisco. So did the Hermit...

In June, Kesey began his stretch on the work farm, which was just a few miles from his old place in La Honda. He worked in the tailor shop. He was let out last November, after serving five months. He went back to Oregon, and he and Faye set up house in a shed on his brother Chuck's farm, up a gravel road south of Springfield. The shed was called the Space Heater House, after a gas heater inside that gave off a jet flame when it lit up.

In February, Neal Cassady's body was found beside a railroad tract outside the town of San Miguel de Allende, in Mexico. Some local Americans said he had been going at top speed for two weeks and had headed off down the railroad track one night and his heart just gave out. Others said he had been despondent, and felt that he was growing old, and had been on a long downer and had made the mistake of drinking alcohol on top of barbiturates. His body was cremated.

In the spring, various Pranksters... Babbs and Gretch, George Walker, Mike Hagen, Hassler, Black Maria... began finding their way to Oregon from time to time. Kesey was writing again, working on a novel. The bus was there, parked beside the Space Heater House.

Author's Note

A NOTE ON THE WRITING OF THIS BOOK . . . I HAVE TRIED NOT ONLY TO tell what the Pranksters did but to re-create the mental atmosphere or subjective reality of it. I don't think their adventure can be understood without that. All the events, details and dialogue I have recorded are either what I saw and heard myself or were told to me by people who were there themselves or were recorded on tapes or film or in writing. I was fortunate to get the help of many unusually talented and articulate people; most notably, Ken Kesey himself. The Pranksters recorded much of their own history in the Prankster Archives in the form of tapes, diaries, letters, photographs and the 40-hour movie of the bus trip. Kesey was also generous enough to allow me to draw from his letters to Larry McMurtry in the chapters on his flight to Mexico. Much of the dialogue and italicized material in Chapters XXI and XXIII is quoted from these letters.

For all the Pranksters, as I have tried to show, the events described in this book were both a group adventure and a personal exploration. Many achieved great insight on both levels. I can think back especially to my talks with Mountain Girl, Hassler, Black Maria, Stewart Brand, Ken Babbs, Page Browning, Mike Hagen, Doris Delay, Hugh Romney, Zonker, George Walker, and Neal Cassady. Sandy Lehmann-Haupt told me about his Prankster days in especially full and penetrating detail.

There were several excellent writers, in addition to Kesey, who were involved in the Prankster saga. Playwright Norman Hartweg recounted his experiences for me in a series of tapes. Ed McClanahan provided me with information about several phases of the Prankster adventure, and Robert Stone told me a great deal about Kesey's fugitive days in Mexico.

Hunter Thompson made available to me several tapes he had made while working on his book, Hell's Angels, *and parts of the book itself dealing with the Pranksters and the Angels were also helpful.*

I was also fortunate to find people like Clair Brush, who wrote for me a 3,000-word description of her experience at the Watts Acid Test, much of which I quote in describing the Test. Of the many other people I talked to or corresponded with, I particularly want to mention Vic Lovell, Paul Sawyer, Paul Krassner, Pat Hallinan, Brian Rohan, Paul Robertson, Jerry Garcia, Gary Goldhill, Michael Bowen, Anne Severson, Paul Hawken, Bill Tara, Michael Laton, Jack the Fluke, Bill Graham, John Bartholomew Tucker, Roger Grimsby, Marshall Efron, Robin White, Larry McMurtry, Larry Schiller, Donovan Bess, Carl Lehmann-Haupt, and Mr. and Mrs. Fred Kesey.

About the Author

TOM WOLFE is the author of a dozen books, among them such contemporary classics as *The Electric Kool-Aid Acid Test, The Right Stuff, The Bonfire of the Vanities,* and *A Man in Full.* A native of Richmond, Virginia, he earned his B.A. at Washington and Lee University and a Ph.D. in American studies at Yale. He lives in New York City.